BUDDHIST IMAGES OF HUMAN PERFECTION

BUDDHIST IMAGES OF HUMAN PERFECTION

The Arahant of the Sutta Piṭaka Compared with the Bodhisattva and the Mahāsiddha

NATHAN KATZ

MOTILAL BANARSIDASS PUBLISHERS
PRIVATE LIMITED • DELHI

First Edition: Delhi, 1982
Reprint : Delhi, 1989, 2004

ISBN: 81-208-0647-6

MOTILAL BANARSIDASS
41 U.A. Bungalow Road, Jawahar Nagar, Delhi 110 007
8 Mahalaxmi Chamber, 22 Bhulabhai Desai Road, Mumbai 400 026
236, 9th Main III Block, Jayanagar, Bangalore 560 011
120 Royapettah High Road, Mylapore, Chennai 600 004
Sanas Plaza, 1302 Baji Rao Road, Pune 411 002
8 Camac Street, Kolkata 700 017
Ashok Rajpath, Patna 800 004
Chowk, Varanasi 221 001

Printed in India
BY JAINENDRA PRAKASH JAIN AT SHRI JAINENDRA PRESS,
A-45 NARAINA, PHASE-I, NEW DELHI 110 028
AND PUBLISHED BY NARENDRA PRAKASH JAIN FOR
MOTILAL BANARSIDASS PUBLISHERS PRIVATE LIMITED,
BUNGALOW ROAD, DELHI 110 007

PREFACE TO THE SECOND EDITION

It is, of course, deeply gratifying that demand for this book has been sufficient to warrant a second printing. The thought that people actually *read* what I write never ceases to amaze and inspire me.

It is now more than a decade since I wrote *Buddhist Images of Human Perfection,* and a decade is more than enough time for reflection upon the complex constellation of issues surrounding a 'western' scholar who writes about an 'eastern' religion. One of these issues is that of privilege. I am acutely aware of how fortunate I have been in having studied Buddhism from Sri Lankan and Tibetan teachers, as well as in American, Indian, and Sri Lankan universities. When I recall that my own father grew up in a dirt-floored farm house in rural, oppressive Ukrainia, my good luck staggers me.

Another such issue is balancing 'objectivity' and 'sympathy'. Both the Academy and my many Buddhist teachers and friends have a moral claim upon my work: the former demands my objectivity, dispassion and honesty: the latter, my love and solidarity. As I write, I hear their collective voices and hope I've managed not to sacrifice one for the other.

Religion is a curious phenomenon. It is so very, very dear to many people, so central to all of our identities, that its civilizing message is often the first casualty in the social-political conflicts we describe as "religious". The academic study of religion is curiouser still without scholarly dispassion and objectivity as our paradigm, what we do in universities is at best a dim shadow of loving study in monasteries *yeshivat,* and *madrasas.* We lose our *raison d'étre* if we give up on the seemingly impossible goal of objectivity. At the same time, without sympathy, appreciation, and a sense of the majesty of religious ideas and practices, we are mere technicians; we sacrifice our heart to our brain, we become intellectual idolaters. As scholars of religion, our dilemmas are acute. As privileged westerners, these dilemmas multiply.

My hope has always been that this book would prod both Buddhists and academics to see the *continuity* of the Buddhist tradition, which is the continuity of wisdom and compassion. I want Mahāyāna Buddhists, and scholars partisan to them, to cease to disparage the Theravāda by calling it "Hīnayāna"—an offensive term when applied to a living religion, yet a meaningful concept in the context of Mahāyāna hermeneutics. Similarly, I see neither wisdom nor compassion in disparaging the Mahāyāna as degenerate, when it is obvious to me that Mahāyāna techniques and ideas "conduce to peace, calm, and tranquility, to nibbâna."

In short, I want the world to cease treating religions as though they were football teams. Religion is concerned with weighty issues—the death of a child, the perfection of society, how to instill kindness and charity, the nature of compulsion and freedom. Religion doesn't need cheerleaders, however sophisticated the cheers. We don't need team banners or pennants under the guise of piety or scholarship. Most of all, we don't need Missionaries masquerading as scholars!

My hope for a more tolerant and open-minded approach to Buddhism was born out of sensitivities inculcated by my existential situation. I am a member of a small, ancient religion which has been the basis for larger, more powerful world religions. Adherents of these other faiths claim to understand my religion better than I do myself. In precisely the same way, some Mahāyānists claim to understand the "Hīnayāna" better than do Theravādins. So quite naturally, I become intrigued by the question of what happens when one religion grows out of, and claims to supplant, an older religion. I have wanted to defend the older, maligned tradition, and this bit of personal history has been the impetus for taking up the question of how Buddhists of different *yānas* misunderstand each other.

My questions and my method are based upon a modest assumption that the *first* step toward understanding a religion is to understand it as members of that religion understand it, or have understood it during various historical eras. In many senses, this is a matter of courtesy: One ought not define the other, even if (especially if ?) one has economic or political *power* over the other, which always entails the semantic power of definitions. For far too long, men have defined women, whites have defined people of color, Christians have defined Jews, the powerful have defined those lacking power. I believe it is incumbent upon scholars to resist facile, imposed definitions. Now it is time for us to *listen* to those whom we *study*. It is my dearest hope that such listening, to teachers from both the Theravāda and the Mahāyāna has been the basis of the book.

NATHAN KATZ

Tampa, Florida,
U.S.A.
May 1989

PREFACE : THREE SKETCHES

The Arahant

A fierce tropical sun rises over the *dagoba*, its pure white surface reflecting brilliant rays, causing the saffron-robed bhikkhus to squint. As they silently and deliberately gather to hear the *bane* preaching of the well-known thera, said by some to be an arahant, or perhaps an *anāgāmī*, there is a sense of anticipation. The thera approaches, smiling and joking kindly with some of his closer disciples. Amidst the eerie jungle sounds of birds and the constant hum of mosquitos, the thera preaches serenely and insightfully. Several lay disciples receive blessings for the *poya* full moon day of retreat and contemplation, and the thera retires for his last meal of the day, taken before noon. After his meal, he leads a *satipaṭṭhāna* sitting, counsels, monks and laypeople about their meditational practice. Then he walks, deliberately and mindfully, to his small hermitage where he feeds a family of monkeys before entering into his *jhānā* meditations.

The Bodhisattva

The preceptor-bodhisattva beats a gong, as six of his disciples raise their eyes, returning from meditation on *bodhicitta*, the heart/mind of compassion/enlightenment. Perhaps with some hesitation, they recite their vows : to forsake any thought of *nirvāṇa*, to freely accept rebirth in the hells to benefit the sufferings of beings there, to give even their bodies should that be required, to realize the futility of seeking happiness through the satisfaction of desires, to realize that through infinite rebirths, every sentient being—their enemies, the bed bugs which plague the monastery, a woman who has slightly aroused their interest—have at one time or another been their own mothers, and that they must relate with them with appropriate compassion. A *thang ka* painting of Chenrezik, the manifestation of compassion, views these proceedings with his eleven heads : eleven because upon seeing as-it-is the sufferings of the world, he became so overwrought with empathy that his head split into ten additional parts, only to be rescued by Opakme, of whom he is the reflex, who restores his new heads to his body. These six disciples are about to spend the traditional three years, three months and three days in solitary retreat in crude cave-dwellings in the western Himalayas, all out of compassion for all sentient beings.

The Mahāsiddha

A poor layman is addicted to over-eating, but is unable to buy food because of shortages. A strange looking fellow approaches him, but he cannot discern whether it is merely some drunkard, or perhaps even a saint of some sort. This fellow has long, matted hair and wears ragged clothing. The layman complains to this stranger that he is suffering the pains of hunger, and the stranger asks him to meditate on his hunger; that as his stomach is empty, so all phenomena are empty; that as he is passionate about his food, so he should become passionate in serving others. The stranger then asks for payment for this teaching : a bottle of *chang*, a type of beer, which he drinks greedily. Following this curious stranger, the layman sees him approach a Hindu temple in which is a *lingam* noted for its spiritual power. The stranger psychokinetically destroys the *lingam*, shattering it into hundreds of shards. Excitedly, the brahmin of the temple approaches the stranger, telling him that if he is one of those cursed Buddhists, then the least he could do is to act more compassionately. In haunting verses, the stranger replies that in destroying the *lingam*, his actions were purely compassionate. He asks for some more beer, and then he leaves.

ACKNOWLEDGEMENTS

I wish to express my appreciation to the following :

For generous financial support throughout my graduate career, I am indebted to the Department of Religion and to the Graduate School of Temple University; for a Fulbright-Hays research fellowship, my thanks to the United States Educational Foundation in Sri Lanka and to the Institute for International Education.

For facilitating my field work in Sri Lanka and India, I am most grateful to Mr. Bogoda Premaratna and Mr. L. Aelian Fernando, directors of the U.S.E.F./S.L., Colombo; and to Mr. C. S. Ramakrishnan, director of the U.S. Educational Foundation in India, New Delhi, and to the staff members of both these offices.

While in Sri Lanka, I was affiliated with the Vidyalankara Post-Graduate Institute of Buddhist Studies, Kelaniya. I am grateful to its director, the Venerable Dr. Hewapole Ratnasara, and to Professor L. P. N. Perera, head of the Department of Buddhist Thought, for assistance, especially with my study of Pali.

In India I was affiliated with the Department of Philosophy, Delhi University, and I am grateful to its head, Professor Ram Chandra Pandeya, for kind assistance. Most of my time in India was spent at the Library of Tibetan Works and Archives in Dharamsala, and Mr. Gyatsho Tshering, the director, was most generous with hospitality and the Library's facilities; the Venerable Geshe Ngawang Dargyey provided some illuminating lectures and discussions; the librarian, the Venerable Achok Rinpoche, and my research assistant, Mr. Lozang Gyaltsen, helped me to find my way through the Library's voluminous collections.

Two bhikkus in Sri Lanka were most generous with their time, and provided me with some delightful visits and discussions. My deepest thanks and respects go to the Venerable Nyāṇaponika Mahāthera of the Buddhist Publication Society in Kandy, and to the Venerable M. Vajiragñāṇa Thera of the Belanwilla Rāja Mahāvihāra in Boralesgamuwa and of the British Buddhist Association in London.

For very valuable discussions, I am indebted to : Professor M. W. Padmasiri de Silva, head of the Department of Philosophy at Peradeniya University of Sri Lanka; to the Venerable Dodrup Chen Rinpoche of the Sikkim Research Institute of Tibetology : to Professor Donald K. Swearer of Swarthmore College for some valuable conversations about the 'two wheel' theory of Buddhism; to Professor James W. Gair of Cornell University and to Professor John Ross Carter of Colgate University, both of whom were researching in Sri Lanka at the same time I was, for friendship and encouragement; and most especially to Professor Herbert V. Guenther, head of the Department of Far Eastern Studies at the University of Saskatchewan, for a most valuable and encouraging correspondence about my researches; and also to Professor Reginald Ray, head of the Department of Buddhist Studies, Naropa Institute, for valuable discussions about approaches to Tantric Buddhism and the mahāsiddha image especially.

To the readers of my dissertation, Professor Richard J. DeMartino and Professor Rabbi Zalman M. Schachter, for encouragement and for keen observations, go my gratitude and respect.

Most of all, I am indebted to my major professor, Professor Bibhuti S. Yadav, for patiently training me about Buddhism, for encouragement and deep friendship, for necessary rebukes, for sharp and delightful conversations in Philadelphia and Madras, and for the inspiration to study Buddhism on its own terms and in its own contexts. Daniabad, Professorji.

The President and Trustees of Williams College, and especially Professor Francis Oakley, Dean of the Faculty have been most generous in providing a partial subvention for the publication of this book, and I am deeply grateful for their support.

My appreciations also go to Sri N. P. Jain of Motilal Banarsidass, Delhi, for diligence in seeing my manuscript through the process of publication.

Nathan Katz

Williamstown, Massachusetts
April, 1980

TABLE OF CONTENTS

INTRODUCTION

The arahant, the bodhisattva and the mahāsiddha all call themselves Buddhists; living teachers from any of the three main forms of Buddhism—the Theravāda, the Mahāyāna and the Vajrayāna—readily grant that the goal of which they speak is identical with the goals of the other forms. Yet our three images of human potentiality, our conceptions of the perfected person in these three forms, radically diverge. How to both reconcile this divergence and maintain the identity of the goal, while at the same time maintaining the integrity of each of these three traditions, is the task of this essay.

The larger phenomenon which we are studying—that is, how a religious tradition which bases itself on an older tradition, yet claims to have its own conceptual and mythic identity, deals with the tension of this continuity and divergence—is not a problem unique to Buddhists. We find a similar problem in Christianity, which claims to be both a continuation of Judaism and an abrogation of Judaism, both at the same time—just as Mahāyāna Buddhism claims to be based on the teachings of the Buddha as found in the earlier Buddhist canon, yet also claims to have its own identity distinct from what they disparagingly call the 'Hīnayāna'. However, in Buddhism there was never anything like the Council of Nycaea which formulated the fundamental dogmatics by which Christianity differed from Judaism; Buddhism flowered with a magnificent proliferation of systems, schools, mythologies, symbols, practices and rituals, yet also maintained its continuity among all forms of Buddhism, expressed by such teachings as '*buddhayāna*' and '*ekayāna*', the teaching that there is, beneath these diverse flowerings, a continuous heart of the matter.

Much of the confusion with which scholars have become enmeshed on this question has revolved around naive understandings of religious language. For example, in this essay we shall consider the language of the arahant (arhat, dgra bcom pa). In the Pali literature, a close analysis of which forms the largest part of this essay, the arahant is the perfected human, one who has completed everything there is to do, a finished product, a

Buddha. In much of the Sanskrit and Tibetan literatures, however, the arhat is described as selfish, one who is interested only in his own salvation and not in the sufferings of others, one who is arrogant and conceited. Now, following from a naive understanding of how religious language works, one might be tempted to assume a real difference between the arahant and the bodhisattva, whom the Mahāyāna raises as an alternative symbol of the perfected person; that the '*nirvāṇa* of the bodhisattva' is different from and higher than 'the *nirvāṇa* of the arhat'; that the bodhisattva is, in some sense, the contradiction and/or abrogation of the arahant. Precisely the same problem arises when the mahāsiddha is proposed by Tāntric Buddhism to abrogate the bodhisattva, who is seen as narrowly scholastic, as addicted to the pleasures and refuge of the monastic life, who is moralistic and aloof from the sufferings of the world.

However, religious language does not work so simplistically. This is to say that simply because we find the term arahant/arhat in both the Pali and Sanskrit litetratures, it does not follow that they both refer in the same way. In fact, religious language is not referential language at all, but such a naive conception of language as referential leads one to take at face value the Mahāyāna claims about the arhat, and scholars and some Buddhist hermeneuticians have indeed taken arhat-talk in precisely this naive way.

Therefore, a new approach to these interrelated issues is needed, and we propose a close contextual reading of primary and commentatorial literatures from the Pali, Sanskrit and Tibetan sources. To use a phrase currently in vogue, what we are doing is returning Pali arahant-talk to its original language-game, and Sanskrit arhat-talk to its own linguistic home, and so also Tibetan arhat-and bodhisattva-talk. In other words, our question is : In what contexts and for what reasons do Mahāyāna authors say both that (a) the arhat is selfish and conceited; and (b) there is only one Buddha-vehicle by which all Buddhists attain to full bodhi ? When a Sanskrit author says that the arhat is selfish and conceited, what is really being said ? Following from our claim that religious language is not referential language, we are left with this question : If indeed Sanskrit arhat-talk does not refer to the arahant notion in the Pali canon, to what does it refer (if it refers at all) ?; what is really being said ? And we find that some Buddhist hermeneuticians were well aware of this problem, and devised some ingenious methods for its dis-solution.

Such a question entails a close study of the Pali arahant concept. This, as we have said, forms the major portion of this essay, and we have undertaken a close, contextual reading of the literatures on this subject. By a 'close, contextual reading' we mean an analysis of the language of talking about the arahant, a very tricky problem in Buddhism because of its unique understanding of the nature of language itself. In every form of Buddhism we have studied, we have found a very suspicious attitude towards language: from the Buddha himself to the late Tantras, language is heuristic and pedagogical. Philosophical language is diseased language, language which has degenerated from its useful context, language which no longer serves us, but of which we have become servants. Whether an arahant, a bodhisattva or a mahāsiddha, language is an expression, language is useful, language is a skill to be developed by analysis and meditation; but language is not philosophical or referential. Precisely for this reason, our method is contextual : to see what is being said in particular circumstances; not to develop any type of meta-language by which we evaluate given Buddhist statements, but to expose and reveal by contextual analysis the utility of a given statement in Buddhist literature. It is by just this method that we seek to demonstrate that arhat-talk in the Sanskrit cannot be seen as referring to arahant-talk in the Pali; to hold that it does would be to make a meta-language out of everyday language, and we would argue that this is precisely to miss the point of Buddhism, which seeks to liberate language, to return to a natural discourse within clearly proscribed limits and goals of the attainment of *bodhi*, and not to develop a philosophy in the usual sense of the term.

While there has been excellent work done on the arahant concept previously, and on the bodhisattva concept as well, we feel that this study is unique in the history of Buddhist scholarship. It is unique for two basic reasons : (a) its scope, namely a study of these three Buddhist ideals; and (b) its method, which is a contextual study of the language of talking about the perfected person, which does not develop any meta-language, and which returns, for example, Sanskrit arhat-talk to its original pedagogical home.

The implications of this study fall into two areas generally. The first implies a re-appraisal of the dynamics of Buddhism and Buddhist language itself : that talk about these perfected persons, about *yānas* and so forth, is not referential talk; that the Mahāyāna criticisms of the arahant do not refer to the arahant of the Pali canon, and that Tibetan criticisms of the bodhisattva (byang chub sems dpa') do not refer to the bodhisattva as found in Sanskrit literature. The second area is implied by our methodology, which we feel could well be applied to other issues, both within Buddhism and outside of it. Within Buddhism, such a contextual study could prove most fruitful for a study of the notion of 'body' in these three yānas, or to the notion of monastic vows, et cetera. In the larger context of the history of religions, this method might be helpful in sorting out, for example, talk about 'messiah' and 'mosheakh' and the contexts in which early Christians talked about Jesus as 'messiah' as viewed in the context of an extended discussion of what Jews might have meant by 'mosheakh'. If one were to assume that they meant the same thing, then the questions which were personified by the 'Judiazers' and the 'Zealots' of early Christianity would work out very differently than if such a contextual study would show that these two terms were used very differently.

We beg the reader's indulgence with the great deal of highly technical data we consider in our extended treatment of the Pali arahant concept. We must point out that Buddhism is not a simple subject, and that in order to get clear about arahant/arhat language, a great deal of subsidiary terminology about meditation, about emotions, about the path, about one's relatedness to society, about 'views' (*diṭṭhi*), et cetera, is necessarily involved. With the reader's patience, however, we will proceed to paint a picture of the arahant in a way that it has not been painted before, and we shall also analyze Mahāyāna claims about this arahant/arhat.

As to the question of why *three* portraits of the perfected person, we could only offer the following, albeit tentatively : that the person is not a one-dimensional being; that the depths, psychological tendencies, methods of teaching and relation to society, et cetera, require a three-dimensional portrait; that human potentiality, of which the arahant, the bodhisattva and the mahāsiddha are symbols, is varied and vast, and that it could not be fully portrayed by any one image; that to tell the 'whole story' we need to compile many 'stories', and that the strength of Buddhism as a vital religion is precisely that it is so multi-dimensional that it can accommodate varying, but not necessarily contradictory, portraits of what it means to be most fully human, which is to say, to become perfected.

Nathan Katz

CHAPTER I

FORMULAE, EXPRESSIONS, OCCASIONS AND SYMBOLS OF THE ARAHANT

A. *General*

It has been clearly established that the term 'arahant' is derived from the root $\sqrt{}$arh, "to be worthy" or "to deserve."[1] I. B. Horner[2] gives us the following four Pali forms of the noun : *arahā, arahat, arahant,* and *arahan.* It may also be used as a verb, which in Pali turns out to be *arahati*, "to be worthy" (Sanskrit : *arhati* and the nominal *arhat*). Etymologically, then, the arahant is "the worthy one."

In Buddhist literature, however, we find such contrived and suggestive etymologies as : derived from *ārakā*, distant, because all unskilful (*akusala*) states are distant from the arahant;[3] deriving from *ari* (enemy)+*han* (destroyer), because the arahant is one who has destroyed the enemies, the *kilesā*, which is the etymology by which the Tibetan translators came up with *dgra bcom pa*, from *dgra* (enemy) and *bcom* (subduer);[4] "and because of absence of secret (*a-raha*) wrongdoing."[5]

More useful than etymologies for our preliminary observations about the use of the term *arahant*, however, would be to look

---

1. T. W. Rhys-Davids and William Stede, *Pali-English Dictionary*, repr. New Delhi : Oriental Books Reprint Corp., 1975 (London : Pali Text Society, 1921-1925), p. 77. [Hereinafter : *PTS Dictionary*]. See also William Dwight Whitney, *The Roots Verb-Forms and Primary Derivatives of the Sanskrit Language*, repr. New Haven : American Oriental Society, American Oriental Series, Vol. 30, 1945. (Leipzig : Druk und Verlag von Breitkopf und Härtel, Bibliothek Indogermanischer Grammatiken, Band II, Anhang II, 1885), p. 4. [Hereinafter : "Whitney"]

2. Isaline B. Horner, *The Early Buddhist Theory of Man Perfected : A Study of the Arahan*, London : Williams & Northgate Ltd., 1936, p. 52. [Hereinafter : *EBTMP*]

3. M.I.280. Confer DhA.IV228, and As1.349.

4. Sarat Chandra Dass, *A Tibetan-English Dictionary*, repr. Delhi : Motilal Banarsidass, 1970. (Calcutta : Baptist Mission Press, 1902), p. 277.

5. Horner, *EBTMP*, p. 179.

into the *Sutta Piṭaka*, where one finds some rather standardized formulae about the arahant. Given the very central doctrinal position of the arahant concept in early Buddhism, it is not surprising that there are a good number of such formulae. For the present, our purpose will be satisfied by a listing of these formulae by *nikāya* of the *Sutta Piṭaka*, leaving in-depth analyses for later sections of this essay.

B. *Arahant-Formulae in the Sutta Piṭaka*

1. *From the Dīgha Nikāya*

In the Mahā-Nidāna Sutta[6] we find the Buddha giving the following formula to Ānanda :

> Yato kho Ānanda bhikkhu n' eva vedanaṃ attānaṃ samanupassati, no pi appaṭisaṃvedanaṃ attānaṃ samanupassati, no pi "Attā me vediyati, vedanā dhammo hi me attā" to samanupassati, so evaṃ asamanupassanto na kiñci loke upādiyati, anupādiyaṃ na paritassati, aparitassaṃ peccataṃ yeva parinibbāyati, "Khīṇā jāti, vusitaṃ brahmacariyaṃ, kataṃ karaṇīyaṃ nāparaṃ itthattāyāti" pajānāti.
>
> Now when a brother, Ānanda, does not regard soul under these aspects,— either as feeling, or as non-sentient, or as having feelings,— then he, thus refraining from such views, grasps as nothing whatever in the world; and not grasping he trembles not, he himself attains to perfect peace. And he knows that birth is at an end, that the higher life [*brahmacariyaṃ*] has been fulfilled, that what had to be done had been accomplished, and that after this present world there is no beyond.

The theme of the arahant as one who does not subscribe to varying views (*diṭṭhi*) about the self shall be taken up in detail in a later section, as this seems to be one of the most significant aspects of the formula. Additionally, it should be noted that the phrase—*Khīṇā jāti, vusitaṃ brahmacariyaṃ, kataṃ karaṇīyaṃ nāparaṃ itthattāyāti*—is perhaps the most common characterization of the arahant as found in the *nikāyas*. This also shall be taken up.

In the Pasādika Suttanta[7] we find the Buddha offering us the following arahant formula :

6. D.xv.32. (PTS translation)
7. D.xxix.26. (PTS translation).

Yo so āvuso bhikkhu arahaṃ khīṇāsavo vusitavā katakaraṇiyo ohita-bhāro anuppata sedattho pāraikkhīṇa-bhava-saṃyojano sammad-aññā vimutto.

The brother who is arahant (is one) in whom the intoxicants [*āsavā*] are destroyed, who has done his task, who has laid low his burden, who has attained salvation, who has utterly destroyed the fetter of rebirth, who is emancipated by true gnosis [*sammad-aññā*]......

This formula is a loaded one, as it is filled with terms that need a great deal of clarification. Just to point to these difficult usages, we might mention *khīṇāsavo*, which Horner[8] finds to be the most common epithet of the arahant and which we corroborate as such in our readings, and which Rhys-Davids[9] translates as "in whom the intoxicants are destroyed." We shall embark upon an extended discussion of the term *āsava* below, a term which has been translated as "intoxicants,"[10] "cankers,"[11] "deadly outflows,"[12] and "drugs,"[13] and which we feel best remains untranslated. In any case, a *khīṇāsavo* is one who overcomes or loosens the grip of the *āsavā*, which is to say that he has overcome the world (*saṁsāra*; *loka*), the totality of human suffering. Another difficulty is raised by calling the arahant *vusitavā katakaraṇīyo*, "one who has completed his task." This became a highly controversial point at the Council of Pāṭaliputra, where Mahādeva and the Mahāsaṁghikas launched a strong challenge to this notion of the arahant as a completed product.[14] In fact,

---

8. Horner, *EBTMP*, pp. 121-122.

9. *Dialogues of the Buddha*, London : Pali Text Society, 3 vols., 1899-1921, III, p. 125.

10. Rhys-Davids, in *Dialogues of the Buddha*, as above, *passim*.

11. E. M. Hare, in *The Book of Gradual Sayings*, vols. III-V, London: Pali Text Society, 1934-1936, *passim*.

12. So Edward Conze translates *āśrava* in *The Short Prajñāpāramitā Texts*, London : Luzac & Co., 1973.

13. Lord Chalmers, in *Buddha's Teachings, being the Sutta-Nipāta or Discourse-Collection*, Cambridge : Harvard University Press, Harvard Oriental Series, ed. C. R. Lanman, Vol. 37, 1932, *passim*.

14. For an account of this controversy, see Bhāvaviveka (Legs Idan 'byed pa), *Nikāyabhedavibhaṅgavyākhyāna* (*sDe pa tha dadpar 'byed pa dang rnam par bshad pa*), *bsTan 'gyur*, Peking edition, *mDo 'grel*, Vol. U, Otani no. 5640, fascs. 177a-187b. See also Louis de la Vallée Poussin, "The 'Five Points' of Mahādeva and the *Kathāvatthu*," *Journal of the Royal Asiatic Society*, 1910, pp. 413-423.

the very rise of the mahāyāna hinges, to a large extent, on Mahādeva's attack on this concept. We shall see below, however, that the arahant as a completed product is fully within the range of consistent interpretations which follow from the body of the *Sutta Piṭaka*. The arahant, further, is one who *parikkhīṇa-bhava-saṃyojano*, "has cut off the fetter of rebirth," which is crucial for the Theravāda notion of the arahant. The notion of fetters (*saṃyojanāni*) shall be taken up in its own right below. Finally, the idea that the arahant *sammad-aññā vimutto*, "is freed by *aññā*," indicates the vital role of *aññā*, which Rhys-Davids translated above as "gnosis," in the entire soteriological process of Buddhism. Again, this shall be taken up below.

2. *From the Majjhima Nikāya*

In the Vatthūpama Sutta[15] we read :

Alattha kho Sundarikabhāradvājo brāhmaṇo Bhagavato santike pabbajjaṃ, alattha upasampadaṃ.

Acirūpasampanno kho pan' āyasmā Bhāradvājo eko vūpakaṭṭho appamatto ātāpī pahitatto viharanto nacirass' eva yass' atthāya kulaputtā samma-d-eva agārasmā anagāriyaṃ pabbajanti tad anuttaraṃ brahmacariyaṃ pariyosānaṃ diṭṭhe va dhamme sayaṃ abhiññāya sacchikatvā upasampajja vihāsi : khīṇā jāti, vusitaṃ brahmacariyaṃ, kataṃ karaṇīyaṃ nāparaṃ itthattāyāti abbhaññāsi, aññataro kho pan' āyasmā Bhāradvājo arahataṃ ahosīti.

Then the brahmin Sundarika-Bhāradvāja received the going forth [*pabbajjaṃ*] in the Lord's presence, he received ordination. Soon after he had been ordained, the venerable Bhāradvāja, abiding alone, aloof, diligent, self-resolute, not long afterwards, by his own super-knowledge [*abhiññāya*], having precisely here-and-now realized the matchless culmination of the Brahma-faring [*brahmacariyaṃ*] for the sake of which young men of family rightly go forth from home into homelessness, abided in it. He comprehended : Destroyed is birth, brought to a close the Brahma-faring, done is what was to be done, there is no more of being such and such. So the venerable Bhāradvāja became one of the perfected ones [*arahataṃ*].

This formula is actually a formula about how one goes about

15. M.I.50-51.

becoming an arahant; consequently some new issues are raised. For example, a question which becomes of vital importance in the Mahāsaṁghika-Sthaviravāda schism was the status of the laity, and the entire path described above indicates the necessity of one's becoming a monk : Bhāradvāja receives the "going forth" (*pabbajjaṃ*), which is reinforced as the way by which men of good family (*kulaputtā*) seek the end of suffering (*kulaputtā samma-d-eva agārasmā anagāriyaṃ pabbajanti tad anuttaraṃ brahmacariya-pariyosānaṃ*). From this formula we gather that it was a matter of course that, at the time of the Buddha, leaving home (*pabbajjā*) was a standard method for entry into spiritual practices. This spiritual path (*brahmacariyaṃ*), which shall be discussed in detail in sections on meditation and the four *ariyā maggā*, culminates in arahantship (*arahattā*), which is attainable in this very life (*diṭṭhe va dhamme*). Bhāradvāja's comprehension (*vihāsi*) is identical to the phrase found in the *Dīgha Nikāya* :[16] *Khīṇā jāti, vusitaṃ brahmacariyaṃ, katam karaṇīyaṃ nāparaṃ itthattāyāti abbhaññāsi*. The comprehension comes about by super-knowledge (*abbhiññāya*), which shall also be the topic for full discussion below. We find the same formula repeated identically and in full of Seniyo in the Kukkuravatika Sutta,[17] and also of Brahmadeva.[18]

A second arahant formula found in the *Majjhima Nikāya* is put into the mouth of Sāriputta :[19]

> Yato kho āvuso ariyasāvako evaṃ akusalaṃ pajānāti evaṃ akusalamūlaṃ pajānāti, evaṃ kusalaṃ pajānāti, evaṃ kusalamūlaṃ pajānāti, so sabbaso rāgānusayaṃ pahāya paṭighānusayaṃ paṭivinodetvā asmīti diṭṭhimānānusayaṃ samūhanitvā avijjaṃ pahāya vijjaṃ uppādetvā diṭṭhe va dhamme dukkhass' antakaro hoti. Ettāvatā pi kho āvuso ariyasāvako sammādiṭṭhi hoti ujugatā 'ssa diṭṭhi, dhamme aveccappasādena samannāgato, āgato imaṃ saddhamman ti.
>
> When, friends, an ariyan disciple understands unskill (*akusala*) as it is, understands the basis of unskill as it is, understands skill as it is, and understands the basis of skill as it is, he has rid

16. D.xv.32.
17. M.I.391-392.
18. S.I.140.
19. M.I.46-47. (My translation)

himself of all lustful addictions (*rāgānusayaṃ*), has dispelled all aversion addictions (*paṭighānusayaṃ*), has got rid of all addictions of speculation of egoism (*asmīti diṭṭhimānānusayaṃ*), has overcome ignorance, has, by here and now causing wisdom to arise, is one who has made an end to suffering. In this sense, friends, is the ariyan disciple one of right view, who is upright in view, who has full confidence in Dhamma, who has come to this good Dhamma.

There are several important points in this formula. In it we do not find the term "arahant," but instead "one who has made an end of suffering" (*dukkhass' antakaro*). This formula revolves around the term "skill" and "unskill" (*kusala* and *akusala*), and "right or perfect view" and "addiction" (*sammādiṭṭhi* and *anusaya*). Unskill and the basis of unskill (*akusala* and *akusala-mūla*) are to be known, as are skill and the basis of skill. We shall later argue that these two concepts are the basis for the activity of the arahant, just as merit and evil (*puññā* and *pāpa*) are the basis for the activity of the non-arahant. We shall also argue that these two poles of *kusala* and *puññā* are not discrete, as most scholars have held,[20] but the development of activities which are considered meritorious can habituate one to that which is considered skilful. It is true that the arahant does not perform *puññā*, which is kammatically binding, but he does that which is *kusala*; but rather than to dichotomize these two ethical concepts, we shall seek to demonstrate their contiguity. *Sammādiṭṭhi* in this formula is contrasted with *anusaya*: "right view," a philosophically complex notion is Buddhism, in contrast with "addiction," primarily the addiction to a latent belief in self (*diṭṭhimānā-nusayaṃ*). Further, *sammādiṭṭhi* leads to a full confidence in Dhamma (*imaṃ saddhamman ti*). The question of view (*diṭṭhi*) as addiction (*anusaya*), and right view (*sammādiṭṭhi*) shall be taken up for philosophical clarification towards the end of this essay.

---

20. See, for example, Melford E. Spiro, *Buddhism and Society: A Great Tradition and its Burmese Vicissitudes*, New York : Harper & Row, 1970, *passim*. See also Winston King, *In the Hope of Nibbana*, La Salle : Open Court, 1964, *passim*., but especially p. 168. A critique of this dichotomization was presented by Harvey B. Aronson, "Measureless States: The Relationship of the Karmic to the Nirvanic," a paper read at the first annual meeting of the International Association of Buddhist Studies, New York City, September, 1978.

A third *Majjhima* arahant formula is found in the famous Alagaddūpama Sutta:[21]

Ayaṃ vuccati bhikkhave bhikkhu ukkhittapaligho iti pi, sankiṇṇaparikho iti pi, abbūḷesiko iti pi, niraggaḷo iti pi, ariyo pannaddhajo pannabhāro visaṃyutto iti pi.

Monks, such a monk is said to have lifted the barrier, and he is said to have filled the moat, and he is said to have pulled up the pillar, and he is said to have withdrawn the bolts, and he is said to be a pure one, the flag laid low, the burden dropped, without fetters.

The commentarial gloss on these analogies is given by Rhys-Davids.[22] 'Lifted the barrier' (*ukkhittapaligho*) means that ignorance is cut down like a palm tree stump so that it cannot rise again. 'Filled the moat' (*sankiṇṇaparikkho*) refers to the impossibility of future rebirths. 'Pulled up the pillar' (*abbūḷesiko*) refers to the eradication of craving (*taṇhā*), which shall be taken up again. 'Withdrawn the bolts' (*niraggaḷo*) means the destruction of the five fetters which bind one to the lower shore (*orambhāgiyāni saṃyojanāni*), a topic which we shall treat in detail below. The commentary tells us that the rest of the verse refers to the destruction of all addiction to egoistic speculations (*diṭṭhimānānusaya*). The arahant here is referred to simply as a 'pure one' (*visaṃyutto*), or one who has become purified.[23]

Another formula is found in the same Alagaddūpama Sutta :[24]

ye te bhikkhū arahanto khīṇāsavā vusitavanto katakaranīyā ohitabhārā anuppattasadatthā parikkhīṇabhavasaṃyojanā samma-d-aññā vimuttā, vaṭṭaṃ na 'tthi paññāpanāya.

Those monks who are arahants, who have destroyed the *āsavā,* who have lived the life, done what there was to be done, laid down their burdens, attained their goal, who have fully destroyed all fetters of becoming, who are freed by profound wisdom,—one cannot know their course.

The first part of this formula is identical (save for its plural grammar) to what we have already found in the *Dīgha* and

21. M.I.139. (PTS translation) Repeated at A.III.84.

22. I. B. Horner, tr., *The Middle Length Sayings*, London: Pali Text Society, 1954-1959, Vol. I, pp. 178-179.

23. This, incidentally, is the Tibetan etymology of Buddha, *sang rgyas*, which literally would mean 'fully purified one.'

24. M.I.141. (My translation).

Majjhima Nikāyas.[25] There are two new key ideas introduced here, however : The first is the notion of *samma-d-aññā*, which we have here translated as 'profound knowledge', and which has its use in a way of indicating by what means an arahant becomes such. The two key terms in this compound, *samma*, which has the sense of genuine, proper, or profound, and *aññā*, which is specifically used in the sense of that knowledge which makes an arahant an arahant, and which shall be discussed in detail below, are often said of the arahant. Perhaps even more noteworthy is the notion that one cannot know the course of the arahant : *vaṭṭaṃ tesaṃ na 'tthi paññāpanāya*. We shall conclude our entire discussion of the arahant notion in the *Sutta Piṭaka* by returning to this notion which, we feel, indicates the highest philosophic standards of Buddhism.

The last arahant formula found in the *Majjhima Nikāya* has already been alluded to. It is based on a play on words, and we read :[26]

> Kathañ ca bhikkhave bhikkhu arahaṃ hoti : ārakā 'ssa honti pāpakā akusalā dhammā saṅkilesikā punabhavikā sadarā dukkhavipākā āyatiṃ jātijarāmaraṇiyā.
>
> By what reason is a monk called an arahant? Because far from him (*ārakā*) are evil and unskilled factors (*pāpakā akusalā dhammā*) which are joined with the defilements (*kilesā*), and fearful rebirths (*punabhavikā sadarā*), which lead to *dukkha*, which is future birth, old age and death.

The import of the Pali verse is the pun on the words *arahaṃ* and *ārakā*, which, we feel, has led to some questionable but light-hearted etymologizing. Of course, *dukkha* as expressed by *jātijarāmaraṇiyā* is but a way of talking about *saṃsāra*, the world of suffering, and this verse merely points out that the arahant is far from all of this. We shall take up a more systematic discussion of the notion of the world as found in the *Sutta Piṭaka* below, as one major trend in thinking about the arahant is that he is the very resolution of the world, and therefore a clear idea of what is meant by 'world' should be undertaken. Of course, all of this is merely hinted at by this verse.

---

25. D.xv.32 and M.I.51.
26. M.I.280. (My translation)

3. *From the Saṃyutta Nikāya*

We find one arahant formula in the *Saṃyutta Nikāya*, which[27] is in *gāthā* verse :

Sukkhino vata arahanto / taṇhā tesaṃ na vijjati //
Asmimāno samucchinno / mohajālaṃ pedālitam //
Anejanto anuppatā / cittaṃ tesaṃ anāvilaṃ //
loke anupalittā te / brahmabhūtā anāsavā //
Pañcakkhande pariññāya / sattasaddhammagocarā //
pasaṃsiyā sappurisā / puttā buddhassa orasā //
Sattaratanasampannā / tīsu sikkhāsu sikkhitā //
Ạnuvicaranti mahāvīrā / pahīnabhayabheravā //

which F. L. Woodward[28] translates poetically as :

Ah, happy saints, the Arahants ! In them no craving's seen.
The 'I'-conceit is rooted up; delusion's net is burst,
Lust-free they have attained; translucent is the heart of them.
These god-like beings, drug immune, unspotted in the world,
Knowing the fivefold mass, they roam the seven domains of good.
Worthy of praise and worthy they—sons of the Wake true born,
The wearers of the sevenfold gem, in the threefold training trained—
These mighty heroes follow on, exempt from fear and dread :
Lords of the tenfold potency, great sages tranquillised :
Best beings in all the world; in them no craving's seen.
They've won the knowledge of adepts. This compound is their last.
That essence of the holy life that they have made their own.
Unshaken by the triple modes, set free from birth to come,
The plane of self-control they've won, victorious in the world.
Upward or crossways or below—no lure is found in them.
They sound aloud their lion's roar "Supreme are they that wake."

In this *gāthā*, the arahant is first called 'happy' or 'blissful' (*sukha*), a theme repeated in a few places in the *Sutta Piṭaka*.[29]

27. S.III.83-84.

28. *The Book of Kindred Sayings, op. cit.*, Vol. I, pp. 69-70.

29. Such as at *Udana*, p. 11; and a critical discussion of *sukha/dukkha* is found at S.V.209-210, and which will be considered in our discussion of the arahant and the emotions.

No craving (*taṇhā*) can be found in them, an important aspect of the arahant : in fact, it appears that this is the *sine qua non* of *arahattā*.[30] This shall be taken up again in our discussion of unskilful factors (*akusalā dhammā*).

The 'I'-conceit, Woodward's translation of *asmimāno*; delusion's net (*mohajāla*), and freedom from lust (*anejanto anuppattā*) are most often expressed as the three root causes (*mūla-paccayā*) of the whole of *saṃsāra* : lust (*rāga*), hatred (*dosa*) and ignorance (*moha*), the three *kilesā* from which the arahant is far.[31] Woodward's "unspotted in the world" for *loke anūpalittā* is a bit ambiguous, as it might call to mind references of the unknowability of the course of the arahant (*vaṭṭaṃ tesaṃ na 'tthi paññāpanāya*), which is another matter entirely. In this case, *anūpallita* means "untainted" or "cleansed." The arahant is also "godlike" (*brahmabhūtā*), and he is also *anāsavā*, not of the āsavā, which has been discussed above.

The arahant knows the five *khanda* thoroughly (*pañcakkhande pariññāya*), which reflects his full comprehension of the Buddha's teaching of *anattā*, the non-substantiality of self, which is tantamount to saying, as above, that there is no *asmimāno*, or 'I'-conceit, in the arahant. The arahants "roam the seven fields of good" (*sattasaddhammagocarā*), or the seven good *dhammā*, which the commentary[32] lists as : (1) faith or conviction (*saddhā*); (2) a sense of shame (*hiri*); (3) religious dread (*ottappaṃ*); (4) truth (*saccaṃ*); (5) energy (*viriya*); (6) mindfulness (*sati*); and (7) wisdom (*paññā*). These are also indicated by *sattaratana-sampannā*, "they possess the sevenfold gem," which the commentary identifies with the seven factors of enlightenment (*sattā bojjhaṅgā*), which will be discussed below.

The arahants are the true sons of the Buddha (*puttā buddhassa orasā*), an imagery we find most frequently in the Therīgāthā,[33] where it becomes an adaptation of Brahma-mythology. As the brahmins in the Puruṣa Hymn of the *Ṛg Veda*[34] are said to be born from the mouth (or speech) of Brahmā, so some arahants claim to be born from the mouth of the Buddha.

30. See S.II.53-54.
31. See DhA.228.
32. See the footnote at *Kindred Sayings*, Vol. III, p. 69.
33. *Thig.*, verses 335-336.
34. *Ṛg Veda*, X, 90, 72.

The arahants are trained in the threefold training (*tīsu sikkhāsu sikkhitā*), which the commentary glosses as training in higher morality (*adhisīla*), higher thought (*adhicitta*) and higher wisdom (*adhipaññā*), but it seems that this could just as well be a reference to the threefold lore of the arahant, which is a common manner of speech about arahants.[35]

That the arahant should be free from fear and dread (*pahīna-bhayabheravā*) is an extension of the idea that all fear and dread can be found to be rooted in the notion of a self which, if existentially negated, makes fear and dread an impossibility. It is a common motif in tales of the arahants that they should not fear, and some rather humorous anecdotes in the regard have been found in the Singhalese commentatorial and chronicle (*vaṃsa*) traditions.[36] To indicate a line of thought that could be developed further, modern existential philosophy makes much of an honest confrontation with fear and dread, as Kierkegaard's *angst*, Sartre's *nausée*, et cetera. A closer analysis will reveal, however, that according to the Buddha, fear and dread is an egoistic morbidity which must be passed through quickly for there to be true spiritual growth.[37]

They are "lords of the tenfold potency" (*dasaṅgehi sampannā*), a reference to the arahant's ten powers (*dasabalāni*), which[38] in some places are listed nearly identically as the well-known ten powers of a Tathāgata (*dasatathāgatabalāni*).[39] This will be discussed in detail in our discussion of the arahant and the buddha, but we find this reference significant to indicate the spiritual equivalence of the arahant and the Tathāgata in the *Sutta Piṭaka*.

The arahants are called mahānāgā, great *nāgas*, for which Woodward's "great sages" is inadequate. Nāgā symbolism is one of the ways the arahant is discussed in both canonical and

35. M. I. 481-483.

36. Walpola Rahula, *History of Buddhism in Ceylon: The Anurādhapura Period*, Colombo : M. D. Gunasena, 1966 (1956), pp. 217-229. [Hereinafter : Rahula, HBC.]

37. See M. W. Padmasiri de Silva, *Tangles and Webs: Comparative Studies in Existentialism, Psychoanalysis and Buddhism*, Colombo : Lake House, 1976, pp. 46-59.

38. A.V.174-176.

39. M.I.69-71.

popular Buddhist literature, and this shall be discussed in our section on arahant symbolism.

They are beyond any further training (*asekhā*). The distinction between *sekha* and *asekha* becomes significant as one of the ways of speaking which grew into the whole notion of the paths and fruitions of the four noble persons (four *ariyā puggalā maggā* and *phalāni*), to which a section below is devoted. They have completed the essence of the spiritual life (*yo sāro brahmacariyassa tasmim aparapaccayā*), and are set free from future rebirths (*vippamuttā punabbhavā*), which is the goal of *brahmacariya*. They are victors (*vijitāvino*), a notion which becomes embellished in the Mahāyāna and Vajrayāna Buddhist traditions, who speak about the *jina* or *rgyal ba* as the perfected person. Nothing in the world can be a lure (*nandi*) for them, as they are unshakable (*akopya*).[40] This also became an issue of great controversy in the Mahāyāna, and much has been controverted as to at which point along the *magga* one becomes unshakable.[41] This was especially crucial in the bodhisattva path and the notion of the ten *bhūmis*, or levels, of the career of the bodhisattva (*bodhisattvayāna*), and which is discussed at length in such texts as the *Daśabhūmikasūtra* and the *Bodhisattvabhūmi*.[42]

Finally, the arahants are said to sound their lion's roar (*nandanti sīhanādaṃ*). The whole idea of a lion's roar and its grammatical cousin of a public expression of the arahant's insight (*aññā vyākaronti*) will be discussed in the very next section, but it is important that an arahant express his spiritual attainment. According to this *gāthā*, what is declared is that the buddha (here used in its generic sense of an awakened one) is supreme in the world : *buddhā loke anuttarāti*.

40. See Edward Conze, *Buddhist Thought in India*, Ann Arbor : University of Michigan Press, 1967 (1962), p. 167.

41. Various positions on this topic are enumerated by Kong sprul blo gros mtha' yas in his monumental work, *Theg pa'i rgo kun las btus pa gsung rab rin po che'i mdzod bslab pa gsum legs par ston pa'i bstan bcos shes bya ba*, or as it is more widely known, the *Snes bya kun khyab*, New Delhi : International Academy of Indian Culture, 1970, '*grel* (auto-commentary), Vol. III, fasc. 523. He concludes that the *śrāvaka* becomes unshakable in his practice at the level of the *prayogamārga* known as the *rigs pa'i sa*, the "great patience and exalted Dharma levels."

42. See *Bodhisattvabhūmi* by Asaṅga (Thogs med), *rNal 'byor spyod pa'i sa las byang chub sems dpa'i sa, bsTan, 'gyur*, Peking edition, *mDo 'grel*, Vol. shi, facs. 131a-245a.

4. *From the Aṅguttara Nikāya*

In the *Aṅguttara Nikāya* we find three new arahant formulae, one of which is a modification of one with which we are already familiar. The first[43] is very brief :

Kāyamuniṃ vācāmuniṃ cetomuniṃ anāsavaṃ muniṃ
moneyyasampannaṃ āhu sabbappahāyinan ti.

This could be translated in two ways, depending on how one reads the term *muni*. The term is derived from the Vedic √*muni*, which means "to be silent"[44] and which became identified with one who took vows of silence. From this derivation, we get *muni* as "a sage." Based on the earlier usage, this verse could be read as : "Silent with regard to body, speech and mind, the silent one (*muni*) is blessed with silence, and is called one who has given up or renounced all." Following the later usage, we would get : "Sagacious in body, speech and mind, the sage (*muni*) is blessed with sagacity and is called one who has given up or renounced all." Given the time of the compilation of these texts, the latter reading is more likely, although the first is of more philosophic interest, as we want to contend that the arahant is one who can be silent, not merely in speech but, as the verse says, also with body, which is to say, an intentionality, and mind.[45] 'Renouncing all" (*sabbappahāyinaṃ*) is, of course, not new to what we have already seen about the arahant.

The next formula[46] is an adaptation of the most common formula about becoming an arahant, and one with which we are quite familiar. However, the first part of this section regarding energy (*viriya*) is most interesting, and it is addressed by the Buddha to Soṇa :

Evam eva kho Soṇa accāraddhaviriyaṃ uddhaccāya saṃvattati atilīnaviriyam kosajjāya saṃvattati. Tasmā ti ha tvaṃ Soṇa viriyasamataṃ adhiṭṭhaha indriyānañ ca samataṃ paṭivijjha tattha ca nimittaṃ gaṇhāhī ti.....Atha kho āyasmā Soṇo

43. A.I.273. (My translation)
44. *PTS Dictionary*, p. 538.
45. Talk about body, speech and mind is quite important throughout Buddhism, but it is especially important in the *tantrayāna*. For an example of this language, see the second entreaty in Indrabhūti's *rDo rje theg pa'i rtsa ba dang yan lag gi ltung ba'i bshags pa*, *bsTan 'gyur*, sNar thang edition, *rgyud 'grel*, Vol. Pu, fascs. 114b-115b, especially fasc. 115b.
46. A.III.376. (My translation).

> aparena samayena viriyasamataṃ adhiṭṭhahi indriyānañ ca samataṃ paṭivijjhi tattha ca nimittaṃ aggahesi. Atha kho āyasmā Soṇo eko vūpakaṭṭho ātāpi pahitatto viharanto na cirass' eva yass' atthāya kulaputtā samma-d-eva agārasmā anagāriyaṃ pabbajanti, tad anuttaraṃ brahmacariyapariyosānaṃ diṭṭh' eva dhamme sayaṃ abhiññā sacchikatvā upasampajja vihāsi. "Khīṇā jāti vusitaṃ brahmacariyaṃ kataṃ karaṇīyaṃ nāparaṃ itthattāyā ti abhiññāsi. Aññataro ca panāyasmā Soṇo arahataṃ ahosi.
>
> Even so, Soṇa, energy, when overstrong, ends in flurry, when over-lax, in idleness. Wherefore, Soṇa, stand fast in the mean of energy; pierce the mean (in the use) of the faculties; and therein grasp the real worth.....And presently, the venerable Soṇa stood fast in the mean of energy; pierced the mean in the faculties; and grasped therein the mark; and living alone, secluded, ernest, ardent, resolute, entered and abode, not long after, here amid things seen, by his own power, in the realisation of that end above all of the godly life [*brahmacariyaṃ*], for the sake of which clansmen [*kulaputtā*] rightly go forth from home to the homeless life; and he knew : "Birth is ended, the godly life lived, done is what was to be done, there is no more of this." And the venerable Soṇa was one of the arahants.

Energy (*viriya*) is one of the faculties (*indriyāni*) of which there are said to be three[47] or five.[48] If energy is overstrung (*accāraddhaviriyaṃ*), one ends up in a state of flurry (*uddhaccā*), which is usually understood as a state of psychological and intellectual restlessness. On the other hand, if too lax in energy (*atilīnaviriyaṃ*) then the result is indolence (*kosajja*), which is fully explained in the commentatorial literature.[49] Soṇa is asked to find the mean (*samataṃ*) of energy, an indication of the role played by the notion of the middle way (*majjhimā paṭipadā*) in matters of practice in early Buddhism. This term first comes up in the very first *sutta* spoken by the Buddha, the Dhammacakkappavattana Sutta.[50] As the notion of *majjhimā paṭipadā* developed in Buddhist thought, it became more related to philosophical

47. S.V.204.
48. S.V.193-194; See also S.V.202.
49. Vbh. 369.
50. S. 41.11.

issues than to practical ones, and the use of the term in relation to the thoroughly practical matter of *viriya* or energy is therefore significant in that it indicates the orientation of the Buddhism of the *Nikāyas* regarding the notion of the middle way. This does not, however, exclude more philosophic implications, as we shall see in our discussion of the philosophy of the arahant towards the end of this essay. It is by piercing this mean (*samataṃ*) of *viriya* that Soṇa becomes an arahant by the usual formula.[51]

In the same *sutta* we find a modification of another familiar arahant formula, this time the improvisation coming at the end of the verse. We read Soṇa's words :[52]

Yo so bhante bhikkhu arahaṃ khīṇāsavo vusitavā katakaraṇīyo ohitabhāro anuppattasasattho parakkhīṇabhavasaññojano samma-d-aññā vimutto, so cha ṭṭhānāni adhimutto hoti : nekkhammādhimutto hoti, pavivekādhimutto hoti, avyāpajjhādhimutto, taṇhakkhayādhimutto hoti, upādānakkhayādhimutto hoti, asammohādhimutto hoti.

Lord, the arahant monk has destroyed the cankers [*āsavā*], lived the life, done what was to be done, set down the burden, won self-weal, shattered life's fetters and is freed by perfect gnosis [*samma-d-aññā*], has applied himself to six things : to dispassion, detachment, harmlessness, destroying craving, destroying grasping and to non-delusion.

The *cha ṭṭhānāni*, which we would prefer to translate as 'six behaviors'[53] are: intention for renunciation (*nekkhamādhimmutto*); intention for detachment (*pavivekādhimutto*); intention for non harmfulness (*avyāpajjhādhimutto*); intention for the destruction of craving (*taṇhakkhayādhimutto*); intention for the destruction of grasping (*upādānakkhayādhimutto*); and intention for non-delusion (*asammohādhimutto*). These six behaviors were not, to the best of our knowledge, developed under these terminologies, but they are grammatical cousins of the faculties (*indriyāni*), the factors of enlightenment (*bojjhaṅgā*) and the powers (*balāni*), all skilful things (*kusalā dhammā*).

---

51. Which is also found at M.I. 50-51, D.xv.32, M.I. 391-392, S.I.140, et cetera.

52. A.III.376.

53. See *PTS Dictionary*, *s.v. ṭhāna*, II, 2, p. 289.

5. *From the Khuddaka Nikāya*

In the *Khuddaka Nikāya* we find one more arahant formula, and also one *Dhammapada* verse, of significance in our present context. The arahant formula is from the *Itivuttaka*[54] and is a *gāthā* :

Yassa rāgo ca doso ca avijjā ca virājitā /
taṃ bhāvitattaññataraṃ brahmabhūtaṃ tathāgataṃ /
buddhaṃ verabhayātītaṃ āhu sabbapahāyinan ti //

which Woodward[55] translates as :

Who lust and hate and ignorance hath left, him they call 'one whose self is made to grow', 'One become Brahma', 'He who has thus come', 'Awakened One', 'who hath passed fear and dread', And 'one who hath the all abandoned'.

The first verse characterizes the arahant as one who has gone beyond the three *kilesā* of lust (*rāga*), hatred (*dosa*) and ignorance (*avijjā*), which is more commonly called, in this context, *moha* or delusion. The appellations of the arahant in this formula are interesting, as he is called :

1. *bhāvitattāaññtaraṃ*, for which Woodward's "one whose self is made to grow" seems inadequate. This term is a compound of three words : *bhāvita*, the passive verbal form of *bhāvanā*, "to make become" or "to develop," which gives us the sense of "is developed or cultivated"; *attā*, self, but in this context meaning *citta* or mind;[56] and *aññatara*, a pronominal adjective meaning simply "a certain one" or "a."[57] The compound, therefore, could better be translated as "a person who has cultivated his mind," which is simpler than Woodward's "one whose self is made to grow," and which also does not bring a philosophic muddle into the picture.

2. *brahmabhūtaṃ* means one who has become like *brahma*, which is more or less the way Woodward translates it. The term *brahma* in Buddhist usage is employed to talk about spiritual matters, as in *brahmacariya*, and has no theistic or metaphysical implications, as would be the case in its brahmanical

54. Iti. 57.

55. F. L. Woodward, tr., *The Minor Anthologies of the Pali Canon* Part II, London : Pali Text Society, 1948. (1935), p. 159.

56. *PTS Dictionary*, p. 503.

57. *Ibid.*, p. 14.

contexts. This context prohibits a reading of "become one with Brahma" or any such theological interpretation which would, however, be applicable in a certain discourse given by Sāriputta[58] and which shall be discussed below.

3. *tathāgataṃ* need not be translated. What is of interest to us is that the arahant can rightfully be called a *tathāgata*. The *Itivuttaka* is one of the very oldest texts in the *Tipiṭaka*, and we see in this usage, as well as in the next appellation, *buddhaṃ*, that there was no significant distinction between arahant, *tathāgata* and *buddha* in the earliest literature.

4. *buddhaṃ* has just been discussed.

5. *verabhayātītaṃ* means that one need not fear (*bhaya*) the *verabhayā*, known as the 'fivefold guilty dread' which arises from breaking the five fundamental ethical precepts of Buddhism, the *pañcaśīla*. This shall be taken up below.

6. *sabbapahāyinaṃ* has been discussed in our considerations of the *Aṅguttara Nikāya*.[59]

The *Dhammapada* verse about the arahant is :[60]

N' eva devo na gandhabbo / na māro saha brahmunā /
Jitaṃ apajitaṃ kayirā / tathārūpassa jantuno //

This verse simply tells us that the arahant is beyond the range of the gods, Māra even together with Brahmā. The relationship of the arahants to the gods has been fully and competently discussed by M. M. J. Marasinghe,[61] so we shall not be concerning ourselves with this topic in the present essay. But it is vital to Buddhism that the arahant be beyond the gods, who are relocated into just another sector of *saṃsāra*, albeit a pleasant and more enduring sector. This is an elementary point in Buddhism, and our field researches in Sri Lanka have indicated that it is well understood by Buddhists. In Sri Lanka, Buddhists pray to the gods, but they are quite aware that what they pray to them for is "secular"—wealth, love, successful missions, et cetera. Hindus in Sri Lanka believe that the gods can be their *kalyāṇamitta*,

58. M.I.182ff.
59. A.I.273.
60. Dhp. VIII.6.
61. M.M.J. Marasinghe, *Gods in Early Buddhism : A Study in their Social and Mythological Melieu as Depicted in the Nikāyas of the Pāli Canon*, Kelaniya : Vidyalankara Campus Publications, 1974, *passim*. [Hereinafter : Marasinghe, *GEB*].

or 'spiritual friend,' bestowing upon them religious as well as secular benefits. This is firmly denied by even the most rural Buddhists. The gods, according to them, can indeed bestow material benefit, but spiritual fruits are totally a matter of the individual's control and effort.

6. *Conclusions*

We have found thirteen arahant formulae in the *Sutta Piṭaka.* Undoubtedly there is some overlap among them; yet we feel that each contributes something unique to our picture of the arahant. The *P.T.S. Dictionary*,[62] for the sake of comparison, extracts just these four formulae, which are listed as :

1. khīṇā jāti vusitaṃ brahmacariyaṃ kataṃ karaṇīyaṃ nāparaṃ itthattāya, which is found at : Vin.1.14, 35, 183; D.I.84, 177, 203; M.I.139, II.39; S.I.140, II.51, 82, 95, 120, 245, III.21, 45, 55, 68, 71, 90, 195, 223, IV.2, 20, 35, 45, 86, 107, 151, 383, V.72, 90, 144, 222; A.I.165, II.211, III.93, IV.88, 179, 302; V.155, 162; Sn., p. 16; Pug., p. 61; et cetera.

2. eko vūpakaṭṭho appamatto ātāpī pahitatto, which is found at : D.I.177, II.153; S.I.140, 161, II.21, III.36, 74, IV.64, V.144, 166; A.I.282, II.249, III.70, 217, 201, 376, IV.235.

3. arahaṃ khīṇāsavo vusitavā katakaraṇīyo ohitabhāro anupattasadattho parikkhīṇa-bhava-saññojano samma-d-aññā vimutto, which is found at : D.III.83, 97; M.I.4, 235; S.I.71, III.161, 193, IV.125, V.145, 205, 273, 302; A.I.144, II.359, 376. IV.362, 369, 371 sq.; It., p. 38.

4. ñāṇañ ca pana me dassanaṃ udapādi akuppā me cetovimutti ayaṃ antimā jāti natthi dāni punabbhavo, which is found at : S.II.171, III.28, IV.8, V.204; A.I.259, IV.56, 305, 448.

Closely related to our discussion of formulae, by which the arahant is described or characterized, is our discussion of the arahant's public expression of his *arahattā,* which is known as *aññaṃ vyākaroti,* and which is the next topic to be taken up. It is under this head that we shall consider the fourth formula from the *P.T.S. Dictionary's* list above.

C. *Expressions of Arahattā*

In the early texts, the arahants publicly express that they have attained their goal (*attha*). We find these formal expressions in

62. *PTS Dictionary*, p. 77.

all of the *nikāyas*, and there is one text compiled almost exclusively of similar expressions, the *Thera* and *Therīgāthā* of the *Khuddaka Nikāya*. The grammar of these declarations is usually expressed as *aññā vyākaroti*, "to express *aññā*." All of this rightly leads us to question the meaning and use of the term *aññā* as a preliminary to our discussion of its expressions (*vyākaroti*).

Aññā comes from the Sanskrit root √*jñā*, "to know,"[63] and it finds itself in the same linguistic family with other *jñā*-derivatives such as : *ñāṇa* (Skt. *jñāna*), *paññā* (*prajñā*), *saññā* (*saṁjñā*) and *viññāṇa* (*vijñāna*).[64] The *P.T.S. Dictionary*[65] gives us : "knowledge, recognition, perfect knowledge, philosophic insight, knowledge *par excellence*, viz. Arahantship, saving knowledge, gnosis." Buddhadatta[66] gives us : "perfect knowledge, arahantship," and Nyāṇatiloka[67] offers : "highest knowledge, gnosis, refers to the perfect knowledge of the saint." *Paññā*, the term which stems closest in usage, is defined as : "intelligence, comprising all the higher faculties of cognition, intellect as conversant with general truths";[68] or "wisdom, knowledge, insight";[69] or "understanding, knowledge, wisdom, insight, comprises a very wide field. The specific Buddhist knowledge or wisdom, however, as part of the noble eightfold path....is insight (*vipassanā*), i.e. that intuitive knowledge which brings about the four stages of holiness [four *ariyā maggā*] and the realisation of nibbāna... and which consists in the penetration of the impermanence, misery and impersonality of all forms of existence."[70]

63. Whitney, p. 56.

64. David J. Kalupahana ("Aññā," *s v.*, *Encyclopadia of Buddhism*, Colombo: Government of Ceylon, 1961 on), and Alex Wayman ("Regarding the Translation of the Buddhist Terms saññā/samjñā and viññāna/vijñāṇa,," in *Malalasekera Commemoration Volume*, Colombo : 1976, pp. 325-335) have been of considerable assistance in sorting out this confusion of terms, and we want to develop some of the points they suggest.

65. *PTS. Dictionary*, p. 14.

66. A. P. Buddhadatta Mahāthera, *Concise Pāli-English Dictionary*, Colombo : Colombo Apothecaries' Co., 1968, p. 5.

67. Nyāṇatiloka Mahāthera, *Buddhist Dictionary*, Colombo : Frewin & Co., 1972, p. 15.

68. *PTS Dictionary*, p. 390.

69. Buddhadatta, *op. cit.*, p. 154.

70. Nyāṇatiloka, *op. cit.*, p. 122. Elsewhere (Nathan Katz, "Nāgārjuna and Wittgenstein on Error," in Katz, ed., *Buddhist and Western Philosophy* :

Aññā is generally distinguished from *pannā* in that it is used in the restricted sense of that knowledge or intuition that brings about the fruition (*phala*) of *arahattā*. As such, the commentaries equate it with arahantship itself : *sambahulehi kira bhikkhūhi Bhagavato santike aññā vyākatā, "Khīṇā jāti. . . ."*[71]

It seems that all of these grammatical cousins derived from the root √*jñā* refer to cognitive processes, and in the *Sutta Piṭaka* we find specific derivatives used to point to specific aspects of cognition. *Aññā* is used most often to speak about that cognition which is coterminous with the attainment of *arahattā*. This is not a hard and fast rule, as the Buddha declares his attainment at the Bodhi-tree by the more general term *ñāṇa*.[72] *Pannā*, as Kalupahanna[73] suggests, is "only a means to the attainment of release and that is not an end in itself."

The *aññā vyākaroti*, or expression of *aññā*, therefore means the same as expressing *arahattā*. It would seem that the best way to get clear about the notion of expressing *aññā* or *arahattā* would be to look at some such expressions from the *Sutta Piṭaka* and see what is usually involved.

Probably the most well-known *vyākaroti* is made by Soṇa, and which we have already considered under our discussion of arahant formulae. It[74] reads : "Lord, the arahant monk who has destroyed the cankers [*āsavā*], lived the life, done what was to be done, set down the burden, won self-weal, shattered life's fetters and is freed by perfect gnosis [*samma-d-aññā*], has applied himself to six things. . . ." This expression involves the most standard arahant formula (*khīṇā jāti*, etc.) followed by reference to the six behaviors (*cha ṭṭhānāni*), or intentions to practice.

Other expressions of *arahattā* utilize rather standardized

A Critical Comparative Study, New Delhi : Sterling, forthcoming we have tried to get straight about the grammar of *paññā/prajñā* in its Mahāyāna usages with specific regard to whether this type of 'insight' entailed a referrent. We concluded that it did not.

71. As quoted in *Gradual Sayings*, Vol. II, p. 85, fn. 2.

72. M.I.167.

73. Kalupahana, *op. cit.*, p. 695; in reference to M.I.204.

74. A.III.376. (PTS translation).
Yo so bhante bhikkhu arahaṃ khīṇāsavo vusitavā katakaraṇīyo anuppattasadattho parikkhīṇabhavasaññojano sammadaññā vimutto, so cha ṭṭhānāni adhimutto hoti.

systems of Buddhist symbolism of the arahant, which shall be considered in detail below. For example, we find the *gāthā* of the Therī Uttarā[75] as :

Having practiced with body, speech and mind,
and having overcome the root of thirst,
I am cooled, *nibbāna-ed.*

Here the Therī is telling us that, by having practiced or disciplined herself with regard to body or intentionality, speech and mind, she has overcome all thirst as well as the possibility (*mūla*) of thirst. She has become cooled (*sītībhūta*), which is to say that she has quenched the fever of the passions, and thus is *nibbāna-ed* (*nibbutā*), which etymologically means "blown out" or extinguished.

A common phrase in the *vyākaroti* of the *Therī* and *Theragāthā* is : "deep reflection arose in me" (*tato me manasīkāro udapajjatha*), which is found, for example, in the *gāthā* of Thera Nāgasamāla and Thera Sundarasamudda[76] and which go on to say: "Attention to the fact and to the cause/ The misery of it all was manifest/Distaste, indifference, and mind possessed."

Occasionally the *vyākaroti* gives specific reference to standard Buddhist doctrinal formulations. In the case of the Therī Jentī we find mention of the seven factors of enlightenment, the *satta bojjhaṅgā*, which was a way of talking about the entire *magga* of the Buddha, namely : mindfulness (*sati*), investigation of Dhamma (*dhammavicaya*), energy (*viriya*), ecstacy (*pīti*), tranquility (*passaddhi*), concentrative meditation (*samādhi*) and equanimity (*upekkhā*). She says in *gāthā* :[77]

The seven factors of enlightenment (*satta bojjhaṅga*),
Ways by which *nibbāna* is actualized,
I have developed all of them,
as has been taught by the Buddha.

---

75. Thig., verse 15. (My translation).
kāyena saṃvutā āsiṃ vācāya uda cetasā /
samūlaṃ taṇham abbuyha sītībhūta 'mhi nibbutā //

76. Thag., verses 269-270 and 464-465 respectively. (PTS translation).
ādīnavo pāturahū, nibbidā samatiṭṭhata /
tato cittaṃ vimucci me, passa dhammasudhammataṃ /
tisso vijjā anupattā, kataṃ buddhassa sāsanan ti. //

77. Thig., verse 21. (My translation).
ye ime satta bojjhaṅga maggā nibbānapattiyā /
bhāvitā te mayā sabbe yathā buddhena desitā //

While it is true, as we have discussed, that the arahant is beyond the range of the gods, who are understood in Buddhism as denizens of *saṃsāra* as humans are, nevertheless we do find occasionally a Buddhist re-adaptation of Vedic mythology.[78] An example of this Buddhist confiscation of Vedic mythology is found in the *gāthā* of Therī Sundarī,[79] who tells us that her new birth as an arahant is structurally similar to the Vedic understanding of the birth of the *brāhmaṇa* caste from the mouth (or speech) of Brahman :

Having left Banaras, I came to you.
Sundarī reverences the feet of you, declared as the great hero (*mahāvīra*).
You are Buddha. You are the Teacher. I am your daughter, born from your mouth, true Brahman.
[I have] done my task, [and am] beyond the *āsavā*.

Other expressions which refer to the gods are numerous. In one, the Thera Sunīta[80] reports a vision in which he beheld, after his *bodhi*-experience at a sunrise, Indra and Brahmā approaching him and hailing him for his attainment of *arahattā*. The Therī Selā, in her *gāthā*,[81] taunts Māra, as she is now beyond his reach. One other reference to the gods in this context is in a story about Bāhiya[82] where he wonders whether or not he has become an arahant. A *devatā* assures him that he has not, and directs him to the Buddha.

Three expressions in the *Therī-Theragāthā* strike one because of their beautiful use of nature imagery, reminiscent of the flavor of Zen Buddhism. The first of these is expressed by Therī Cittā :[83]

---

78. This is discussed in detail by Étienne Lamotte, *Histoire du bouddhisme indienne : des origines á l'ere Saka*, Louvain : Publications Universitaires, Biblio-théque du Muséon, Vol. 43, 1958, p. 689. [Hereinafter : Lamotte, *HBI*.] See also D.III.84, S.II.221, Iti.29.

79. Thig, verses 335-336. (My translation).
Bārāṇasito nikkhamma tava santikam āgatā /
sāvikā te mahāvīra pāde vandati Sundarī //
tuvaṃ buddho tuvaṃ satthā tuyhaṃ dhīta mhi brāhmaṇa /
orassāmukhato jātā katakiccā anāsavā //

80. Thag., verses 628-631.

81. Thig., verses 58-59 : evaṃ jānāhi pāpima nihato tvam asi antaka.

82. Udāna, pp. 6-7.

83. Thig., verse 126. (PTS translation).
saṃghāṭiṃ nikkhipitivāna pattakaṃ ca nikujjiya /
sele khambhesiṃ attānaṃ tamokkhandhaṃ padāliya //

Thrown from my shoulder hangs my cloak, o'erturned
My little bowl. So 'gainst the rock I lean
And prop this little self of me, and break away
The wildering gloom that long had closed me in.

and another expressed by Therī Paṭācārā :[84]

One day, bathing my feet, I sit and watch
The water as it trickles down the slope.
Thereby I set my heart in steadfastness,
As one doth train a horse of noble breed.
Then going to my cell, I take my lamp,
And seated on my couch I watch the flame
Grasping the pin, I pull the wick right down
Into the oil......
Lo ! the *nibbāna* of the little lamp !
Emancipation dawns ! My heart is free !

and finally, the one expressed by Thera Vanavaccha :[85]

Crags of a pleasant blue color,
having the purity of cold water,
whose rocks have 'the herds of Indra'-beetle;
in these I delight.

The significance of these three *gāthās* shall be discussed again in our discussion of the arahant and emotions, but let it suffice for the moment to note the keenly-developed aesthetic sensibilities of these therī and thera (elders). Those who see in various forms of Buddhist poetry, be they the *haiku* of Japan, the *dohā* of Bengal, the *gītī* (Tibetan *glu*) of Tibet, or the devotional forms of naturalistic bent of Tibet again, something inimical to the spirit of Buddhism, are requested to re-think their original position, which appears to us as rather narrow. Aesthetic appreciation is indeed more emphasized in the naturalistic Sahajayāna and

---

84. Thig., verses 114-116. (PTS translation).
pāde pakkhālayitvāna udake so karom' ahaṃ /
pādodakañ ca disvāna thalato ninnam āgataṃ /
tato cittaṃ samādhemi assaṃ bhadraṃ va jāniyaṃ //
tato dīpaṃ gahetvāna vihāraṃ pāvisiṃ ahaṃ /
seyyaṃ olokayitvāna mañcakamhi upāvisiṃ //
tato sūciṃ gahetvāna vaṭṭiṃ okassayām' ahaṃ /
padīpasseva nibbānaṃ vimokkho aho cetaso //

85. Thag, verse 13. (My translation).
Nīlabbhavaṇṇā rucirā sītavārī śucindharā
indagopakasañchannā te selā remayanti man ti.

other tantric forms, as well as in Zen, but it is present in very early Buddhist writings as well, and no amount of overly-scholastic interpretations of the Theravāda can negate their presence and their integrality to Pali Buddhism.

In these eleven instances of *aññā vyākaroti*, we have found the following typology : doctrinal (Soṇa, Nāgasamāla, Jentī, Sundarasamudda, Selā and Uttarā); devotional (Sundarī); visionary or mystical (Sunīta); and naturalistic (Cittā, Paṭācārā and Vanavaccha).

Having seen some instances of *aññā vyākaroti*, it would now be well to see what is said about this phenomenon. A very well known comment about these expressions of *arahattā* is made by the Buddha after hearing Khema's expression. Khema[86] says :

> Sir (*bhante*), the monk who is an arahant, who has overcome the *āsavā*, who has completed his task, laid down the burden, attained his goal, who has completely destroyed the fetters of rebirth, who is freed by profound knowledge, to him it does not occur "there is a superior" or "there is an equal" or "there is an inferior."

This expression contains a standard arahant formula, save for the last line which contends that the arahant does not compare himself with others. The Buddha takes up this last important point of Khema's and says :[87]

> So it is, monks, when a son of family (*kulaputtā*) expresses *aññā*. The goal is declared, but a self is not mentioned. But some stupid people express *aññā* pridefully. Then they meet with distress.

And the Buddha adds this *gāthā* :[88]

86. A.III.359. (My translation)
yo so bhante bhikkhu arahṃ khīṇāsavo ohitabhāro anuppattasadattho parikkhīṇābhavasaññojano samma-d-aññā vimutto, tassa na evaṃ hoti 'atthi me seyyo' ti vā 'atthi me sadiso' ti vā 'atthi me hīno' ti vā.

87. A.III.359. (My translation).
Evaṃ kho bhikkhave kulaputtā aññaṃ vyākaronto.
Attha ca vutto attā ca anupanīto. Atha ca pana idh' ekacce moghapurisā hasmāmakā maññe aññaṃ vyākaronti, te pacchā vighātaṃ āpajjantīti.

88. A.III.359. (My translation).
No ussesu na umesu samatte nopanīyare
Khīṇā sañjāti vusitaṃ brahmacariyaṃ caranti
Saññojanavippamuttā ti.

Influenced by neither "greater," "lesser," nor "equal,"
they abide, having overcome further rebirth,
having fulfilled the spiritual life,
fully released from all bonds.

There are two significant points being made here. The first is that any expression of *aññā* is made without reference to self or any comparison with others, indicating the egolessness of the goal (*attha*). An expression of *aññā* that did refer to self would be an extreme case of *asmimāno*, conceitedness, for, as Buddhaghosa says in his *Visuddhimagga* :[89]

Suffering is, but not one who suffers.
Action is, but no actor.
Extinction [*nibbuti*] is, but no extinguished person.
There is a path [*magga*], but no one who goes.

Another point being made by the Buddha is simply that because one gives the semblance of an expression of *arahattā* it does not necessarily follow that this expression is genuine or profound (*samma-d-aññā*).

As the Buddha says of his Dhamma, and which we could also apply to these expressions of *aññā*, is that it is both subjective or personal (*ajjhataṃ*) as well as objective (*bāhīraṃ*).[90] As is pointed out by Johansson,[91] the subjective (*ajjhataṃ*) aspect is tantamount to the expression. At one point, the Buddha claims that these expressions cannot be questioned :[92] "Sāriputta, however a son of family (*kulaputto*) expresses, just that expression is to be seen as such."

However, from the Buddha's observation above that certain expressions of *aññā* may be prideful and therefore not genuine

---

89. Vism., HOS edition, p. 436. (My translation).
Dukkham eva hi, na koci dukkhito /
kārako na, kiriyā va vijjati /
atthi nibbuti, na nibbuto pumā /
maggam atthi, gamako na vijjatī ti //

90. S.IV.4ff.

91. Rune E. A. Johansson, *The Psychology of Nirvana : A Comparative Study of the Natural Goal of Buddhism and the Aims of Modern Psychology*, Garden City, N. Y. : Anchor Books, 1970. (London : George Allen & Unwin, 1969), pp. 114-115. [Hereinafter : Johansson, *P.N.*]

92. S.II.51. (My translation)
Yena kenaci pi Sāriputta pariyāyena kulaputto vyākaroti, atha kho vyākatam vyākatato daṭṭhabbanti.

or profound, and also from another comment[93] that "there are monks who declare *aññā* by pride or conceit," some method of judging these expressions is indicated, and we find this developed in two distinct ways.[94]

The first of these ways is found in the *Majjhima Nikāya*[95] and is discussed by I. B. Horner :[96]

> Sutta 112 sets forth six ways in which a monk's claim to be an arahant can be scrutinized by other monks : they may ask him about things he has seen, heard, sensed or cognized; about the five groups of grasping; about the six elements; about the six sense-fields; and about this consciousness-informed body and the phenomena external to it. In answer to each group of questions the monk who claims arahantship for himself relates the process by which he reached this height.

This, then, would be one of the objective (*bāhīraṃ*) criteria of *arahattā*. But this method has its shortcomings, as discussed in the *Aṅguttara Nikāya*,[97] as a clever monk may be able to sham the answers to this interrogation. We are left, then, with only one foolproof method : namely, mindreading (*cetasā ceto paricca*) by a monk proficient in the meditations (*jhāna*), supernormal powers (*iddhi*) and higher knowledges (*abhiññā*). We shall consider some of the implications of this in our section on the *abhiññā* and *iddhi*, but let us simply state at this point that these supernormal powers played an important role in Dhamma as found in the *Sutta Piṭaka*, this function being only one example.

It was not always an easy matter to find a *bhikkhu* able to exercise such *abhiññā* to test another *bhikkhu's aññā vyākaroti*, especially as Mahā Kassapa observes that the number of arahants has been decreasing,[98] to which the Buddha ruefully replies that an increase in precepts is often accompanied by a decrease in arahants. Thus, in the *Vinaya Piṭaka*[99] a false claim of *arahattā* was considered a *pārājika* offense, the penalty for which was

93. M.II.252. (My translation).
santi pan'idh' ekacce bhikkhū adhimānena pi aññaṃ vyākaṃsu.
94. M. III.29-30; and A.V.161-164.
95. M.III.29-30.
96. *Middle Length Sayings*, III, pp. xiv-xv.
97. A.V.161-164.
98. S.II.224.
99. Vin.III.90.

expulsion from the *saṅgha.* Consequently, the custom of expressing *arahattā* publicly died out, the penalties for a false expression being too severe.

As the Buddha's dialogical method was largely to investigate the conditions given which a claim came to be made, rather than focusing on the claim itself, Ānanda[100] applies this method to the case of expressing *aññā* :

"... when anyone, be it monk or nun, proclaims in my presence that he had attained arahantship, all do so by virtue of four factors [*aṅgehi*] or one of these four."

The first of these four factors is :

> Herein, your reverences, a monk develops insight [*vipassanā*] preceded by calm [*samatha*]. In him thus developing insight preceded by calm is born the way [*magga*]. He follows along that Way, makes it grow, makes much of it. In him following, developing, making much of that Way, the fetters [*saṁyojanāni*] are abandoned, the lurking tendencies [*anusayā*] come to an end.

The other three factors involve *vipassanā* and *samatha* as well. The second is : "he develops calm preceded by insight" (*vipassanā-pubbaṅgamaṃ samathaṃ bhāveti*). The third is : "*vipassanā* and *samatha* conjoined" (*samathavipassanaṃ yuganaddhaṃ bhāveti*). And the last is : "his mind is utterly cleansed about perplexities about Dhamma" (*dhammuddhacciggahītamanā hoti*). This analysis by Ānanda ultimately rests on two key notions : insight (*vipassanā*) and calm (*samatha*), which are also the terms used to talk about the two chief meditational systems of Buddhism. In this context, *samatha* is used in its meditational sense, while *vipassanā* seems to be a synonym for *paññā*. This distinction resulted in the entire *paññāvimutto-cetovimutto* question, a question which very nearly led to a schism in Laṅkā,[101] and one

---

100. A.II.157. (My translation)
yo hi koci āvuso bhikkhu vā bhikkhuni vā mama santike arahattapttiṃ vyākaroti sabbo so catuhi aṅgehi etesaṃ vā aññatarena.

101. Nathan Katz, *Meanderings of the Wheel of Dhamma : A Comparative Study of Some Buddhist Missions*, Kandy : Buddhist Publication Society, Wheel Series No. 257, p. 23, fn. 5 : "The intellectual emphasis of the Theravāda was underscored in the first century C.E. by the *ganthadhura*, *vipassanādhura* debates. While these two methods of learning and meditative insight are not viewed as antithetical in Theravāda literature, the primacy of an intel-

which shall be taken up in detail below. The commentary refers this entire analysis to the arising of the *magga* in the sense of entry into the path of the stream-winner (*sotāpattimagga*),[102] but it is clear from Ānanda's original statement that he is discussing how one comes to the fruition of *arahattā* (*arahattāphala*). Although the terminology of the fourth factor (*dhammauddhacciggahitamanā*, etc.) is the terminology of the *sotāpanna* or streamwinner, the context dictates that this is significant only in the sense of from where one has arrived at *arahattāphala*.

Another issue we may touch upon in our discussion of *aññā vyākaroti*, but which shall be considered in detail below, is whether or not such an expression entails the attainment of the supernormal powers (*iddhi*). An expression such as the one Therī Uppalavaṇṇā[103] makes certainly does, as it has specific reference to these powers :

How erst I lived I know : the Heavenly Eye,
Purview celestial, have I clarified;
Clear too the inward life that others lead;
Clear too I hear the sounds ineffable;
Powers supernormal have I made my own;
And won immunity from the deadly Drugs [*āsavā*].
These, the six higher knowledges are mine.
Accomplished is the bidding of the Lord.
With chariot and horses four I came,
Made visible by supernormal power [*iddhi*],
And worshipped, wonder working, at his feet,
The wondrous Buddha, Sovran of the world.

This expression contains specific reference to the six higher knowledges (*abhiññā*), which are : (1) *iddhi-vidhā* or supernormal

lectual comprehension of Dhamma is a distinguishing mark of the Singhalese Theravāda. Of course, meditation has always been vital, as in any form of Buddhism......."

102. Mrs. Rhys-Davids, tr., *The Book of Kindred Sayings*, vols. I and II only, London : Pali Text Society, 1917, 1922, II, p. 157, fn.

103. Thig., verses 227-229. (PTS translation)
pubbenivāsaṃ jānāmi dibbacakkhuṃ visodhittaṃ /
ceto paricca ñāṇañ ca sotadhātu visodhitā / /
iddhi pi me sacchikatā patto me āsavakkhayo /
cha me abhiññā sacchikatā kataṃ buddhassa sāsanaṃ //
iddhiyā abhinimmitvā caturassaṃ rathaṃ ahaṃ /
buddhassa pāde vanditvā lokanāthassa sirīmato //

or magical powers; (2) *dibba-sota*, the divine ear or clairaudience; (3) *ceto-pariya-ñāṇa*, or mind-reading; (4) *dibba-cakkhu*, the divine eye or clairvoyance; (5) *pubbe-nivāsānussati*, or remembering former existences; and (6) *āsvakkhaya*, the overcoming of the *āsavā*. The first five are reckoned mundane (*lokiyā*), and the last is supermundane (*lokuttara*). These six are mentioned in all of the *nikāyas* on many occasions.[104] In this verse, Uppalavaṇṇā arrives to worship the Buddha by *iddhi*-produced (*iddhiyā*) chariot and horses. Although this topic is found by some to be embarrassing,[105] we shall take it up in detail below.

Despite Uppalavaṇṇā's verses, an expression of *arahattā* is not always understood as entailing *iddhi* and *abhiññā* (save for the sixth *abhiññā* of *āsavakkhaya,* of course). In one place, Susīma[106] asks some members of the *saṅgha* who had already declared *aññā* whether or not their expressions entailed the various *iddhividhā*. They reply that this is not the case, because"...we are *paññāvimuttas*, venerable Susīma" (*paññāvimuttā kho mayaṃ āvuso Susīmāti*), meaning that they have attained liberation (*vimutta*) by insight (*paññā*) rather than being liberated by or through the heart/mind (*cetovimuttā*). Such *paññāvimuttā* arahants come to be known rather disparagingly as "dry-visioned" (*sukkhavipassaka*),[107] and this whole question shall be considered in detail below. However, while some expressions of *arahattā* or *aññā* make vivid references to *iddhi* and *abhiññā*, this is not entailed in the expression itself.

Anyone familiar with Buddhist literature will quickly see parallels between this phenomenon of *aññā vyākaroti* and the "lion's roar" tradition (*sīhanāda*). It would seem well that we distinguish between these two phenomena. Both are spontaneous verbal expressions of an enlightened mind. Both are included in the canonical traditions of all schools of Buddhism, and other similar phenomena, such as *dohā*, *gīti* and *haiku*, were maintained in the Buddhist cultures of Bengal, Tibet and Japan.

---

104. See Nyāṇatiloka, *op. cit.*, p. 2, for a list of references.

105. See Louis de la Vallée Poussin, "Le Bouddha et les Abhijñās," *Le Muséon*, 1931, pp. 335-342.

106. S.II.121 ff.

107. Nārada Mahāthera, *The Buddha and his Teachings*, Colombo : Vajirārāma, 2nd ed., 1973 (1964), pp. 537-583.

Let us look at how the Buddha characterizes his sīhanāda teachings :[108]

> For the Samaṇa Gotama both utters forth his lion's roar, and that too in assemblies where men congregate, and in full confidence in the justice of his claim, and men put their questions to him on that, and on being questioned he expounds the problem put, and by his exposition thereof satisfaction arises in their hearts, and they hold it worthy to listen to his word, and in listening to it they experience conviction, and being convinced they give outward signs thereof, and they penetrate even to the truth, and having grasped it they are able also to carry the truth out.

A superficial analysis of the *sīhanāda* and *aññā vyākaroti* phenomena might yield some sort of distinction along the lines that whereas *sīhanāda* is teaching, the *aññā vyākaroti* is expression. This distinction would not hold up, we feel, because it could be argued that the Buddha's teaching is also expression. The distinction of teaching and expression is especially tenuous in Buddhism : teaching is expression, and vice-versa. We would offer that one uses the term *aññā vyākaroti* to indicate the tradition of a newly-realized arahant making his first important public expression, which is considered within Buddhism a highly significant event, as these expressions are often remembered and investigated. The *sīhanāda* tradition—and this is not only restricted in its application to the Buddha, as even in the *Sutta Piṭaka* we find other arahants expressing in this way—is an especially fearless form of exposition, and certain discourses get called *sīhanāda* because of their adjudged importance. A *sutta* which is considered to be a *sīhanāda* may be called such in its title,[109] or it may not be, as the Dhammacakkappavattanā Sutta,[110] which is perhaps the most reknown *sīhanāda*. A *sutta*, it seems, may be judged important enough to be called *sīhanāda* either

---

108. D.viii.22. (PTS translation)
Sīhanādañ ca Samaṇo Gotamo nadatī, parisāsu ca nadati, visārado ca nadati, pañhañ ca naṃ pucchanti, pañhañ ca nesaṃ puṭṭho vyākaronti, pañhassa veyyākaraṇena cittaṃ ārādheti, sotabbañ ci assa maññanti, sutvā ca pasīdanti, passanā ca pasannākāram karonti, tathattāya ca paṭipajjanti, patipannā ca ārādhentīti.

109. D.viii.

110. S.41.11.

because of its intrinsic import in content, or because of the importance of the occasion on which it was uttered.

It might also be mentioned that while *aññā vyākaroti* is used primarily to refer to the expression of *arahattāphala*, the fruition of *arahattā*, one also finds such *vyākaroti* for different stages of the four *maggā* and *phalāni* (paths and fruitions), especially that of the streamwinner (*sotāpatti*).[111] This shall be taken up in more detail when we discuss the four noble persons (*ariyā puggalā*), but we wish to indicate here the wider application of the term *vyākaroti* than simply to that expression at the time of *arahattāphala*.

D. *Occasions of Arahattā*

To help us become familiar with the use of the term arahant, it would be well if we were to look at some instances in the *Sutta Piṭaka* and the commentaries of actual attainment of *arahattā*, the occasions of *bodhi*. It must be mentioned that *nibbāna* or *arahattā* is not conceived by Buddhists as the result of these occasions, as the Buddha was very clear that *nibbāna* is not in any sense caused; it is the very antithesis of that which could be caused, because that which is caused is marked by the *tilakkhana* or three characteristics of suffering (*dukkha*), impermanence (*anicca*) and egolessness (*anattā*), and *nibbāna* could not be characterized by these three. Yet it is useful to look at the occasions at which *nibbāna* is attained, in order to indicate to us when and how the term for one who attains it, namely arahant, is used.

As we shall see, the most frequent occasion of the attainment of *arahattā* is upon hearing a sermon from the Buddha, or even just hearing a snippet of Dhamma. Also quite common are rather dramatic deathbed stories where, collecting oneself in the face of old age/ sickness / death, the bhikkhu is able to overcome them. We also find some less-readily explainable occasions, such as watching a flame, hearing a song, contemplating a corpse, et cetera.

Before we actually consider these occasions, it should be pointed out that in the early Buddhist texts, there were no caste, age, or

111. As, for example, S.II.68-70; A.III.211; and A.IV.405.

sex barriers to *arahattā*. To this point, Mrs. Rhys-Davids[112] reminds us that Māṇava, Adhimutta, Rāhula, Sāna, Kumāra-Kassapa and many others became arahants as youth, and that Bhadda, Saṅkicca, Sīvali, the Sopākas and Sumana became arahants as children, all according to the commentary on the *Therī-Theragāthā* by Dhammapāla. Using the same source, her census of the caste-origins of the 259 poets of the *Theragāthā*[113] reveals that 113 of them were brahmins, sixty were khattiyas, seven were owners or tenants of land, fifty-three were merchants or the like, nine were craftsmen, mahouts or caravan guides, one was an actor, ten were pariahs, laborers, slaves or fishermen, three were bastards of royalty or *saṅgha*-members, and three were 'sone of simple lay-adherents.' Thus neither age nor caste nor learning was an insurmountable barrier, although there is quite a disproportionate number of brahmins. (In fact, there remained a disproportion of brahmins among those who became bodhisattvas or mahāsiddhas as well.) The mere presence of the *Therīgāthā* in the *Sutta Piṭaka* indicated that sex was not a barrier either.

A paradigm for the instance of attaining *arahattā* on hearing the Buddha preach Dhamma is the case of Soṇa, to which we have referred twice before. In this case,[114] Soṇa hears the Buddha discoursing on energy (*viriya*), and in the next verse we hear Soṇa's *aññā vyākaroti*, which is in terms similar to the ones used by the Buddha in his discourse.

The case of Sāriputta[115] is quite well known. Before he entered the *saṅgha*, he was a leading disciple of Sañjaya, and he was one of those referred to by Brahmā as "having little dust on their eyes" in his inducing the Buddha to teach. All that Sāriputta needed for entrance into the supramundane path (*lokuttara magga*) was hearing the formula of *paṭiccasamuppāda*. He then joined the *saṅgha* and became an arahant in seven days.[116]

112. Mrs. Rhys-Davids, tr., *Psalms of the Brethren*, London : Pali Text Society, 1964 (1913), "Translator's Introduction," pp. xxix-xxx.

113. *Ibid.*, p. xxviii.

114. A.III.376.

115. An excellent biography of Sāriputta has been written by Nyāṇaponika Mahāthera, *The Life of Sāriputta*, Kandy : Buddhist Publication Society, Wheel Series Nos. 90/91/92, 1966.

116. Nārada Mahāthera, *op. cit.*, pp. 565-566.

This type of example is found in many places in the *Sutta Piṭaka*. But the point to note is that it was not the simple hearing of the Dhamma, but one's open and ripe interaction with it, that yielded this occasion of *arahattā*. This is beautifully described in the *Udāna*,[117] where the leper Supabuddha hears the Buddha discoursing and attains streamwinning (*sotāpatti*). The point of interest in this citation is how the mind of Supabuddha is described as fully prepared and ripe to hear Dhamma :

> Then just as a white cloth, free from stains, is ready to receive the dye, even so in Supabuddha, the leper, as he sat there in that very seat, arose the pure, stainless dhamma-sight, the knowledge that whatsoever is of a nature to arise, that also is of a nature to end. And Supabuddha, the leper, saw dhamma, reached dhamma, understood dhamma, plunged into dhamma, crossed beyond doubting, was free from all questionings, won confidence, and needing none other in the Master's message, rose from his seat, advanced to the Exalted One, and sat down at one side.......[118]

This brings us to the next most frequent occasion of *arahattā* as found in the *Sutta Piṭaka*: the deathbed. The Buddha refers directly to the value of the deathbed for spiritual growth :[119]

---

117. Udāna, p. 49. (PTS translation)
seyyath' āpi nāma suddhaṃ vatthaṃ apagatakālakaṃ sammad eva rajanaṃ paṭigaṇheyya, evem eva Suppabuddhassa kuṭṭhissa tasmiṃ yeva āsane virajaṃ vītamalaṃ dhammacakkhuṃ udapādi; yaṃ kiñci samudayadhammaṃ, sabban taṃ nirodhadhamman ti. Atha kho Suppabuddho kuṭṭhī diṭṭhadhammo pattadhammo viditadhammo pariyogāḷhadhammo tiṇṇavicikiccho vigatakathaṃkatho vesārajja-ppatto aparappaccayo satthu sāsane uṭṭhāy' āsanā yena bhagavā ten' upasaṅkami, upasaṅkamitvā bhagavantaṃ abhivādetvā ekamantaṃ nisīdi...

118. Parenthetically, it might be pointed out that the notion of *bodhi* being occasioned by hearing the Dhamma is the basis for the Tibetan tradition of *bar do thos grol*, a text which has twice been translated as "The Tibetan Book of the Dead." *Thos grol* means "liberation by hearing," which is done in the state between death and rebirth (*antarabhava; bar do*).

119. A.III.381. (PTS translation)
Puna ca paraṃ Ānanda bikkhuno pañcahi orambhāgiyehi saṃyojanehi cittaṃ avimuttam hoti. So tamhi samaye maraṇakāle na h'eva kho labhati Tathāgataṃ dassanāya, api ca kho Tathāgatasāvakaṃ labhati dassanāya. Tassa Tathāgatasāvako dhammaṃ deseti adikalyāṇaṃ majjhe kalyāṇaṃ pariyosānakalyāṇaṃ sāttham savyañjanaṃ

> Consider, Ānanda, the monk whose mind is not wholly freed from the five lower fetters, but, when dying, is able to see the Tathāgata : the Tathāgata teaches him Dhamma, lovely in the beginning, lovely in the middle, lovely in the end, its goodness, its significance; and makes known the godly life [*brahmacariyaṃ*], wholly, fulfilled, perfectly pure. When he has heard the Dhamma teaching, his mind is wholly freed from the five lower fetters.

Of course, the Buddha here is referring specifically to the fruition of the path of the streamwinner, and not to *arahattā*. However, our central point here—that the deathbed is a very rich occasion for spiritual growth—is what the Buddha is saying. Therefore it is not unexpected that we read of many instances in Buddhist texts of the attainment of *arahattā* on the deathbed. Incidentally, this is precisely the context in which the Tibetan "liberation-through-hearing" texts (*thos grol*) are ritually employed.

Two *suttas* of the *Saṁyutta Nikāya*[120] are parallel. In both of these *suttas*, a bhikkhu is seriously ill, and the Buddha calls on him to see if he has any last-minute questions about the Dhamma. In both cases, the bhikkhu says that he doesn't fully understand the Dhamma, and the Buddha asks him the extent to which he doesn't understand it.

The first bhikkhu replies :[121] "Passion and the destruction of passion, lord, that is what I understand to be the Norm [*sic.* : Dhamma] taught by the Exalted One." Then the *sutta* comments :[122] "In that brother arose the pure and flawless eye of the Norm [*sic.* : *dhammacakkhu*], so that he saw whatsoever is of a nature to arise, all that is of a nature to cease." This formula is that of a streamwinner (*sotāpatti*).

---

kevalaparipuṇṇaṃ parisuddhaṃ brahmacariyaṃ pakāseti. Tassa taṃ dhammadesanaṃ sutvā pañcahi orambhāgiyehi saṃyojanehi cittaṃ vimuccati.

120. *Suttas* 74 and 75. S.IV.46–48.

121. S.IV.46. (PTS translation)
Rāgavirāgatthaṃ khvāham bhante Bhagavatā dhammaṃ desitam ājānāmīti.

122. S.IV.46. (PTS translation)
imasmiṃ ca pana veyyākaraṇasmiṃ bhaññamāne tassa bhikkhuno virajaṃ vītamalaṃ dhammacakkhum udapādi. Yaṃ kiñci samudayadhammaṃ sabbantaṃ nirodhadhammanti.

The second bhikkhu replies :[123] "Final emancipation without grasping, lord, I take to be the meaning of the Norm [Dhamma] taught by the Exalted One." The *sutta* continue:[124] "The heart of the brother was released from the *āsavas* without grasping." This, of course, is an arahant formula, and it seems that this bhikkhu's earlier protest about not fully understanding Dhamma is contrived. What is indicated is that his deathbed conversation with the Buddha was the occasion of his *arahattā.*

An inversion of this theme is found in the encounter between Sāriputta and Upasena.[125] In this case Upasena, on his deathbed, preaches to Sāriputta, who had come to visit him. Upasena had been bitten by a snake and was carried on to a couch. Sāriputta comes and remarks that Upasena looks none the worse for it all, and Upasena uses the opportunity to give a very brief discourse before dying :

> Friend Sāriputta, he who should think, 'I am the eye,' 'the eye is mine,' or 'I am the tongue,' 'the tongue is mine,' or 'I am the mind,' 'the mind is mine'—in him there would be a change for the worse in his faculties. But I, friend, have no such ideas. How could there be any change in my body, and change for the worse in my faculties ?

Other occasions of *arahattā* revolve around entry of the individual into the *saṅgha.* We have one instance of a bhikkhu attaining *arahattā* at the moment he entered the order :[126]

---

123. S.IV.48. (PTS translation)
Anupādāparinibbanatthaṃ khvāhaṃ bhante Bhagavatā dhammaṃ desitaṃ ājānāmīti.

124. S.IV.48. (PTS translation)
imasmiñca pana veyyākaraṇasmiṃ bhaññamāne tassa bhikkhussa anupādāya āsavehi cittaṃ vimuccatīti.

125. S.IV.40. (PTS translation)
Yassa nuna āvuso Sāriputta na evaṃ hoti. Ahaṃ cakkhunti Mama cakkhunti vā...la...Ahaṃ jivhā ti vā Mama jivhāti vā. Ahaṃ mano ti vā Mama manoti vā, tassa āvuso Sāriputta siyā kāyassa vā aññathattam indriyānaṃ vā pariṇāmo. Mayhañca kho āvuso Sāriputta na evaṃ hoti. Ahaṃ cakkhunti vā Mama jivhāti vā. Ahaṃ manoti vā Mama manoti vā, tassa mayham āvuso Sāriputta kiṃ kāyassa vā aññathattam bhavissati indriyānaṃ vā vipariṇāmoti.

126. Thag., verses 181-182. (My translation)
Yato ahaṃ pabbajito sammāsambuddhasāsane /
vimuccamāno uggacchiṃ, kāmadhātuṃ uppaccagaṃ //

Since I went forth (*pabbajito*)
into the religion (*sāsane*) of the fully perfect Buddha,
I rose liberated, going beyond
the realm of sensuality (*kāmadhātuṃ*).
As the Brahmin looked at me,
my heart / mind (*cittaṃ*) was liberated,
unshakable (*akuppā*) in my freedom, all fetters overcome.

And similarly we have the story of Mahāśiva[127] who, by reflecting upon the spotless purity of his conduct since his ordination (*upasampadā*), attained *arahattā*.[128]

Perhaps the most famous tale of the attaining of *arahattā*, and this one under fire as it were, is that of Ānanda.[129] After the passing of the Buddha, a council was held to collect the various discourses as remembered by his disciples. Ānanda, having been closer to the Buddha than any of the others, and in possession of an acute memory, was vital to this project. The problem was that the council was to be composed entirely of arahants, and Ānanda was not yet an arahant. The 499 arahants did not allow him to attend the convocation of the council, and Ānanda at that point made supreme effort and was able to attain *arahattā*, completing the traditional number of five hundred arahants for the council, and to contribute his recollections of the discourses.[130]

Another instance of attaining *arahattā* under fire is found in the commentary to the *Dīgha Nikāya*,[131] and is recounted by Rahula :[132]

> [A] mahāthera of Kaṇṭhatakasāla Pariveṇa lay on his death-bed at the age of 80, groaning in severe pain. King Vasabha went to see the thera, and hearing his groans was disappointed and turned back at the door remarking that he would not

---

Brahmuno pekkhamānassa tato cittaṃ vimucci me /
akuppā me vimuttīti sabbasaṃyojanakkhayā 'ti //

127. Man.I.40-42.
128. E. W. Adikaram, *Early History of Buddhism in Ceylon, or State of Buddhism in Ceylon as Revealed by the Pāli Commentaries of the 5th Century A.D.*, Colombo : M. D. Gunasena, 1953 (1946). p. 116. [Hereinafter : Adhikaram, *EHBC*.]
129. Buddhist Legends, Vol. III, p. 160.
130. Nārada Mahāthera, *op. cit.*, p. 149.
131. DA.205.
132. Rahula, *HBC*, p. 233.

worship a monk who, even after 60 years in the order, was not able to bear a little pain. The attendant monk informed the dying thera that the king had heard his groans and had gone away in disappointment : 'Sir, why do you thus disgrace us ?' 'Then leave me alone,' said the thera, and, suppressing his pain, attained arahantship. He then asked the attendant to tell the king to come and worship him.

The presence of even another's death can be a very strong spiritual stimulus in Buddhism. Kulla Thera describes the situation in which he attained *arahattā*[133] in which he comes across a rotting, worm-filled, untended corpse lying in a field. He thinks : "Behold the four compound, Kulla, diseased, impure, dripping, exuding, pride of fools !" He then contemplates the corpse, relating it to what he calls his own self, and attains *arahattā*.

We discussed earlier the *aññā vyākaroti* of Therī Paṭācārā[134] where she watches the flame of her little lamp become extinguished (*nibbānaṃ*), whereat she cries : "Lo ! the *nibbāna* of the little lamp ! Emancipation dawns ! My heart is free !" (*padīpasseva nibbānaṃ vimokkho ahu cetaso*).

Dhammapāla's commentary on the *Udāna*[135] tells the story of the brahmin Bhāradvāja, who carried a large bowl to collect scraps. The Buddha did not allow him to carry it with a strap (*ṭhavika*), so the bowl, which had been a possession of pride, became reduced to mere shards. Seeing his beloved bowl in such a state, Bhāradvāja became an arahant. One could speculate that Bhāradvāja, living an austere life, had identified very strongly with his bowl, or, in psychological terminology, had invested a great amount of ego in it. On seeing it reduced to shards, he felt his self so reduced, which was his liberating experience.

It is said[136] that the sight of the Mahācetiya, the chief shrine at the classical Singhalese capital of Anurādhapura, was capable of producing subtle emotions in those who saw it, and that

133. Theg., verses 393-398.
āturaṃ asuciṃ pūtiṃ passa Kulla samussayaṃ /
uggharantaṃ paggharantaṃ bāḷānaṃ abhinanditaṃ //

134. Theg., verses 114-116.

135. Quoted in *Kindred Sayings*, Vol. IV, p. 68, fn. 1.

136. Sum.Vil,III.899; and Pap.Sn. 882; cited in Adikaram, *EHBC*, p. 108.

numberless bhikkhus, in reflecting on these subtle emotions, attained *arahattā*. This shall be taken up in our discussion of the arahant and emotions, but we note it here to indicate that occasionally some object, such as Paṭācārā's lamp, Bhāradvāja's bowl, and the Mahācetiya, plays a key role in occasioning *arahattā*.

Adikaram[137] comments on another such occasion :

> Buddhism entered so intimately into the activities of everyday life that we find even songs sung by the ordinary folk to be pregnant with deep religious sentiment. Thus, it is said, sixty bhikkhus attained arahantship by hearing a Singhalese song sung by a girl who was keeping watch over a rice field.

There is a very interesting milenniarian note in the traditions surrounding the death of Mahā-Saṅgharakkhita. Lamotte has discussed the milenniarian traditions regarding the arahants elsewhere,[138] but in this case the thera did not want to attain *arahattā* until the coming of Metteyya, so he delayed it. As he was dying, a great crowd of devotees gathered. Since they would be disappointed if he died as a worldling (*puthujjana*), he gave up his idea of seeing Metteyya, attained *arahattā* on the spot, and died.[139]

In one case[140] the *devatā* plays a role in the attainment of *arahattā*. Kumāra-Kassapa is asked a riddle by a *devatā* which he cannot answer, and the *devatā* sends him to the Buddha.[141] Marasinghe[142] cites the commentary's claim that this riddle led directly to his attainment of *arahattā*.[143]

One other interesting tradition surrounding the attainment of *arahattā* is its prediction. In one place[144] Bakkula invited his fellow bhikkhus to attend on him that afternoon, as he would

---

137. Citing Pj.II.2.397; and SA.I.273.
138. Lamotte, *HBI*, p. 217.
139. Vism., p. 36; discussed by Rahula, *HBC*, pp. 222-223.
140. M.I.142.
141. One is herein reminded of the *mkha' 'gro ma* (Skt. : *ḍākinī*) sending future mahāsiddhas to their tantric masters. This is discussed in Nathan Katz, "Anima and *mKha' 'gro ma* : A Critical, Comparative Study of Jung and Tibetan Buddhism," Dharamsala : *The Tibet Journal*, II, 3, Autumn 1977, pp. 13-43.
142. Marasinghe, *GEB*, p. 87.
143. SS., p. 132.
144. M.III.127-128.

then attain *arahattā*. He does so, and the commentary[145] adds that as he did not want his corpse to burden his fellow monks, he attained "the realm of heat" (*tejodhātu*). Flames emitted from his body which "burnt like ghee." This tradition is kept alive today in Tibetan Buddhism's teaching of the 'rainbow body' by which the corpse of the saint is said to vanish.

As interesting to us as the occasions of *arahattā* are a few references in the *Majjhima Nikāya* to its non-occasions. At one place[146] the Buddha analyzes five conditions given which the path to *arahattā* could be said to arise, and at another place[147] he gives four conditions which lead to the non-arising of this path. The five *kusala* conditions are :[148] (1) that a monk has conviction or faith (*saddhā*) in the Tathāgata as one who is able to teach the path; (2) the monk should be in good health, have good digestion, et cetera; (3) the monk should present himself honestly to the Tathāgata; (4) he should be endowed with energy (*viriya*); and (5) he should possess wisdom (*paññā*) and discrimination (*nibbedhikāya*). Conversely, the four conditions that are not conducive to *arahattā* are :[149] (1) taking one's teacher to be omniscient (*sabbaññā*) and accepting his teaching on this basis; (2) accepting a teaching based on tradition; (3) accepting a teaching based on reasoning (*takka*) alone; and (4) accepting a stupid teacher who resorts to eel-wriggling (*amarāvikkhepa*) or worthless, positionless disputation which is based on a fear of blame and error, rather than on a confidence in truth.

The most famous story of a non-occasion of *arahattā* is that of Upaka and the Buddha.[150] After the Buddha's *bodhi* at Buddha-Gaya, and as he is wandering towards Sarnath to turn the wheel of Dhamma, he meets Upaka en route. Upaka is an Ājīvika, one who is sick of teaching and philosophy, a stoic. Seeing the Buddha's unworldly demeanor, Upaka asks who he is, to which the Buddha replies that he is one who has discovered the four noble truths (*cattāri ariyā saccā*) which lead to the utter destruction of craving and sorrow. Upaka mutters that this

145. MA.IV.196.
146. M.II.95-96.
147. M.I.519-520.
148. M.II.95-96.
149. M.I.519-520.
150. M.I.170-171.

may be the case, and he goes on his way. Entailed in Upaka's walking away from the Buddha is his conviction that no amount of self-effort can cure man's illness of life, and that all doctrines are simply pride and conceit. This incident as recorded in the *Majjhima Nikāya* seems to be faithful to the Ājīvika position of weariness with philosophy and religion, and Upaka emerges as something of a heroic fellow. He does not contend against the Buddha, he does not reject his claim, and does not question him. His reply indicates his feeling that while all that the Buddha has to say about *dukkha, magga* and *nibbāna* may be true, but Upaka simply does not care, and he stoicly goes on his way. He is an atheist not in the sense that he does not believe in a god, because he doesn't care about god rather than disbelieving in him. He is an atheist in the sense that he doesn't care about religion, dhamma and *magga*, and he is a good contrast to the disciples of Buddha who do solve life's multi-lemma, as the weariness and sceptical attitude he demonstrates are antithetical to energy (*viriya*) and conviction (*saddhā*), which is evidenced in the disciples' lives. It is to the credit of the compilers of the *Majjhima* that this story comes down to us in such an unadulterated form, for it might have been embarrassing to them that the first ascetic whom the Buddha meets after his enlightenment should walk away from him, despite his implied offer of teaching. This would tend to indicate the historical validity of something much akin to the way in which this encounter is described.

E. *Symbolism of the Arahant*

1. *General*

In the *Sutta Piṭaka*, the most common genre of symbolism for the arahant and his task employs metaphors of water : flood (*ogha*), stream (*soto*), sea or ocean (*samudda*), pool (*rahada*) and river (*Gaṅgā, nadī*); and the things in relation to water : crossing over (*tiṇṇa*), bank (*kūla*), this shore and other shore (*pāram apāraṃ vā*); and the range of 'going beyond' images (*pāragato*). Also common, but not quite as frequent, are images of fire (*āditta*), fever (*patiḷāha*), being cool (*sītibhūta*) and being extinguished (*nibbuta*). One also finds a range of *nāga* symbolism, and this symbol is used for an arahant, a cobra and an elephant. Other images are those of the warrior, royalty, *devas* and the divine tree (*pāricchattaka*), health and illness, a corpse, the diamond (*vajira*) and a mountain. We shall consider first the two most important metaphor ranges, that of water and then that of fire and cooling. Then we shall discuss the *nāga*, and then the other symbols.

2. *Water Symbolism*

In our discussion of water symbolism and the arahant, it seems evident that the image of the flood (*ogha*) is the most important. According to Sāriputta.[151] there are four floods : the flood of sensuality (*kāmogha*); the flood of will-to-be (*bhavogha*); the flood of views (*diṭṭhogha*); and the flood of ignorance (*avijjogha*). These four floods are identical to the four *āsavā*,[152] and, as we shall demonstrate in our considerations of the arahant as *khīṇāsavo*, one who overcomes the *āsavā*, the overcoming of the *āsavā* is the *sina qua non* of *arahattā*; and, in our context of the arahant as one who crosses over the floods, this crossing is *arahattā*. In our discussion of the notion of the world (*loka*), we shall see that the four *ogha*, or the four *āsavā*, are identical conceptually with the world. Thus, the world as the lived experience of the person in terms of self and other, is herein expressed as the four floods. The Buddha[153] is one who teaches us how to cross over these floods.: "He showed a way for the crossing over of the floods, and we who have been shown this ambrosia of deathlessness (*amata*) stand unshakable, seeing Dhamma."

It seems that "a way for crossing the floods" (*oghassa nittharaṇaṃ paññāpenti*) was a phrase in use at the time of the Buddha to indicate a religious teaching, as Sālha the Licchavi[154] refers to some other teachings as : "...there are some *samaṇas* and *brahmaṇas* who show a twofold method for crossing the floods, by reason of virtue (*sīla*), and that be extreme asceticism (*tapo*)."

151. S.IV.257.
152. Given at M.I.9 and elsewhere.
153. Theg., verse 1243. (My translation)
aghassa hi nittharaṇatthaṃ anekavihitaṃ maggaṃ akkhāsi / tasmiñ ca amate akkhāte dhammadassā ṭhitā asaṁhīrā //
154. A.II.200. (My translation)
santi...eke samaṇabrahmaṇā dvayena oghassa nittharaṇaṃ paññāpenti sīlavisuddhihetu ca tapojigucchāhetu ca.

The Buddha's response is that *sīla* may play some role in this crossing over, but it is not sufficient in itself; and that *tapo* is most often counterproductive to the goal. At another place[155] Hemavata asks the Buddha what sort of person is able to cross the floods, and the Buddha replies :

Across the raging flood in safety fares
the virtuous, of comprehending mind,
serene, reflective, watchful evermore.
The abyss engulfs him who—quit of lust
for pleasure, quit of trammels, freed from bonds—
has stifled hankerings for life on life.

Stream imagery is bivalent. In one sense, the stream (*soto*) refers to the way (*magga*) taught by the Buddha. In this sense we get the image of the person who is intent on Dhamma being called a streamwinner (*sotāpatti*). In its other sense, *sota* means the streaming of *saṁsāra*, the flooding we have just discussed. In this sense, the Buddha says of his teaching :[156] "Monks, the true way of speaking about renunciation is as against the stream" (*paṭisoto ti kho bhikkhave nekkhammassetaṃ adhivacanaṃ*). There seem to be two opposed streams : that of the path, and that of *saṁsāra*.

There is one other unique reference to a stream in the *Sutta Piṭaka*.[157] In this verse, which is addressed to the Buddha by Pahārāda, the streams stand for those completing the path of the arahant, and the ocean into which these streams flow in *nibbāna*. He says :

Just as all the streams that flow into the ocean,
all the rains that fall from the sky, affect neither the emptiness
nor the fullness of the ocean; even so, though many monks

155. Suttanipāta, pp. 29-30. (HOS translation)
Sabbadā sīlasampanno paññavā susamāhito ajjhattacintī satimā oghaṃ tarati duttaraṃ. Virato kāmasaññāya sabbasaṃyojanātigo-nandībhavaparikkhīṇo, so gambhīro na sīdati.

156. Iti.114-115. (My translation)

157. A.IV.199. (PTS translation)
Puna ca param bhante yā kāci loke savantiyo mahāsamuddaṃ appenti, yā kāci antalikkhā dhārā papatanti, na tena mahāsamuddhassa ūnattaṃ vā pūrattaṃ vā paññāyati. Yam pi bhante yā kāci loke savantiyo mahāsamuddaṃ appenti, yā kāci antillikhā dhārā papatanti, na tena mahāsamuddhassa ūnattaṃ vā pūrattaṃ vā paññāyati.

become completely cool in the cool element to which naught attaches, yet neither the emptiness nor the fullness of that cool element is affected.

Other water symbolism revolves around rivers, banks, crossing over and going beyond. In one place,[158] arahants are likened to bulls who have been brought across (*patāreti*) the Ganges by a skilled shepherd, the Buddha, and have reached the opposite bank. The *Dhammapada*[159] comments that : "Few are there amongst men who go beyond; the rest of mankind only run about on the bank." We are familiar with the image of 'this bank or shore' for *saṁsāra*; now we are introduced to the concept of going beyond, which[160] is equated with *arahattā* : *pāragato ti arahattaṃ patto*. 'Going beyond' means reaching the solid ground on the other shore :[161] "He has come out from the depths and reached the solid ground."

Of course, the most famous analogy in the *Sutta Piṭaka* of crossing over is the analogy of the raft, which is found in the Alagaddūpama Sutta.[162] Some of the conceptual and philosophic implications of this analogy will arise throughout this essay, as we feel it is a crucial one for any understanding of Buddhism. It is so well known that we shall not cite it at length, just the Buddha's concluding remark :[163]

> So it is, monks, that this teaching (*dhamma*) of the analogy of the raft is preached by me for crossing over, not for holding onto. You, monks, by understanding this analogy of the raft, should get rid of *dhammas*, all the more so non-*dhammas*.

Along these same lines is a verse from the *Dhammapada*.[164] We

---

158. M.I. 255.
159. Dhammapada.VI.10. (Nārada translation)
Appakā te manussesu—ye hanā pāragāmino /
Athāyaṃ itharā pajā—tītamevānudhāvati //
160. SnA.35.
161. S.IV.207. (My translation)
sa ce pātāle paccuṭṭhāsi atho gādham pi ajjhagāti.
162. M.I.134-135.
163. M.I.136. (My translation)
Eva evaṃ kho bhikkhave kullūpamo mayā dhammo desito nittharaṇatthāya no gahaṇatthāya. Kullūpamaṃ vo bhikkhave ājānantehi dhammā pi vo pahātabbā, pag eva adhammā.
164. Dhammapada.XXVI.3. (Nārada translation)
Yassa pāraṃ apāraṃ vā, pārāpāraṃ na vijjati /
Vītaddaraṃ visaṃyuttaṃ, taṃ ahaṃ brūmi brāhmaṇaṃ //

find it curious that in Horner's otherwise excellent discussion of *tiṇṇa*[165] there is no reference to it. The Buddha says there :

For whom there exists neither the hither nor the farther shore,
nor both the hither and the farther shore,
he who is undistressed and unbound—
him I call a brāhmaṇa.

Both this *Dhammapada* verse and the raft analogy indicate the provisional, pedagogical and heuristic nature of the Buddha's Dhamma. His teaching, like the raft, is to be used, and is not, therefore, the proper topic for philosophizing. No literal interpretations of his words are allowed according to the *Dhammapada*, as even the notion of the other shore, the goal of Dhamma, is to be discarded. Some of the implications of these startling verses shall be discussed in our section of the philosophy of the arahant, most especially in our considerations on the arahant and *diṭṭhi* and language analysis.

As well as floods (*oghā*) and streams (*sotā*), *saṁsāra* is also likened to the ocean (*samudda*), an ocean replete with denizens of the deep. We read in the *Itivuttaka* :[166]

Who lust and ignorance and hate hath left,
He hath crossed o'er this ocean with its sharks,
With its demons and fearsome waves impassable.
Bond-free, escaped from death and without base,
Transcending sorrow, to become no more,
Evanished, incomparable one—
He hath befooled the King of Death, I say.

Another similar verse is found in the *Saṁyutta Nikāya*,[167] which Horner[168] glosses :

...whosoever conquers the impulses arising from the data peculiar to each of the six senses 'has crossed over the ocean (*samudda*) with its waves and whirlpools, its sharks and demons. ...The brahmin has crossed over (*tiṇṇo*) and going beyond (*pāraṅgato*) stands on dry land (*thale tiṭṭhati*).

Of course the image of crossing over is also extremely important in Mahāyāna Buddhism, as expressed at the very end of the

165. SnA.35.
166. S.IV.207. (My translation)
167. S.IV.157.
168. Horner, *EBTMP*, pp. 257-281.

Hṛdayaprajñāpāramitāsūtra by the great *mantra* :[169] *Gate gate paraṁgate parasaṁgate bodhi svāhā.*

Horner, whose work on this range of symbolism is excellent, except for her surprising neglect of *Dhammapada* verse XXVI.3, summarizes :[170]

> Thus, as in the case of *tiṇṇa*. we find that *pāra* has a metaphorical meaning in addition to its primary significance. Further, we shall expect to find that when it is used metaphorically, it occurs not merely alone, but in connection with the metaphorical meanings of the flood (*ogha*) and other conditions which have been crossed over (*tiṇṇa*). So long as *pāraṅgata* or *pāragū* is the corollary of *oghatiṇṇa*, crossing over and getting beyond the flood, it is often accompanied by similes of rafts and ships, and by descriptions of denizens of the seas or rivers. In the *Sutta Nipāta* (sn. 771) there is an exhortation to discard desires for pleasure, and then having dispelled them to cross the flood. When a man has, as it were, baled out the ship, he is called *pāragū*. Or if a man is travelling on a well-made raft, it will carry him beyond, and then there will be no more need for the raft (sn. 21; M.I. 134f.).

We find two other analogies of the arahant and water. In the first, he is likened to a pool.[171]

> Like the earth, a balanced and well-disciplined person resents not. He is comparable to a pillar (*indakhīla*). Like a pool, unsullied by mud, is he; to such a balanced one (*tādi*), life's wanderings do not arise.

And in the *Saṁyutta Nikāya*[172] we find the well-known analogy of the arahant and the lotus which grows in muddy water :

> Just as, brethren, a dark blue lotus or a white lotus, born in

169. Edward Conze, tr., *Buddhist Wisdom Books*, New York : Harper Torchbooks, 1972 (1958), pp. 101-102.
170. Horner, *EBTMP*, p. 297.
171. Dhammapada.VII.6. (Nārada translation)
Paṭhavi samo no virujjhati, indakhīlūpamo tādi subbato /
Rahado' va apetakadhammo, saṁsārā na bhavanti tādino //
172. S.III.140. (PTS translation)
Seyyathāpi bhikkhave uppalaṃ vā padumaṃ vā puṇḍarīkaṃ vā udake jātam udake jātam udake samvaddhaṃ udaka accuggamma ṭhāti anupalittam udakena. Evam eva kho bhikkhave Tathāgato loke saṃvaḍdho lokam abhibhuyya viharati anupalitto lokenāti.

> the water, come to full growth in the water, rises to the surface and stands unspotted by the water, even so, brethren, the *Tathāgata*, having been born in the world, having come to full growth in the world, passing beyond the world, abides unspotted by the world.

3. *Symbolism of Fire and Cooling*

One use of the fire metaphor is to indicate the existential urgency of the Buddha's teachings. The Buddha tells his disciples :[173]

> Just as, monks, when one's turban or head is aflame, for the extinguishing thereof one must put forth intense desire, effort, exertion, impulse, unobstruction, mindfulness, and attention, even so must that person put forth intense desire, and the rest, for the attainment of those profitable states.

In the *Suttanipāta*[174] the metaphor is nearly identical : there it is one's home that is ablaze, and this is reminiscent of the crucial analogy in the *Saddharmapuṇḍarīka*[175] of the father who beckons his children out of a burning house with toys, which the *sūtra* says is analogous to the Buddha's offering a naively-understood *nirvāṇa* to the *śrāvakas.*

More, however, than urgency is carried in this metaphor. Fire becomes a symbol for the totality of our *saṁsāric* experience. In the famous Ādittaṃ sutta,[176] known in the west as the Fire Sermon, the Buddha tells us that all our senses and their objects are ablaze. Parenthetically, this *sutta* became very well known in the west because of its adaptation by the brilliant absurdist-

173. A.II.93. (PTS translation)
Seyythāpi bhikkhave ādittacelo vā ādditasīso vā, tass' eva celassa vā sīsassa vā nibbapapanāya adhimattaṃ chandañ ca sampajaññañ ca kareyya, evam eva kho bhikkhave tena puggalena tesaṃ yeva kusalānaṃ dhammānaṃ paṭilābhāya adhimatto chando ca.........sampajaññañ ca karaṇīyaṃ, so aparena samayena lābhī c' eva hoti ajjhattaṃ cetosamathassa lābhī adhipaññādhammavipassanāya.
The same metaphor is found at S.I.13, S.I.108, S.III.143. S.V.440, A.III.308, A.IV.320, and A.V.93.

174. Suttanipāta, p. 114.

175. *Saddharmapuṇḍarīkasūttra, or the Lotus of the True Law*, tr. H. Kern, Delhi : Motilal Banarsidass, Sacred Books of the East Series, Vol. XXI, 1968 (1884), pp. 30-59.

176. S.IV.19-20, and repeated S.III.71.

dadaist playwright, Eugene Ionesco, in his monumental *La Cantatrice Chauve*.[177] Ionesco's understanding of the Buddha as an absurdist would not be concurrent with most modern scholarship, and no study of his adaptation has been undertaken. After discoursing on the fiery nature of *saṁsāra*, the *sutta* tells us :[178] "And when the teaching was thus expounded, the hearts of those brethren were utterly set free from the *āsavas*," which is to say that they attained *arahattā*. It is cardinal in Buddhism that a dispassionate and clear seeing of things-as-they-are (*yathābhūtadassanañāṇa*), regardless of the hedonic quality of things, leads to spiritual growth. The Buddha does not want us to become obsessed with either unpleasant or blissful interpretative experiences of the given; rather, an open encounter with the given leads to *arahattā*. Thus, a heightened awareness (*paññā*) of the fire of *saṁsāra* can cool or extinguish us.

As *saṁsāra*, the totality of our experience in terms of self and other, is fiery, so the arahant, according to the texts,[179] is cool (*sītibhūto*) :

> Surely at all times happily doth rest the arahant in whom all fire's extinct; Who cleaveth not to sensuous desires, cool with all his being, rid of all the germs that bring new life, all encumbrances cut out; subdued the pain and pining of the heart; Calm and serene he resteth happily, for in his mind he hath attained to peace.

Similarly, in the *Therīgāthā*,[180] the Therī Uttarā describes herself as "cool am I now, I know nibbāna's peace" (*sītibhūta 'mhi nibbutā*). In another place[181] the Buddha says that one who practises the concentrative meditations (*jhānā*) will become cooled : *sītibhavussanti*. Similarly, the *Dhammapada*[182] says :

---

177. *The Bald Soprano*, first performed in Paris in 1950.
178. S.IV.20. (PTS translation)
Imasmiṃ ca pana veyyākaraṇasmiṃ bhaññamāne tassa bhikkhusahassassa anupādāya āsavehi cittāni vimucciṃsūti.
179. S.I.212. (PTS translation)
Sabbadā ve sukhaṃ seti, brāhmaṇo parinibbuto /
yo na limpati kāmesu, sītibhūto nirūpadhi //
sabbā āsattiyo chetvā, vineyya hadaye daraṃ /
upasanto sukhaṃ seti, santim pappuyya cetasā ti //
180. Thig., verse 15.
181. M.III.244-245.
182. Dhammapada.VII.1. (Nārada translation)
Gataddhino visokassa, vippamuttassa sabbadhi sabbaganthappahīnassa, parilāho na vijjati.

For him who has completed the journey, for him who is sorrowless, for him who from everything is totally free, for him who has destroyed all ties (*gantha*), the fever exists not.

We also get the notion that, as for fire to burn there need be fuel, so for *saṁsāra* to persist in its fieriness, there must be something which nourishes (*āharā*) these existential flames. Thus, we find in the *Suttanipāta* the idea that *nibbāna* is like a fire which has burned itsélf out :[183]

'The old is dead, no fresh
growths rise,' cry saints, who, quit
of germs and hopes, reject
all life to come, and pass
away like lamps unfed.
The gem the Order holds;
—and may that truth bless all !

We have already considered a very similar notion found in the Therīgāthā,[184] wherein the Therī Paṭācārā attains *arahattā* while watching her little lamp become extinguished as the fuel runs out. This is the most frequent type of fire analogy found in the *Sutta Piṭaka*. However, we have found one instance of a fire metaphor employed in an opposite sense, this from the *Therāgāthā*.[185] In this unusual case, the arahant Kañkhārevato says that the Tathāgata is like a fire because he is a giver of light. Despite this single contrary use of fire symbolism, however, the *Sutta Piṭaka* usages of fire metaphors are all in the sense that we have been indicating : that fire is an image for the totality of *saṁsāra*, as is symbolism of flooding (*oghā*). As a fire depends on fuel, so *saṁsāra* relies upon the *āsavā* for its continued persistence; and, when the fuel becomes exhausted, *saṁsāra*, like the flame, becomes extinguished (*nibbutā*). Thus the arahant is one who is cool, just as he is one who has crossed over.

183. Suttanipāta, pp. 41-42. (HOS translation)
'Khīṇaṃ purāṇaṃ navaṃ n'atthi sambhavaṃ,'
virattacittā āyatike bhavasmiṃ
te khiṇabījā avirūḷchandā
nibbanti dhīrā yathāyam padīpo,
idam pi Saṃghe ratanaṃ paṇītaṃ,
etena saccena suvatthitoti.

184. Theg., verses 114-116.

185. Theg., verse 3.

4. Nāga *Symbolism*

The term *nāga* is applied to three beings in the *Sutta Piṭaka* : to the cobra, the elephant, and the arahant. That the cobra is a symbol of the arahant is explicit in the Vammīka Sutta.[186] The Venerable Nyāṇaponika Mahāthera has discussed the cobra/arahant analogy in two monographs,[187] so we need only briefly mention his findings here. He points to a central Buddhist analogy of the Dhamma being likened to a snake in the sense that, if grasped wrongly, it becomes extremely dangerous. So Dhamma, when extracted from its linguistic home of pedagogical talk leading to *nibbāna,* becomes yet another vicious *diṭṭhi*. This metaphor was taken up again by Candrakīrti[188] who says that a wrongly-understood *śūnyatā* is similar to a wrongly-grasped snake. Another similarity between the arahant and a cobra, Nyāṇaponika[189] tells us, is :

> Just as the serpent does not hesitate to fulfil the biological 'law of its kind' in shedding its old skin, so will right renunciation not waver or shrink from those acts of giving up which right understanding of reality demands.

The *nāga* as elephant is likened to the arahant in three ways. The first way is that they both enjoy solitude in the forests :[190] "Herein agreed mind with mind, of sage and elephant whose tusks are like a plough pole, since both alike love forest solitude."

The second sense is that both are fearless :[191] "Monks, these two tremble not at a thunder-clap. What two ? A monk who

---

186. M.I.142-145.

187. Nyānaponika Mahāthera, *The Snake Similie : Alaggadūpama Sutta*, Kandy : Buddhist Publication Society, Wheel Series, Nos. 48/49, 1962; and *The Worn-Out Skin*, Kandy : Buddhist Publication Society, Wheel Series, Nos. 241/242, 1977.

188. Ācāriya Candrakīrti (sLob dpon zla ba grags pa), *Mūlamadhyamikavṛttiprasannapadā nāma* (*dBu ma tshig gsal*), Dharamsala : The Council of Cultural & Religious Affairs of His Holiness the Dalai Lama, 1968, pp. 400-439

189. Nyāṇaponika Mahāthera, *The Worn-Out Skin*, p. 15.

190. Udāna, p. 42. (PTS translation)
etaṃ nāgassa nāgena īsādantassa hatthino, sameti
cittaṃ cittena yaṃ eko ramatī vane 'ti.

191. A.I.77. (PTS translation)
Dve 'me bhikkhave assaniyā phalantiyā na santasanti.
Katame dve? Bhikkhu ca khīṇāsavo hatthājāniyo ca.

has destroyed the *āsavas*, and an elephant of noble breed." In the Singhalese commentatorial tradition, this led to many implications, some serious and some rather light-hearted, and which shall be considered farther when we discuss the arahant and the emotions. However, one of these incidents might be mentioned in this context. Rahula[192] quotes from the Samantapāsādikā :[193] "...even if a thunderbolt fell on his head, an arahant would not be frightened or disturbed, but if he showed signs of fear, he should be rejected as no arahant."

One other analogy with the elephant is found in the Therāgāthā,[194] where the Thera Soṇa Poṭiriyaputta says that an arahant should strive like a noble warrior-elephant, and by which we are reminded of the Tibetan etymology for *dgra bcom pa* (arahant) : "If in fight my warrior-elephant advanced, 'twere better, fallen from his back, dead on the field and trampled should I lie, than beaten like a captive to the foe." Dhammapāla's commentary on this verse says that Soṇa Poṭiriyaputta had been a warrior before taking up the robes.

It might surprise the reader to learn that *arahattā* could be discussed, even in poetic analogy, in such militaristic terms. However, we find it discussed in almost all terminologies imaginable, and this seems consistent with the nature of the use of language in Buddhism as something indicative rather than denotive, as something heuristic and pedagogical. Thus the Buddha tells us that it is to be expected that different arahants would express *arahattā* very differently, owing to individual differences in temperament, experience, inclinations and so forth.[195]

5. *Other Symbols*

The other symbols by means of which the arahant is discussed

192. Rahula, *HBC*, p. 220.
193. Samantapāsādikā, p. 350.
Khīṇāsava nāma asaniyāpi matthake pataya mānāya bhayaṃ vā chambhitattaṃ vā lomahaṃso vā na hoti. Sacassa bhayaṃ vā chambhitattaṃ vā lomahaṃso vā uppajjati, na tvaṃ arahāti apanetabbo.
194. Theg., verse 194. (PTS translation)
hatthikkhandhāvapatittaṃ kuñjaro ce anukkame, saṃgāme me mataṃ seyyo yañ ca jīve parājito 'ti.
195. S.IV.191-195.

in the *Sutta Piṭaka* include : the arahant as a mountain, the symbolism of the divine tree (*pāricchattaka*) and of the gods generally, as royalty, diamond (*vajira*) symbolism, and the whole range of images of sickness and health.

In one place[196] the arahant is likened to a mountain crag because, like the mountain, he is never moved. The mountain is unmoved by wind as the arahant is unmoved by the senses, by likes or dislikes.

Marasinghe[197] discusses the metaphor from the *Aṅguttara Nikāya*[198] where :

> .. steps of progress in the higher life and the attainment of arahanthood are compared to the different stages in the blossoming of the divine tree *Pāricchattaka* in the Tāvatiṃsa heaven. When a disciple attains arahanthood, all the devas are delighted and show appreciation of this : news of such an event reaches as far as the Brahmaloka in an instant, such being the power (*ānubhāva*) of an arahant.

And in some other places we find the arahant identified with some of the *devas* themselves. Horner[199] discussed this range of symbolism of the *devas* of purification (*visuddhadevas*):

> In the *Vibhaṅga* (Vbb. 422) arahans are identified with the *visuddhadevas*, or *devas* by purification. The Commentary explains (VbhA. 518) this to mean 'devas by purification of all the corruptions (*kilesā*), worthy of veneration (*pūjārahā*) of all the *devas*.' The *Majjhima* Commentary (MA.I.33) says that the *visuddhadevas* are arahans devoid of the *āsavas*. These *visuddhadevas* form dogmatically the highest class of *devas*. Other classes of *devas* are 'conventional *devas*' (*sammutideva*), such as kings and princes; and *devas* by rebirth (*uppattideva*). This distinction is current only in the later canonical works (Vbh.422, and cf. Khu.123; VvA.18; Nd.II.307). In the *Vimānavatthu* Commentary the *visuddhadevas* (or arahans) are associated with a term, *devātideva*, the *deva* of the *devas*

196. A.III.379.
Selo yathā ekanghano vātena na samirati, evaṃ rūpa rasā saddā gandhā phassā ca kevalā, iṭṭhā dhammā aniṭṭhā ca na ppavendhenti tādino, ṭhitaṃ cittaṃ vippamuttaṃ. vayañ c' assānupassatī ti.

197. Marasinghe, *GEB*, p. 273.

198. A.IV.117.

199. Horner, *EBTMP*, p. 157.

(VvA.18), which in post-canonical works appears as an epithet of Gotama. The Commentary says: 'He seeing all the teaching of the *devātideva* means : because he is a *deva* by purification he is said to be of the nature of the supreme *deva* or of the *devas* by purification.'

This might appear as puzzling, as one way in which the Buddha's teaching is unique is in that human potentiality (*arahattā*) is greater than any of the gods. The gods, of course, remain enmeshed in *saṁsāra* from which the arahant is free. This tradition of equating the arahant with the *visuddhadevas* seems a condescension of the notion of the arahant, as the arahant is said to be beyond all of *saṁsāra* in which the *devas*, like humans, animals, *petas* and denizens of hell, reside. One possible key to this puzzle lies in the notion of the anāgāmī, the non-returner, who is very nearly an arahant and will take rebirth spontaneously in a god-realm, and there attain *arahattā* without returning to this world. This is only conjecture, but if the arahant is beyond *saṁsāra* in which all the *devas* reside, and if there is some identification of a certain class of *devas* with any of the noble persons (*ariyā puggalā*), then it would seem that it should be the *anāgāmī* rather than the arahant with whom these *visuddhadevas* are associated.

The symbols of royalty are often borrowed and adapted to the arahant. In one place,[200] the seven *bojjhaṅgā*, or factors or limbs of enlightenment, of which the arahant is in possession, are analogous to the seven treasures (gems, *ratanāni*), traditionally emblems of authority of a *mahārāja*.

One *Aṅguttara sutta*[201] discusses three types of persons, the third of which bears a significant epithet. The first type of person is *arukūpamacitta*, or one with a mind like an open sore that festers at the slightest stimulation. The second is the *vijjūpamacitta*, the one with a mind like lightning, who is capable of seeing things-as-they-are (*yathābhūtaṃ pajānāti*) in a flash. The last is the *vajirūpamacitta*, the one with a mind like a diamond, who has destroyed the *āsavā*.[202] The third of these is most interesting

200. S.V.99.
201. A.I.123-124.
202. A.I.124.
Sayyathāpi bhikkhave vajirassa n' atthi kiñci abhejjaṃ maṇi vā pāsāṇo vā, evaṃ eva kho bhikkhave idh' ekacco āsavāṇaṃ khayā... pe...sacchikatvā upasampajja viharati.

to us because of the continuity of *vajira* (Skt. : *vajra*; Tib. : *rdo rje*) symbolism from the earliest Pāli to the latest Tibetan texts.

The first image above, that of the one with a mind like a festering sore, carries us to the next range of arahant symbolism : that of sickness and health. The Buddha[203] tells us about the university of mental disease (*cetasikā ārogya*):

> Monks, there are to be seen beings who can admit freedom from bodily disease for one year, for two years, for three, four, five, ten, twenty, thirty, forty, fifty years; who can admit freedom from bodily disease for even a hundred years. But, monks, those beings are hard to find in the world who can admit freedom from mental disease even for one moment, save only those in whom the *āsavas* are destroyed.

Mental disease in the Buddhist sense is found anywhere there is egoism (*āmimāna*), anywhere the *āsavā* have not been destroyed, in any case where the floods (*oghā*) have not been crossed (*tiṇṇa*); it is universal. and this psychosis is the manifestation of addiction to belief in self (*attavādupādānaṃ*), which is the hub of the turning of the wheel of becoming (*bhavacakka*).

The canonical images of mental health have been described quite neatly by Johansson :[204]

> Of special interest to the psychologist are a number of definitions in terms of health. M.I.511 : *Evam eva kho Māgandiya ahañ c' eva te dhammaṃ deseyyaṃ : idan taṃ ārogyaṃ, idan taṃ nibbānaṃ passeyyāsi*, 'Even so, Māgandiya, if I were to teach you the doctrine saying, this is that health, this is that *nibbāna*, you might know health, might see *nibbāna*.' We find *abyādhi*, 'freedom from disease,' as a synonym for *nibbāna* in M.I.172, and *anītika*, 'health,' in S.IV.371. In S.III.4f, Sāriputta explains how it is possible to have a healthy mind (*no āturacitto*) in spite of a sick body : a healthy mind is to have a correct insight as to the nature of the *khandhā* and to avoid identifying oneself with them. The definition is very similar

202. A.I.143. (PTS translation)
Dissanti bhikkhave sattā kāyikena rogena ekam pi vassaṃ ārogyaṃ paṭijānamānā, dve pi vassāni ārogyaṃ paṭijānamānā, tiṇi pi... cattari pi... paññasam pi vassāno ārogyaṃ paṭijānamānā. Te bhikkhave sattā dallabhā lokasmiṃ ye cetasikena rogena muhattam pi ārogyaṃ paṭijānanti annatta khīṇāsavehi.

204. Johansson, *PN*, p. 26.

to the explanation of *vimutti* given in S.II.124ff, so *nibbāna* is both mental health and interior freedom.

One further symbol of health, paradoxically, is the dead man. One Therāgāthā verse[205] is interesting because two other religious traditions speak of their ideal person as a dead man : the Sufi who has practiced the *fanas*, annihilations, and the Zen man is a 'living dead man.'[206] In this verse, Sāriputta Thera says :[207] "Whoso serene and calm, dead to the world, Can utter wisdom's runes with wit unswelled, Unruffled, he doth shake off naughty things, As they were forest-leaves, by wind-god blown." The arahant is dead to the world, because the world exists only so long as the conditions that support it, *viz.*, the *oghā*, *āsavā*, *saṃyojanāni*, et cetera, continue to sustain it. For this reason these conditions are called *ahārā*, nutriments, because they sustain *saṁsāra*. In the absence of these conditions, the world, as a system of relationships between self and other, lacks productive cause. As Marasinghe aptly writes :[208] "A sentient being exists in the world only so long as it continues to share in the same qualities as the world..." and these qualities, such as *āsmimāna*, et cetera, are not present in the arahant; hence he is as dead to the world as it is to him. Unlike religions which would seek to overcome death without giving up life as well. Buddhism confronts the life/death dilemma more directly and honestly, and holds that the arahant, who is dead to the world, is its ideal person.

---

205. Theg., verse 1006.

206. Richard J. DeMartino discusses the symbolism of the Zen man as a 'living dead man' in his essay in Eric Fromm, D. T. Suzuki and R. J. DeMartino, *Zen Buddhism and Psychoanalysis*, New York: Grove Press, 1960.

207. Theg., verse 1006. (PTS translation)
Upasanto uparato mantabhāṇī anuddhato /
dhunāti pāpake dhamme dumapattaṃ va māluto //

208. Marasinghe, *GEB*, pp. 57-58.

CHAPTER II

MEDITATION AND *ARAHATTĀ*

A. *Introductory*

1. *Scope of this Discussion*

Because it is so truly alien to western traditions, the entire question of meditation and the arahant has become a veritable tangle of muddles. Much of this muddle is terminological, as the family of words relating to mental discipline cannot be clearly distinguished by simple translations. Therefore, our preliminary task in this discussion shall be an attempt to sort out terms like *samādhi*, *bhāvanā*, *sati* and *satipaṭṭhāna*, *samatha* and *vipassanā*, and *jhāna*.

In the teaching of Buddhism to undergraduate students, one question which invariably arises is whether or not proficiency at the *jhānā* and other mental disciplines constitutes *nibbāna* or *arahattā*. Of course it does not, and we shall see that the Buddha was most emphatic in maintaining this point. We shall consider some of the implications of this distinction by the Buddha, and we shall argue that this distinction is crucial for the philosophic and religious identity of Buddhism as distinct from other Indian systems, at least in terms of Buddhism's perception of itself.

In discussing the range of issues around meditation, several subsidiary questions arise. One is the terminology of *cetovimutti*, 'one who is liberated by or through the heart/mind,' and *paññāvimutti*, 'one who is liberated by or through *paññā* or wisdom.' We find this distinction repeated throughout the *Sutta Piṭaka*, and we shall attempt to show its significance. We shall conclude this chapter with an analysis of the Buddhist path as traditionally understood in the language of the four noble paths and their fruitions (*cattāri ariyā maggā* and *phalāni*).

2. *The Relationship of Meditation to* Arahattā

The first point we wish to take up, that skill at meditation is not coterminous with *arahattā* or *nibbāna*, is rather elementary. It is also very basic: therefore, it must be established before pursuing our discussion.

The most common distinction of types of meditation is : *samatha* (calm); and *vipassanā* (insight). The most common technique for the former are the *jhānā*, and *sati* for the latter. We shall discuss these typologies below, but for the present we want to consider two comments of the Buddha about these two basic forms.

Of the first type, the *jhānā*, the Buddha says :[1] "Whatever is thought through and maintained by higher thinking, that one knows to be impermanent, of the nature of destruction." And of *sati* meditation, the Buddha says :[2] "Monks, may your minds be delightfully well established in the four arisings of mindfulness; but do not confound that with that which is beyond birth and death (*amatam*)."

In the first reference above, the Buddha is reminding us that all of worldly experience, including the various meditative experiences, are conditioned (*saṅkhāta*), and hence unsatisfactory, impermanent and insubstantial. Only *nibbāna*, it must be remembered, is taught as unconditioned (*asaṅkhāta*). That all worldly experience is conditioned and therefore unsatisfactory is expressed in the first of the four noble truths : *sabbe saṅkhārā dukkhā*. To hold otherwise, to claim that the *jhānā* or any other experience, including experiences of God, mystical experiences, et cetera, are ultimately satisfactory, permanent or substantial, is explicitly rejected by the Buddha[3] when he claims that this was precisely the problem of his two teachers, Āḷāra Kāḷāma and Uddaka Rāmaputta. At another place,[4] just this position is condemned as a deadly heresy.

The Buddha's remark about not confusing *sati* meditation with the *amata*, another name for *nibbāna* or *arahattā*, makes the same point of not confusing the means with the end. As we shall see below, the *jhānā* and their resulting powers are not indispensable, at least theoretically, for the attainment of *arahattā*. Whether or not *arahattā* could be possible in the

1. A.V.346. (My translation)
   yaṃ kho pana kiñci abhisaṃkataṃ abhisañcetayitaṃ, tad aniccaṃ nirodhadhamman 'ti pajānāti.
2. S.V.161. (My translation)
   Catusu bhikkhave satipaṭṭhānesu supatiṭṭhitacittā viharatha, ma vo amatam panassa.
3. M.I.164 ff.
4. D.I.137 f.

absence of this *jhānā* practice shall also be considered. Johansson[5] has also noticed Buddhism's radical separation of meditation and the goal of meditation :

> Meditation does not automatically lead to a realisation of *nibbāna*, as Anuruddha points out, A.I.282 : ..."Strenuous and unshaken is my energy. Mindfulness is set up in me untroubled. My body is calm, not perturbed. My mind is concentrated, one-pointed. Yet for all that, my mind is not freed from the obsessions without grasping."[6] In M.II.37-44 it is said that also an evil man may be able to practice meditation and reach the eighth level.

3. *Meditation and Spontaneity*

One other question which often arises in discussions of Buddhism, is that if *nibbāna* could rightly be characterized as a free, spontaneous and unconditioned mind (*asaṅkhārika kusala citta*), then how could it be reached by a rather tedious disciplining, which appears to be the antithesis of spontaneity ? We shall discuss this type of question in detail when considering the sociology and psychology of the arahant, but the Venerable Nyāṇaponika Mahāthera[7] offers a crucial hint : in Buddhism, *asaṅkhārika-kusala-citta* is rooted in *sasaṅkhārika-kusala-citta*, which is to say that meditation as a formal practice inclines us toward freedom, that the goal of Buddhism is something to which we gradually become habituated. While there is no doubt that, in one sense, it is a breakthrough (*vimokkha*) from all conditioning, nevertheless such formal practices as ethics and meditation can serve as a basis—though never a condition—for this attainment. This will become significant for our discussion when we look at the sociology of the arahant in terms of the "two wheels of Dhamma" theory which has been applied to Buddhism by many scholars. This theory holds that the goals of (a) *nibbāna* and (b) ethics, as bases for social organization,

---

5. Johansson, *PN*, pp. 98-99.
6. A.I. 282.
   Āraddhaṃ kho pana ma viriyaṃ asallīnaṃ sati asamuṭṭhā passaddho kāyo asāraddho samāhitaṃ cittaṃ ekaggaṃ. Atha ca pana me na anupādāya āsavehi cittaṃ vimuccatī 'ti.
7. Nyāṇaponika Mahāthera, *The Power of Mindfulness* Kandy : Buddhist Publication Society, Wheel Series Nos. 121/122, 1976 (1968), p. 39.

are radically discrete and that therefore two distinct forms of social organization, the monastic and the lay, evolved along entirely different premises. These premises have been called '*nibbānic* Buddhism' and '*kammatic* Buddhism' by Spiro,[8] the former tending towards *arahattā* for the members of the *saṅgha*, the latter towards the heavens (*sagga*) for the laity. Our position is that this dichotomization, while useful for some scholarly distinctions, can become dysfunctional if pushed too far in one's attempts to understand the Buddhist world. Thus our premise is that, as Nyāṇaponika offers, spontaneity (*asaṅkhārika-kusala-citta*) can be rooted in disciplined habit (*sasaṅkhārika-kusala-citta*).

This issue also becomes significant in terms of the psychology of the arahant : how can psychological freedom, in the highest sense, be developed by psychological discipline ? Another expression of just this problem is found in the question of two Buddhist ethical terms : merit (*puññā*) and skilfulness (*kusala*). A terminological confusion, as P. D. Premasiri[9] argues, has led to such claims as the arahant being an-ethical. The case which we shall develop is that while *puññā* is *kammatically* binding and *kusala* is not, the former is the habituating ground of the latter. In the context of our present discussion, however, it is sufficient for us to indicate that the freedom which is the goal of meditation can be habituated by the strict discipline of meditation, although the former could never be said to be caused by the latter, as freedom is defined in Buddhism as antithetical to the *tilakkhana* (unsatisfactoriness, impermanence and insubstantiality) which characterize the world of cause and effect. But we shall discuss these issues later.

B. *Samādhi*

Meanwhile we proceed to sort out meditational terminology in the *Sutta Piṭaka*. The most common generic term for the various types of mental discipline is *samādhi*, which is also the eighth member of the eightfold path (*magga*) taught by the

8. Spiro, *op. cit., passim.*

9. P. D. Premasiri, "Interpretation of Two Principle Ethical Terms in Early Buddhism," Peradeniya : *The Sri Lanka Journal of the Humanities*, 2, 1, June 1976, pp. 63-74.

Buddha. Lancaster[10] finds a paucity of useful material on *samādhi* in the *Sutta Piṭaka*; however, in Buddhaghosa's *Visuddhimagga*,[11] seven forms of meditation are subsumed under his discussion of *samādhi*. He writes :[12]

> Herein, as to enumeration : it was said above 'from among the forty meditation subjects.' Herein, the forty meditation subjects [*kammaṭṭhānāni*] are these : ten *kasinas* (totalities), ten kinds of foulness, ten recollections, four divine abidings, four immaterial states, one perception, one defining.

Buddhaghosa says that it is impossible to offer a definition of *samādhi*, due to its wide range of usages, but it could be discussed in this way :[13]

> In what sense is it concentration [*samādhi*] ? It is concentration in the sense of concentrating [*samādhāna*]. What is this concentrating ? It is the centering [*ādhāna*] of consciousness and consciousness-concomitants evenly [*samaṃ*] and rightly [*sammā*] on a single object: placing, is what it means. So it is the state, in virtue of which consciousness and its concomitants remain evenly and rightly on a single object undistracted and unscattered, that would be understood as concentrating.

The Buddha has this to say about *samādhi* :[14] And of what sort, monks, is the *indriya* (faculty, power) of *samādhi* ? Here,

---

10. Lewis R. Lancaster, "Samādhi Names in Buddhist Texts," Colombo : *Malalasekere Commemoration Volume*, 1976.

11. Vism., chapters 3-12.

12. Vism., p. 89, III, paragraph 104. (Ñāṇamoli translation)
Tattha saṅkhāṭaniddesato ti, ca tālīnāya kammaṭṭhānesu iti hi vuttaṃ : tatr' imāni cattālīsa kammaṭṭhānāni : dasa kasiṇā, dasa asubhā, dasa anussatiyo, cattāro brahmavihārā, cattāro āruppā, ekā saññā, ekaṃ vavayyjānan ti.

13. Vism., III, paragraph 3. (Ñāṇamoli translation)
Ken' aṭṭhena samādhī ti ? Samādhāanṭṭhena samādhi. Kim idaṃ samādhānaṃ nāma ? Ekārammaṇe cittacetasikānaṃ samaṃ sammā ca ādhānaṃ : ṭhapanan ti vuttaṃ hoti. Tasmā yassa dhammass' ānubhāvena ekārammaṇe cittacetasikā samaṃ sammā ca avikkhipamānā avippakiṇṇā ca hutvā tiṭṭhanti, idaṃ samādhānan ti veditabbaṃ.

14. S.V. 197. (My translation)
Katamañ ca bhikkhave samādhindriyaṃ ? Idha bhikkhave ariyasāvako vossaggārammanaṃ karitvā labhati samādhiṃ labhati citassa ekaggataṃ.

> monks, the noble disciple, having made relinquishing his object, grabs hold of *samādhi*, grabs hold of one-pointedness of mind.

In this *sutta*, the Buddha is especially concerned with carefully distinguishing *samādhi* from *sati* and *vipassanā*, which he also characterizes for purposes of clarification. Of the former, *sati*, he says :[15]

> ...the Ariyan disciple is mindful, possessed of supreme discrimination, one who calls to mind and remembers things said and done long ago.

And of the latter, *vipassanā*, he says :[16]

> ...the Ariyan disciple is possessed of insight [*vipassanā*] thus : he has insight for tracing out the rise and fall of things, insight which is Ariyan, penetrating, going on to the utter destruction of ill.

Other characterizations of *samādhi* in the *Sutta Piṭaka* link it up with 'one-pointedness of mind' (*citass' ekaggatā*),[17] as the Buddha has done in this *sutta*, all of which gives us a sense of 'concentration' for *samādhi*.

Samādhi, then, is defined by the *P.T.S. Dictionary*[18] as : "concentration; a concentrated, self-controlled intent state of mind and meditation, which, concomitant with right living, is a necessary condition to the attainment of higher wisdom and emancipation." From our observations of some usages of the term from the *Visuddhimagga* and the *Sutta Piṭaka* as above, it seems to be used as a general term for the traditional forty meditational practices, and is characterized by an even distribution of awareness (*ādhāna, sammaṃ*), and as a centering of the mind (*citassa ekaggatā*). It is also one of the three headings, along with *sīla* and *paññā*, of the noble eightfold path, under which is subsumed *sammā sati* and *sammā samādhi*. As one of

---

15. S.V. 197. (PTS translation)
ariyasāvako satimā hoti paramena satinepakkena samannāgato cirakataṃ cirabhāsitam pi saritā anussaritā.
16. S.V. 197. (PTS translation)
ariyasāvako paññavā hoti, udayatthagāminiyā paññāya samannāgato ariyāya nibbedhikāya
sammādukkhakkhayagāminiyā.
17. M.I. 301.
18. *P.T.S. Dictionary*, p. 685.

these three headings, it has the use of covering the whole range of meditation, as in Buddhaghosa's usage above. In the other use, it seems to indicate the culmination of a particular meditative exercise, as it can be applied to the *jhānā*, *sati*, et cetera. It would seem, from these uses, therefore, that one would not be far wrong in using the term *samādhi* as both (a) a general term for meditation, as well as (b) to indicate the culmination of a given meditative process : hence its translation in many places as 'concentration,' and its canonical equivalence to 'one-pointedness of mind' (*citassa ekaggatā*), and as an even distribution of awareness over consciousness and its concomitants, as in Buddhaghosa.

C. *Bhāvanā*

Bhāvanā is a derivative of the root √*bhu*, 'to be,' and is defined in the *P.T.S. Dictionary*[19] as : "producing, dwelling on something, putting one's thoughts to, application, developing by means of thought or meditation, cultivation by mind, culture." We find this term used in all of the above senses in the *Sutta Piṭaka.* The Buddha[20] in one place applies bhāvanā to the thirty-seven factors conducive to enlightenment (*bodhipakkhika dhammā*) :

> Monks, although a wish such as this may arise in the heart of a monk, as he lives without applying himself to making-become [*bhāvanā*] : "Oh that my heart might be freed of the cankers [āsavā] and be without attachment !"—yet his heart is not so freed. And what is the reason ? Let it be said : "It is lack of making-become." Making-become of what ? The four arisings of mindfulness, the four right efforts, the four bases of psychic power, the five controlling faculties, the five powers, the seven parts in awakening and the eightfold Ariyan Way.

---

19. *P. T. S. Dictionary*, p. 503.
20. A.IV.125-126. (PTS translation)
Bhāvanaṃ ananuyuttassa bhikkhave bhikkhuno viharato kiñcāpi evaṃ icchā uppajjeyya 'aho vata me anupādāya āsavehi cittaṃ vimuccati. Taṃ kissa hetu ?
'Abhāvitattā ti 'ssa vacanīyaṃ. Kissa abhāvitatta ? Catunnaṃ satipaṭṭhānānaṃ catunnaṃ sammappadhānānaṃ catunnaṃ iddhipādānaṃ pañcannaṃ indriyānaṃ pañcannaṃ balānaṃ sattannaṃ bojjhaṅgānaṃ ariyassa aṭṭhaṅgikassa maggassa.

We shall be discussing these thirty-seven factors—*satipaṭṭhāna, pahāna, iddhipāda, indriyāni, balāni, bojjhaṅgā* and *magga*—below, but the point to note is that to all of these the term *bhāvanā* is applied. Here *bhāvanā* is translated by E. M. Hare rather awkwardly as 'making-become,' where the simpler 'cultivation' or 'development' would have been better employed.

The point to note is that the practice of *bhāvanā* may revolve around any particular aspect of the Dhamma. For example, particular views should be developed (*bhāvanā*) to counteract specific unwholesome views :[21]

> There are three mental objects [*dhammā*], monks. Which three ? The view of self-comfort [*assādadiṭṭhi*], the view of egoism [*attānudiṭṭhi*], and the wrong view [*micchādiṭṭhi*]. These, monks, are the three mental objects. To overcome these three mental objects, monks, develop three [other] mental objects. What three ? To overcome the view of self-comfort, cultivate the view of impermanence; to overcome the view of egoism, cultivate the view of *anattā*; and to overcome the wrong view, cultivate the right view. Monks, these three mental objects are overcome by the cultivation of these three [other] mental objects.

At another place,[22] a monk who wishes to develop (*bhāvanā*) himself too quickly, which is contrary to the teaching that the way is gradual, is likened to a cow who lifts the hind leg before having put down the front leg. Here it seems that *bhāvanā* is used in a very wide, non-technical sense of general development or cultivation.

Very common in Burma, and also found in Sri Lanka, are the *bhāvanā-sālā*, halls for *bhāvānā*, utilized primarily by the laity

---

21. A.III.447. (My translation)
Tayo me bhikkhave dhammā. Katame tayo ? Assādadiṭṭhi, attānudiṭṭhi, micchādiṭṭhi. Ime kho bhikkhave tayo dhammā. Imesaṃ kho bhikkhave tiṇṇaṃ dhammānaṃ pahānāya tayo dhammā bhāvetabbā. Katame tayo ? Assadadiṭṭhiyā pahānāya anicca-saññā bhāvetabbā, attānudiṭṭhiyā pahānāya anattasaññā bhāvetabbā, micchādiṭṭhiyā pahānāya sammādiṭṭhi bhāvetabbā. Imesaṃ kho bhikkhave tiṇṇaṃ dhammānaṃ pahānāya ime tayo dhammā bhāvetabbāti.

22. A.IV.418-422.
sā purimaṃ pādaṃ na suppatiṭṭhitaṃ patiṭṭhāpetvā pacchimaṃ pādaṃ uddhareyya.

for the practice of elementary meditation. In this context, *bhāvanā* is used to talk about the actualization of the four *brahma-vihārā*. The four *brahma-vihārā,* which constitute the fundamental ethical notions of Buddhism, are : *mettā, muditā, karuṇā,* and *upekkhā.* Rahula[23] describes them as :

> (1) extending universal love and goodwill to all living beings without any kind of discrimination, 'just as a mother loves her only child,' (2) compassion for all living beings who are suffering, in trouble and affliction (which, according to Buddhism, is a redundancy), (3) sympathetic joy in others' success, welfare and happiness, and (4) equanimity in all vicissitudes of life.

Buddhaghosa[24] devotes a full chapter to specific practices for developing these four *brahma-vihārā*, which generally entail the suppression of the antithetical mental object and the application of each of the *vihārā* to varying objects, beginning with those neutral to the meditator, then to those near, and then to those far or antagonistic.

Bhāvanā in the *Sutta Piṭaka* is applied rather generally to any aspect of the Buddha's teaching, carrying with it the sense of developing or cultivating that particular dhamma. In the case of this term, it seems that its use is quite near to its etymology of 'bringing to life' or 'making-become.' In contemporary use, however, it usually refers to the practice of meditation on the four *brahma-vihārā*, which are fundamental Buddhist ethical principles.

D. *Vipassanā*

The most common distinction of meditational techniques in Buddhism is *samatha*, 'calming,' and *vipassanā*, 'insight,' techniques. Under the first heading we find the *jhānā* techniques, and under the latter, *sati.* This term derives from the Sanskrit root, $\sqrt{}$*smṛ*, 'to remember,'[25] and for which the *P.T.S. Dictionary* offers :[26] "memory, recognition, consciousness...intentness of

23. Walpola Rahula, *What the Buddha Taught*, New York : Grove Press, 1974 (1959), p. 75.
24. Vism., chapter 9.
25. Whitney, p. 199.
26. *P.T.S. Dictionary*, p. 672.

mind, wakefulness of mind, mindfulness, alertness, lucidity of mind, self-possession, consciousness, self-consciousness." The *samatha* techniques are not unique to Buddhism. As we have seen before, the *jhānā* were taught to the Buddha by his early teachers, and Sāriputta uses them to teach Brahma-devotees the way to attain rebirth near their God.[27] What the Buddha uniquely added to the Indian *jhānā* (Sanskrit : *dhyāna*) tradition was the teaching that they, too, were mere products and therefore subject to the three characteristics (*tilakkhana*) of unsatisfactoriness, impermanence and insubstantiality.[28] The *vipassanā* techniques, according to Bhikkhu Ñāṇamoli,[29] are a unique contribution of the Buddha;

> [The Buddha] does claim that the development of insight, *vipassanā*, culminating in the penetration of the Four Truths is peculiar to [his teachings].

Most frequently in the *Sutta Piṭaka*[30] we find these two techniques, *samatha* and *vipassanā*, mentioned together, but gradually in the development of Buddhist thought about meditation, we find more and more emphasis placed on *vipassanā* alone,[31] especially the *satipaṭṭhāna* method. Our experiences in the Theravāda cultures of Burma and Sri Lanka have indicated that this is the most popular monastic meditational venue, and it along with the *bhāvanā* of the four *brahma-vihārā* as the only techniques still employed with any regularity. In the *Sutta Piṭaka* we find two major discourses on *satipaṭṭhāna*,[32] and these *suttas* are so popular that "...often this discourse...is recited at the bedside of a dying Buddhist, so that in the last hour of his life, his heart may be set on, consoled and gladdened by the Master's great message of liberation,"[33] a practice strikingly similar to the Tibetan *bar do thos grol* tradition of reading a

27. M.II.184-197.
28. A. V. 346.
29. Bhikkhu Ñāṇamoli, tr., *The Path of Purification : Visuddhi Magga of Bhadantācariya Buddhaghosa*, Kandy : Buddhist Publication Society, third edition, 1975, "Introduction," p. xxxi.
30. e.g., A.II.56.
31. Nyāṇaponika, *The Heart of Buddhist Meditation*, New York : Samuel Weiser, 1965 (London : Rider, 1962), p. 103. [Hereinafter : *HBM*].
32. *Majjhima* no. 10 and *Dīgha* no. 22.
33. Nyāṇaponika, *HBM*, p. 11.

text said to produce liberation (*vimokkha*; *thos grol*) just at the moment of death and immediately thereafter (*antarabhāva*; *bar do*).

Most *sati* instruction begins with some practices involving mindful concentration (*satisamādhi*; note the use of *samādhi* here conjoined with the particular meditational technique of *sati*) on breathing. An example of this instruction is :[34]

> Intent concentration on in-breathing and out-breathing, Ānanda, is the one state which, if cultivated and made much of, brings the four arisings of mindfulness, if cultivated and made much of, brings the seven limbs of wisdom to completion. The seven limbs of wisdom, if cultivated and made much of, complete knowledge and release.

We shall discuss the seven limbs of wisdom (*sattā bojjhaṅgā*) in another section. One point of interest to us is to note the difference between Buddhist mindfulness of breathing (*ānāpāna sati*) and the Hindu *prāṇāyāma*, or *yoga* of breathing. In the former, the breathing itself is never the meditational objective; rather it is the mindfulness of breathing that is considered important. The breathing itself, while having a calming effect and some benefits to health, is not the purpose of this technique. This point, as presented by Nyāṇaponika,[35] is a principle that could be applied to all Buddhist meditations : their objective is seeing the impermanence of the states produced in meditation, or, expressed differently, observing the meditations mindfully. Undoubtedly some Hindu techniques such as *prāṇāyāma* and *kuṇḍalinī* found their way into Buddhist practice at a later date, but early Buddhism was quite clear in maintaining a different objective for their techniques, especially those associated with *vipassanā*. This could also be held, as we shall see, for the Buddhist understanding of the *jhānā*, as the point of their practice was not mere absorption into the formless (*ārūpya*) realms, but the awareness that these realms, like our poor *kāmaloka*, were marked by the *tilakkhana*.

---

34. S. V. 329. (PTS translation)
Ānāpānasatisamādhi kho Ānanda eko dhamma bhāvito bahulīkato cattāro satipaṭṭhāne paripūreti, cattāro satipaṭṭhānā bhāvitā bahulīkatā satta bojjhaṅge paripūrenti, satta bojjhaṅgā bhāvitā bahulīkatā vijjāvimuttim paripūrenti.

35. Nyāṇaponika, *HBM*, p. 61.

The arahant, also, enjoyed *satipaṭṭhāna* techniques, especially those of *ānāpānasati*. We read :[36]

Moreover, monks, those monks who are arahants, in whom the *āsavas* are destroyed, who have lived the life, done the task, lifted the burden, won their highest good, worn out the fetters of becoming, who by perfect knowledge have become free,—for such also the intent concentration on in-breathing and out-breathing, if cultivated and made much of, conduces both to pleasant living and to mindful composure even in this life.

Now at this point a question could be raised : if the arahant is truly one who has done what was to be done (*katakaraṇīyo*), then for what purpose would he practice any meditation ? Two possible answers, both unacceptable to the Theravāda and which actually were offered by opposing Buddhist schools, were : (1) that the arahant is not such a finished product as one might think, and there are still some things to be done by him; and (2) that the Buddha and, by analogy, the arahants, remained in meditation throughout their lives, and that anything which seemed like a worldly action was done merely in conformity with the practices of the world (*loke vohāra*), a position analogous to the Docetic view of Jesus. The Theravāda view is more down-to-earth : "Both the serenity of *jhānā* and the clear vision of *vipassanā* are so natural to the arahant's mentality, that this seems to be a sufficient reason for their engagement in these meditations and practices though there is nothing further for them to achieve by doing so."[37]

Discussions of *satipaṭṭhāna* usually revolve around four outsets or stations (*upaṭṭhāna*) :[38]

---

36. S.V.326. (PTS translation)
Ye ca kho te bhikkhave bhikkhū arahanto khīṇāsavā vusitavanto katakaraṇīyā ohitabhārā anuppattasadatthā parikkhīṇabhavasaṃyojanā sammadaññā vimuttā, tesam ānāpānasatisamādhi bhāvito bahulīkato diṭṭheva dhamme sukhavihārāya c' eva saṃvattati satisampajaññāya ca.

37. Personal communication from Nyāṇaponika Mahāthera, from Kandy, dated 9.11.77.

38. S.V.141. (My translation)
Ekāyano ayam bhikkhave maggo sattānaṃ visuddhiyā sokaparidevānaṃ samatikkamāya dukkhadomanassānaṃ atthagamāya ñāyassa

> Monks, a certain vehicle which is the way to the purification of beings, to the full going beyond sorrow, going to the goal of destroying pain and sorrow, to the higher way, to the realization of *nibbāna*, is the four foundations of mindfulness. Which four ? Herein, monks, as regards body, a monk dwells observing body, having cut off worldly sorrow by training the ardent application of mindfulness. As regards feeling (*vedanā*), he dwells observing feelings, etc. As regards mind (*citta*), he dwells observing mind, etc. As regards phenomena (*dhammā*), he dwells observing phenomena, etc.

In the Pāsādika Suttanta,[39] this technique is especially recommended for those who speculate regarding the beginning of the world. In two excellent books[40] the topic of *satipaṭṭhāna* has been treated at length and with sympathetic intelligence, so it would be redundant at best to enter into a lengthy discussion here. Let us limit ourselves to saying that the *vipassanā* technique of *satipaṭṭhāna* involves attention to body, feeling, mind and phenomena in a systematic way, all within the context of the four noble truths, and which culminates with insight (*vipassanā*) into these truths.[41] At several places in the *Sutta Piṭaka* we are told that the arahants enjoy this practice, which would mean, from a Theravāda perspective, that it is a natural expression of their attainment, not implying the necessity of further training.

---

adhigamāya nibbānassa sacchikiriyāya. Yad idaṃ cattāro satipaṭṭhānā. Katame cattāro ? Idha bhikkhave bhikkhu abhijjhādomanassam. Vedanāsu vedānupassī viharati ātāpī sampajāno. Citte cittānupassī viharati ātāpī sampajāno. Dhammesu dhammānupassī viharati ātāpī sampajāno satima vinneyya loke abhijjhādomanassaṃ.

39. D.xxix. 40.

40. Nyāṇaponika, *HBM*; and Donald K. Swearer, *Secrets of the Lotus*, New York : Macmillan, 1971.

41. This insight is considered indispensable for the attainment of *nibbāna*, which is analogous to saying, as does Candrakīrti, that the realization of *śūnyatā* is indispensable for the attainment of *nirvāṇa*. See *Prasannapadā*, pp. 351-353, as quoted in T.R.V. Murti, *The Central Philosophy of Buddhism: A Study of the Mādhyamaka System*, London : George Allen & Unwin, 1974 (1955), p. 96, fn. 3 : tad ayam ācā yo yathaivaṃvidhe viṣaye nācāryamatānuvarti tathā pratīpaditaṁ Madhyamakāvatāre 'dūraṅgamāyāṁ tu dhiyādhika ity atreti na punas tad dūṣaṇe yatha āsthīyate.

The insight which emerges from *vipassanā* techniques may also be called *paññā*. The only distinction of the terms *vipassanā* and *paññā* is that the former arises in the context of meditation-talk, and the latter, which has a wider range, presents itself to us in the question of the *paññāvimutti*, the one who is freed by insight, and the *cetovimutti*, the one who is freed through the heart/mind. The former category applies to those arahants who have attained to that state by these *vipassanā* techniques primarily; and the latter to those arahants who have employed the *samatha* techniques and have actualized the *abhiññā* and *iddhividhā* which arise from the *jhānā*, as well as *vipassanā*. We shall enter into this discussion properly after having discussed the *jhānā*.

One other interesting discourse centering on *satipaṭṭhāna* techniques tells us that one may use them both to ward oneself (*attānaṃ rakkhanto*) and to ward another (*paraṃ rakkhanto*). The citation is rather lengthy, but its interesting implications warrant our quoting it in full :[42]

> Once upon a time, monks, a bamboo acrobat set up his pole and called to his pupil, Medakathālika, saying : "Now, my lad, climb the pole and stand on my shoulder !" "All right, master," replied the pupil to the bamboo acrobat, climbed the pole and stood on his master's shoulder. Then said the master to his pupil : "Now, Medakathālika, my lad, you watch me and I'll watch you. Thus watched and warded by each other, we'll show our tricks, get a good fee and come down safe from the bamboo pole." At these words Medakathālika the pupil said to his master : "No, no ! That won't do, master ! You look after yourself and I'll look after myself. Thus watched and warded, each by himself, we'll show our tricks, get a good fee, and come down safe from the bamboo pole. That's the way to do it !" Then said the Exalted One : "Now, monks, just as Medakathālika the pupil said to his master : 'I'll look after myself,' so ought ye to observe the station of mindfulness which means 'I'll ward myself', likewise that which means 'we'll ward another.' By warding oneself, monks, one wards another. By warding another, one wards himself. And how, monks by warding oneself does one ward another ? It is by

42. S.V.168-169. (PTS translation)

> following after, by cultivating, by making much of him. And how, monks, by warding another does one ward himself? It is by forbearance, by harmlessness, by good-will, by compassion towards him. That, monks, is how he wards himself. Monks, ye must observe the station of mindfulness which means 'I'll ward myself.' Ye must observe that which means 'I'll ward another.' It is by warding another that one wards himself."

The commentary[43] says that the way one wards another as entailed in warding himself, is by setting himself up as an example for the other. But this does not seem to be the only valid interpretation. If the practices of *satipaṭṭhāna* entail the cultivation of forbearance (*khanti*), harmlessness (*avihiṃsā*), good-will (*mettā*) and compassion (*anuddaya*), as the text indicates, then more than an example is proferred for the warding of another. The question involved is whether *arahattā*, which is the culmination of these *vipassanā* techniques, entails an active helping of the other, or whether this helping is accidental to *arahattā*, which would seem to follow from the commentary's claim that he wards another merely by example. The latter alternative has been the traditional interpretation, both within the Theravāda tradition and also in modern scholarship. For the present, we merely wish to pose these two alternatives. After further discussions of the arahant, we shall attempt to resolve the question in the context of the sociology of the arahant.[44]

E. *Jhāna*

In the distinction of Buddhist meditational practices into *samatha* and *vipassanā*, we stated earlier that the former category largely subsumes the *jhānā*, and the latter category contains *satipaṭṭhāna*. We also pointed out that the latter was unique to Buddhism, whereas *samatha* was shared with other Indian systems, although the Buddha's interpretation of the *jhānā* as something produced and therefore characterized by the *tilakkhana*

---

43. Quoted at *Kindred Sayings*, p. 48, fn. 1.

44. We favor the former alternative explanation, as the latter would, we feel, make the arahant notion liable to the Mahāyāna criticisms levelled against it, and our contention is that the arahant, bodhisattva and mahāsiddha ideals form a continuity within Buddhism.

of unsatisfactoriness, impermanence and insubstantiality, was also a unique contribution.

Samatha derives from the root $\sqrt{}$*śam*, 'be quiet,'[45] and is defined in the *P.T.S. Dictionary*[46] as "calm, quietude of heart." *Jhāna* derives from the twin roots, $\sqrt{}$*dhyā* and $\sqrt{}$*dhī*, both 'to think,'[47] although Buddhaghoṣa[48] offers a more creative etymology : ". . . called *jhāna* from meditation on objects and from burning up anything adverse" (*ārammaṇ' ūpanijjhānato paccanīkajhāpanato vājhānaṃ*).

We have also stated above that the *jhānā* are not to be confused with the goal.[49] This point is explained by Nyāṇaponika Mahāthera :[50]

> The development of tranquility, *samatha-bhāvanā*, aims at the full concentration of mind, attained in the meditative absorptions, *jhānā*. These absorptions are gained, in different degrees, by the systematic practice of the 38 traditional 'subjects of meditation conducive to tranquility,' *samatha-kammaṭṭhāna*. Through the high degree of mental unification and stillness attained in these absorptions, the fivefold sense perception is temporarily obliterated, and conceptual and discursive thought, being weak in the first stage of absorption, is completely absent in the following stages. From the latter fact alone it can be gathered that, in the Buddha's teaching, the development of tranquility or the meditative absorptions, are only means to an end, and cannot lead, by themselves, to the highest goal of liberation which is attainable only through insight. After rising from these states of absorption, the meditator is therefore advised to continue his meditation with the development of insight.

The connection between the 'topics for meditation' (*kasiṇā*) and the *jhānā* is discussed by Buddhaghoṣa :[51]

---

45. Whitney, p. 171.
46. *P.T.S. Dictionary*, p. 652.
47. Whitney, p. 85 and p. 83.
48. Vism. (PTS edition), p. 150.
49. A.V. 346.
50. Nyāṇaponika, *HBM*, p. 102.
51. Vism., III, paragraph 107. (Ñāṇamoli translation) Jhānappabhedato ti, appanāvahesu c' ettha ānāpanasatiyā saddhiṃ dasa kasiṇā catutthajjhānikā honti. Kāyagatāsatiyā saddhiṃ dasa

> As to the kind of *jhānā* : among those that bring absorption, the ten *kasiṇās* together with mindfulness of breathing bring all four *jhānā*. The ten kinds of foulness together with mindfulness occupied with the body bring the first *jhāna*. The first three divine abidings [*brahma-vihārā*] bring three *jhāna*. The fourth divine abiding and the four immaterial states [*āruppā*] bring the fourth *jhāna*. This is 'as to the kind of *jhānā*.'

At the time when Buddhaghoṣa was writing, there was not yet a sharp division between the *samatha* and *vipassanā* techniques of meditation; thus one finds both systems so interrelated in his writings. As Nyāṇaponika points out,[52] the radical separation of the two comes much later. In reading source materials on the *jhānā*, however, one finds a type of discourse about four and/ or eight *jhānā*, as well as the distinction of *rūpa* and *āruppa jhānā*. The clearest discourse involving all eight *jhānā*, four *rūpa* and four *āruppa*, is taught by Moggallāna[53] and deserves to be cited at length.

Of the first *jhāna*, which is one of the four *rūpa jhānā*, Moggallāna says :[54]

> Herein a brother, aloof from sensuality, aloof from evil states, attains the first trance [*jhāna*] which is accompanied by thought directed and sustained, which is born of solitude, full of zest and ease, and abides therein. This is called 'the first trance.'

The first point to note is the claim that in the first *rūpa jhāna*, the meditator is aloof from sensuality (*kāma*). In Buddhist thought, the world in which we live is called *kāmaloka*, the realm of sensuality, and it is through sensuality that we are born into it. Of the five (or, in later traditions, six) realms of possible rebirth, as symbolized by the *bhavacakka* (Sanskrit : *bhavacakra*; Tibetan : *srid pa'i 'khor lo*), one of the oldest Buddhist 'maps'

---

asubhā paṭhamajjhānikā. Purimā tayo brahmavihārā tikajjhānikā. Catutthabrahmavihāro cattāro ca āruppā catutthajjhānikā ti. Evaṃ jhānappabhedato.

52. Nyāṇaponika, *HBM*, p. 103.

53. S.IV.263-269.

54. S.IV.263. (PTS translation)
Idha bhikkhu vivicceva kāmehi vivicca akusalehi dhammehi savitakkaṃ savicāraṃ vivekajam pītisukhaṃ pathamaṃ jhānam upasampajja viharati. Idaṃ vuccati pathamaṃ jhānanti.

of existence, *kāmaloka* is said to be comprised of humans, animals, et cetera. For Buddhists there are two other worlds (*lokā*) : *rūpaloka* and *ārupaloka*, both of which are the realms of the various deities, spirits, and meditators. By leaving behind sensuality here is meant leaving *kāmaloka* and the entry into the *rūpaloka*, the 'world of forms.' The first four *jhānā* belong to this realm; the four higher *jhānā* are *āruppa*, or formless.

There are five *jhānic* activities which gradually wither away as one progresses in the *jhānā*. These five activities are : *vitakka*, which means the initial drawing of attention to an object, translated here as 'directed thinking'; *vicārā*, the dwelling upon or perhaps investigation of the object, here translated as 'sustained thought'; *pīti*, which is joy, rapture or zest; *sukha*, which is ease or pleasantness; and *ekaggatā*, which as we saw before was equated with *samādhi* in one context and which is a concentration or one-pointedness of mind. In this first (*pathamaṃ*) *jhāna*, we find that all five of these activities are present. However, it is said elsewhere[55] that speech (*vācā*) is the only activity that has ceased, and that all of these five remain.

The second *rūpa jhāna* is described by Moggallāna thus :[56]

> Herein when a brother, by the calming down of thought directed and sustained, attains the inward calm, that one-pointedness of will, apart from thought directed and sustained, born of concentration, zestful and full of ease, which is the second trance, and abides therein, this is called the second trance.

In this *jhāna*, the activities of *vitakka* and *vicāra* have ceased, which has a calming effect on the meditator. He is left with joy and ease (*pītisukha*).

Moggallāna describes the third *rūpa jhāna* as :[57]

---

55. S.IV.217.

56. S.IV.263-264. (PTS translation)
Idha bhikkhu vitakkavicārānaṃ vūpasamā ajjhattaṃ sampasādanaṃ cetaso ekodibhāvaṃ avitakkam avicāraṃ samādhijjam pītisukhaṃ dutiyaṃ jhānam upasampajja viharati. Idaṃ vuccati dutiyaṃ jhānan ti.

57. S.IV.264. (PTS translation)
Idha bhikkhu pītiyā ca virāgā upekkhako ca viharati, sato ca sampajāno sukhañca kāyena patisaṃvedeti. Yan tam ariyā ācikkhanti upekkhako satimā sukhavihārīti. Tatiyaṃ jhānam upasampajja viharati. Idaṃ vuccati tatiyaṃ jhānan ti.

> Herein a brother, by the fading out of zest, abides balanced and remains mindful and composed and experiences with the body that ease of which the Ariyans aver : "The balanced, thoughtful man dwells happily." Thus he enters on and abides in the third trance. This is called 'the third trance.'

Here joy or zest (*pīti*) has been left behind, and we find the introduction of equanimity (*upekkhā*). We shall see that after the fourth *jhāna*, when all other activities have fallen away, *upekkhā* or *ekaggatā* is all that remains.

As for the fourth *rūpa jhāna*, Moggallāna says :[58]

> Herein a brother, rejecting pleasure, rejecting pain, by the coming to an end of the joy and sorrow which he had before, enters on and abides in the fourth trance, which is freed from pleasure, freed from pain, but is a state of perfect purity of balance and equanimity. This is called 'the fourth trance.'

Here Buddhism insists that there can be no overcoming of pain unless there is an overcoming of pleasure as well and, just as one cannot overcome death without overcoming life as well, both are given up in the fourth *rūpa jhāna*. Elsewhere,[59] this is put differently. The Buddha says of this fourth *rūpa jhāna* : "both inbreathing and outbreathing are extinguished," which is to say that the hedonically neutral (*upekkhā*) one-pointedness of mind (*citass' ekaggatā*) is fully developed.

Lama Anagarika Govinda[60] gives us a very useful chart to discuss these activities in relation to the *jhānā*. However, we have devised our own chart relating to these *Saṃyutta* verses :

---

58. S.IV.265. (PTS translation)
Idha bhikkhu sukhassa ca pahānā dukkhassa ca pahānā pubbeva somanassadomanassānam atthagamā ca adukkhaṃ asukhaṃ upekkhā-sati-pārisuddhiṃ catutthaṃ jhānam upasampajja viharati. Idaṃ vuccati catutthaṃ jhānan ti.

59. S.IV.217-218 : catutthaṃ jhānaṃ samāpannassa assāsapassāsā niruddhā honti.

60. Lama Anagarika Govinda, *The Psychological Attitude of Early Buddhist Philosophy, and its Systematic Representation according to Abhidhamma Tradition,* New York : Samuel Weiser, 1961, p. 85. [Hereinafter : Govinda, *PAEBP*].

JHĀNĀ	ACTIVITIES
pathamaṃ	*vitakka, vicāra, pīti, sukha*
dutiyaṃ	*pīti, sukha*
tatiyaṃ	*sukha, upekkhā*
catutthaṃ	*upekkhā* (= *ekaggatā*)

We also find that these *rūpa jhānā* activities may be specifically proscribed to counteract various unskilful factors (*akusalā dhammā*). In one place,[61] the five hedonic tones of : (a) the faculty of pain (*dukkhindriyaṃ*); (b) the faculty of pleasure (*sukhindriyaṃ*); (c) the faculty of unhappiness (*domanassindriyaṃ*); (d) the faculty of happiness (*somanassindriyaṃ*); and (e) the faculty of equanimity (*upekkhindriyaṃ*); are all overcome, each in turn, by the skilful application of these activities in various *jhānic* practices. This could be schematized as follows :

INDRIYAṀ	*JHĀNA*	ACTIVITY
dukkhindriyaṃ	*pathamaṃ*	*vitakka* and *vicāra*
domanassindriyaṃ	*dutiyaṃ*	*pīti, sukha* (*samādhijaṃ*)
sukhindriyaṃ	*tatiyaṃ*	*"yan tam ariyā ācikkhanti upekkhako satinā sukhavihārīti"* = *upekkhā*
somanassindriyaṃ	*catutthaṃ*	*upekhāsatipārisuddhiṃ*
upekhindriyaṃ	*"Bhikkhu sabbaso nevassaññānāsaññayatanaṃ samati kamma saññāvedayitanirodhan"*	= *āruppā jhānā*

What all of this indicates is that pain may be overcome by the activities of attention and investigation (*vitakka* and *vicāra*); unhappiness may be overcome by joy and ease; pleasure may be overcome by equanimity (*upekkhā*); happiness by the application of equanimity leading to purification; and equanimity itself by the four higher *jhānā*, which we shall now consider.

The first *āruppā jhāna* is called *ākāsānañcāyatana*, the realm (*āyatana*) of the infinity of space (*ākāsa*). This is the first of the four states which are knowable only by a purified mental consciousness apart from the sense organs,[62] the other three being

61. S.V.213-216.
62. M.I.293 : nisaṭṭhena pañcahi indriyehi parisuddhena manoviññāṇena.

the rest of the *āruppā jhānā.* It is said[63] that this *ākāsānañcāyatana* is revealed through objects, which is to say that with the withering of objects, this realm becomes apprehendible, as Moggallāna explains :[64]

> Herein a brother, passing utterly beyond the perception of objects, by the coming of an end of the perception of resistance, by not attending to perception of diversity, with the idea of 'infinite is space,' enters upon and abides in the realm of infinite space. This is called 'the realm of infinite space.'

Now, much has been debated about the translation of *saññā* as 'consciousness,' and, as was indicated earlier, these √*jñā*-derivatives in Buddhist languages pose an extremely difficult problem for the scholar. We have left the P.T.S. translation to stand above, but now we would like to offer 'idea' or 'notion' as a better rendering of *saññā* in this context, an alternative offered by Wayman,[65] and which is superior to Ergardt's[66] maintaining 'perception.' This seems especially appropriate since the next *āruppā jhāna* is called 'the realm of infinite consciousness' (*viññāṇañcāyatana*), and the Buddhist *suttas*, if examined closely, reveal a terminological sophistication such that it would be unlikely that both *saññā* and *viññāṇa* would be used in the same discourse with identical or ambiguous reference. If we opt for 'idea' for *saññā*, then we are left with saying something to the effect that if one gives up the idea of object, then one has entered the realm of infinite space. This seems precisely the point, because *ākāsa* is used in Buddhism to symbolize precisely that of which an object could not be made; it is non-objectifiable and is used to indicate that open dimension of our existence which is beyond subject and object distinctions; it is spontaneity; it, like *nibbāna*, is uncompounded (*asaṅkhāta*); it is an image of the freedom

---

63. S.II.104-105.
64. S.IV.266. (PTS translation)
Idha bhikkhu sabbaso rūpasaññanaṃ samatikkamā paṭighasaññānaṃ amanasikārā atthagamā nānattasaññānam amansikārā Anatto ākāso ti ākāsānañcāyatanam upasampajja viharāmi. Tassa mayham āvuso iminā vihārena viharanto rūpasahagatā saññā manasikārā samudāranti.
65. Alex Wayman, *op. cit., passim.*
66. Jan T. Ergardt, *Faith and Knowledge in Early Buddhism : An Analysis of the Contextual Structures of an Arahant-Formula in the Majjhima Nikāya*, Leiden : E. J. Brill, Supplements to *Numen*, XXXVII, 1977, p. 11.

which our objectifying modality of being negates. This, we feel, is better indicated by treating *saññā* as 'idea' in the sense of a *blik* by which our experience is interpreted. This would give us the sense of a going beyond our *bliks* into an open spontaneity. In later Buddhism, *ākāśa* was very deliberately employed in this sense, and elsewhere we have discussed how, in some Tibetan texts, *mkha'* (*ākạśa*) becomes a symbol for no-thing-ness (*śūnyatā*), and how it becomes embodied into such a symbol as the *mkha' 'gro ma* (Sanskrit : *ḍākinī*) to indicate the faculty of inspiration.[67]

Like all of the *jhānā*, *ākāsānañcāyatana* is not an end in itself. The self-transcending nature of Buddhism as a system for spiritual development is underscored by Moggallāna's insistence that each of the *jhānā* points beyond itself to the next stage of growth. Thus he says :[68]

> Herein a brother, passing utterly beyond the realm of infinite space, with the idea : 'Endless is consciousness,' enters upon and abides in the realm of infinite consciousness. This is called 'the realm of infinite consciousness.'

Thus the structure of the *jhānā* is such that they lead systematically and progressively from one to the next.

This is further demonstrated by Moggallāna's comments about the third *āruppā jhāna* :[69]

> Herein a brother, passing utterly beyond the realm of infinite consciousness, with the idea of 'there is nothing at all,' enters on and abides in the realm of nothingness. This is called 'the realm of nothingness.'

This brings us to the last *jhāna*, which Moggallāna discusses :[70]

---

67. See Nathan Katz, "Anima and *mKha' 'gro ma*," *op. cit., passim.*
68. S.IV.266. (PTS translation)
Idha bhikkhu sabbaso ākāsānañcāyatanaṃ samatikkamma Anattaṃ viññaṇanti viññāṇañcāyatanaṃ upasampajja viharati. Idaṃ vuccati viññāṇañcāyatanan ti.
69. S.IV.267. (PTS translation)
Idha bhikkhu sabbaso viññāṇañcāyatanaṃ samatikkamma Natthi kiñcīti ākiñcaññāyatanam upasampajja viharati. Idaṃ vuccati ākiñcaññāyatanam ti.
70. S.IV.268. (PTS translation)
Idha bhikkhu sabbaso ākiñcaññāyatanaṃ samatikkamma nevasaññā nāsaññ āyatanam upasampajja viharati. Idaṃ vuccati nevasaññā nāsaññ āyatanan ti.

> Herein a brother, passing utterly beyond the realm of nothingness, with the idea of 'neither consciousness nor unconsciousness,' enters upon and abides in the realm of neither consciousness nor unconsciousness. This is called 'the realm of neither consciousness nor unconsciousness.'

Notice the structure of the idea of the realm of nothingness (*ākiñcaññāyatana*). While nothingness (or as some scholars suggest, no-thing-ness) indicates that the notion of a 'thing' is an habituated prejudice, this too must be gone beyond to yet another *jhānic* realm. Structurally, this reminds us of the dialectical teaching of the Mahāyāna philosopher Nāgārjuna, for whom *śūnyatā*, which has also been translated as 'nothingness,' 'no-thing-ness', or 'emptiness', is used as a corrective device against prejudiced thinking.[71] Yet this *śūnyatā* of Nāgārjuna, like the *ākiñcaññāyatana* of the *jhānā*, is utterly misunderstood if taken as something final. Thus Moggallāna warns us to continue to the next realm, the one termed *nevasaññānasaññāyatana*, which is also not the final one.

However, Moggallāna's discourse does not end with the last *jhānā*. All of the *jhānā* must be gone beyond, so we are told :[72]

> Herein a brother, paying no attention to all or any distinguishing marks, enters on and abides in that rapture of heart which is without conditions. This is called 'the unconditioned heart' (*cetosamādhi*).

We feel that the translator has missed an important variation on the highly formalized Pali of this *sutta*. The discussion of each other *jhāna* ends with "it is called" (*idaṃ vuccati*) and then the name of that particular meditative practice. In only this one, which is not properly a *jhāna* at all but the going beyond all *jhānā*, we find "I call it" (*ayaṃ vuccati*). This adds both a personal touch as well as emphasis. The emphasis is on the crucial point that all of the *jhānā*, singularly as well as collectively, are finally left behind. This is called 'the signless concentrated heart' (*animitto cetosamādhi*). Another *sutta*[73] says that when

---

71. We have discussed this aspect of Nāgārjuna's teaching in Nathan Katz, "Nāgārjuna and Wittgenstein on Error," *op. cit.*, *passim.*

72. S.IV.268-269. (PTS translation)
Idha bhikkhu sabbanimittānam amansikārā animittaṃ cetosamādhim upasampajja viharati. Ayam vuccati animitto cetosamādhīti.

73. S.IV.218.

one goes beyond *nevasaññānāsaññāyatana*, then one arrives at the cessation of lust, hatred and ignorance (*rāgo-, doso-* and *moho-niruddho*), and has become a *khīṇāsavo*, an arahant.

In one place[74] the arahant is described as one who is able to focus on any of the *jhānā* and see that they are impermanent. The most exquisite of recluses (*puggalo samaṇesu samaṇasukhumālo*)[75] is able to attain any of the *jhānā* and abide in them without difficulty. We shall see that the arahant who is 'liberated in both ways' (*ubhatobhāgavimutto*) is fluent in attaining the *jhānā*, as well as aware of their ultimate unsatisfactoriness. Were he not so aware, he would fall into the same problem as the teachers of the Buddha, Āḷāra Kāḷāma and Uddaka Rāmaputta, who thought that these meditations were something final.[76] Their problem was that they saw permanence where there is impermanence, which is one of the five lower fetters (*orambhāgiyāni saṃyojanāni*).[77]

F. *Cetovimutti* and *Paññāvimutti*

The Kīṭāgiri Sutta[78] gives us the Buddha's typology of his disciples. In it, seven are delineated : the *ubhatabhāgavimutto*, the *paññāvimutto*, the *kāyasakkhī*, and *diṭṭhippatto*, the *saddhāvimutto*, the *dhammānusārī* and the *saddhānusārī*. Of these first two types—the *ubhatabhāgavimutto*, which could be rendered as one who is liberated (*vimutto*) from both (the ablative *ubhato*) portions (*bhāga*), or "one who is emancipated in two ways";[79] and the *paññāvimutto*, one who is liberated by insight or wisdom—the Buddha says[80] that they, having seen through *paññā*, their *āsavā* are totally destroyed, which is to say that they are arahants. Of the last five, the Buddha says :[81] "Monks, I say that this monk has something yet to be done diligently," that he is *sekhā*, still in the stages of training, and not yet an arahant. These five,

---

74. M.III.244-245.
75. A.II.87-88.
76. M.I.164 ff.
77. S.V.61.
78. M.I.477.
79. *P.T.S. Dictionary*, s.v. *ubhato*, p. 154.
80. M.I.477-478 : paññāya disvā āsavā parikkhīṇā honti.
81. M.I.478-479 : imassa kho ahaṃ bhikkhave bhikkhuno appamādena karaṇiyan ti vadāmi.

by means of *paññā* and/or *saddhā*, which is conviction or faith, have attained some degree of understanding of the Buddha's teachings, and may have developed some of the faculties, but they have not yet fully actualized *nibbāna*. The first two, on the other hand, have completed their training (*asekhā*), are arahants, and thus will be the basis of our discussion.

Some scholars take these two terms to refer to the method of meditation and the method of analytic study. Bhikshu Sangharakshita[82] contends that the notion of *paññāvimutti* is merely a theoretical acknowledgement of the possibility of *arahattā* apart from meditation. Nalinaksha Dutt[83] believes the *ubhatabhāgavimutti* to be clearly the superior. The Buddha, however, seems less certain of the superiority of one over the other. He says[84] that such judgements are no easy matter : *na khv ettha . . . sukaraṃ ekaṃsena vyākātuṃ.*

Nor does it seem that these were merely theoretical concessions. We find that we cannot accept Sangharakshita's view on the *paññāvimutti* because we find the Buddha specifically referring to some of his disciples by this term, so at least according to our text[85] there actually were some *paññavimutti* arahants. According to our sources, the Buddha is engaged in discussion with Sāriputta about his five hundred arahant disciples, of which three hundred and eighty are claimed by the Buddha to be *paññāvimuttā*. In the same place, he says that of these three hundred and eighty, along with the other one hundred and twenty, assumedly *ubhatabhāgavimuttā*, that there is nothing, in either body or speech, for which they could be blamed : *na kiñci garahāmi kāyikaṃ vā vācasikaṃ vā.*

Returning to the Kīṭāgiri Sutta, we find the Buddha describing the *ubhatabhāgavimutto* in this manner :[86]

---

82. Bhikshu Sangharakshita, *A Survey of Buddhism*, Bangalore : Indian Institute of World Culture, third edition, 1966 (1957), p. 379. [Hereinafter : Sangharakshita, *Survey*].

83. Nalinaksha Dutt, *Early Monastic Buddhism*, Calcutta : Firma K. L. Mukhopadhyay, second edition, 1971 (1960), p. 267. [Hereinafter : Dutt, *EMB*].

84. A.I.120.

85. S.I.191.

86. M.I.477. (My translation)

Katamo ca bhikkhave puggalo ubhatabhāgavimutto : Idha bhikkhave

> Monks, which is the *ubhatabhāgavimutto* person, the one who is liberated in both ways ? Monks, in this case a certain person dwells, having come into intimate (*kāyena*) contact with the peaceful liberations (*vimokkhā*), which, having gone beyond form are formless. Having seen thus through wisdom, the *āsavā* are totally destroyed.

As discussed, the eight *vimokkhā* are the transcending culminations of each of the eight *jhānā*, so the *ubhatabhāgavimutti* has fully mastered these techniques. By *pañña*, he has attained the total destruction of the *āsavā*, and is an arahant.

As for the *paññāvimutti*, the Buddha says :[87]

> Monks, who is the *paññāvimutto* person, the one who is freed by wisdom ? Monks, in that case a certain person dwells, not having come into intimate contact with the peaceful *vimokkhā* which, having gone beyond form, are formless. Having thus seen through wisdom, the *āsavā* are totally destroyed.

In this context, then, the *ubhatabhāgavimutti* is distinguished from the *paññāvimutti* by virtue of his mastery of the *jhānā*, although the aim of their methods is identical, *viz*., the total destruction of the *āsavā*.

The *ubhatabhāgavimutti* is also called the *cetovimutti*.[88] While *ceto* is derived from the Sanskrit root $\sqrt{}$*cit*, 'to perceive, know, or appear,'[89] in Buddhism its use indicates emotively toned thinking. While it may be "the seat and organ of thought,"[90] this basis is always dispositional and conative.[91] The case for translating *citta* or *ceto* as 'heart' in a psychological sense, has been made by Mrs. Rhys-Davids,[92] so the question of its

---

ekacco puggalo ye te santā vimokhā atikamma rūpe āruppā te kāyena phassitvā viharati, paññāya c' assa disvā āsavā parikhīṇā honti.

87. M.I.477-478. (My translation)
Idha bhikkhave ekacco puggalo ye te santā vomikhā atikamma rūpe āruppā te na yāyena phassitvā viharati, paññāya c' assa disvā āsavā parikkhīṇā honti.
88. As at A.I.234; Vin.I.111; D.I.156; S.II.265; etc.
89. Whitney, p. 47.
90. *P.T.S. Dictionary*, p. 266.
91. *Idem.*
92. Rhys-Davids, *Buddhist Psychological Ethics*, Chapter II; as cited in *P.T.S. Dictionary, s.v.*

translation need not be raised here again. In the context of *vimutto*-language, what is being suggested is that one who is 'freed in both ways' has done so by a systematic training of this *citta* or *ceto* by means of the *jhānā*.

In the context of our earlier distinction of *samatha*, or calming meditation, and *vipassanā*, or insight meditation, the Pali commentatorial tradition has distinguished the *ceto*- or *ubhatabhāga-vimutti* from the *paññāvimutti* thus : the former follows the *samatha* practices, most especially the *jhānā*, while the latter follows the *vipassanā* practices.[93] One implication of this distinction is that the *cetovimutti* has attained the five *abhiññā*, including the *iddhividhā*, while the *paññāvimutti* has not. This is borne out in a *sutta*[94] where Susīma the Wanderer asks those members of the *saṅgha* who had expressed *aññā*, which is to say, those who were arahants, whether or not that expression entailed the various knowledges of psychic powers (*iddhividhā*). The arahants tell him that it did not, since they had been freed by *paññā* : *paññāvimuttā kho mayaṃ āvuso Susīmāti*.

Another commentatorial distinction was between the *suddha-vipassanā*, or those who attain insight by purification, and which corresponds to the *cetovimutti*; and the *sukha-vipassanā*, those whose insight is dry, the *paññāvimutti*. Sangharakshita[95] finds a danger inherent in this second type :

> This type of emancipation is no doubt possible for persons possessing a certain type of temperament. But the theoretical recognition of the possibility, by providing the merely intellectual with an apparently valid excuse for the neglect of meditation, was potentially a source of danger. In the absence of any experience of the *jhānas* a merely rational understanding of the Dharma could easily be mistaken for insight.

Were Sangharakshita's claim taken seriously, however, the Buddhist might be forced into holding that *nibbāna* is somehow dependent upon or conditioned by the *jhānā*, a position categorically denied by the Buddha, as demonstrated at the very outset

---

93. See Shwe Zan Aung and Mrs. Rhys Davids, *Compendium of Philosophy : being a Translation Now Made for the First Time from the Original Pali of the Abhidhammattha-Sangaha with Introductory Essays and Notes*, London : Pali Text Society, 1972 (1910), p. 55 and p. 75.

94. S.II.121ff.

95. Sangharakshita, *Survey*, p. 379.

of our discussion of meditation and the arahant. Walpola Rahula[96] apparently thinks that just such a problem arose in Lanka by the *ganthadhura-vipassanādhura* debates of the first century C.E. At that time a question arose in the Theravāda as to whether meditation (of the *vipassanā* type) or study (*gantha*) was primary in the monastic life. Of course, this is not an either/or question, and monks in Lanka did not, in fact, neglect meditation, even though it was held that the *gantha*-venue was primary. It was not *jhānic* meditation which was the Buddha's new and vital contribution to the history of religions; this had been taught *to* him. It was his penetrating analysis of the ultimate unsatisfactoriness of any of the meditational experiences, which were seen by him as no more than a particular sub-set of worldly experience. This was expressed by his contention that all of the three realms, *kāmaloka*, *rūpaloka* and *arūpaloka* (the latter two being attainable only by the gods, anti-gods and meditators), comprised *saṃsāra* as they did not give lasting satisfaction. It was only by going beyond the limits of the world that suffering could be eradicated.[97] Thus the very crucial doctrinal expression that all meditative experience is ultimately unsatisfactory, underlies any Buddhist meditational practice to the extent that it could be called Buddhist. In advocating the primacy of study over meditation, the Theravāda hardly denied or neglected practice, but chose to emphasize the doctrinal context in which meditation could be said to be Buddhistically significant. Thus it seems that Sangharakshita's fears about an overly-intellectualized *saṅgha* are not well-founded, but result from a lack of appreciation of the issues involved in these *ganthadhura-vipassanādhura* debates.

Further, it seems that these debates had a precedent even during the Buddha's lifetime. In the *Aṅguttara Nikāya*[98] we read of two groups of the Buddha's disciples called *dhammayogā*, those attached to the Dhamma, and *jhānīyā*, practitioners of the *jhānā*. The latter are : "they who live with their whole being in tune with the deathless,"[99] and would correspond to the

96. Rahula, *HBC*, pp. 159-160.

97. S.I.60.

98. A.III.365.

99. A.III.356 : ye amataṃ dhātuṃ kāyena phusitvā viharanti.

cetovimuttā, according to Mahā Cunda. The former are : "they who with insight penetrate and see the deep way of the goal,"[100] the *paññāvimuttā*. In this *sutta*, Mahā Cunda counsels both groups to praise the other. Both the *dhammayogi* and the *jhānīyo*, he says, are rare in this world, and as such are worthy of the respect of all the *saṅgha*, irrespective of which path one adopts for oneself. Thus Mahā Cunda, even during the lifetime of the Buddha, averts a potential schism along the lines of one group which cultivates insight, and another group which practises the *jhānā*.

Certainly, the polemicization of these types was a later development; during the time of the Buddha, the correct attitude, as expressed by Mahā Cunda, was that the goal of *arahattā* was rare and worthy of respect and praise, regardless of the way in which one got there. One function of this distinction was to indicate the radical doctrinal separation of meditation in general, and *arahattā*. The latter, being free from that which could produce suffering, is therefore defined as free from all causes and conditions, including the very practices which incline towards it. As we have seen earlier, *arahattā* is coterminous with insight into the nature of existence, expressed as *tilakkhana*, which is to say, the destruction of the *āsavā*. The distinction of *cetovimutti*, or *ubhatabhāgavimutti*, and *paññāvimutti*, merely indicates that while this insight (*paññā*) is coterminous with *arahattā*,[101] we use the term *ubhatabhāgavimutti* to indicate the path which includes the useful but not essential practice of the *jhānā*, along with their resultant *abhiññā*. As to which of these two types was the Buddha, there is no doubt that he was an *ubhatabhāgavimutti*,[102] as he says that he is able to attain any of the *vimokkhā* at will, and that he has mastery over the *abhiññā*.

G. *Four Maggā and Four Phalāni*

We must return again to the problem presented to us in the Kīṭāgiri Sutta.[103] We saw there that the Buddha's disciples

100. A.III.356 : ye gambhīraṃ atthapadaṃ paññāya ativijjha passantī ti.

101. As at M.I.477 : paññāya c' assa disvā āsavā parikkhīṇā honti.

102. S.II.221-222.

Ahaṃ kho āvuso āsavānaṃ khayā anāsavanaṃ cetovimuttiṃ paññāvimuttiṃ diṭṭheva dhamme sayam abhiññā sacchikatvā upasampajja viharāmi.

103. M.I.477.

were roughly classified into two groups : (1) those who had no need of further training (*asekhā*), which is to say the arahants or, as expressed in the *sutta*, the *paññāvimuttā* and the *ubhatabhāgavimuttā*; and (2) those who were still undergoing training (*sekhā*), but had nonetheless already made significant spiritual progress in the path (*magga*). This rather elementary distinction was developed canonically and in the commentaries into the doctrine of the four paths and the four fruitions (*cattāri ariyā maggā* and *phalāni*), a teaching which became known in the Mahāyāna as the "eight holy persons" (*aṣṭa ariyā pudgalā*). Various systems of classification of these holy people do not always yield the same eight. Therefore, our procedure in this complicated matter will be to present, first of all, the simplest systematization, and then to add other holy people as mentioned elsewhere. We will contend that all subsequent systems can be fitted into the simpler system, producing a sort of chart of Buddhistically-understood spiritual growth.

The simplest statement of these persons is found in the Sampasādaniya Suttanta,[104] where we read :

> Unsurpassable, Lord, is the way in which the Exalted One teaches the Norm [Dhamma] concerning modes of (receiving) instruction, namely, that there are four such modes : (1) The Exalted One knows through his own (method of) systematic thought, that a given individual, when carrying out what he has been taught, by the complete destruction of three fetters, will become a streamwinner [*sotāpanna*], saved from disaster

---

104. D.xxviii.13. (PTS translation)

Aparam pana bhante etad ānuttariyaṃ yathā Bhagavā dhammaṃ deseti anusāsana-vidhāsu. Catasso imā bhante anusāsana-vidhā. Jānāti bhante Bhagavā parapuggalaṃ paccattaṃ yoniso-manasikārā, —Ayaṃ puggalo yathānusiṭṭhaṃ tathā paṭipajjamāno, tiṇṇaṃ saṃyojanānaṃ parikkhayā sotāpanno bhavissati avini-pāta-dhammo niyato sambodhi-parāyano ti. Jānāti bhante Bhagavā parapuggalaṃ paccattaṃ yonisomanasikārā, —Ayaṃ puggalo yathānusiṭṭhaṃ tathā paṭipajjamāno, tiṇṇaṃ saṃyojanānaṃ parikkhayā rāga-dosa-mohānaṃ tanuttā sakadāgāmī bhavissati, sakid eva imaṃ lokaṃ āgantvā dukkhass' antaṃ karissatīti. Jānāti bhante Bhagavā para-puggalaṃ paccattaṃ yonisomanasikārā, —Ayaṃ puggalo yathānusiṭṭhaṃ tathā paṭipajjamāno āsavānaṃ khayā anāsavaṃ ceto-vimuttiṃ paññā-vimuttiṃ diṭṭhe va dhamme sayaṃ abhiññā sacchikatvā upasampajja viharissatīti. Etad ānuttariyaṃ bhante anusani-vidhāsu.

> thereafter, certain to attain enlightenment; (2) by the complete destruction of three fetters, will have so diminished passion and hate and illusion that he will become a once-returner [*sakadāgāmī*], and returning but once to this world will make an end of ill; (3) by the complete destruction of the five ulterior fetters [*orambhāgiyāni saṃyojanāni*], will be reborn in a *deva*-world, there to pass utterly away, thence never to return [*anāgāmī*]; (4) by the destruction of the Intoxicants [*āsavā*] will come to know and realize for himself, even in this life, emancipation of intellect [*cetovimutto*] and emancipation of insight [*paññāvimutto*], and there will abide. Unsurpassable, Lord, is this concerning modes of receiving instruction.

This discourse gives the four *puggalā*; the four *maggā* are simply the practices which lead to these fruitions (*phalāni*).

It is clear from this and other sources that talk about these four persons is connected with talk about the various fetters (*saṃyojanāni*), so it will be necessary to consider at this point just what is meant by these *saṃyojanāni*. A *saṃyojana* is simply that which binds,[105] hence its translation as 'fetter'. Most lists give ten such fetters, although we also find discussions of three,[106] five,[107] and seven.[108] Talk about ten fetters is usually in two groups of five : the five lower fetters (*pancamāni orambhāgiyāni saṃyojanāni*); and the five higher fetters (*pancamāni uddhambhāgiyāni saṃyojanāni*). The five lower fetters are[109]: (1) *sakkāyadiṭṭhi*, which is the belief (*diṭṭhi*) in some abiding personality; (2) *vicikicchā*, or doubt; (3) *kāmacchando*, desire for sensuality; (4) *sīlabbataparāmāso*, the belief in the efficacy of naïve ritualism; and (5) *vyāpādo*, malevolence. The five higher fetters are : (6) *rūparāgo*, passion for forms; (7) *arūparāgo*, desire for the formless; (8) *māno*, egoism or pride; (9) *uddhacam*, restlessness; and (10) *avijjā*, ignorance. Thus, as a preliminary we may say that the first of the holy persons, the one who has entered into the stream of the Buddha's teachings, the *sotāpanno*, has destroyed the first three of the fetters which bind him to

---

105. *P.T.S. Dictionary*, p. 656.
106. E.g. : M.I.9; A.I.233; S.V.406.
107. S.V.61; M.I.141.
108. Nett.14.
109. S.V.61

saṃsāra, namely : the belief in an abiding personality, *sakkāya-diṭṭhi*; doubt about the fundamentals of this teaching, *vicikicchā*; and belief in the efficacy of ritualistic religions, *sīlabbataparāmāso*. The second of the holy persons, the once-returner to the realm of fivefold sensuality (*kāmaloka*), the *sakadāgāmī*, has additionally made significant progress in the destruction of desire for sensuality, *kāmacchando*, and of malevolence, *vyāpādo*. The *anāgāmī*, the one who does not return to *kāmaloka*, has totally destroyed *kāmacchando* and *vyāpādo*. The arahant, the fourth of the holy persons, has also completely destroyed the five higher fetters (*uddhambhāgiyāni saṃyojanāni*) : passion for either form or formlessness (*rūparāgo* or *arūparāgo*); egoism (*māno*); restlessness (*uddhaccam*); and ignorance (*avijjā*).

A *sotāpanna* is one who may justly say :[110]

> I am he for whom perished is purgatory, perished the womb of beasts, perished the *peta*-realm, perished is the waste, the woeful way, the downfall. Streamwinner am I ! Not for me is the falling back. I am sure, having enlightenment is my goal.

Such is his *vyākaroti*, structurally similar to the arahant's *aññā vyākaroti*. He is freed from 'the fivefold dread and hatred' (*pañca bhayāni*), which is anxiety over breaking any of the five fundamental precepts (*pañca sīla*).[111] He also has the 'four limbs of the streamwinner' (*cattāri sotāpattiyaṅgāni*), which are also called the 'mirror of dhamma' (*dhammādāsaṃ*),[112] which are : (a) faith in the Buddha; (b) faith in the Dhamma; (c) faith in the *Saṅgha*; and (d) the virtues valued by the *sāsana*. Further, he has some understanding of causality and the causal origin of things (*hetu c' assa sudiṭṭho, hetusamuppannā ca dhammā*).[113]

The *sotāpanno* has an understanding of the four noble truths as taught by the Buddha, and he does not doubt them.[114] He is deeply engrossed in the practice of the eightfold noble path.[115]

---

110. S.II.70. (PTS translation)
khīṇanirayomhi khīṇatiracchānayoniyo khīṇapettivisayo khīṇāpāya-duggativinipāto sotāpanno 'ham asmi avinipātadhammo niyato sambodhiparāyano ti.

111. A.IV.405; S.II.68.

112. See : S.II.68; S.V.356-357; S.V.345; and A.IV.405.

113. A.III.441. See also S.II.69.

114. S.III.203.

115. A.II.89.

He is described as one who has entered the path to surety : *apaṇṇakataṃ paṭipadaṃ paṭipanno hoti.*[116] He is in training and lives attached to the 'highest rest from the toil' : *sekho hoti, appattamānaso anuttaraṃ yogakkhemaṃ patthayamāno viharati.*[117] And he is fully committed to the destruction of the *āsavā* : *āraddhā hoti āsavānaṃ khayāya.*[118]

It is also said that the *sotāpanno* has begun the development of the five faculties (*indriyāni*).[119] The term *indriya* in Vedic means 'belonging to Indra,'[120] and its Pali usage indicates that which is powerful, like Indra, or that which has power over. F. L. Woodward's 'controlling power'[121] gives a good sense of the term in this context. The *indriyāni*, in the usual list of five,[122] are : *saddhindriyaṃ*, the controlling power of faith or conviction; *viriyindriyaṃ*, the controlling faculty of energy; *satindriyaṃ*, the controlling power of mindfulness; *samādhindriyaṃ*, the controlling power of meditation; and *pannindriyaṃ*, the controlling power of wisdom or insight. Other systems of *indriyāni*[123] are rare, and we are told that, for one who has mastered these controlling powers, their exercise is as easy and swift as a man opening and closing his eyes.[124] The complete mastery of these *indriyāni* is identical with *arahattā*, but a gradual mastery is reflected in this doctrine of the holy persons : the less the degree of mastery, the person is considered an *anāgāmī, sakadāgāmī* or a *sotāpanno.*

A *sakadāgāmī*, as discussed above, is one who, like the *sotāpanno*, has destroyed the first three *saṃyojanāni,* but he has also made significant progress with the next two, *kāmarāgo* and *vyāpādo.* Although his title might indicate that he has only one more birth in *kāmaloka*, this may or may not be the case; he may, according to the texts, have anywhere from seven to one more rebirth. He is described[125] in this manner :

---

116. A.II.76.
117. A.II.90.
118. A.II.76.
119. S.V.193-200.
120. *P.T.S. Dictionary*, p. 121.
121. *Kindred Sayings, passim.*
122. S.V.193-194.
123. As at S.V. 202.
124. M.III.299.
125. A.I.233. (PTS translation)
Idha bhikkhave sīlesu paripūrakārī hoti samādhismiṃ mattasokārī

He trains himself in the rules of the training by undertaking them. Such a one, by destroying three fetters, is destined to seven more births at most : seven times more at most he fares and wanders up and down among *devas* and mankind and then makes an end of ill. Or, such a one again, by destroying three fetters, is a 'one seeder' [*ekabījī*] : he takes just one rebirth as a man and then makes an end of ill. This monk, by destroying three fetters and weakening those of lust [*rāgo*], malice [*dosa*] and delusion [*moha*], is a once-returner. He comes back to this world only once and makes an end of ill.

Thus the *magga* of the *sakadāgāmī* commences when the first three fetters have been completely destroyed, and he has made significant progress on the next two, *kāmarāgo* and *vyāpādo*, or, as expressed here, *rāgadosamohā*. At this point he is said to have seven more births. The fruition (*phala*) of the *sakadāgāmī* arises when he has but one birth remaining, at which point he is called by the more specific term, *ekabījī*.

The *anāgāmī*, according to the Alaggadūpama *Sutta*,[126] are : ". . .those monks in whom all the five lower fetters are destroyed. All of them are of spontaneous uprising; they attain *parinibbāna* there, and will not return from that world." They have freed themselves from personality-belief, from doubt in the *sāsana*, from belief in naïve ritualism, from passion for sensuality, and from malevolence; but there remain the fetters of passion for the realms of form and formlessness, some degree of egoism, restlessness and ignorance. The first five, the *orambhāgiyāni saṃyojanāni*, are said to be fetters of the lower realm, or the realm of fivefold sensuous desire (*kāmaloka*). The last five, the *uddham-*

---

paññāya mattaso kārī. So yāni tāni khuddānukkaddakāni sikkhāpadāni tāni āpajjati pi vuṭṭhāti pi. Taṃ kissa hetu ? Na hi m' ettha bhikkhave abhabbatā vuttā. Yāni ca kho tāni sikkhāpadāni ādibrahmacariyakāni brahmacariyasāruppāni tattha dhuvasīlo ca hoti ṭhitasīlo ca samādāya sikkhati sikkhāpadesu. So tiṇṇaṃ saṃyojanānaṃ parikkhayā sattakkhattuparamo hoti sattakkhattuparamaṃ deve ca mānuse ca sandhāvitvā saṃsāritvā dukkhassa antaṃ karoti. So tiṇṇaṃ saṃyojanānaṃ parikkhayā rāgadosamohānaṃ tanuttā sakadāgāmī hoti sakid eva imaṃ lokaṃ āgantvā dukkhassa antaṃ karoti.

126. M.I.141. (PTS translation)
yesaṃ bhikkhūnaṃ pañc' orambhāgiyāni saṃyojanāni pahīnāhi sabbe te opapātikā tattha parinibbāyino anāvattidhammā tasmā lokā.

bhāgiyāni saṃyojanāni, are the fetters of the higher realms of *rūpaloka* and *arūpaloka*; thus the *anāgāmī* still is attached by the fifth and sixth fetters, as well as some degree of pride and restlessness and, of course, by ignorance. While he is not subject to future rebirths in *kāmaloka*, he will still be reborn spontaneously (*upapātika*) in one of the higher *lokā*, where he will attain *parinibbāna*, according to this *sutta*.[127]

On two canonical occasions, the fruition of the *anāgāmī* is attained by a lay person, an *upāsaka*. The Buddha mentions[128] that some one hundred and forty lay people attained this fruition at Nātika. In the *Therīgāthā*[129] we learn that Anopamā attained this *anāgāmī phala* as a laywoman. She says that after this, she became ordained and soon became an arahant. There was a controversy as to whether or not the highest fruition, that of an arahant, was attainable by a lay person, or whether one needed to become a *saṅghika*. One position was that the *anāgāmī phala* was the highest to which the laity could attain; another was that while one could become an arahant while a lay person, it would be necessary for him or her to enter the *saṅgha* immediately; and others held that *arahattā* was open to all. It would seem that this *Therīgāthā* tends to support the first option.

It is said[130] that the *anāgāmī* is familiar with the eight *vimokkhā* which, as we have indicated in our discussion of the *jhānā*, are the culminations of the eight *jhānic* meditational practices, each *vimokkha* being the full comprehension of the ultimate unsatisfactoriness of any meditational experience, since they are all compounded phenomena (*saṅkhātā dhammā*). Nārada Mahāthera[131] points out that both *anāgāmī* and arahants ". . .could experience *nibbānic* bliss for as long as seven days in this life" which is then called *nirodha-samāpatti* and ". . .is the highest form of bliss possible in this life." It seems that the *anāgāmī* and the arahant have more than the *vimokkhā* in common. In the Dvayatānupassanā Sutta[132] it is said that a full comprehension

127. See also Dutt, *EMB*, pp. 263-264.
128. S.V.358-360.
129. Thig., verses 154-156.
130. A.II.87.
131. Nārada Mahāthera, *BHT*, pp. 560-561.
132. Suttanipāta (PTS edition), p. 140.

of the four noble truths leads to one of two results, either *arahattā* or *anāgāmi-phala*. The practice of the *iddhipada* is said[133] to lead also to either of these two results, as does meditation on a corpse.[134] The highest degree of ambivalence between the arahant and the *anāgāmī* is found in this statement[135] about the *jhānā* :

> Whatsoever is even a higher product, produced by higher thought, even that is impermanent, of a nature to end. Fixed on that idea, he wins destruction of the cankers [*āsavā*]; and if not that, yet by his passion for dhamma, by his delight in dhamma, he utterly making an end of the five fetters belonging to this world, he is reborn spontaneously and in that state passes utterly away, never to return (hither) from that world.

Here the very situation in which it is possible for one to attain to *arahattā*, the destruction of the *āsavā*, namely the full understanding of the impermanence and ultimate unsatisfactoriness of the *jhānā*, may also be the occasion of one's attaining the *phala* of the *anāgāmī*.

There seem to be two other terms for talking about the *anāgāmī* : 'one who goes up the stream,' *uddhaṃ-soto*; and 'one who goes to the pure lands,' *akaniṭṭha-gāmī*. We read : "Having fully destroyed the five lower fetters, he is one who goes up the stream, one who goes to the pure lands."[136] In one other place,[137] these two terms are used in a discussion of the four holy persons in place of the usual *anāgāmī*.

All of this tends to indicate that one who is adept at the *jhānā*, but has not yet overcome desire for the products of the *jhānā*, is "caught," so to speak, in the *jhānā*, or he is spontaneously born (*upapātika*) there until such time as he overcomes this

133. A. III 81-82.

134. S.V.129.

135. A.V.346. (PTS translation)
yaṃ kho pana kiñci abhisaṃkhataṃ abhisañcetayitaṃ, tad aniccaṃ nirodhadhamman' ti pajānāti. So tattha ṭhito āsavānaṃ khayaṃ pāpuṇāti; no ce āsavānaṃ khayaṃ pāpuṇāti, ten' eva dhammarāgena tāya dhammanandiyā pañcannaṃ orambhāgiyānaṃ saṃyojanānaṃ parikkhayā opapātiko hoti tattha parinibbāyī anāvattidhammo tasmā lokā.

136. A.I.233. (My translation)
So pañcannaṃ orambhāgiyānaṃ saṃyojanānaṃ parikkhayā uddhaṃ-soto hoti akaniṭṭhagāmī.

137. A.II, 133-134.

desire, which may be understood as a form of egoism (*māno*) or of restlessness (*uddhacco*), since, in Buddhist cosmology, that is said to be one of the characteristics of the higher realms. This seems to be his situation until such time as there is a total destruction of the last fetter, that of ignorance, at which time he becomes an arahant. Such a person is said to go up the stream (*uddam-soto*), and he has gone to the purely blissful realms (*akaniṭṭha-gāmī*), which is a way of characterizing what it means to be an *anāgāmī*.

Perhaps the simplest and most cogent use of the term *anāgāmī* is found in the *Itivuttaka*,[138] one of the oldest parts of the *Sutta Piṭaka* :

> Monks, one who is bound by the bond of passion, who is bound by the bond of becoming, is a returner, he comes back to life in this world. Monks, he who is freed from the bond of passions and freed from the bond of becoming, also is an arahant, one who has destroyed the cankers [*āsavā*].

Much has been said already about the fourth holy person, the arahant, and it will not be necessary to repeat those materials here. He is, of course, one who has destroyed all ten fetters which bind to both the lower world of sense-desire, and also to the higher worlds of form and formlessness. He is[139] "...one who has overcome the *āsavā*, lived the life, done what there was to be done, put down the burden, won his goal, destroyed the fetters of becoming, here and now freed" (*khīṇāsavo vusitavā katakaraṇīyo ohitbāro anuppattasadattho parikkhīṇabhavasaññojano sammadaññā vimutto*).

The image of the four holy persons became popular in Buddhist culture. The 'great chronicle' of Ceylon, the *Mahāvaṃsa,* tells us about the construction of the Lohapāsāda, a famous monastic building known popularly as the 'Brazen Palace' and found at Anurādhapura in Lanka.[140] This nine-story structure was said to

---

138. Iti.95. (PTS translation)
Kāmayogayutto bhikkhave bhavayogayutto āgāmī hoti āgantā itthattaṃ; kāmayogavisaññuto bhikkhave bhavayogayutto anāgāmī hoti anāgantā itthattaṃ; kāmayogavisaññuto bhikkhave bhavayogavisaññuto arahā hoti anāgantā khīṇāsavo ti.

139. S.III.161 and elsewhere.

140. Mahāvaṃsa.27.42ff. See also Adikaram, *EHBC*, p. 63.

hold ordinary *bhikkhus* on the first story, especially learned *bhikkhus* on the second story, *sotāpannā* on the third, *sakadāgāmī* on the fourth, *anāgāmī* on the fifth, and arahants on the upper four floors. The same text[141] says that the architects of such a place were themselves arahants.

As highly-structured and restricting as this scheme might seem, what with all its paths and fruitions of paths, the Buddha himself was not concerned with the possibility of a monk's intentness on any goal, but with that monk's spiritual development. Thus, in the Bhūmija Sutta[142] he says that what matters is not a practitioner's fixedness on any goal, but his commitment to the practice itself. If the practices be properly done, his thoughts about goals or no-goals will have no effect. Rather, the practice itself will naturally have its own fruition.

Sāriputta, in his conversation with Mahā Koṭṭhita,[143] makes a similar point. Rather than emphasize these four *maggā* and *phalāni* as discrete, he recommends the same meditational practices, in this case, contemplation of the five *kkhandā*, for all of the holy persons, be they streamwinners, once-returners, or non-returners. The Buddha's lack of concern for goals, but emphasis on practice, as well as Sāriputta's proscription of the same practices for all of the holy persons, indicates that these four *maggā* and *phalāni* should not be understood as rigid boundaries which are readily distinguishable, but as a map, of sorts, of Buddhistically-understood spiritual growth and development.

This point may be understood by way of a brief discussion of the addenda to this list of four persons. The first addition was that if all of these persons could be called 'holy' (*ariyā*), then what could be said about the rest of humanity ? They are called *puthujjana*, which is literally 'one of the many folk.'[144] Mediating between the *puthujjanā* and the *sotāpannā* were the *gotrabhū*, literally 'one who has become a member of the (spiritual) family.' There seems to be some confusion as to whether he is to be considered one of the holy people or not.

141. Mahāvaṃsa.27.3.

142. M.III.138.

143. S.III.167-169.

144. Nyāṇatiloka, *Buddhist Dictionary*, p. 146.

In one place,[145] there is a discussion of nine, rather than the usual eight, holy people, a list which includes the *gotrabhū*. Nalinaksha Dutt[146] gives us a long discussion about whether the *gotrabhū* is the highest of the *puthujjanā* or the lowest of the *ariyā puggalā*, drawing largely from the commentatorial literature, the details of which need not be repeated here. We would like to indicate, however, that the whole notion of a *gotra* becomes extremely important in both the *bodhisattvayāna* and the *tantra-yāna*, which often speak about prerequisites for entry into a given spiritual practice. These prerequisites are often discussed in the language of *gotra* (family) and *kūlu* (clan), both of which are translated into Tibetan as *rigs*.

The *gotrabhū* were further divided into two typologies : the *dhammānusāri*, 'the one devoted to dhamma', and the *saddhānu-sāri*, 'the one devoted to faith.' In one place,[147] the former is said to be superior to the latter. In another place,[148] it is said that the former are bound for enlightenment (*sambodhiparāyanā*), while the latter are bound for heaven (*saggaparāyanā*). Dutt[149] seems to think that these are two separate categories in addition to the *gotrabhū*, but our readings have not found an instance wherein both *gotrabhū* and these two are mentioned together; rather, they seem to be alternate ways of speaking about the same category. However, the problem is complicated by the observation that if, as the Buddha maintains, the *saddhānusārī* are bound for heaven rather than *sambodhi*, then they could not be considered as holy people, as they are considered holy precisely because they are on the path which leads to *arahattā* and not to heaven. So if the *dhammānusārī* and the *saddhānu-sārī* are simply a way of talking about the *gotrabhū* and not separate categories, as our reading seems to indicate, then they should not be considered as among the holy people, who are holy because they are bound for *arahattā*. Some further research on this topic is in order, and it might well pursue the connections, if any, between the *dhammānusārī* and the *paññāvimutti*, and the *saddhānusārī* and the *cetovimutti*, especially as these issues were

145. A.IV.373 : puggalā āhuneyyā pāhuneyyā dakkhiṇeyyā añjalikaraṇīyā.
146. Dutt, *EMB*, pp. 253-254.
147. S.V.200.
148. M.I.142.
149. Dutt, *EMB*, pp. 254-255.

presented in the *ganthadhura-vipassanādhura* debates of the first century C.E.

We have already referred to the sub-category of the *sakadāgāmī* called the *ekabījī*, the one who has only one more birth in *kāmaloka*. Actually, two terms are involved here : the first is the *kolaṃkola*, one who will go from family to family and who has attained the controlling powers that are not of the *āsavā* (*anāsavayāni indriyāni*);[150] and the *ekabījī*, the one who is to have but one more rebirth in *kāmaloka*. Buddhaghoṣa[151] says that both of these are higher than the *sotāpanno*, which would support our view that these are but a way of talking about the *sakadāgāmī*, indicating whether he has but one or more than one rebirth in *kāmaloka*. The Buddha, however, says[152] that both of these are in truth *sotāpannā*, which is of course prior to the stage of the *sakadāgāmī*. Dutt[153] gives some indications of both the Sanskrit and Pali commentatorial glosses on this point, but clearly some further research is here necessary.

We shall conclude this discussion with a chart. This will clearly indicate our understanding of these various people, *puthujjanā* or *ariyā*, that comprise the Buddhist path as understood in the Pali canon. These are tentative hypotheses, not conclusions, as the questions are open as to whether the *gotrabhū* is an *ariya* or a *puthujjana*, or something in between as we believe. It is also unclear as to whether the *saddhānusārī* and the *dhammānusārī* are merely sub-categories of the *gotrabhū* or if they indicate different persons entirely. Likewise, it is difficult to know just where the *kolaṃkola* and the *ekabījī* should be placed; despite some contrary canonical evidence, we have opted to place them as sub-categories of the *sakadāgāmī*, for reasons given above. Finally, we have included the *saṃyojanāni* in the chart, indicating at which phase of spiritual growth the person is understood to have eradicated any given fetter.

150. Dutt, EMB, pp. 261-262.
151. Vism., p. 709.
152. A.V.120.
153. Dutt, *EMB*, pp. 261-262.

PUGGALĀ	SUB-CATEGORY	TRAINING	SAṂYOJANĀNI ERADICATED
Puthujjana	——	None	None
Gotrabhū	Saddhānusārī	Sekha	None
	Dhammānusārī	Sekha	None
Ariyā			
Sotāpanno	——	Sekha	Sakkāya-diṭṭhi; Vicikicchā; Sīlabbataparāmāsa
Sakadāgāmī	Kolaṃkola Ekabījī	Sekha	Kāmarāga; Vyāpāda (PARTIALLY)
Anāgāmī	——	Sekha	Kāmarāga; Vyāpāda
Arahant	Paññāvimutti Ubhatabhāgavimutti	Asekha	Rūparāga; Aruparāga; Māna; Udhacca; Avijjā.

CHAPTER III

THE ARAHANT AND THE BUDDHA

A. *Introductory*

Having briefly surveyed Buddhist meditational practices, and having indicated the canonical understanding of the Buddhist path, we may now proceed to what is for us a crucial issue : is the Buddha in any sense significantly different from the arahant ?

Our contention is that the *ubhatabhāgavimutto* arahant and the Buddha are identical, the only difference is that of precedence, which may or may not be considered significant. The Buddha came first, and he showed his disciples, some of whom became arahants, the path which leads to the *arahant-phala.* In terms of spiritual attainments, as well as in terms of skill at the 'higher knowledges' (*abhiññā*) and the 'psychic powers' (*iddhividhā*), however, there are no grounds for their conceptual separation. The *paññāvimutto* arahant is said to be the equal of the Buddha in terms of spiritual attainment, as they have both completely overcome the *āsavā*; however, the *paññāvimutto* has not developed these *abhiññā* and *iddhividhā* as has the Buddha, and therefore he is not so readily able to express and teach Dhamma as the Buddha and the *ubhatabhāgavimutto* are.

In order to present our case of the fundamental identity of the Buddha and the arahant, we shall first consider these *abhiññā* and *iddhividhā*, demonstrating their integrality to the early Buddhist notion of a Buddha. According to Mahāyāna sources,[1] the Buddha is perfected both in terms of wisdom or insight (*prajñā*; *shes rab*), and also in terms of his ability to express and teach Dharma to others (*upāya*; *thabs*). This is found to be

1. Tsong kha pa, *sNgags rim chen mo*, in *rGyal ba btsong kha pa chen po'i bka' 'bum* ("The Complete Works of Tsong kha pa"), vol. dza. Chapter one (fascs. 2b-37a) has been translated in Jeffrey Hopkins, *Tantra in Tibet : The Great Exposition of Secret Mantra*, London : George Allen & Unwin, Wisdom of Tibet Series, no. 3, 1977, p. 68. [Hereinafter : *sNgags rim chen mo*].

implicit in the Pali canon as well. Since the *abhiññā* and the *iddhividhā* are equally developed by the *ubhatabhāgavimutto*, then he will be shown to be the equal of the Buddha, both pedagogically, in terms of what the Mahāyāna calls 'skilfulness' (*upāya kauśaliya*), and also in terms of wisdom, as defined in the Pali canon.

While others of the so-called 'Hīnayāna' schools allowed that the arahant was spiritually inferior to the Buddha, and to the *pacceka-buddha* (Sanskrit : *pratyekabuddha; Tibetan* : *rang sangs rgyas*) as well,[2] we find that the Theravāda made no such concessions. By maintaining the integrity of the arahant concept, by maintaining his equality with the Buddha, the Theravāda avoided many of the Mahāyāna criticisms of the arahant notion; so much so, in fact, that even the fourteenth century Tibetan author, Tsong kha pa,[3] expressed some puzzlement as to how and for what reasons the arahant (or the so-called 'Hīnayāna' generally) could be distinguished from the Buddha (or the Mahāyāna and Vajrayāna). Tsong kha pa, following the claim of the *Pañcaviṃśatisāhasrikā Prajñāpāramitā* which asserts the spiritual identity of the arahant and the Buddha,[4] as both are said to equally 'course in the perfection of wisdom,' yet manages to maintain the coherence of the notion of a '*yāna*' (Tibetan : *theg pa*) by maintaining that the *śrāvakayāna*, the *buddhayāna* (or *bodhisattvayāna*) and the *tantrayāna* are significantly distinguishable in terms of method only, but not in terms of wisdom,[5] which is to say that while they are spiritually equal, they are not equally pedagogically skilful.

Of course, Tsong kha pa knew nothing of the Theravāda, but was responding to the claims and positions of schools like

2. *Saddharmapuṇḍarikasūtra*, ed. by P. L. Vaidya, Buddhist Sanskrit Texts, No. 6, Darbhaṅga : The Mithila Institute, 1960, p. 29.

3. Tsong kha pa, *sNgags rim chen mo*, p. 43.

4. *Pañcaviṃśatisāhasrikā Prajñāpāramitā*, tr. Edward Conze, *The Large Sutra on the Perfection of Wisdom*, Berkeley : University of California Press, 1975, p. 58.

5. Tsong kha pa, *sNgags rim chen mo*, p. 99.

See also Nāgārjuna (kLu sgrub), *Rin po che'i 'phreng pa*, tr. and ed. by Jeffrey Hopkins, Lati Rinpoche and Anne Klein, *The Precious Garland and the Song of the Four Mindfulnesses*, London : George Allen & Unwin, Wisdom of Tibet Series, no. 2, 1975, p. 390 and p. 393.

the sarvāstivāda, especially as represented in texts like the *Abhidharmakośa*,[6] which conceded a significant difference between the arhat and the Buddha. We find the Theravāda position more challenging : namely, if the *ubhatabhāgavimutto* also cultivates the *abhiññā* and the *iddhipādā*, and if the *abhiññā* and the *iddhividhā* are religiously significant in Buddhism in terms of one's ability to teach Dhamma, as we believe, then Tsong kha pa's distinction in terms of method becomes even more tenuous. In short, his method issue would then become merely an issue of *types of method* employed, and not one of *method in general.* According to the Theravāda, we maintain, the *ubhatabhāgavimutto* arahant, by virtue of his development of these *abhiññā*, is as methodically skilful as the Buddha; the only possible distinction being that of precedence.

We contend that the Theravāda's maintaining of the integrity of the arahant notion is related to their maintaining the humanness of the Buddha; that if the Buddha is superhuman, or divine, or a metaphysical principle, rather than a person, then indeed he is different from any of the arahants, who at least began their careers as persons. But insofar as the Theravāda maintains that the Buddha, too, at least began as a person, then it also maintains his equivalence with the arahants in all significant senses.

Thus, for one to hold, as we do, the identity of the perfected person, be he Buddha, arahant, bodhisattva, mahāsiddha or whatever, throughout Buddhism, then the sarvāstivāda concession on this point must be seen as a submission to external pressures, as a form of conceptual backsliding, and one must accept something like the Theravāda's maintaining both the essential humanity of the Buddha and, consequently, his equivalence with the arahant.

In making this sort of case, we shall consider such possible objections as that of the Buddha's omniscience (*sabbaññā*) as compared with the limited knowledge of the arahant. However, an understanding of the notion of omniscience must be undertaken in a Buddhist context, and we propose to analyze this question in just this manner. We shall see whether 'omniscience' in a

6. Ācārya Vasubandhu, *Chos mngon pa mdzod kyi bshad pa*, 2 vols., Dharamsala : Council of Cultural and Religious Affairs of His Holiness the Dalai Lama, n.d.

Buddhist sense provides any reasonable grounds for distinguishing conceptually the Buddha and the arahant.

B. *The Abhiññā*

For scholars of the previous generation, the entire topic of the six (or five) *abhiññā* was sensitive. Following from the prejudice that Buddhism, or at least that part of it taught by the Buddha, was thoroughly rationalistic and non-mystical, many scholars ignored or even denied the existence of the considerable body of canonical references to these 'higher knowledges' (*abhiññā*), and especially to the 'psychic powers' (*iddhi*). Louis de la Vallée Poussin was one of the few who faced these issues squarely, and for doing so was criticized by Dasgupta, who said:[7]

> Is it even necessary to say that there is neither sorcery nor thaumaturgy in the Buddhism of the Buddha ?. . .It is difficult to believe that a scholar of the quality of La Vallée Poussin is capable of abandoning himself so strongly to such baseless and uncritical fantasies.

For the Buddha, on the other hand, the acceptance of such "fantasies" was manifest. Mahā Kassapa says, with the Buddha's approval :[8]

> It were as easy, friend, to imagine that an elephant seven to eight cubits high could be hidden under a young palm leaf, as to imagine that the six Super-knowledges [*abhiññā*] of me could be hidden.

What we propose in this section is a discussion of the six *abhiññā* which will show their position and development from the practice of the *jhānā*, their indispensability in both the formulation of Buddhist thought, as well as in the teaching of that doctrine, and as a bridge between the *ceto-* or *ubhatabhāgavimutto* arahant and the Buddha.

In the Dasuttara Suttanta,[9] the Buddha is discussing the six teachings that are to be actualized (*cha dhammā sacchikātabbā*)

---

7. Louis de la Vallée Poussin, "Le Bouddha et les Abhijñās," *op. cit.*, p. 335.

8. S.II.217 (PTS translation)
Sattaratanam vā āvuso nāgam aḍḍhaṭṭaratanaṃ vā tālapattikāya chādetabbam manneyya yo me cha abhiññā chādetabbaṃ maññeyyāti.

9. D.xxxiv.1.7.x. (My translation)

by his disciples. These are the six *abhiññā*, which are said to be :

1. "a brother enjoys *iddhi* in various ways : being one, he becomes many. . .he becomes. . .invisible. . .he goes, without obstruction, through a wall, solid ground. . .on water. . .in the sky...he reaches the realm of Brahmā with his body." (*bhikkhu aneka-vihitaṃ iddhividham paccanubhoti. . .pe. . .yāve Brahmalokā pi kāyena vasaṃ vatteti*).

2. "by his purified divine ear (clairaudience), which surpasses that of other people, he hears divine and human sounds, both far and near." (*dibbāya sota-dhātuyā visuddhāya atikkanta-mānusikāya ubho sadde suṇāti dibbe ca mānuse ca, ye dūre santike ca.*)

3. "with his own heart/mind, he knows the heart/mind of other people, he knows the impassioned heart/mind as impassioned, the liberated heart/mind as liberated, and the unliberated heart/mind as unliberated." (*para-sattānam para-puggalānaṃ cetasā ceto paricca pajānāti, sarāgaṃ va cittaṃ. . .pe. . .avimuttaṃ vā cittaṃ avimuttaṃ cittan ti pajānāti.*)

4. "he remembers previous lives in the past : one, two, or more, in full detail." (*aneka-vihitaṃ pubbe-nivāsaṃ anussarati seyyathīdaṃ ekam pi jātiṃ dve pi jātiyo. . . .*)

5. "with the purified divine eye (clairvoyance), which surpasses that of other people, he knows the farings of beings according to their *kamma* (actions)." (*dibbena cakkhunā visuddhena atikkanta-mānusakena...pe...yathā kammūpage satte pajānāti.*)

6. "the *āsavā* destroyed, he dwells, having attained the higher knowledges, here and now liberated through wisdom and liberated through the heart/mind, free from the *āsavā*." (*āsavānaṃ khayā anāsavaṃ ceto-vimuttiṃ pannāvimuttiṃ diṭṭheva dhamme sayaṃ abhiññā sacchikatvā upasampajja viharati.*)

These six *abhiññā* are termed : (1) *iddhividhā*, or knowledge of psychic powers; (2) *dibbasota*, the divine ear or clairaudience; (3) *paracittavijāñāṇa*, the ability to discern another's mind/heart, or mind-reading; (4) *pubbenivāsānussatiñāṇa*, knowledge of former lives of oneself and others; (5) *dibbacakkhu*, the divine eye or clairvoyance; and (6) *āsavakkhaya*, the destruction of the *āsavā*.[10]

10. This list of six is found in many places, such as : D.34; M.4.6.77; A.III.99; V.23; S.xv.9; and Pug.27, 39, according to Nyāṇatiloka Mahāthera, *Buddhist Dictionary*, p. 2.

We shall reserve our discussion of *iddhividhā* for a bit later, as the last five are more crucial in a formal, doctrinal sense. Of these latter five, the last—*āsavakkhaya*—means *khīṇāsavā*, the destruction of the *āsavā*, which is to say *arahattā* itself. The remaining four—clairaudience, knowledge of former lives, mind-reading and clairvoyance—are our immediate concern.

Before we discuss the *abhiññā* as such, however, a brief note must be inserted on Buddhism as *ehipassaka* teaching.[11] *Ehipassaka* means simply "come and see," and this was the Buddha's invitation to his disciples. Jayatilleke[12] has admirably demonstrated that the Buddha did not allow authority (*sabda*), logic (*takka*) or mystical experiences (such as the *jhānā*), to serve as a basis for conviction (*saddhā*). Nor do we believe, as Jayatilleke and many modern Theravāda scholars do, that the Buddha was a logical positivist in the sense that the meaning of his *sāsana* depends on its scientific or theoretical verifiability. In fact, this position has been the object of criticism from another Theravāda scholar, A. D. P. Kalansuriya,[13] who argues that meaning in Buddhism is not defined in a positivist sense.[14] Certainly the Buddha used language in such a way that allowed for meaningful symbolic and analogic statements to be accepted, statements which had nothing to do with the principle of verification which underlies any positivistic approach. However, in a non-technical sense, the *ehipassaka* principle was employed by the Buddha. He did not allow Sāriputta to hail him as omniscient, since Sāriputta was speaking beyond what was meaningful in the sense that is was beyond his experience to make such a claim; that he would have had to have been omniscient himself to hail the Buddha as such.[15] Therefore, if the Buddha did not allow him to speak beyond his experience, and if he did not allow his disciples to do so, then what sort of experience could serve as a basis for talk about rebirth, the fruition of *kamma*,

11. See Soma Thera, *Kālāma Sutta : The Buddha's Charter of Free Inquiry*, Kandy : Buddhist Publication Society, Wheel Series No. 8, 1963.

12. K. N. Jayatilleke, *Early Buddhist Theory of Knowledge*, London : George Allen & Unwin, 1963, pp. 171-204. [Hereinafter : *EBTK*].

13. A. D. P. Kalansuriya, "Wittgenstein, Meaning Model and Buddhism," Pune : *Indian Philosophical Quarterly*, IV, 3, April 1977, pp. 381ff.

14. *Ibid.*, p. 384.

15. D.xvi.1.16.

et cetera ? It is here that the *abhiññā* rescue Buddhism from a mere dogmatism, at least for the Buddha himself and those disciples who had developed these *abhiññā*.

Clairaudience (*dibbasota*) means hearing sounds, divine and human, far and near. Without this faculty, talk about the five or six realms of rebirth, about the trilochosm (the three worlds of desire, forms and formlessness), et cetera, would be mere dogmatism. There are many canonical references to this particular *abhiññā*, especially on the part of the Buddha in overhearing distant conversations, such as the one between Bhāradvāja the brahmin and Māgandiya the wandering ascetic.[16] It was assumed to be a real possibility for his disciples, as Sunakkhatta complains that, although he could occasionally see divine forms, he could not yet hear them.[17] The arahant Uppalavaṇṇā claims that she had developed this faculty.[18]

Mind-reading (*paracittavijñāṇa*) was a most useful tool by which the Buddha taught. Perhaps the most unique contribution of his teaching method was that, when confronted with a question, he chose to analyze the conditions given which such a question could be raised in the first place. For Buddhism, there is no such thing as an innocent question; they are not raised from mere curiosity. They are raised by the process of *paṭiccasamuppāda,* which is to say that one cannot coherently speak of any result (here the question itself) independent of the causal nexus from which it arises. Therefore, to treat a question as independent of its questioner would be the epitome of Buddhist bad faith. A question, therefore, is not an intellectual entity, not innocent; it is the outcome of a subtle psychological process. To answer a question, our usual procedure is to ignore the basis of the question, the causes given which the question could be asked. No significant religious question could be justly treated in such isolation, and by investigating the psychological heat over which questions (or positions) percolated, the Buddha showed that all questions and positions were rooted in one of several extreme views about the lived world. Both canonically and logically, Buddhism begins with the Brahmajāla Sutta,[19]

16. M.I.502.
17. D.I.152.
18. Thig., verse 227.
19. D.1.

a systematic analysis of sixty-two religio-philosophic positions held potentially or actually by his Indian co-religionists of his day. There he describes his teachings as a net (*jāla*) in which are entrapped all positions, and in which they flounder in the light of the Buddha's psychoanalysis of them. Philosophically he is analytically silent, which is to say that by psychoanalysis he silences the subconscious gossip from which all questions and positions emerge. This analysis is not merely logical but psychological, and his quieting of Maluṅkyaputta's[20] philosophical outburst indicates the method by which he employs mind-reading in order to bring out into the forum that which underlies more superficial pseudo-issues. For the Buddha, a significant religious question is that which leads the questioner to raise a question, that which is not logically (or positivistically) apparent.

This type of mind-reading might be similar to a sensitive psycho-therapist's 'reading' of his therapands. One need not assume that all canonical instances of this *abhiññā* be mystifying. Some others might seem to us more mysterious, as one other canonical use of this mind-reading faculty, which was to ascertain the validity of expressions of *aññā* by the disciples. In one place,[21] we find a discussion of what happens when a monk makes this expression of *aññā*. In the first place, the Tathāgata or one of his disciples who is skilled in the *jhānā* examines him. The monk in question is asked how this *aññā* came to be, and his replies are scrutinized. However, the point is raised that these replies could be simulated, not necessarily emerging from genuine *arahattā*. Finally the Buddha says that the only certain method for evaluating these expressions is that a monk who has actualized this faculty of mind-reading must read his mind/heart with his own (*cetasā ceto paricca*). Apparently this faculty became more and more uncommon, as by the time the *Bhikkhu-pāṭimokkha* was codified, the fourth offence for which expulsion from the *saṅgha* was mandatory (*pārājika*) was :[22]

> Should any bhikkhu while having no acquaintance of it suggest that some superior human state worthy of the Noble Ones'

---

20. M.63.
21. A.V.161-164.
22. Ven. Ñāṇamoli Thera, *The Paṭimokkha : 227 Fundamental Rules of a Bhikkhu*, Bangkok : King Mahā Makutala Academy, 1961, pp. 68-69.

knowledge and vision is present in himself saying "I know thus, I see thus" and afterwards on another occasion should he, whether examined or not examined, having fallen into the fault and being desirous of purification, say thus, "Friends, not knowing, I said 'I know' ; not seeing, I said 'I see'; what I said was vain and false", then unless it was through over-estimation, he is defeated and no more in communion also.

Thus it appears to us that the faculty of mind-reading was of use to the Buddha as a pedagogical underpinning, as well as essential in evaluating the *aññā* expressions of the disciples. It also seems that this faculty had become uncommon by the time of the codification of the *Pāṭimokkha,* as this once common practice of *aññā vyākaroti* became one of the four severest transgressions for the *saṅgha,* along with engaging in sexual intercourse, thievery and murder, requiring a penalty of expulsion from the *saṅgha.*

The knowledge of former lives (*pubbenivāsānussatiñāṇa*) is essential in the formulation of Buddhist doctrine. Without it, there could be no teaching of *kamma* and rebirth. It is said to follow from the development of *sati,*[23] and canonical references to it are numerous, as when the Buddha is called upon to locate a departed disciple or acquaintance. On many occasions he related homiletic stories about past lives, which were the foundation of the *jātaka* traditions, which themselves were the foundation for the bodhisattva teachings of the Mahāyāna. Since Buddhism accepts no mediated reward or punishment for one's actions (*kamma*), an impersonal principle of retribution was necessary in order to maintain any correspondence between actions and their fruits, and this principle could be known only by this type of knowledge by which the Buddha would often discuss the careers of his disciples and interlocators.

Yet this knowledge in itself was not sufficient for the development of the Buddha's teachings about rebirth. In the Brahmajāla

---

Yo pana bhikkhu anabhijānaṃ uttarimanussadhammaṃ attūpanāyikaṃ alamariyañāṇadassanaṃ samudācareyya : "Iti jānāmi, iti passāmi" ti, tato aparena samayena samanuggāhiyamāno vā asamanuggāhiyamāno vā āpanno visuddhāpekkho evaṃ vadeyya, "ajānam evaṃ āvuso avacaṃ, 'jānāmi' apassaṃ, 'passāmi'. Tucchaṃ musā vilapin" ti. Aññatra adhimānā, ayam 'pi pārājiko hoti asaṃvāso.

23. A.II.183.

Sutta again,[24] he shows that an eternalism could be a false derivative of this knowledge, whereby brahmins remember upto several hundred thousand births, and conclude from this that the world must be eternal. Thus, while remembering past births would be necessary as a foundation for the Buddha's teachings, without the sixth *abhiññā*, knowledge of the destruction of the *āsavā*, one could, and brahmins in fact did, draw erroneous eternalistic conclusions from it.

Clairvoyance, especially as it yields knowledge of the farings of beings to the heavens and hells according to their *kamma* (*yathākammūpagatañāṇa*), is also fundamental for Buddhist doctrine. It is the way in which an arahant knows another arahant; it is the experiential base for the doctrine of *kamma* and rebirth; and it is the basis for the teachings of the five destinies (*gāti*) within *saṃsāra*. In its wider use as clairvoyance, it is by this power that the Buddha knows of the presence of his five former colleagues at Isipatana,[25] and Jayatilleke[26] notes that it is similar to the Jaina notion of *avadhi*, the basis for Mahāvīra's claim to omniscience; except insofar as the Buddhist clairvoyance is temporally limited, whereas *avadhi* extends to all times. The foremost disciple in this faculty was Anuruddha, who was able to see a thousand worlds.[27] However, although Anuruddha can see so many heavens and hells, it is stated that he had not attained the faculty of the knowledge of former lives,[28] so apparently these faculties may be developed independently of each other.

These *abhiññā* were not taught to all of his disciples by the Buddha. In the Pāṭika Sutta,[29] Sunakkhatta complains that the Buddha has neglected him in this regard. The Buddha replies, just as he does to Māluṇkya's insistence on philosophic teaching, that since he had never promised to give such teachings, Sunakkhatta, like Māluṇkya, had better concentrate on what was essential to his *sāsana*. Of course, these *abhiññā* were the outcome of the practice of the *jhānā*, and as we have found in the preceding section on the *paññāvimutti* and the *cetovimutti*, the

24. D.I.128.
25. M.I.170.
26. Jayatilleke, *EBTK*, p. 441.
27. M.I.213.
28. S.IV.243f.
29. D.xxiv.1.4.

practice of the *jhānā* was not essential for the attaining of *arahattā*. The *abhiññā*, in fact, were said to arise as one began the practice of the fifth *jhāna*, which is the first of the supramundane, or formless (*āruppā*) *jhānā*.[30]

We have already demonstrated that that which characterizes an arahant is the destruction of the *āsavā*, which means the completion of the task of overcoming *avijjā* and the attainment of *nibbāna*. All of this also characterizes the Buddha, but he is additionally able to formulate and teach the doctrine which enables others to do the same. As we have just shown, these *abhiññā*, along with *iddhividhā*, are essential to the formulation and teaching of Dhamma. Further, we have shown that the Buddha would be the *ubhatabhāgavimutto*, the one freed in both ways—that of the practice of the *jhānā*, and that of the development of *paññā*,[31] as were some sixty of his five hundred arahant disciples.[32] Thus, while some distinction could be drawn between the Buddha as *ubhatabhāgavimutto* and some of his arahant disciples, one can find no distinction at all—except in terms of precedence—between the Buddha and his *ubhatabhāgavimutto* arahant disciples. This case shall be developed further, but attention must now be paid to the first of the *abhiññā* we mentioned, the *iddhividhā*, which are chiefly pedagogical aids.

C. *Iddhi*

Iddhi derives from the root $\sqrt{}$*ardh*, 'to prosper,'[33] and carries the sense of psychic potency.[34] Scholars of Buddhism are particularly squeamish about this topic, as with all of the *abhiññā*,[35] and from a reading of the canonical material on this topic, it seems that the Buddha himself had some ambivalence. For

30. See Nārada Mahāthera, *BHT*, p. 538; and cf. Sangharakshita, *Survey*, p. 487.

31. S.I.221-222.

32. S.I.191.

33. *P.T.S. Dictionary*, p. 120.

34. Franklin Edgerton, *Buddhist Hybrid Sanskrit Dictionary*, repr. Delhi : Motilal Banarsidass, 1977 (New Haven : Yale University Press, 1953) s.v., *ṛddhi*, p. 151. [Herinafter : *BHSD*].

35. See *P.T.S. Dictionary*, s.v., especially section 3.

example, in one place[36] he says : "Monks, I call the four bases of *iddhi* the way which leads to the unconditioned (*asaṅkhāta*, or *nibbāna*)," which indicates that these practices, associated with the specific cultivation of *iddhi*, were of the highest religious value. Elsewhere[37] he tells his disciples that the public practice of *iddhi* is a wrong act (*dukkaṭa*), indicating some shortcomings or dangers of this method. In this section we shall discuss *iddhi*, the method of its cultivation, as well as the Buddha's ambivalence about it. We shall resolve this latter issue by indicating the canonical distinction, which was maintained from the time of the Buddha right on through contemporary vajrayāna practice, of mundane and supramundane magic.

Standardized lists of approximately ten *iddhividhā* appear throughout the *Sutta Piṭaka*, all of which describe the monk possessing *iddhi* similarly to this from the Sāmaññaphala Sutta :[38]

> He enjoys the Wondrous Gift [*iddhi*] in its various modes—being one he becomes many, or having become many he becomes one again; he becomes visible or invisible; he goes, feeling no obstruction, to the further side of a wall or rampart or hill, as if through air; he penetrates up and down through solid ground, as if through water; he walks on water without breaking through, as if on solid ground; he travels cross-legged in the sky, like the birds on wing; even the Moon and the Sun, so potent, so mighty though they be, does he touch and feel with his hand; he reaches in the body even up to the heaven of Brahmā.

Undoubtedly this listing is a stereotype; Mrs. Rhys-Davids[39] finds it and its basic variants repeated eighteen times in the five *nikāyas*, and three times in the basic commentaries (*aṭṭhakathā*).

---

36. S.IV. 360. (My translation)
Cattāro iddhipādā ayaṃ vuccati bhikkhave asaṅkhatagāmi maggo.
37. Vin.II.112.
38. D.ii.87. (PTS translation)
So aneka-vihitaṃ iddhi-vidhaṃ paccanubhoti—eko pi hutvā bahudhā hoti, bahudhā pi hutvā eko hoti, āvibhāvaṃ tiro-bhāvaṃ tiro-kuḍḍaṃ tiro-pākāraṃ tiro-pabbataṃ asajjamāno gacchati seyyathā pi udake, udake pi abhijjamāno gacchati seyyathā pi paṭaviyam, ākāse pi pallaṅkena kamati seyyathā pi pakkhī sakuṇo, ime pi candima-suriye evaṃ mahiddhike evaṃ mahānubbhāve pāṇinā parimasati parimajjati, yāve Brahma-lokā pi kāyena va saṃvatteti.
39. *P.T.S. Dictionary*, p. 120.

The *iddhividhā* are cultivated by means of the practice known as the four steps leading to *iddhi* (*cattāro iddhipādā*) or, as it is commonly translated, 'the four bases of psychic power.' These *cattāro iddhipādā* are listed and discussed at many places in the *Sutta Piṭaka*, such as in the Saṅgīti Suttanta,[40] which is a gloss on the fundamental teachings of the Buddha :

> The four steps to *iddhi* : Herein, friends, a monk :
> (a) develops the step to *iddhi* that is composed of a concentration of desire [*chanda*] together with [*saṅkhāra*] effort; (b) develops the step to *iddhi* that is composed of a concentration [*samādhi*] of the heart/mind [*citta*] together with effort; (c) develops the step to *iddhi* that is composed of a concentration of energy [*viriya*] together with effort; and (d) develops the step to *iddhi* that is composed of a concentration of investigation [*vīmaṃsā*] together with effort.

In the Janavasabha Suttanta[41] the Buddha says that he himself has successfully employed just these practices, thereby acquiring the *iddhividhā*. Further, it is said in the Ākaṅkheyya Sutta[42] that one who cultivates these practices ". . .should be one who fulfils certain moral practices, who is dedicated to internal mental calm, who meditates uninterruptedly, who has vision and frequents empty places."

Many of the canonical and commentatorial examples of *iddhi* arise in the context of the teaching situation. One such instance is related by the arahant Subhā in the Therīgāthā.[43] One day her way is blocked by a certain young man of Rājagaha, who has become infatuated with her. She predictably responds by discoursing on the unsatisfactoriness of sensual pursuits, the

---

40. D.xxxiii.1.11. (My translation)
Cattāro iddhipādā. Idh' āvuso bhikkhu chanda-samādhi-padhāna-saṃkhāra-samannāgataṃ iddhipādaṃ bhāveti. Citta-samādhi-padhāna-saṃkhāra-samannāgataṃ iddhipādaṃ bhāveti. Viriya-samādhi-padhāna-saṃkhāra-samannāgataṃ iddhipādaṃ bhāveti. Vīmaṃsā-samādhi-padhāna-saṃkhāra-samannāgataṃ iddhipādaṃ bhāveti.

41. D.xviii.22. Ahaṃ pi kho bho imesaṃ yeva catunnaṃ iddhipādānaṃ bhāvitattā bahulikattā evam mahiddhiko evam mahānubhāvoti.

42. M.I.34. (My translation)
sīlesv-ev' assa paripūrakārī ajjhattaṃ cetosamatham annuyutto anirākaṭajjhāno vipassanāya samannāgato brūhetā suññāgārānaṃ.

43. Thig., verses 366-399.

value of renunciation in particular, and the Dhamma in general. As might be expected in such a situation, her words fall on deaf ears, and the young man sustains his pursuit. Seeing that the young man is especially enamoured of her eyes, she pulls one of them from its socket, saying that if he loves her eyes, he should have one of them. The young man is horrified, his lust is dissipated, and he begs forgiveness and instruction. Turning to face the direction of the Buddha, Subhā's eye is restored, and the young man becomes a disciple. Here we find the *iddhi* of magical healing to be of pedagogical utility in a case when discoursing would have been to no avail. Had *iddhi* not been available to this arahant, one can well imagine that the young man's lust would have remained incurable (*atekicca*).

On another occasion,[44] the Buddha and Moggallāna, who was known as his foremost disciple in terms of *iddhi*, are in conversation. The Buddha comments on his displeasure with the general status of his disciples : that they have become lax in their practice. He tells Moggallāna to go and shake them up a bit.[45] Then, with his big toe, Moggallāna set the building in which the monks were staying to shaking.[46] The frightened monks run to the Buddha, and he tells them that it was merely Moggallāna's *iddhividhā* that had shaken their house. He exhorts them that they, too, could develop such *iddhividhā* were they to become more diligent in their practice. Here, *iddhi* is effectively used to shake up both the house and the monks' lackadaisical attitude. It is also interesting to note the use of the promise of *iddhi* to encourage the monks to practice diligently.

That *iddhi* was assumed by both the Buddha and his contemporaries is illustrated in his dialogue with Upāli, a follower of Jaina teachings.[47] The issue in this discussion is whether the most serious offences are those of body, of speech, or of mind. Following Mahāvīra's interpretation of *ahiṃsā*, Upāli contends that the offences of body are the most serious, while the Buddha, following the principle that mind is the forerunner of all states,[48]

44. S.V. 269-270.
45. S.V.269 : gaccha Moggallāna te bhikkhū saṃvejehīti.
46. *Idem.* : tathārūpam iddhābhisaṅkhāram abhisaṅkhāresi. yathā pādaṅguṭṭhakena sampacālesi.
47. M.I.378-379.
48. Dhammapada.I.1. manopubbaṅgamā dhammā.

contends that offences of mind are the most serious. The Buddha both convinces and converts Upāli by pointing out that whereas as many as fifty warriors, upon entering Nālandā, would be unable to slay the city's population in an instant by use of their swords, only one accomplished meditator could do so by means of the *iddhividhā*. Therefore, the Buddha concludes, offences of mind are more serious than those of the body.

That the Buddha, at least as he is represented in the *Sutta Piṭaka*, took the *iddhi* quite seriously and literally, is demonstrated in a conversation he holds with Ānanda.[49] Ānanda asks whether he can reach as far as the *Brahmaloka* by means of his mind-made body (*manomayena kāyena*). After telling Ānanda that he can, he is asked whether he can reach the *Brahmaloka* both with the mind-made body and 'this physical body made of the four great elements' (*iminā cātumahābhūtikena kāyena*), and the Buddha replies that he can. In another place,[50] he emphasizes that he is adept at magic (*māyā*) :

> They who speak thus, headman, that I know magic, do speak in accordance with my view. They do not misrepresent me by stating what is wrong. They do speak in conformity with my teaching, so that no one who is of the same view as I, who is a follower of my view, could give opportunity for censure.

Thus it is clearly evident that the Buddha considered himself to be adept at these magical *iddhi*, and he certainly was not one to hesitate to employ them when appropriate. One of the *iddhividhā* we find him exercising is that of flying. In the *Udana*,[51] we read of the Buddha finding the Ganges at flood, so

49. S.V.282.

50. S.IV.340. (PTS translation)

Ye te gāmaṇi evam āhaṃsu Samaṇo Gotamo māyaṃ jānātīti vuttavādino ceva me te na ca mam abhūtena abhācikkhanti. dhamassa cānudhammaṃ vyākaronti. na ca keci sadadhammiko vādānapato gāroyhaṃ ṭhānam āgacchatīti.

51. Udana, p. 90.

We find an identical motif in some of the hagiographies (*rnam thar*) of the mahāsiddhas (*grub thob*), an example of which is found in the hagiography of Virupa, found in the *sLob bshad khrid yig* by 'Jam mgon mkhyen rtse, page 6, na, 5, and as discussed by Khetsun Sangpo, *rGya gar paṇ chen rnams kyi rnam that ngo mtshar padmo'i 'dzum zhal gsar pa*, Vol. I, Dharamsala : Library of Tibetan Works and Archives, 1973, p. 335.

he flies across it, together with his retinue of disciples. The ease with which this *iddhi* is accomplished is likened to the ease with which a strong man bends his arm. Of course, this particular episode nicely correlates with our discussion of 'crossing-over' symbolism, but in the context of our discussion of *iddhi*, it is also typical of the exercise of these psychic powers.

We find examples of the public display of the *iddhividhā* for pedagogical purposes. In the *Saṃyutta Nikāya*[52] we find the householder (*gahapati*) Citta asking the arahant Mahaka for a demonstration of *iddhi*. Mahaka agrees and instructs Citta to place his cloak on the verandah, along with a bundle of grass. Then Mahaka retired into the house and shot a bolt of fire through the keyhole, igniting the grass but leaving the cloak undamaged. From this incident, Citta's determination for practising Dhamma is uplifted, and he also promises to become Mahaka's patron. It seems, then, that the use of *iddhi* for stimulating the disciples' practice was considered appropriate, as evidenced by this story of Mahaka, and also by Moggallāna's magical exhortations.

Since, as we contend, *iddhi* was used appropriately in the pedagogical context, it is not surprising that we find several death-bed demonstrations of *iddhi*. We have indicated several times in this essay that death, in Buddhism, is a highly potent teaching situation, and we find the arahant Dabba[53] publicly attaining what is called the realm of heat (*tejodhātu*) at the moment of his death. This realm of heat, which is very similar to the tantric 'rainbow body' teachings, means that, at the moment of death, one's body is consumed with flames, psychically generated.

While all of the above examples of the demonstration of *iddhi* occur in a teaching context, we also find instances that were considered appropriate which had as their aim the generation of religious sentiments. Finding no flowers to offer to the Mahā-cetiya at Anurādhapura, magically conjured flowers are used as a substitute to enhance religious feelings.[54]

According to the *Visuddhimagga*,[55] one may employ *iddhi* to investigate another's expression of *aññā*, similar to the use of the *abhiññā* of mind-reading (*paracittavijāñāṇa*), as discussed

52. S.IV.290-291.
53. Udana, p. 92.
54. MA.699; cited in Rahula, *HBC*, pp. 226-227.
55. Vism., pp. 476ff.

above. In this story, Mahānāga of Uccavālika thought himself to be an arahant. His student, Dhammadinna, one of the most renowned of the arahants of classical Lanka, decided to challenge his teacher's false assumption. Dhammadinna asked Mahānāga whether he had attained arahattā, and he was told that it had been attained sixty years previously. Dhammadinna then asked if the teacher was able to accomplish *samādhi.* Receiving an affirmative reply, Dhammadinna asked Mahānāga to conjure up an elephant for him. When Mahānāga did this, the elephant began trumpeting and frightened the elder. Seeing his teacher afraid, Dhammadinna asked him if it were possible that an arahant be afraid of anything. Realizing his longstanding error, Mahānāga begged to become Dhammadinna's disciple, and soon thereafter attained *arahattā.* Once again, the use of *iddhi* here is clearly pedagogical.

All of the above instances of *iddhi* were considered to be appropriate. One thread that runs through them was that they all involve either the teaching of Dhamma or the expression of religious sentiment. One major inappropriate use of *iddhi*, however, is found in the *Culavagga.*[56] In this story, a certain rich man of Rājagaha offered a fine almsbowl to any religious teacher who could take it from its perch atop a tall bamboo pole. Teachers such as Pūraṇa Kassapa and Makkhalī Gosāla were unable to reach it, and finally Piṇḍola Bhāradvāja arrived, ascended in the air, and took the bowl. When the Buddha learned of this episode, he scolded Piṇḍola Bhāradvāja saying :[57]

> Bhāradvāja, it is unsuitable, unseemly, improper, not done in keeping with a *samaṇa*, unfitting, a thing that should not be done. How can you, Bhāradvāja, indulge in the performance of superhuman miracles for the sake of a wretched wooden bowl ? Just as a woman exhibits her nudity for the sake of a wretched little coin, even so, Bhāradvāja, a performance of

56. Culavagga, pp. 203-205; cited in Rahula, *HBC*, pp. 226-227.

57. *Ibid.*, p. 204. (Rahula translation)
Ananucchavikaṃ Bhāradvāja, ananulomikaṃ appatirūpaṃ assāmaṇakaṃ akapiyyaṃ akaraṇīyaṃ. Kathaṃ hi nāma Bhāradvāja, chavassa dārupatassa kāraṇā gihīnaṃ uttarimanussadhammaṃ iddhipāṭihāriyaṃ dassessasi ? Seyyathāpi Bhāradvāja, mātugāmo chavassa māsakarūpassa kāraṇā hirokopīnaṃ dassetī, evam eva kho tayā Bhāradvāja, chavassa dārupattassa kāreṇā gihīnaṃ uttarimanussadhammaṃ iddhipātihāriyaṃ dassitaṃ.

superhuman miracles is given by you to the laity for the sake of a wretched wooden bowl.

It seems that the Buddha's criterion in determining this use of *iddhi* to be inappropriate is that Bhāradvāja did it for the sake of some gain, whereas the appropriate use of *iddhi* should be pedagogical, inspirational and/or religious. The *Culavagga*[58] goes on to tell us that it was on this occasion that the Buddha instituted the rules governing the use and display of *iddhi*.

The regulation, which is found in the *Vinaya Piṭaka*,[59] is strictly negative : bhikkhus are not allowed to display *iddhi* to the laity at the risk of committing a misdeed (*dukkaṭa*). It should be noted here that the regulations governing monastic discipline in Buddhism are invariably negative; that the whole notion of monastic discipline (*pāṭimokkha*) means "a restraint of body and speech (from misdeeds),"[60] and thus all early Buddhist monastic regulations have a negative character of restraint. This is less the case in the bodhisattva *prāṭimokṣa*, where there are both positive and restraining regulations.[61] In the tantric *prāṭimokṣa* tradition, which is called *samaya* (Tibetan : *sdom pa*), none of the fourteen injunctions are negative or restraining in character, but indicate positive mental attitudes which are to be cultivated.[62] The negative injunctions regarding the *iddhividhā* in the Theravāda canon need not, then, be understood as a denial of their religious validity. It is simply a matter of style that the Pali *pāṭimokkha* speaks a negativistic language. We have indicated many Pali sources which confirm that there is an appropriate religious use of the *iddhividhā*, and it would be an unwarranted generalization to assume from the Vinaya reference that the Buddha did not appreciate the value of *iddhi*. He merely indicated appropriate and inappropriate circumstances for its use. Given the negativistic character of the Theravāda *pāṭimokkha* literature, it would

58. Culavagga, p. 205.

59. Vin.II.112.

60. *Abhidharmakośa-ṭikā* : lus ngag sdom pa'i phyir so so thar pa'i sdom pa zhes bya'o.; cited in Kong sprul, *Shes bya kun khyab*, *op. cit.*, 'grel, Vol. II, p. 38.

61. See *Bodhisattva Prāṭimokṣa Sūtra*, ed. Nalinaksha Dutt, *Indian Historical Quarterly*, VII, 1931, pp. 259-286.

62. See *rDo rje theg pa'i rtsa ba dang yan lag gi ltung ba'i bshags pa*, by Indrabhūti, *bsTan 'gyur*, sNar thang edition, sNgags, Vol. pu., fascs. 114b-115b.

not have been consistent with its genre to make positive statements in this context.

The fact remains that, despite many instances when the use of *iddhi* was clearly appropriate, the Pali sources remain ambivalent as to its value. By sheer weight of numbers, however, we are led to the tentative conclusion that there is more to be said in favor of *iddhi* than against it. By way of evidence of the value of the *iddhividhā*, we would indicate the following statements by the Buddha :

1. "Monks, I call the four steps to *iddhi* a way which goes to the unconditioned."[63]
2. By practising the four *iddhipādā*, the bhikkhu "becomes one for successful breaking through, he becomes one for awakening, he becomes one for winning the incomparable security from the bonds."[64]
3. "Monks, these four bases of psychic power [*iddhipādā*], if cultivated and made much of, conduce to downright revulsion, to dispassion, to cessation, to calm, to full comprehension, to the wisdom, to *nibbāna*."[65]
4. These four *iddhipādā* give rise to "the Ariyan way that goes on to utter destruction of ill."[66]
5. These four *iddhipādā* lead one to become a "tathāgata, who is called arahant, a fully enlightened one."[67]

Yet despite all these extremely positive remarks about the value of the *iddhipādā*, we have found one place[68] where the Buddha expresses his ambivalence about them, or perhaps he is expressing the notion that the *iddhividhā* are essentially neutral, as he says

---

63. S.IV.260. (My translation)
cattāro iddhipādā ayaṃ vuccati bhikkhave asaṅkhatagāmi maggo.
64. M.I.104. ‹(PTS translation)
Sa kho bhikkhave evaṃ ussoḷhipannarasaṅgasamannāgato bhikkhu bhabbo abhinibbhidāya, bhabbo sambodhāya, bhabbo anuttarassa yogakkhemassa adhigamāya.
65. S.V.255. (PTS translation)
Cattāro me bhikkhave iddhipādā bhāvitā bahulīkatā ariyā niyyānikā niyyanti takkarassa sammādukkhakkhayagāmī.
66. S.V.255. : ariyo maggo sammādukkhakkhayagāmī.
67. S.V.257. : tathāgato arahaṃ sammasambuddha ti vuccatiti.
68. S.V.254 : Cattāro 'me bhikkhave iddhipādā bhāvitā bahulīkatā aparāparaṃ gamanāya samvattanti.

that they "...conduce to going neither to the hither nor to the further shore."

This ambivalence is also expressed about magic (*māyā*) generally. The Buddha says that while he knows magic, and how to utilize magic to advantage, nevertheless for the common magician, this practice leads to rebirth in the lower realms.[69] This ambivalence on the part of the Buddha may properly reflect the cardinal notion that it is not an act per se, but the intentionality which gives rise to the act, which determines the ethical quality of the act. Following from this principle that it is the mind and not the mere action that determines the *kammatic* quality of an event, in the Sampasādaniya Sutta[70] the Buddha distinguishes between (a) that *iddhi* which is associated with the *āsavā*, and (b) that *iddhi* which is not so associated. The *iddhividhā* themselves are discussed in identical terms, but those which are not associated with the *āsavā* are called holy (*ariya*), and those which are associated with the *āsavā* are called unholy (*anāriya*). Therefore, as to whether one concludes that the *iddhividhā*, in and of themselves, conduce towards *nibbāna* or conduce against *nibbāna*, or both, or neither, seems to depend upon which *suttas* one focuses on, and what predispositions one has about this topic. It seems that the practice of *iddhi* is appropriate when related with either (a) teaching Dhamma, (b) inspiring others, or (c) expressing religious sentiments. No act in Buddhism can be judged apart from the contextual matrix of the act, which is its intentionality. Thus, there is no one, simple criterion for evaluating the practice of *iddhi* in early Buddhism. Certainly, one does not fairly represent the tradition by claiming that the *iddhividhā* are alien to Buddhism, an example of the Buddha's concessions to popular Indian religions of his day; or by denying their existence entirely, as some scholars do. It cannot be doubted that, given certain situations, the *iddhi* are rightfully employed by the Buddha and his arahant disciples, and we offer that no picture of the perfected person in early Buddhism could be complete without some account of his practice of these *iddhividhā*.

---

69. S.IV.342.
Māyancāhaṃ gāmaṇi pajānāmi māyāna va vipākaṃ. yathāpaṭipanno ca māyāvī kāyassa bhedā param maraṇā apāraṃ duggatiṃ vinipātaṃ nirayam upapajjati tanca pajānāmi.

70. D.xxviii.18.

Returning the discussion of these *iddhividhā* to their context as one of the six *abhiññā*, one can see that our case that these are integral aspects of early Buddhism's perfected person, is even more clear. Without such *abhiññā* as the knowledge of former lives (*pubbenivāsānussatiñāṇa*), or that type of clairvoyance (*dibbacakkhu*) which gives knowledge of the faring of beings according to their *kamma* (*yathākammūpagatañāṇa*), there could be no doctrine of *kamma* and rebirth, an essential feature of all forms of Buddhism. Without this knowledge of his former lives, the Buddha, obviously, could not have spoken about his former lives, and there would have been no Theravāda *jātaka* tradition and, consequently, no Mahāyāna doctrine of the bodhisattva. Mind-reading (*paracittavijāñāṇa*) proves in the *Sutta Piṭaka* to be an invaluable pedagogical aid, although it seems that its immediate effect on the formulation of the Dhamma by the Buddha was not so great. The ability to hear extensively in both the human and divine realms (*dibbasota*) does not seem to be as important as the other *abhiññā*, although an extension of this principle becomes significant in the Avalokitesvara tradition of the *bodhisattvayāna,* especially in terms of the development of the sensitivity to the sufferings of others, as expressed in the teachings which seek to develop the adept's *karuṇā*. This last of the *abhiññā*, which some scholars do not wish to consider an *abhiññā* at all, is the destruction of the *āsavā* (*āsavakkhaya*) which, as we have seen, is the *sine qua non* of *arahattā*. Despite repeated statements in the *Sutta Piṭaka* that it is to be so considered,[71] those who do not wish to consider this to be an *abhiññā* are those who feel squeamish about these *abhiññā* and *iddhividhā* dimensions of early Buddhism in the first place.

Both the Buddha and all of his *ubhatabhāgavimutto* have developed these six *abhiññā,* as they are all natural outcomes of the practice of the *jhānā,* although never the goal of this practice. *Arahattā* could never be said to be in any way dependent on this *abhiññā*, or on the *jhānā,* as we have seen that the *paññāvimutto* or *sukhavipassaka* arahants have not practised them, yet they are still arahants. However, these meditational practices, along with the resulting *abhiññā*, we contend, are essential to the notion

71. See footnote 9 of this chapter for a list of canonical references to the six *abhiññā,* all of which include *āsavakkhaya.*

of a Buddha as one who is able to discover and teach the Dhamma. We have demonstrated that these *abhiññā* are essential to the formulation of the Dhamma, as they are to its verification (in the *ehipassaka* sense of verification) by the disciples of the Buddha. They are also extremely useful pedagogical aids.

The next topic we shall consider, that of the relationship of an arahant and the Buddha, therefore follows naturally from our discussion of these *abhiññā*. For an arahant to be identical to the Buddha, which is what we contend, then it is vital that the arahant has developed these faculties.

D. *The Arahant and the Buddha*

In this discussion, we shall first point out that there are three general trends of thinking in the *Sutta Piṭaka* regarding the comparative status of the Buddha and the arahant. The first of these three, which we find to be the most common understanding, is that the Buddha and the arahant are, in every significant sense, identical in terms of spiritual achievement. As a very general rule, this seems to be the position found in the oldest sections of the *Sutta Piṭaka*, such as the *Khuddaka Nikāya*. The second position is that the Buddha differs from the arahant only in the very special sense that he is 'a shower of the way' (*maggakkhayin*), which is to say that the notions of the Buddha and the arahant differ only in precedence, the Buddha being the discoverer and original promulgator of the Dhamma in a given aeon (*kalpa*). A third understanding, and the most significant one in terms of traditional understandings of the rise of Mahāyāna Buddhism, is that the Buddha and the arahant are radically different, that the Buddha is possessed of qualities and attributes that would be inapplicable to the arahant.

The textual ambivalence led to serious hermeneutical difficulties for both Buddhists and scholars of Buddhism. To pose the problem most briefly, we find that at the Council of Pāṭaliputra, one Mahādeva raised five well-known 'points' regarding the spiritual status of the arahant, all of which indicated the spiritual imperfection of the arahant notion.[72] In the schism that developed at that council, the Mahāsaṅghikas accepted Mahādeva's

72. See Chapter I, footnote 14.

position, whereas the Sthaviravāda (Theravāda) rejected it, choosing to maintain the spiritual integrity of the arahant concept. By the time of the promulgation of the *Lotus Sūtra* (*Saddharmapuṇḍarīkasūtra*), we find the arahant as a spiritually inferior being, defined as one who thinks he has accomplished more than he actually has.[73] The radical divergence of this position from that found in the Pali *Sutta Piṭaka* is striking, of course, and it was statements such as those found in the *Lotus* that led to some of the chief hermeneutical difficulties which Buddhists faced, and were integral to the formulation of the bodhisattva doctrine. The problem, to put it simply, is that if, as Mahādeva and the *Lotus* tell us, the arahant is a spiritually inferior person, one possessed of the arrogance of believing that he had accomplished more than he had, then the arahant notion becomes unsatisfactory as a goal of the religious life—at least, this has been the traditional understanding of the problem. We shall argue that such a formulation of the issue misses the point, and that when the *Lotus* and other Mahāyāna texts speak derogatorily of the arahant, they do not do so in a way which refers to the arahant notion as found in the Pali canon. The Mahāyāna redefined what they meant by an arahant, which for them means a basically spiritually arrogant psychological type, and it was an arahant thus understood and defined which was the object of Mahāyāna polemics. . .*and not the arahant of the Pali canon.* Nor do such efforts at Buddhist hermeneutics as discussed by Robert Thurman,[74] which follow the traditional Mahāyāna analysis of the arahant as the pursuer of 'pacification of self,' as opposed to the bodhisattva who pursues 'pacification of others,' help us to get out of the problem. One easily forgets that other Mahāyāna texts contemporaneous with the *Lotus*, such as the 25,000 *Line Prajñāpāramitā* (*Pañcaviṃśatisāhasrikā Prajñāpāramitā*), set up the problem much differently. It is an assumption of such texts that all Buddhist careers (*yānas*), that of the *arhat*, the *pratyekabuddha*, and the *buddhayāna*, pursue

73. *Saddharmapuṇḍarīkasūtra*, Vaidya ed., p. 26 : "they imagined having attained what they had not attained; they imagined having understood what they had not understood." Cf. Kern, tr., p. 38.

74. Robert A. F. Thurman, "Buddhist Hermeneutics," Missoula : *Journal of the American Academy of Religion*, XLVI, 1, March 1978, pp. 19-40.

their goal(s) in the same wisdom (*prajñā*). It was this type of position that led keen Buddhist hermeneuticians, such as Tsong kha pa in his *sNgags rim chen mo*,[75] to raise the question that if the arahant and the Buddha cannot be distinguished in terms of wisdom, with what basis are we left to speak of different Buddhist careers at all ?

This digression has been merely to indicate a serious problem with which Buddhists have been confronted. Our point, for the moment at least, is that prior to any discussion of the Mahāyāna or vajrayāna understandings of the arahant ideal, is a full and clear elucidation of the arahant ideal in its original context : the Pali texts. Only after such a contextual elucidation will it become coherent to present the contextual uses of the arahant notion as found in later Buddhist writings.

Returning to our immediate problem, which is to discern the position of the Pali canon *vis-à-vis* the arahant/Buddha issue, we find three main trends : (1) that the Buddha and the arahant are identical; (2) that the Buddha is an arahant, but also 'something more than' an arahant, either in principle or due to precedence; and (3) that the Buddha and the arahant are separable notions.

The standard 'definition' of the Buddha, found in many places in the *Sutta Piṭaka*,[76] is :

> Now regarding the venerable Gotama, such is the reputation that has been noised abroad—That Blessed One is an Arahant, a fully awakened one, abounding in wisdom and goodness, happy, with knowledge of the worlds, unsurpassed as a guide to mortals willing to be led, a teacher for gods and men, a Blessed One, a Buddha.

Thus far from this 'definition,' we can clearly see that the notion of Buddhahood entails *arahattā*; that a Buddha is an arahant. However, what is not clear is whether or not a Buddha is 'something more than' an arahant as well. The text continues :[77]

---

75. See footnote 1 to this chapter.

76. But we are citing from the Soṇadaṇḍa Sutta, D.iv.2. (PTS translation) Taṃ kho pana Bhagavantaṃ Gotamaṃ evaṃ kalyāṇo kittissado abhuggato : 'Iti pi so Bhagavā arahaṃ sammāsambuddho vijjā-caraṇa-sampanno sugato loka-vidū anuttaro purisa-dhamma-sārathī setthā deva-manussānaṃ buddho bhagavā.

77. D.iv.2. (PTS translation) So imaṃ lokaṃ sadevakaṃ samārakaṃ sabrahmakaṃ sassamaṇa-

He, by himself, thoroughly knows and sees, as it were, face to face this universe,—including the worlds above the gods, the Brahmās, and the Māras, and the world below with its recluses and brāhmaṇas, its princes and peoples,—and having known it, he makes his knowledge known to others. The truth, lovely in its origin, lovely in its progress, lovely in the spirit and in the letter, the higher life doth he make known, in all its fullness and in all its purity.

This citation raises several issues, which shall be pursued. First of all, as we have noted, the text tells us that the notion of a Buddha entails the notion of an arahant; thus one of the epithets of Gotama is *arahaṃ*, the affirmation that he is indeed an arahant. However, we shall leave open for the moment the question as to whether the notion of a Buddha involves more than being an arahant, in either the sense of a being who is intrinsically more than an arahant, or who is accidentally so, which would merely be in terms of precedence.

Another question from this text is that of omniscience (*sabbāññā*). What does it mean to say that the Buddha knows all of these worlds ? Is this knowledge omniscience, or is some other sort of knowledge involved ? And if it is omniscience, what might that mean within a Buddhist context ? And, to return more immediately to the issues which confront us, whether this knowledge is understood as omniscience or not, do the arahants have the same knowledge ?

One characteristic of the Buddha, according to this text, is that he makes this knowledge known to others, that he is a teacher. If the arahant is also a teacher, then he and the Buddha, at least in this sense, are equal. If he is not intrinsically a teacher, then one of the Mahāyāna hermeneutical conclusions, that the arahant is interested only in self-pacification, whereas the Buddha, via the bodhisattva career, is involved with the pacification of others, and therefore significantly different than and, according to Mahāyāna standards, superior to the arahant is right. This shall be the specific topic for our discussion of the sociology of the

---

brāhmaṇiṃ pajaṃ sadevamanussaṃ sayaṃ abhiññā sacchikatvā pavedati. So dhammaṃ deseti ādikalyāṇaṃ majjhe kalyāṇaṃ pariyosāna-kalyāṇaṃ sātthaṃ savyañjanaṃ, kevala-paripuṇṇaṃ parisuddhaṃ brahmacariyaṃ pakāseti. Sādhu kho pana tathā-rūpānaṃ arahataṃ dassanaṃ hoti.

arahant, where we find that the arahant is intrinsically a teacher; but it does seem appropriate to at least raise this key issue at this juncture in our discussion.

Just as the term arahant is a standard epithet of the Buddha, we also find that in some places the term 'buddha' is an epithet of the arahant. In one *gāthā* section of the *Majjhima Nikāya*,[78] we find a poetical discussion of what it means to be an arahant :

> He knows his previous lives; he sees the heavens and hells; he has actualized the destruction of (re-)birth; a sage, accomplished in the *abhiññā*. He knows that his heart/mind is completely purified; freed from all passion; beyond birth and death; complete in the religious life; [he knows] all empassioned *dhammā*; such a one is called *buddha*.

We see very clearly in this verse that one who has followed the full training of an arahant, including the *jhānā*, is entitled to the epithet '*buddha*'. The *jhānā* are involved in this verse because it indicates that one who is called *buddha* is one who has mastered the *abhiññā*, specifically the knowledge of former births (*pubbenivāsānussatiñāṇa*), the divine eye which extends to the heavens and the hells (*dibbacakkhu*), and, of course, the destruction of the *āsavā* (*āsavakkhaya*). So according to this verse, the *ubhatabhāgavimutto* arahant, at least, may properly be called a *buddha*.

The Buddha in another place[79] considers what it means to be called a *brāhmaṇa*, which in the Buddhist sense means the true religieux. Once again in *gāthā* we read :

> He who has cut the strap [hatred], the thong [craving], and the rope [heresies], together with the appendages [latent tendencies], who has thrown the cross-bar [ignorance], who is enlightened [*buddha*]—him I call a *brāhmaṇa*.

Here we see, in an even earlier *gāthā*, the application of the epithet *buddha* to one whom, by its own terms, we would call a *paññāvimutto*. There are no references to the *abhiññā*, either

---

78. M.II.144. (My translation)
Pubbenivāsaṃ yo vedi saggāpāyañ ca passati,
Atho jātikkhayaṃ patto, abhiññā vosito muni.
Cittaṃ visuddhaṃ jānāti muttaṃ rāgehi sabbaso
Pahīnajātimaraṇo brahmacariyassa kevalī
Pāragū sabbadhammānaṃ Buddho tādi pavuccatīti.

79. Dhammapada.XXVI.16. (Nārada translation)
Chetvā naddhiṃ varattañ ca sandāmaṃ sahanukkamaṃ.
Ukkhittapaḷighaṃ buddhaṃ taṃ ahaṃ brūmi brāhmaṇaṃ.

explicit or implied, yet the term *buddha* is employed. This verse is clearly referring to one who is enlightened in the dry sense (*sukhavipassako*).

Of course, the question might be raised that in the standard epithets of the Buddha, we find not only arahant but also *sambuddha*, and it might be argued that perhaps, while the arahant might be a *buddha* and vice versa, it might be that the epithet *sambuddha*, which could only be applied to Gotama and the Buddhas of each aeon, has a connotation different from and wider than the simple *buddha*. Just this question was anticipated by Lord Chalmers,[80] one of the pioneers of modern Pali scholarship. He writes :

> Whilst the title of '*Sambuddha*' (or more fully : '*Bhagavā Arahaṃ Sammā-sambuddha*') is restricted to him whom we call 'the Buddha' (or to his apocryphal seven—later twenty-five—forerunners of other aeons), and whilst the uncompounded form '*buddha*' throughout the Canon usually has the same denotation, there are in the *Sutta-Nipāta* some half dozen instances of its use in a more extended sense so as to embrace '*catusacca-buddhā ariya-puggalā*' (Pj.II.374), i.e. 'the Noble ones who are alive to the Four Truths' of Buddhism. These instances of the plural use of *buddhā* in the *Sutta-Nipāta* occur, it will be found, in *triṣṭubh* stanzas, indicated above as the oldest material of this book; and it seems *a priori* probable that what was in Buddhism at first a title open to all bhikkhus of highest 'comprehension' or 'enlightenment' (cf. verse 386 d.), came later to be confined to the Founder alone.

This restriction of a particular epithet for the founder of a religion was the practice in Jainism, not Buddhism. Miss Horner[81] tells us that the Jaina usage of the term 'arahant' differs primarily in that it was restricted to the founders (or discoverers, *tirthantika*) of the religion, and was inapplicable to the saints of the religion in general. Of course, in Jainism the founder of the religion was considered omniscient in a very different sense than the Buddha was thought to be omniscient, if indeed he could be so considered in any sense. Thus, the scope of knowledge of the Jaina religious leader was in principle different from that avail-

80. Lord Chalmers, "Introduction" to *Buddha's Teaching*, *op. cit.*, p. xix.
81. Horner, *EBTMP*, pp. 72-73.

able to the practitioners of that faith; thus the reservation to him alone of his epithets, including 'arahant,' seems to follow from the logic of his being claimed to be omniscient. If, however, the Buddha is understood as either (a) not omniscient, or (b) omniscient in a particular sense such that we could all, in principle, be omniscient, then there would not be this reason for reserving any particular epithet, be it 'arahant,' '*buddha*,' or even '*sammāsambuddha*,' for the Buddha alone. We shall explore these possibilities in more detail below; but for the moment let us content ourselves with the tentative claim that in Buddhism, especially in the earliest texts, thus far we have found no epithet that could not be applied to both the Buddha and an arahant.

In one place[82] the Buddha is asked if he knows of any others who are his equal in the particular sense of having mastered the three *pāṭihāriya*. The *pāṭihāriya*, which could be rendered as 'miracles,' are :[83] (1) the miracle of psychic power (*iddhi-pāṭihāriya*); (2) the miracle of telepathy or mind-reading (*ādesanā-pāṭihāriya*); and (3) the miracle of teaching (*anusāsanī-pāṭihāriya*). Especially significant for our discussion is the third of these miracles, and we shall return to the arahant as teacher below. The greater import of this *pāṭihāriya* of teaching is acknowledged by the Buddha in another *sutta*.[84] The question thus posed, the Buddha replies :[85]

> Yes indeed, brahmin. The monks possessed of these three marvellous powers are not just one or two or three, four or five hundred, but much more than that in number.

Thus, at least in terms of this one significant doctrinal formula, the three *pāṭihāriya*, the Buddha readily admits that many of his followers are his equal.

The Buddha also says that the method by which he became liberated is the same method by which his followers could so become. We read :[86]

---

82. A.I.172.
83. See Nyāṇatiloka, *Buddhist Dictionary*, p. 136.
84. A.III.61.
85. A.I.172. (PTS translation)
Na kho brāhmaṇa ekaṃ yeva sataṃ na dve satāni na tīṇi satāni na cattāri satāni na pañca sattāni atha kho bhiyyo va ye bhikkhū imehi tīhi pātihāriyehi samannāgatā ti.
86. S.IV.105. (My translation)
Mayhaṃ kho bhikkhave yoniso manasikārā yoniso sammappadhānā

> Monks, I have won the freedom that is beyond the world [*anuttarā vimutti*], I have actualized the freedom that is beyond the world, by means of thorough application of mind [*yoniso manasikārā*] and by means of thorough right effort [*yoniso sammappadhānā*]. You, also, win the freedom that is beyond the world, actualize the freedom that is beyond the world, by means of thorough application of mind, and by means of thorough right effort.

Thus it would seem that if the method by which one attains the *vimutti* that is beyond the world is the same for the Buddha and for the potential arahant, then the possibility of a significant difference between the Buddha and the arahant is diminished. Put simply, if the method by which one attains a goal is identical, then it would seem to follow that the goal is also identical.

The Buddha, in another place,[87] seems to be saying just that. Here the Buddha is discoursing about all the *jhānā* and *iddhi* that he has attained, and that Mahā Kassapa has attained as much. He concludes this discourse by saying :[88]

> I, monks, dwell, having actualized here and now the higher knowledges [*abhiññā*], freed through the heart/mind and freed through wisdom. Kassapa, too, monks, dwells, having actualized here and now the higher knowledges, freed through the heart/mind and freed through wisdom.

Here the Buddha is describing, in identical terminology, the spiritual attainments of himself and one of his foremost arahant disciples, Mahā Kassapa. Of course, it should be noted that Mahā Kassapa is clearly the *ubhatabhāgavimutto* type of arahant.

One bit of specious evidence that might be offered in support of this contention that the Buddha and the arahant are equal, is the fact that a Buddha, an arahant, a *paccekabuddha* and a *cakkavatti* are all said by the Buddha to be worthy of having

---

anuttarā vimutti anuppattā anuttarā vimutti sacchikatā. Tumhe pi bhikkhave yoniso manasikārā yoniso sammappadhānā anuttaraṃ vimuttiṃ anupāpuṇātha anuttaraṃ vimuttiṃ sacchikarothā ti.

87. S.II.210-214.

88. S.II.214. (My translation)
Ahañca bhikkhave āsavānaṃ khayā anāsavanaṃ cetovimuttiṃ paññāvimuttiṃ diṭṭheva dhamme sayam abhiññā sacchikatvā upasampajja viharāmi. Kassapo pi bhikkhave āsavānaṃ khayā anāsavanaṃ cetovimuttiṃ paññāvimuttiṃ diṭṭheva dhamme sayam abhiññā sacchikatvā viharatīti.

their relics worshipped in a *thūpa* (Sanskrit : *stūpa*; Tibetan : *mcod rten*; = reliquary).[89] This does not, however, necessarily imply any sort of equivalence of spiritual attainment. In the commentary to this verse,[90] we are told that a *cakkavatti* is allowed *a thūpa* and not an ordinary saintly monk, for two reasons : (1) because the *cakkavatti* is rare; and (2) if the ordinary saintly monk were afforded a *thūpa*, then the island of Siṃhaladīpa (Lanka) would become too overcrowded. Thus, if one believes the commentary, the criterion for deserving a *thūpa* is not spirituality but singularity—and this for ecological reasons.

One way in which the Buddha is distinct from the arahant is that he is a shower of a way not shown before (*maggakkhayin*).[91] In one place,[92] the Buddha explicitly says that it is this feature of him as *maggakkhayin* that distinguishes him from another monk who is an arahant. A similar point is made in the *Itivuttaka*,[93] also in verse :

> The teacher, the great sage, is the first in the world; second to him is the disciple who has cultivated himself; third is the student [*sekho*] who has heard much [*bahussuto*] and has upheld morality [*sīla*]. These three, teachers of gods and humans, carry the light [*pabhaṃkarā*], preach the Dhamma, open the gates to the deathless [*amata*], and lead many to freedom from that which binds them. They follow the caravan leader, practising the way so well taught, here and now going from suffering to the deathless, practising the Sugata's religion.

From this verse we get the idea of the Buddha as a 'first among equals.' He is the primary focus of the religious life, but is distinguished only in that he is the teacher (*setthā*), and is therefore the first in the world (*loke paṭhamo*). Second are those

89. A.II.245.
90. Cited in *Dialogues of the Buddha*, II, p. 156.
91. M.III.8.
92. S.III.66.
93. Iti.79-80. (My translation)
Satthā hi loke paṭhamo mahesi tass-anvayo sāvako bhāvitatto athāparo pāṭipado pi sekho bahussuto sīlavatūpapanno. Ete tayo devamanussa-seṭṭhā pabhaṃkarā dhammamudīrayantā apāvuṇanti amatassa dvāraṃ yogā pamocenti bahujanaṃ te. Ye satthavāhena anuttarena sudesitaṃ maggamanukkamanti idh-eva dukkhassa karoṇti antaṃ ye appamattā sugatassa sāsane ti.

disciples who have cultivated themselves (*sāvako bhāvitatto*), the arahants; and last are those who are still in training (*sekho*). All of them, according to this verse, are identical in terms of teaching. It should be kept in mind here that these sections of the *Khuddaka Nikāya* are thought by linguists to be the oldest portions of the *Sutta Piṭaka*, and we see here again that it was commonly held at that time that the Buddha and the arahant could not be significantly distinguished. Here—to repeat—the only distinction that could be made is one in terms of precedence.

Similarly, the Buddha says of himself :[94]

> I am one who has gone beyond everything. I know everything. I am detached from all *dhammā*. I have given up everything, freed in the destruction of all craving [*taṇhā*]. [Having actualized] the *abhiññā* by myself, to whom should I point [as my teacher] ?

Miss Horner comments :[95]

> In these respects, not a single monk resembles him; his disciples are not Way-showers but Way-followers, not one of whom was designated either by the Lord or by the Order to be the mainstay, arbiter or support (*paṭisaraṇa*) for the others after his passing.

That the Buddha is offered such greater homage than any of the arahants has been explained to us by this analogy :[96] that while we may respect, say, the manufacturer of a light bulb, we certainly do not revere him as we do Edison, who invented the light bulb. While the bulbs made by Edison and by the factory are the same, it is Edison whom we admire by virtue of his having invented this item. Likewise, it was the Buddha and only he who discovered Dhamma; others may practise it and get identical results, but that does not in any sense equal his magnificent achievement.

Bhikshu Sangharakshita makes the same point :[97]

> It is not when we merely do a thing, but when we do it *for the*

---

94. Dhammapada.XXIV.20. (My translation)
 Sabbābhibhū sabbavidū 'ham asmi; sabbesu dhammesu anūpalitto.
 Sabbañjaho taṇhakkhaye vimutto; sayaṃ abhiñña kam uddiseyyaṃ.

95. I. B. Horner, "Translator's Introduction" to *The Middle Length Sayings*, III, pp. xiii-xiv.

96. Personal communication from Nyāṇaponika Mahāthera.

97. Sangharakshita, *Survey*, pp. 42-43.

> *first time*, that the most formidable obstacles are encountered. We therefore honour the Master not only as an Arahant, or one by whom Nirvāṇa has been attained, but as a Buddha, as one Who, having qualified Himself for the superhumanly difficult task by practising the Ten Perfections for an incalculable number of lives, without a teacher and without a guide breaks through the obstacles which block the road to Nirvāṇa and throws it open once more to the traffic of humanity.

Here Sangharakshita speaks aptly as to why the Buddhist reveres the Buddha so much more than an arahant, but his reference to the practice of the perfections (*pāramitā*) might tend toward some confusion.

The *pāramitā* were the homoletic points of the *jātaka* tradition, which related various incidents in the previous lives of the Buddha, and which are enormously popular in all Buddhist countries. Some of these were taken from the *suttas* themselves; others seem to be later accretions. Well before the codification of the *jātaka*, however, there was the tradition of the *apadāna*, as found in the Mahāpadāna Sutta of the *Dīgha Nikāya*. According to Rhys-Davids,[98] the *apadānā* were the life-stories of an arahant, quite possibly stories from a previous life, since many arahants had developed the *abhiññā* of remembering previous existences. In the *sutta* in question, the term *apadāna* was used for a story of a previous life of the Buddha, and Rhys-Davids quite logically concludes that the term '*apadāna*' was used to refer to the previous life stories of *any* arahant, the Buddha included. Gradually, however, a terminological distinction was arrived at, *apadāna* being reserved for the disciple arahants, and *jātaka* used exclusively for life stories of the Buddha.

One statement we found made about the Buddha, but never about an arahant, is that he is born for the welfare of the world[99]:

> Monks, there is one person whose birth in the world is for the welfare of many folk, for the happiness of many folk, who is

98. Rhys-Davids,"Introduction" to *Dialogues of the Buddha*, II, p. 3.

99. A.I.22.; and cf. M.I.110. (PTS translation)
Ekapuggalo bhikkhave -oke uppajjamāno uppajjati bahujanahitāya bahujanasukhāya lokānukampāya atthāya hitāya sukhāya devamanussānaṃ. Katamo ekapuggalo ? Tathāgato arahaṃ sammā sambuddho. Ayam kho bhikkhave ekapuggalo loke uppajjamāno.

> born out of compassion for the world, for the profit [*atthāya*; a better reading for which would be "for the goal or aim"], welfare and happiness of *devas* and mankind. Who is that one person ? It is a Tathāgata, who is Arahant, a fully Enlightened One. This, monks, is that one person.

We do not wish to decide whether or not the arahant, after attaining *arahattā*, could or could not be said to live for the benefit of the world, et cetera, as the Buddha. This shall be considered in full when we turn to the question of the relationship of the arahant to society. But we must conclude from this statement of the Buddha that only he is born for the benefit of the world, a position which, in time, came to lead commentators to arrive at a type of docetic view of the Buddha.

Also, this verse can serve to introduce us to the term '*tathāgata*,' which, after '*bhagavā*,' is the most frequently used epithet of the Buddha. Derived from either or both *tathā+gata*, 'thus-gone,' or from *tathā+āgata*, 'thus come,' its etymology has been discussed by Buddhaghoṣa. In the *Sumaṅgala-vilāsinī*,[100] he says that:

> . . .the Tathāgatas are those who have come (*tathā āgato*) in the same way as the previous Tathāgatas, i.e., all of them embraced the recluse life, went through a long and arduous process of self-abnegation, perfected themselves in the highest meditation, and ultimately realized the Truth. After rendering benefit to countless human beings, they passed away from the mortal world (*tathā gato*). They realized the same and unchangeable (*tathalakkhaṇa*) Truth. They comprehended and propounded the same four ariyan truths (*ariyasaccāni tathādhamma*). They visualized the phenomenal world in the same manner (*tathādassitā*). They spoke the truth (*tathāvāditā*) only from the day of attainment of bodhi to *mahāparinibbāna*. They acted according to their words (*tathākāritā*). They surpassed (*abhibhavaṭṭhena*) all beings of the highest heaven or the lowliest hell, and lastly they realized the same truth (*tatthāya gato*), which governs the world.

Of course, all of this could be said of an arahant just as well; however, the tradition of successive Buddhas, according to Rhys-Davids,[101]

---

100. *Sumaṅgala-vilāsinī*, pp. 66-68; cited by Dutt, EMB, p. 296.
101. *Dialogues of the Buddha*, II, p. 2.

> . . .presupposes the conception of a Buddha as a different and more exalted personage than an Arahant. Now in our oldest documents, these two conceptions are still in a state of fusion. The word Buddha does not occur in its later, special, technical sense.

Rhys-Davids is indicating a perceived tendency in the Theravāda, and Buddhism in general, toward a more exalted view of the Buddha. This observation is seconded by Adikaram :[102]

> Whatever the reasons [whether the influence of the Lokottaravāda or for internal reasons] were, there is not the least doubt that the Theravādins, too, who 'adhered strictly to the realistic view of the person of their Master' did tend to some extent towards making the Buddha supernatural.

We would opt for the influence from Mahāyāna or quasi-Mahāyāna schools, although it seems that a 'supernatural' Buddha could be derived from the Pali texts, as could a 'naturalistic' one.

Supernatural or not, there are passages in the *Sutta Piṭaka* which emphasize the uniqueness of the Buddha. Most of these, as we have indicated, tell us that the Buddha discovered a way on his own (*sayaṃ*), and that he was a 'shower-of-the-way' (*maggakkhayin*) rather than a follower (*sāvaka*). This is clearly indicated by Ānanda in the Gopakamoggallāna Sutta,[103] where he is asked if there is even one way in which the Buddha is different from all other beings, including the arahant disciples. Ānanda replies :

> There is not even one monk, brahmin, who is possessed in every way and in every part of all those things of which the Lord was possessed, perfected one, fully Self-Awakened One. For, brahmin, the Lord was the one to make arise a Way that had not arisen. . .; he is a knower of the Way, an

102. Adikaram, *EHBC*, p. 96.

103. M.III.8. (PTS translation)

Na 'tthi kho, brāhmaṇa, ekabhikkhu pi tehi dhammehi sabbena sabbaṃ sabbathā sabbaṃ samannāgato, yehi dhammehi samannāgato so Bhagavā anuppannassa maggassa uppādetā asañjātassa maggassa sañjāneta, yehi dhammehi samannāgato so Bhagavā ahosi arahaṃ sammāsambuddho. So hi, brāhmaṇa, Bhagavā anuppannassa maggassa akhātā, maggaññū maggavidū maggakovido. Maggānugā ca pana etarehi sāvakā viharanti pacchā samannāgatā ti.

understander of the Way, skilled in the Way. But the disciples are now Way-followers, following after him.

Perhaps it was just for this reason that it was taught that there could be one and only one Buddha in a given world-system in one aeon. Sakka, chief of one of the classes of the *devā*, says :[104] "Nowhere, gentlemen, and at no time is it possible that, in one and the same world-system, two Arahant Buddhas supreme should arise together, neither before nor after the other. This can in no wise be." One very simple reason for this is that if a Buddha is characterized as one who discovers a way which had not been discovered before, then there simply cannot be two 'firsts' in the same world-system. One need not bring any 'supernatural' Buddha into the exegesis of this *sutta*.

Of course, one way in which talk about the Buddha differs from talk about an arahant is in the canonical *bodhisatta* doctrine, especially as found in the Mahāpadāna Suttanta,[105] and the related doctrines about the *mahāpurisa* and his thirty-two marks.[106] These doctrines become especially important in the bodhisattva doctrine of the Mahāyâna, especially as found in the *Bodhisattva-bhūmi* by Asaṅga,[107] and are also crucial for understanding the development of tantric deity-yoga (*yi dam kyi rnal 'byor*) practices, according to Tsong kha pa.[108] According to these later developments in Buddhism, the miraculous teachings about the bodhisattva as found in Pali and other texts, as well as the doctrine of the thirty-two marks of the great man (*mahāpurisa*), are not merely popular pietism, but have a tremendous symbolic vitality. Perhaps this interpretation of this doctrine, which is found in all forms of Buddhism, is most clearly explicated in tantric practice texts. In the context of our discussion of the

104. D.xix.14. (PTS translation)
Aṭṭhānaṃ kho etaṃ mārisā anavakāso yaṃ ekissā lokadhātuyā dve arahanto sammā-sambuddhā apubbaṃ acarimaṃ upajjeyyuṃ. N' etaṃ ṭhānaṃ vijjati.
Cf.M.III.65. and D.xxviii.19.

105. D.xiv.

106. D.xiv.1.32; cf. Lakkhaṇa Sutta, D.xxx.1.2., which deals specifically with this notion.

107. See Asaṅga (Thogs med), *Yogacaryābhūmanu Bodhisattvabhūmi* (*rNal 'byor spyod pa'i sa las byang chub sems dpa'i sa*), *bsTan 'gyur* 'mDo 'grel, Vol. zhi, Peking edition, fasc. 171b.

108. Tsong kha pa, *sNgags rim chen mo*, pp. 60ff.

Theravāda, this doctrine has received almost no serious attention, and such talk is relegated to the popular realm. However, if *kāya* is understood as an intentionality-structure in the sense that, according to Buddhism, intentionality (*saṅkhāra*) is prior to its embodiment (*kāya*); and if the marks, miraculous birth tales, et cetera, are related to this intentionality-structuring, then perhaps it could be argued that the embodiment into this *kāya*, as symbolically related in the Mahāpadāna Suttanta by the Buddha, indicates the development of a specific type of intentionality which better enables him (or, for that matter, any arahant) to successfully teach the Dhamma, which in the Mahāyāna is precisely this intentionality.[109] To put this matter more simply, one attains a Buddha-body in order to better enable him to teach, and the meditative practices here involve contemplation of these thirty-two marks, miraculous births, et cetera, as a way of motivating one towards that goal.

We hasten to point out, however, that to the best of our knowledge, this type of interpretation was never offered within the Theravāda commentatorial tradition. However, an open-minded reading of the Pali texts would not rule it out, either. Nor would this interpretation conflict with other Theravāda teachings, as there is nothing that would prevent an arahant from assuming the type of intentionality-structure that would be best suited for the promulgation of the Dhamma.

What the Theravāda commentatorial tradition in fact did with these materials, however, was gradually to concede some special status to the Buddha, a status above and beyond that arising from simple precedence. We find such attitudes as early as the *Milindapañha*,[110] and in the *Paramatthajotikā*, the commentary to the *Khuddaka Nikāya*,[111] we find a new classification of sentient

109. Kong sprul, *Shes bya kun khyab*, *op. cit.*, enters upon a lengthy and detailed discussion of the intentionality or aspiration (*smon*) of the bodhisattva, much of which revolves around the language of acquiring a Buddha-body (*lus*) as the way of attaining the means (*thabs*) for perfected teaching. See especially the *'grel*, Vol. II, pp. 100-121.

110. *Milindapañha*, p. 104; as discussed by Maria Anna Geertruida Theresia Kloppenborg, *The Paccekabuddha : A Buddhist Ascetic*, Leiden : E. J. Brill, 1974, pp. 17-18.

111. *Paramatthajotikā*, I.177-178; also discussed by Kloppenborg, *op. cit.*, p. 16.

beings. This classification is rigid, and it starts with animals and then proceeds to humans, who are divided into men and women, the former having a higher status. Men are divided as householders (*agārikā*) and those who have left the household life behind (*anāgārikā*), the latter being higher. This category is then divided between ordinary ones (*puthujjanā*) and holy ones (*ariyā*). These are said to be either in training (*sekhā*) or beyond further training (*asekhā*), or the arahants. These are either *sukhavipassakā*, or the *paññāvimuttā*, or the *samathayānikā*, practitioners of *samatha* meditations, which is to say the *ubhatabhāgavimuttā*. Those *samathayānikā* who have attained the perfections (*pāramitā*) are called *sāvakapāramippattā*, and are higher than those who have not, the *appattā*. Next come the *paccekabuddhā*, who are said to be higher than any of the *sāvakā* by a wide margin, and who in turn are said to be far inferior to a Buddha. Such categorizations resemble closely those found in the Sarvāstivāda text, the *Abhidharmakośa*,[112] and open the Theravāda to the type of criticisms which the Mahāyāna raised against what they perceived as the 'Hīnayāna.' Certainly, by the time of the compilation of this type of commentatorial literature, a lot of water had passed between it and the canonical equation or near-equation of the arahant and the Buddha.

Returning to the *Sutta Piṭaka* and its usual interpretations, we find that one way in which the Buddha is said to be distinct from the arahant is that the former is omniscient (*sabbaññā*), while the latter is not. We reject this interpretation for the following reasons : first of all, if indeed the Buddha is omniscient, he is omniscient in a particular Buddhist sense of something like 'all knowing regarding spiritual matters'; and second, we would maintain that, in this restricted sense, the arahant is equally accomplished. To present our case, we shall consider what is said in the *Sutta Piṭaka* regarding claims of omniscience predicated of the Buddha and some of his contemporaries, especially of or by Mahāvīra, the *tirthantika* of Jainism.

The Buddha is very interested in the causal process (*paṭiccasamuppāda*) by which predications of omniscience arise. In the Cūḷadukkhakkhanda Sutta,[113] the Buddha encounters some

112. See Conze, *BTI*, pp. 169-170.

113. M.I.92-93.

Jaina monks engaged in the practice of austerities. The Buddha asks why they are so engaged, and the monks reply that their leader, Nāthaputta (an appellation of Mahāvīra), being omniscient, teaches that these austere practices lead to the realm of non-flowing (*anavassavo*), which is to say, *dukkhanirodha* or *nibbāna*. The sense in which they define omniscience is :[114] "all-knowing, all-seeing, he claims all-embracing knowledge and vision," a faculty which entails, according to Jaina teachings, that while "walking or standing still or asleep or awake, knowledge-and-vision is permanently and continuously before me." The Buddha does not categorically reject such a claim; rather, he examines it. He asks each of these monks whether or not they themselves have such knowledge, to which they reply that they have not. The Buddha thereby reduces the claim of the Jainas to a belief, that they have claimed that which they have no grounds to claim, and the Buddha might request them that, if they wish to recite poetry, then they should do so outside of the context of making serious, rational statements. Belief as such is taught by the Buddha to be an unsatisfactory basis for a religion. He characterizes his teaching as one in which a monk could express *aññā*, or attain *arahattā*, apart from belief, inclination, hearsay, argument, reflection on reasons or speculation.[115] In one place,[116] he chides Bhaddiya to avoid all teachings which are based on such beliefs, et cetera. Jayatilleke[117] has analyzed the Buddha's attitude towards a religious teaching (*sāsana*) which is based on the claim of a teacher's omniscience, and which is similar to any religious claim based on scripture, such as Nyāya-Vaiśeṣika and the other orthodox Hindu systems, to the extent that a claimed infallible source (either sacred texts or omniscient teachers) is dependent upon the fallible memory and reasoning of a disciple. Both *śruti* (scripture) and *sabbaññā* (omniscience) are described by the Buddha as among the ten unsatisfactory

114. M.I.92. : Sabbaññū sabbadassāvī aparissaṃ ñāṇadassanaṃ paṭijānissati.

115. S.IV.138-139.
yam pariyāyaṃ āgamma bhikkhu aññatreva saddhāya aññatra ruciyā aññatrānussavā aññatrākāraparivitakkā aññatra diṭṭhinijjhāna-khantiyā aññam vyākareyya. . .

116. A.II.191.

117. Jayatilleke, *EBTK*, chapters IV and V; most especially pp. 202-204.

bases for a *sāsana*.[118] In the Sandaka Sutta,[119] religion based on such claims as omniscience is one of the four types which are not necessarily false, but yet unsatisfactory, as the Buddha found that, upon analysis, some claims of those said to be omniscient were indeed valid, but not necessarily so. Furthermore, even in such cases where the claims were found to be valid, their basis was unsatisfactory because it relied not on the effort and direct knowledge (*paññā*) of the practitioner, but on his possibly faulty memory.

The Buddha was unhappy not only with claims of omniscience of the teachers of other systems; he seemed to be unhappy with claims of his own omniscience. There is a well-known example of this attitude in the Mahāparinibbāna Suttanta[120] wherein Sāriputta, who is said by tradition to be the most advanced disciple of the Buddha in terms of wisdom, approaches the Buddha, salutes him and hails him as omniscient, the wisest of all religious teachers. The Buddha notes how grandly Sāriputta is speaking, and asks him if he has personally known all religious teachers of all times. At Sāriputta's confused denial, the Buddha then asks him on what grounds he makes such grand claims, why he sings so ecstatically. Here we find that the Buddha is saying that even if he is omniscient, it would take another omniscient being to know it. The Buddha here is assiduous in maintaining that if he allows even his beloved disciples like Sāriputta to speak beyond that which they have a basis for claiming, even in a fit of piety, he would open up the unwanted possibility of all sorts of religious claiming. He does not want anyone to be hailed as omniscient, be it Mahāvīra or himself, because for Buddhism a highly serious human disease is the tendency to claim despite the lack of grounds for such claiming, an expression of the craving for speculation (*diṭṭhitaṇhā*).

In other instances, the Buddha, after rejecting omniscience as naïvely understood by some of his contemporaries, does give us an indication of what type of knowledge he does have, all of which will lead us to see what a Buddhist use of omniscience (*sabbaññā*)

118. A.I.189.
119. M.I.519-520.
120. D.xvi.1.16; repeated in the Sampasādaniya Suttanta, D.xxviii.1ff.

might be. In the Trivijja-Vacchagotta Sutta,[121] he is asked whether it would be correct to say that he was omniscient in the following sense : "all-knowing, all-seeing; he claims all-embracing knowledge-and-vision, saying : Whether I am walking or standing still or asleep or awake, knowledge-and-vision is permanently and continuously before me." As we have indicated before, this was precisely the type of omniscience which, according to Buddhist sources, was predicated of Mahāvīra and, we may surmise, was the most common denotation of the term '*sabbaññā*' in India at that time, and which is not far from classical western theological notions of omniscience. The Buddha says that such a claim would be incorrect, and that he would prefer his interlocator, Vacchagotta, to say that he was a 'threefold-knowledge man' (*tivijja*), which means that he : (a) knows his former lives; (b) by means of the *dibbacakkhu*, he knows the farings of beings according to their *kamma*; and (c) that he is liberated by means of the destruction of the *āsavā*.[122] We are, of course, quite familiar with these three knowledges (*tivijja*) in the context of the *abhiññā*, as they directly correspond to : (a) *pubbenivāsānussatiñāṇa*; (b) *yathākammūpagatañāṇa*, one of the products of the *dibbacakkhu*; and (c) *āsavakkhaya*. In our discussion of the *abhiññā*, herein presented under the rubric of the *tivijja*, we saw that these were outgrowths of the practice of the *jhānā*, practised by all *ubhatabhāgavimutto* arahants. The implications of this last point shall be taken up below, but here we wish to indicate that rather than be claimed omniscient in the usual sense, the Buddha prefers to be called one having the *tivijja*, and that these three knowledges are none other than three of the six *abhiññā*.

In the Achariyabbhutadhamma Sutta,[123] Ānanda is, like Sāriputta, hailing the Buddha. While he is not specifically

121. M.I.481-483.

122. See also Edward J. Thomas, *The History of Buddhist Thought*, London : Routledge & Kegan Paul, 2nd ed., 1951 (1933), p. 148, for a discussion of this verse.

123. M.III.124. (PTS translation) ¦
Tasmātiha tvaṃ Ānanda idam pi Tathāgatassa acchariyaṃ abbhuta-dhammaṃ dhārehi : Idh' Ānanda Tathāgatassa viditā vedanā uppajj-anti, viditā upaṭṭhahanti, viditā abbhatthaṃ gacchanti; viditā sannā; viditā vitakkā uppajjanti, viditā upaṭṭhahanti, viditā abbhatthaṃ

referring to omniscience, he is discoursing on the wonders and marvellous qualities (*acchariyaṃ abbhutadhammaṃ*) of the Tathāgata, such as his bodhisattvic residence in Tusita, his immaculate conception, miraculous birth, and other such mythic trends found in the *Sutta Piṭaka.* The Buddha does not directly comment on such language, but rather requests Ānanda to pay more attention to that which is more serious, to that which is significant in the *sāsana.* He says :

> Wherefore do you, Ānanda, regard this too as a wonder, a marvellous quality of the Tathāgata's : As to this, Ānanda, the feelings [*vedanā*] that arise in the Tathāgata are known; known they persist; known they go to destruction; perceptions [*saññā*] are known; the thoughts that arise are known; known they persist; known they go to destruction. So do you, Ānanda, regard this too as a wonder, a marvellous quality of the Tathāgata's.

Thus we see a similar structure in the Buddha's encounters with Ānanda and Vacchagotta. In both cases, the Buddha is presented with a supernaturalistic statement about himself, either omniscience in the first case or, in Ānanda's case, a telling of the last birth of the bodhisattva. In neither case does the Buddha deny what is being said, but he directs the speaker's attention to something he considers to be of greater spiritual significance : the three knowledges (*tivijja*), or the mindfulness of feelings, notions and the like. In both cases, that which is considered more spiritually significant is that which is attainable by any follower of the Dhamma. In the first case, the *tivijja* are attainable by the practice of the *jhānā*, and in the second case, the mindfulness of which the Buddha speaks is like a description of *sati* meditation. Of course the former is especially cultivated by the *ubhatabhāgavimutti*, and the latter by the *paññāvimutti.* One point which could be made at this time is that even if the Buddha is omniscient, his *sāsana* is not dependent on this omniscience for its effectiveness : the practices of *jhānā* and *sati* are indicated by the Buddha as being the crux of the matter, and not talk about omniscience.

---

gacchanti. Idam pi kho tvaṃ Ānanda Tathāgatassa acchariyaṃ abbhutadhammaṃ dhārehīti.

In the Kaṇṇakatthala Sutta,[124] the Buddha actually denies the possibility of omniscience as popularly understood by his contemporaries. He says : "There is neither a recluse nor a brāhmaṇa who at one and the same time can know all, can see all—this situation does not exist." This, of course, is precisely the type of omniscience of which the Jaina monks were speaking. Now the question must be raised as to how the Buddha, who refused to allow his disciples to make claims beyond what they could and did actually know, could make such a statement without being so omniscient himself, lest he be a hypocrite who has different grounds for discourse for himself and for his disciples. The answer is that he allows for a special, Buddhist sense of omniscience to be employed and, presumably, since he is denying the Jaina omniscience, he must have the Buddhist sense of omniscience. This special sense is indicated in the same *sutta* when he refuses to say[125] : "There is neither a recluse nor a brāhmaṇa who, all-knowing, all-seeing, can claim all-embracing knowledge-and-vision—this situation does not exist." In refusing to deny this second possibility, and by categorically denying omniscience in a Jaina sense, the Buddha leaves us with the task of analyzing the significant distinctions to be found between these two omnisciences.

The Jaina omniscience means knowing everything at once, a kind of vision which is actually permanently present before the *tirthantika.* The Buddha's omniscience is not continually present; that is to say that he could, if he wished, know all things, but does not actually know everything at one moment. This distinction is emphasized by Mookerjee :[126]

> By omniscience the Buddhist does not mean that the Buddha had necessarily the detailed knowledge of all things and events occurring in the universe in the past, present and future.

---

124. M.II.126-128. (PTS translation)
Na 'tthi so samaṇo vā brāhmaṇo vā yo sakideva sabbañ ñassati sabbaṃ dakkhīti, n' etaṃ ṭhānaṃ vijjatīti.

125. M.II.126-128. (PTS translation)
Na 'tthi samaṇo vā brāhmaṇo vā yo sabbaññū sabbadassāvī aparisesaṃ ñāṇadassanaṃ paṭijānissati n' etaṃ ṭhānaṃ vijjatīti.

126. S. Mookerjee, "The Omniscient as the Founder of a Religion," The Nava-Nalanda-Mahavihara Research Publication, Vol. II, Patna : Nava Nalanda Mahavihara, n.d. (ca. 1960), pp. 1-44, p. 19.

> What he wants to prove is that the Buddha developed an immaculate power of vision to which the secrets of religion, namely, the ways and means of acquiring provisional and eternal blessedness, presented themselves without obstruction. Whether the Buddha knew the entire number of atoms and hairs of his body is a trivial question. Of course to the enlightened vision of the Buddha, nothing is a sealed book and so he must have known all these trivialities if this was the necessary concomitant of the knowledge of the eternal spiritual mysteries, viz., the conditions of heaven and hell and emancipation.

Mookerjee's point, which we feel is well taken, is that the Buddha's omniscience was a spiritual omniscience; he perfected skill in discovering and teaching the Dhamma, the primary characteristic and *sine qua non* of what it means to be a Buddha. Insofar as mundane knowledge (Mookerjee's example of the number of atoms and hairs on his body) is required to present the Dhamma, the Buddha must in principle know it, and therefore it remains meaningful for a Buddhist to talk about the Buddha's omniscience in a mundane as well as a spiritual sense. As there could be no obstacle to the Buddha's teaching the Dhamma, then even mundane trivialities could not block him. Therefore, he had to be able to know, in principle, these details. This is not to say, as did the Jaina monks, that he actually knew them, or that he needed to know them. Rather, the Buddhist is content to say that the Buddha knew whatever was necessary for him to know in order to teach the Dhamma in an unimpeded manner. And this, we would offer, is precisely the Buddhist usage of the term 'omniscience' (*sabbaññā*).

In the Pāṭika Sutta,[127] the Buddha says that he knows *aggañña* and even *uttaritara*. This *sutta* is easily misunderstood as referring to a Jaina-type omniscience, but our analysis will return to its context of omniscience as the ability to teach unobstructedly. The standard translation of the Buddha's remarks is :

> The ultimate beginning of things [*aggañña*] I know, Bhaggava,

127. D.xxiv.2.14. (PTS translation)
Aggaññañ cāhaṃ Bhaggava pajānāmi, tañ ca pajānāmi, tato ca uttaritaraṃ pajānāmi, tañ ca pajānānaṃ na parāmasāmi, aparāmasato me paccattaṃ yeva nibbuti viditā yad abhijānaṃ Tathāgato no anayaṃ āpajjati.

> and I know not only that, but more than that [*uttaritara*]. And while I know that, I do not pervert it. And as one not perverting it, I even of myself have understood that Peace [*nibbuti*], that which realizing, a Tathāgata can fall into no error.

In the first place, a discussion of the terms '*aggañña*' and '*uttaritara*' seems to be in order.

Aggañña means the highest knowledge, although the translator apparently followed the commentatorial gloss of 'the history of the genesis and course of the world' (*lokuppaticariyavaṃsa*), thus deriving 'the ultimate beginning of things,' a reading which is not justified from the text itself. However, one must remember that the world (*loka*), according to Buddhism, is not the naïvely or benevolently given, but a situation in which the 'I' finds itself problematical. Thus, to know both the genesis and the history of the *loka*, in a Buddhist sense, is to know the origin and development of that situation, or succession of situations, in which the person is a problem to and of himself. This verse surely should not be taken in any cosmological sense, as it appears many scholars who claim that the Buddha herein claims himself to be omniscient in a Jaina sense do interpret it. This possibility seems to be followed in the commentary, which glosses *uttaritara*, which simply means 'more than that,' as 'starting from virtue and concentration, I know even up to omniscient insight'. We would offer that, in knowing the origin and development of the human problematic, the Buddha's 'more than that' is that he knows the treatment for such problematics; that he is a therapist as well as a diagnostician. The 'omniscient insight' resulting from this therapy is none other than the ability to teach unobstructedly, the Buddhist sense of omniscience. Thus, the text goes on to discuss how the Buddha teaches without perversion, reinforcing our claim that all Buddhist omniscience-talk, at least that found in the *Sutta Piṭaka*, revolves in the context of perfected teaching, which entails a sort of omniscience in principle insofar as there are no possible obstacles to this type of teaching.

Having indicated the special Buddhist usage of 'omniscience' (*sabbaññā*), we may proceed to consider whether or not even this restricted sense is restricted to the Buddha, or whether it applies to all or some arahants as well. Of course, we have seen that the Buddha would prefer to talk about the three knowledges, or the six *abhiññā*, or even the ten powers (*balāni*), which will be discussed below, rather than to speak about any omniscience apart from its linguistic home of teaching. Still, in this context the Buddha clearly asserts that the arahants have available to them the same tools for teaching perfectly. We read him saying to his arahant disciples :[128]

> I am freed, bhikkhus, from all snares both celestial and human. Ye also, bhikkhus, are freed from all snares both celestial and human. Fare ye, bhikkhus, in a round that may be for the good of the many, for the happiness of the many, for love toward the world, for the advantage, the good, the happiness of gods and men.

His admonition goes on to tell them that, since there are beings who could understand their teachings, then they must go out in different directions to preach the Dhamma. Now what is being said here is that since the Buddha and the arahants are equally freed, therefore they must equally teach. Thus their liberation qualifies them to teach in the same way as the Buddha teaches; and, since this type of teaching entails, for the Buddhist, that it not be obstructed in any way, so the arahant's teaching must not be obstructed in any way. And we have seen that the Buddhist use of *sabbaññā* means the ability to teach without obstruction, then the arahants must also be possessed of *sabbaññā*. Therefore, we conclude that it would be a gross misrepresentation to make the claim that the Buddha and the arahant could be distinguished in terms of omniscience. Such a claim could only arise from a neglect of the contextual use of the term 'omniscience.' We offer that it is only through such contextual studies that the use or meaning of a Buddhist term could be derived, and our contextual studies have led us to the conclusion that a Buddhist sense of omniscience means the ability to teach unobstructedly. Since both the Buddha and the arahants teach unobstructedly, then it follows that omniscience is not a special predicate of the Buddha alone.

---

128. S.I.131-132. (PTS translation)
Mutto-haṃ bhikkhave sabbapāsehi ye dibbā ye ca mānusā. Tumhe pi bhikkhave muttā sa bbapāsehi ye dibbā ye ca mānusā caratha bhikkhave cārikaṃ bahujana-hitāya bahujana-sukhāya lokānukampakāya atthāya hitāya sukhāya devamanussānaṃ.

Along similar lines, we shall consider one more possible objection to our thesis that the Buddha and the arahant cannot be significantly distinguished in terms of their spiritual attainments, including the ability to teach unobstructedly, which is a direct implication of these attainments. While some Buddhists have held that the Buddha could be distinguished from the arahant by some special qualities or powers,[129] we offer that, in the *Sutta Piṭaka*, there is no evidence for such a claim. And rather than present the innumerable lists of attributes of one who is enlightened, we shall consider the powers (*balāni*), which were specifically thought by some Buddhists to indicate a difference between the Buddha and the arahant.

In the Mahāsīhanāda Sutta,[130] we find the following ten *balāni* of a Tathāgata :

1. He knows what actually is causal condition and what is not causal condition. *Ṭhānañca ṭhānato atthānañ ca atthānato yathābhūtaṃ pajānāti.*
2. He knows actually both the causal condition and the result of one's own *kammatic* accumulations in the past, present and future.
   Atītānāgatapaccuppanānaṃ kammassamādānānaṃ ṭhānaso hetuso vipākaṃ yathābhūtaṃ pajānāti.
3. He knows actually the way which goes to all good results. *Sabbatthagāminiṃ paṭipadaṃ yathābhūtam pajānāti.*
4. He actually knows the world in all its diversity of realms. *Anekadhātunādhātu-lokaṃ yathābhūtam pajānāti.*
5. He actually knows the dispositions of beings. *Sattānaṃ nānādhimuttikataṃ yathābhūtam pajānāti.*
6. He actually knows the superior and inferior faculties of other beings. *Parasattānaṃ parapuggalānaṃ indriyaparopariyattaṃ yathābhūtam pajānāti.*
7. He actually knows purification, the emergence from the *kilesā*, the attainments of concentration, the releases of

129. See, for example, the *Mahāvyutpatti*, ed. and tr. Alexander Csoma de Körös, *Sanskrit-Tibetan-English Vocabulary, Being an Edition of the Mahāvyutpatti*, Memoirs of the Royal Asiatic Society of Bengal, Vol. IV, No. 3, 1944, where one finds a discussion of what are called the 'eighteen special Buddhadharmas' (sangs rgyas kyi chos pa 'dris pa'i bco brgyad; āveṇika-buddha-dharmā).

130. M.I.69-71.

the *jhānā. Jhāna-vomokhasamādhi-samāpattīnaṃ saṅkilesaṃ vodānaṃ vuṭṭhānaṃ yathābhūtaṃ pajānāti.*

8. He remembers his many previous lives, [even] up to one lakh of lives. *Anekavihitaṃ pubbenivāsaṃ anussarati seyyathīdaṃ : ekam pi jātim. . .jātisatasahassam pi.*
9. He sees, with his purified clairvoyance, greater than that of other people, beings as they die and are reborn. He knows these beings according to their *kamma* : inferior, wise, handsome or ugly, well-gone or ill-gone. *Dibbena cakkhunā visuddhena atikkantamānusakena satte passati cavamāne upapajjamāne, hīne paṇīte suvaṇṇe dubbaṇṇe sugate duggate.*
10. He dwells, having actualized the *abhiññā*, here and now freed by the heart/mind and freed by *paññā*, the *āsavā* destroyed. *Āsavānaṃ khayā anāsavaṃ cetovimuttiṃ paññāvimuttiṃ diṭṭhe va dhamme sayaṃ abhiññā sacchikatvā upasampajja viharati.*

At another place,[131] the six *balāni* which enable a Tathāgata to 'roar the lion's roar' and 'turn the *brahma*-wheel' (*sīhanādaṃ nadati brahmacakkaṃ pavattati*) are identical to *balāni* numbers one, two, seven, eight, nine and ten above, as cited from the Mahāsīhanāda Sutta. Numbers three, four, five and six are not included in the *Aṅguttara* list. From these two lists of the *balāni* of a Tathāgata, then, the following six are repeated twice: (1) knowing conditions and non-conditions; (2) knowing the actions and results of actions of beings; (3) knowing about the *jhānā*; (4) remembering previous lives; (5) the *dibbacakkhu*; and (6) knowledge of the destruction of the *āsavā*. The following four are mentioned in only one of the lists : (1) knowledge of that which leads to good results; (2) knowing the world in all its diversity of realms; (3) knowing the dispositions of beings; and (4) knowing the faculties of beings.

We have found four separate listings of the *balāni* of the arahant. The numbers of these *balāni* vary greatly. In one list[132] there are ten powers; in another list[133] there are seven;

---

131. A.III.417-418.
132. A.V.174-176.
133. D.xxxiv.1.8.x.

in another[134] there are five; and in one list[135] there is only one power mentioned. In order to discuss the arahant *balāni*, we shall designate the *Aṅguttara* list, which has ten powers, as List #1. The list found in the Dasuttara Suttanta,[136] which has seven members, shall be called List #2. The five-member list from the *Saṃyutta Nikāya* will be List #3. Finally, the one-member list from the Cakkavatti-Sīhanāda Suttanta[137] will be List #4. We shall give the full List #1, and indicate which of these *balāni* are also found in these other *suttas*.

1. All that is compounded is purely, fully and actually known to be impermanent. *Aniccato sabbe saṅkhārā yathābhūtaṃ sammappaññāya suaiṭṭhā.* [This is identical to the first member of List #2.]
2. All that is compounded is purely, fully and actually known to be like charcoal.
   Aṅgārakāsupamā kāmā yathābhūtaṃ sammappaññāya sudiṭṭhā honti. [This is identical to the second member of List #2.)
3. The heart/mind [of the bhikkhu] tends toward detachment, leads to detachment, enjoys detachment, and the possibility of that which produces the *āsavā* has become extinct. *Vivekaninnaṃ cittaṃ hoti vivekapoṇaṃ vivekapabhāraṃ vivekaṭṭhaṃ nekkhammābhirataṃ vyantibhūtaṃ sabbaso āsavaṭṭhāniyehi dhammehi.* [This is identical to the third member of List #2, and to the only member of List #4.]
4. The four outsets of mindfulness are well-cultivated. *Cattāro satipaṭṭhānā bhāvita honti subhāvitā.* [This is identical to the fourth member of List #2, and to the third member of List #3.]
5. The four right efforts are well-cultivated. *Cattāro sammappadhānā bhāvita honti subhāvitā.*
6. The four steps towards psychic power. . . .*Cattāro iddhipādā*. . . .
7. The five faculties. . . .*Pañca indriyāni*. . . .[This is identical to the fifth member of List #2.]

---

134. S.V.249.
135. D.xxvi.28.
136. D.xxiv.1.8.x.
137. D.xxvi.28.

8. The five powers. . . .*Pañca balāni*. . . .[These five powers are the contents of List #3, and they are : conviction or faith (*saddhā*); mindfulness (*sati*), energy (*viriya*); concentration (*samādhi*); and insight or wisdom (*paññā*).]
9. The seven factors of enlightenment. . . .*Satta bojjhaṅgā*. . . . .[This is identical to the sixth member of List #2.]
10. The holy eightfold path is well-cultivated. *Ariya aṭṭhaṅgiko maggo bhāvito hoti subhāvito*. [This is identical to the seventh and last member of List #2.]

Now the question arises as to whether there is anything included in the listings of the ten *Tathāgatabalāni* which is excluded from the various listings of the ten *arahantbalāni*. If there is, then there would be something of which a Buddha is capable that an arahant isn't.

The first of the *Tathāgatabalāni*, the knowledge of what is and what is not a causal condition, is not explicit in the lists of the *arahantbalāni*. However, this closely approximates the first member of that list, namely, the knowledge of the impermanence of all phenomena. The second of the *Tathāgatabalāni* is the knowledge of cause and effect in the context of the farings of other beings. This is also one of the *tivijja*, namely, *yathākammūpagatañāṇa*, which is one of the products of the *abhiññā*, which are developed through the *jhānā*. We find this on the arahant's list under the sub-heading of the *pañca balāni*, the seventh member of List #1, and the fourth of those five *balāni*. The third of the *Tathāgatabalāni* is the knowledge of that which leads to good results, and is entailed in the arahant's tenth power, and also the seventh of List #2, which is his knowledge of the holy eightfold path. The fourth of the *Tathāgatabalāni* is knowing the diversity of realms of the world, which is cultivated by the arahant via the *jhānā*, and appears to us as the knowledge of the farings of various beings, as before. Knowing the dispositions of beings, the fifth power of a Tathāgata, is one of the results of the practice of the *jhānā*, and appears as mind-reading, one of the *abhiññā*, which is cultivated by the arahant as the eighth member of List #1. The same may be said of the sixth of the *Tathāgatabalāni*, which is knowledge of the faculties (*indriyāni*) of various beings. It seems that *balāni* numbers five and six of the Tathāgata are not conceptually separable; they are not listed separately in our alternate *Tathāgatabalāni* listing, but are included in its second member.

The seventh of the *Tathāgatabalāni*, which is knowledge of the *jhānā*, is entailed in the arahant's mastery of the *pañca balāni*, the eighth member of List #1. The remembering of past lives, the eighth power of a Tathāgata, is cultivated by the arahant in the practice of the *jhānā*, the third of the five *balāni*, which comprise the eighth member of List #1. The *dibbacakkhu*, the ninth of the *Tathāgatabalāni*, is also cultivated by the arahant by the practice of the *jhānā*, as above. The last of the *Tathāgatabalāni* is the knowledge of the destruction of the *āsavā*. This is the only one which appears on both *Tathāgatabalāni* lists and on all four of the *arhantbalāni* lists. Certainly it is the most significant.

In this analysis of the *balāni* of the Tathāgata and the arahant, then, we conclude that there is nothing of which a Tathāgata is capable, of which an arahant is not capable. Our analysis of these canonical lists, then, supports our thesis of the significant identity of the Buddha and the arahant.

E. *Summary and Conclusions*

Our discussion of the arahant and meditation has revolved around several intertwined themes : a sorting out of meditation terminology, and pointing out that the Buddha's unique contribution in this sphere was not the development of new meditational techniques, so much as a new interpretation of the meditational practices current in India at his time; and that this new interpretation of meditative techniques and experiences as being marked, as all products, by the *tilakkhana* of unsatisfactoriness, impermanence and insubstantiality, gives rise to a view of the perfected human independent of his meditative accomplishments, basing human freedom on insight rather than on technique, leading these to be separable notions, as indicated by the language of *paññāvimutti* and *cetovimutti*.

Despite our conclusion that talk about spiritual development, as expressed in the system of the eight holy persons (*aṭṭha ariyā puggalā*), is founded largely in talk about meditation, especially the *jhānā*, we have found that Buddhism, at least that Buddhism as found in the *Sutta Piṭaka* and related texts, has been consistent in maintaining the equation of : *khīṇāsava* (one who has destroyed the *āsavā*) = *paññā* (the wisdom which overcomes the ignorance of self and other) = *arahattā*; all without bringing into the equation meditation language.

However, to say (as we maintain) that the conceptions of the Buddha and the arahant cannot be significantly distinguished, the *jhānā* and their concomitant powers, the *abhiññā*, must be included in our notion of the arahant. This is especially important when we remember that the Buddha is one who discovers and teaches the Dhamma. For the discovery of the Dhamma, which is not the mere product of scripture, reasoning, or any infallible source of knowledge, such higher knowledges as *pubbenivāsānussatiñāṇa* and the *dibbacakkhu* are necessary. For the teaching of the Dhamma, the faculties of the *iddhividhā*, *paracittavijāñāṇa* and *yathākammūpagatañāṇa*, are commonly utilized by the Buddha and the arahants. Our studies lead us to the conclusion that the Buddha and the *ubhatabhāgavimutto* arahant are indistinguishable, and that, in terms of *āsavakkhaya*, he is identical to the *paññāvimutto* arahant *as well.*

Chapter IV

THE PSYCHOLOGY OF THE ARAHANT

A. *Introductory*

In this chapter we will argue two fundamental points : (1) that the arahant is beyond the world (*saṃsāra*; *loka*); and (2) that the arahant is not simply one who is beyond all feeling and emotion. Both of these points are controversial both for Buddhists and for scholars of Buddhism. Moreover, it might be held that these two points are contradictory, arguing something like since the world arises because of craving or desire (*taṇhā*), and since emotion is likewise rooted in *taṇhā*, then either the arahant is beyond the world and therefore also beyond emotion, or that he is in the world and emotional. We feel that this type of objection, as raised by the Uttarāpathakas,[1] is based on both a faulty understanding of what is meant by 'world' (*saṃsāra*; *loka*) in the first place, and also on a confusion of Pali terminology such as *taṇhā* and *chanda*, both of which are commonly rendered as 'desire' in English. Our reading of the basic texts leads us to conclude that the emotions play a key role both in the *magga* which leads to *arahattā*, and in the enlightened life of the arahant. Maintaining this position, we feel, is crucial for any understanding of the arahant, especially in the context of his continuity with later Buddhist images of the perfected person, the bodhisattva and the mahāsiddha.

B. *The Arahant and the World*

It is well-known that the Buddha taught a method which led to the cessation of the world (*tiṇṇ loke visattikan ti*),[2] but what is not so well-known is what the Buddha meant by 'world.' In this case, the term employed is *loka*, and we also find the term

1. *Kathāvatthuppakaraṇa-Aṭṭhakathā*, tr. Bimala Churn Law, *The Debates Commentary*, London : Pali Text Society, 1969 (1940), IV, 3, pp. 212-213.

2. S.I.60.

saṃsāra, usually raised in the context of talk about rebirth, and also *jagat*, used in the sense of the place where one goes,[3] a use to be considered below.

Ānanda, commenting upon some remarks by the Buddha,[4] equates *loka* with *lokasaññī*, which is to say that the world is our experience of the world. 'World' means a lived world; it is our experience, and is therefore the relational, objectified world. It is not a given, a place in which humankind is born and dies; and not the *a priori* stage of our drama, but is the drama itself. The world is derived not from some first cause, but from our desire that there be a world for us (*bhavataṇhā*); its circular matrix (*paṭiccasamuppāda*) revolves around ignorance (*avijjā*). The world is our experience of the world in the sense that one need not grant any world apart from our experience.

Occasionally the term '*jagat*' is used for some sense of what English speakers mean by 'world.' This term is interestingly derived from the Vedic √*gam*,[5] meaning 'go,'[6] therefore the place where one goes, a very different etymology and usage from *loka*. This distinction is sharpened by the Buddha[7] when Rohatissa asks him whether *loka* can be exhausted by going (*gamanena*). The Buddha clearly denies this possibility, indicating two things : (1) the distinction between *jagat*, the physical world to which one goes, and *loka*, the world in a Buddhist sense; and (2) that the entire question of the world, according to his Dhamma, is not a mere question of geography, physics and science. The Buddha says that while one cannot reach the end of the world by physical means (*gamanena*), yet he still teaches a way which leads to the end of the world.[8] This point is emphasized in another place[9] where the Buddha says : "Monks, there is no going to the end of the world by knowing, seeing or going,

3. As A.II.15; and S.I.186.
4. S.IV.95.
5. *P.T.S. Dictionary*, p. 277.
6. Whitney, p. 34.
7. S.I.60.
8. S.I.60.
9. S.IV.93. (My translation)
Nāham bhikkhave gamanena lokassa antaṃ nātayyaṃ pattayyan ti vadāmi, na ca panāham bhikkhave apatvā lokassa antaṃ dukkhassa antakiriyaṃ vadāmi ti.

I say. Monks, I say that without having gone to the end of the world, there is no making an end of suffering."

The same emphasis is found in the Kevaddha Sutta[10] where the Buddha is asked where the cessation of the four great elements (*mahābhūtā*) could be found. The Buddha says that the question is wrongly put, and that rather than asking about any location for the cessation of the *mahābhūtā*, it would be more sensible to ask where do these *mahābhūtā*, and such notions as long and short, fine and coarse, pure and impure, and name and form, cease and lack any basis. The point being made by the Buddha is that any talk about the world apart from someone's lived experience of the world is incoherent; that a religiously significant question about a world apart from man's being in the world is impossible. The answer to this re-phrased question is, of course, in *arahattā*, which is the cessation of the world and all notion of world. As the *Dhammapada*[11] says : "Mind precedes *dhammā*; mind [is their] leader, mind creates [them]," (*manopubbaṅgamā dhammā manoseṭṭhā manomayā*), the world about which the Buddha speaks is the experienced, objectified, psychological world. It is well-known that the Buddha often demonstrated that all claims about the world are, upon examination, found to be existential-psychological statements; that psychoanalysis was a more profitable spiritual undertaking than metaphysical analysis. Here we see that Ānanda's equation of the world (*loka*) with the experience (or idea, perception or notion) of the world (*lokasaññī*), similarly indicates that, since there could be no coherent notion of 'world' as the *a priori* of human existence, then Buddhists must be careful to note their special use and significance of the term 'world' within the context of their religious discipline : *ayaṃ vuccati ariyassa vinaya loko.*[12]

This leads us to some interesting questions. First of all, we have seen that, in Buddhist terminology, the 'world' (*loka*) means our experience of world (*lokasaññī*), the lived world. It

10. D.xi.
Kattha āpo ca paṭhavī tejo vāyo na gādhati ? Kattha dīghañ ca rassañ ca thūlaṃ subhāsubhaṃ ? Kattha nāmañ ca rūpañ ca asesaṃ uparujjhatīti ?

11. Dhammapada.I.1. (My translation)

12. S.IV.95.

was for this reason that the Buddha was able to present us with such startling analyses of various philosophical positions in the Brahmajāla Sutta.[13] In this *sutta*, all sixty-two possible views on the world, the self, and other metaphysical issues current in his day, are psychoanalyzed. For example, eternalistic views (*ātmavāda*) are reduced to superficial conclusions drawn from meditative experiences of former lives, or to mere addiction to reasoning (*takkī hoti vīmaṃsī*).[14] Claiming that the world is infinite or finite is merely a trancic hallucination:[15] believing the world to have been created at a given point in time derives from one's imagining oneself to have been Brahmā in a former life, but actually the meditator was merely one of the "fallen gods debauched by pleasure" (*khiddā padosikā nāma devā*) who are obsessed with guilt and jealousy;[16] those who believe the world arose by chance (*adhicca samuppanikā*) are confused because they are unable to recall previous lives as unconscious beings (*asaññā sattā*);[17] and the sophist-like 'eel-wrigglers' (*amarā vikittepaṃ*) do not equivocate out of conviction, as they would have us believe, but out of fear of exposing their stupidity.[18] In this Brahmajāla Sutta, the Buddha is providing his disciples with a divine net (*brahmajāla*) with which to ensnare all metaphysical positions, a net which is the methodology of the psychoanalysis of metaphysical claims.

'Going to the end of the world' means crossing over the floods (*oghā*), and the four floods are :[19] the flood of sensuality (*kāmogha*); the flood of becoming (*bhavogha*); the flood of metaphysics (*diṭṭhogha*); and the flood of ignorance (*avijjogha*). 'Going to the end of the world' means overcoming the tendency to grasp (*upādāna*), and the four graspings are :[20] grasping after sensuality (*kāmupādāna*); grasping after metaphysics (*diṭṭhupādāna*); grasping after primitive ritualism (*sīlabbatupādāna*); and grasping after an egoistic eternalism (*attavādupādāna*). 'Going

13. D.i.
14. D.i.2.28-36.
15. D.i.2.16-22.
16. D.i.2.1-15.
17. D.i.2.30-34.
18. D.i.2.23-29.
19. S.IV.257.
20. S.IV.258.

to the end of the world' means *arahattā*, the overcoming of the fiction of self (*anattā*), which leads us to saying that, for Buddhism, the self and the world are coterminous and coextensive. This point is clearly made by Marasinghe :[21]

> . . . a sentient being exists in the world only so long as it continues to share in the same qualities as the world, qualities such as impermanence (*aniccatā*), unsatisfactoriness (*dukkhatā*), non-substantiality or soul-lessness (*anattatā*), etc. Something that does not share in the above qualities of the world, something that is permanent, abiding, etc., cannot exist within it. On the other hand, an individual, sharing in similar characteristics as the phenomenal world, being able to exist only within the world, cannot, being in that state, go beyond the geographical boundaries of the world. Or in other words, he cannot go beyond the limitations of time and space as long as he himself remains a part of the world. Therefore, the further he goes, he is actually taking the world also with him. Hence, he can never come to the end of the world. Thus the individual and the world are coterminous.

C. *The Arahant and the Emotions*

This brings us to a crucial question. If, as we have argued, the Buddhist notion of '*loka*' is psychological in the sense of lived and not *a priori* world, then would it not follow that emotions, which are certainly psychological, would find no place in that which is beyond the world, in *arahattā* ? Our response to this type of position, which has found its way into both traditional and western scholarship, is that it assumes too narrow an understanding of human emotions. The detachment of the arahant, which is the detachment from self (*attā*), from the *āsavā*, from all grasping (*upādāna*) and desire (*taṇhā*), is not a bland neutrality or indifference. The Buddha tells us[22] that indifference or neutrality (*upekhindriya*) is of the same nature as happiness (*sukhindriya*), ease (*somanassindriya*), pain (*dukkhindriya*), and discomfort (*domanassindriya*). This is to say that indifference or neutrality is not a goal of Buddhism; that it,

---

21. Marasinghe, *GEB*, pp. 57-58.
22. S.V. 210.

like all other similar emotional tones, is not satisfactory and should be gone beyond. Buddhist detachment means the non-reference of feelings to self, not merely the cultivation of a hedonic or emotive banal neutrality. Neutrality (*upekhindriya*) should not be cultivated, but simply regarded as a feeling like other feelings : "Similarly [as with pleasant and unpleasant feelings], monks, neutrality or indifference must be seen [merely] as a feeling which is neither painful nor pleasurable."[23]

To return to our immediate problem : if the world and the self are coterminous and co-extensive, and that the world is a product of grasping and desire, then what type of emotions could there be said to remain after the overcoming of self ? Or, to rephrase this question, is there a type of emotion which is not contingent merely upon self ? We offer that, in Buddhism, there is, and to present our case we must consider in what sense the Buddha taught that the world is a product of our desire, and what other senses of desire there might be. We feel that a problem in this regard has been the muddle relating to two key terms, '*taṇhā*' and '*chanda*', both translated into English as 'desire' but with differing and even contradictory usages.

That the lived world is neither created nor random was expressed by the Buddha in the well-known formula of *paṭicca-samuppāda* or dependent co-arising :[24] "By this being, that is; from the arising of this, that rises; By this not being, that isn't; from the cessation of that, this doesn't arise." (*Imasmiṃ sati idaṃ hoti; imass' uppādā idaṃ uppajjati*; *imasmiṃ asati idaṃ na hoti; imassa nirodhā imaṃ nirujjhati*.) This concise form of *paṭicca-samuppāda* has several extended forms, all of them including *taṇhā* as the eighth member of the circular series.[25] In one place there are said to be three *taṇhā*,[26] namely : the desire for sensuality (*kāmataṇhā*); the desire for becoming (*bhavataṇhā*); and the desire for non-existence (*vibhavataṇhā*). Following from the principle that "*imasmiṃ asati idaṃ na hoti*," we see that given the not-being of *taṇhā*, then the whole of the world

23. S.V. 210. (My translation)
Tatra bhikkhave yadidam upekhindriyam adukkhamasukhā sā vedanā daṭṭhabbā.
24. M.II. 32. (My translation)
25. See D. xxii.
26. S.V. 257.

[expressed as the trilochosm of the world of sensuality (*kāmaloka*), the world of form (*rūpaloka*), and the world of formlessness (*āruppaloka*)] ceases. In another place,[27] we learn that there are six types of *taṇhā* corresponding to the six sense-fields; elsewhere[28] we learn that the three aspects of the trilochosm derive from our desire for these three worlds.

The most literal meaning of the term '*taṇhā*' is 'thirst'; and Rhys-Davids and Stede[29] have suggested its possible philological relation to its English cognate. We also learn[30] that the destruction of *taṇhā* (*taṇhakkhaya*) is identical to the destruction of the *āsavā* (*āsavakkhaya*), which is to say that it is identical to the cessation of the world, or *arahattā*.

Thus, the world is the product of our desiring that there be a world. Birth-and-death, which is to say suffering, is the product of the multi-lemma that I wish I were here but know that I will not be here (*bhavataṇhā*), and that I wish that I might not be here despite that fact that I am and will continue to be here (*vibhava-taṇhā*). The *Suttanipāta*[31] indicates the strong connection between our views of the world and our desires :

> That which in the world is called 'being' or 'non-being',
> desire sufficiently gives rise to it.
> Having seen the becoming and annihilation of form, beings in the world make judgements.

One should note in this passage the use of the term '*chanda*' ("desire") where one might expect to find '*taṇhā*.' In many cases, these terms are interchangeble. In this passage, we have translated it as 'desire' much as we would had the term been '*taṇhā*.' This new term, '*chanda*,' derives from the root $\sqrt{}$*skandh*, 'to leap,'[32] and gives us the sense of jumping at, and therefore intention, resolution, will, motivation,[33] or desire. We shall

---

27. D.xv.
28. D.xxxiii.
29. *P.T.S. Dictionary*, p. 294.
30. Nyāṇatiloka, *Buddhist Dictionary*, p. 178.
31. Suttanipāta, p. 169. (My translation)
'Sātaṃ, asātan' ti yam āhu loke, tam ūpanissāya pahoti chando, rūpesu disvā vibhavaṃ bhavañ ca, vinicchayaṃ kurute jantu loke.
32. Whitney, p. 190.
33. *P.T.S. Dictionary*, p. 274.

return to its use as 'motivation' shortly, but its usage in the compound '*kāmacchanda*' is identical to '*kāmataṇhā*.'

Chanda is a most interesting term in the *Sutta Piṭaka*, one which underscores for us the necessity of close, contextual readings of these materials. Nyāṇatiloka Mahāthera[34] carefully distinguishes three distinct ranges of usage : (a) as used in *Abhidhamma* literature in a very neutral sense of intention, generally one of the mental concomitants (*cetasikā*); (b) as 'desire' in the sense of that which binds us to *saṃsāra*, such as one of the five *nivaraṇā*;[35] and (c) as desire in a positive sense, a usage which we shall consider below, in connection with a Buddhist sense of motivation.

One comes across this positive sense of *chanda* most often in discussions of the cultivation of the *iddhipādā*, which have already been discussed and cited as practices conducive to *nibbāna*.[36] In order to cultivate these practices, one must conjoin *chanda* into his meditations : *chanda samādhi padhāna saṅkhāra samannāgataṃ iddhipādaṃ bhaveti*.[37] After a discourse on the necessity of incorporating desire (*chanda*) into religious practices, Ānanda is asked by a brahmin[38] if this were a coherent statement, since if the goal of the Buddha's teaching is the overcoming of desire, then to utilize desire in the overcoming of desire would leave us with a sort of infinite regress. Ānanda is not troubled with this objection. He makes the analogy of going to a park : the going thereto is usually preceded with the desire, energy, thought and reflection (*chando*, *viriyaṃ*, *cittaṃ* and *vīmaṃsā*) that one go to the park, and therefore that desire, etc., were appropriate (*tajjo*). Ānanda concludes :[39]

---

34. Nyāṇatiloka, *Buddhist Dictionary*, pp. 40-41.

35. Which, at A.ix.40, are listed as : desire for sensuality (*kāmacchanda*), malevolence (*vyāpāda*), torpor (*thīṇa-middha*), restlessness and worry (*uddhaccakukkucca*), and doubt (*vicikicchā*).

36. S.IV. 360.
Cattāro iddhipādā ayaṃ vuccati bhikkhave asaṅkhatagāmi maggo.

37. D.xxxiii.1.11.

38. S.V. 272-273.
Evaṃ sante kho Ānanda santakaṃ hoti no asantakam chandena ca chandam pajahissatī ti netam ṭhānaṃ vijjatīti.

39. S.V. 273. (My translation)
Evam eva kho brāhmaṇa yo so bhikkhu arahaṃ khīṇāsavo vusitavā

So it is, brahmin, that the arahant monk, the destroyer of the *āsavā*, fulfilled, doer of what was to be done, laid down his burden, actualizer of his goal, who has fully destroyed the fetters to this worldly existence, liberated by the supreme wisdom; that former desire (energy, thought, reflection) which he has used for attaining *arahattā*, [now that] *arahattā* is attained, that desire which so arose [or : 'appropriate'] is satisfied.

It should be noted that Ānanda is not saying that all *chanda* is abated; he is merely indicating that desire or motivation is appropriate in the spiritual life, and that the culmination of the spiritual life means that one need no longer desire that culmination. We cite this dialogue to indicate that the Buddha and his disciples did have some sort of notion of appropriate and inappropriate use of desire or motivation.

The idea of motivation or desire entails that which gives rise to activity, and there is a great deal of material to convince one that the arahant notion in the *Sutta Piṭaka* is a very active ideal. For example, Subhūti's short verse in the *Theragāthā* reads in part :[40] "My mind is well composed, freed; I dwell actively." The sphere and nature of this activity shall be considered in detail in our discussion of the sociology of the arahant, but basically it refers to a very active and compassionate (*mettā-cittena*) teaching. At the moment, however, we are concerned with making the case that the arahant is active, and that the notion of activity entails the notion of motivation (*chanda*), and that the motivations of the arahant are rooted in the emotions. Of course, it has been held that the Buddha or an arahant is the paradigm of a motiveless life, but we wish to point out that this motivelessness is only a coherent concept within the context of an understanding of motivation as rooted in egoism (*asmi-māna*). We are offering that there can be, should be, and is in Buddhism a different and significant sense of motivation, emotion and activity.

---

katakraṇīyo ohitabhāro anuppattasadattho parikkhīṇabhavasaṃyojano sammadaññā vimutto, tasso yo pubbe chando [viriyaṃ, cittaṃ, vīmaṃsā] ahosi arahattapatiyā arahatte yo tajjo chando ca paṭippassaddho.

40. Thag., verse 1. (My translation)
cittaṃ me susamāhitaṃ vimuttaṃ, ātāpī viharāmi.

In the *Itivuttaka* we learn that exertion (*padhāna*) is rooted in a certain type of emotion called *saṃvega* :[41]

> Monks, with two *dhammā* a religiously-inclined monk dwells happily and at ease in this life, very firm about the destruction of the *āsavā*. Which two ? By emotions [when there is] cause for emotion, and from that emotion he exerts himself strongly.

The text goes on to say[42] that the wise man should be emotional when there is cause for emotion : *saṃvejanīyesu ṭhānesu saṃvijjetheva paṇḍito.* Buddhaghoṣa[43] discusses *saṃvega* in its compounded form, *saṃvega-vatthu,* which is to say, those occasions by which *saṃvega* is aroused. There are said to be eight such occasions, namely : birth, old age, sickness, death, suffering in the lower realms of rebirth, suffering in *saṃsāra* in the past, present and future. The Buddha says that there are four causes for *saṃvega,*[44] namely the four places of Buddhist pilgrimage : Lumbini, the place of the birth of the Buddha; Buddha Gayā, the place where he attained *bodhi*; Sārnāth, where he preached the first sermon, setting the wheel of the Dhamma into motion; and Kusinārā, the place where he attained *parinibbāna.* Thus *saṃvega* is a type of spiritually productive emotion, which Buddhaghoṣa interprets as something like the feeling of disgust at the misery of the world, which is to say a feeling of disgust with that which we experience as a world, following from Ānanda's equation of *loka* with *lokasaññī.* Buddhaghoṣa's interpretation seems to follow from the dictum of the Buddha :[45] "That which the outsiders [i.e., non-Buddhists] call happiness, that the holy ones [i.e., advanced Buddhists] call suffering." (*Yam pare sukhato āhu, tad ariyā āhu dukkhato.*) Another *sutta* helps to explain this. An analysis of that which is called pleasurable (*sukhato āhu*) finds that since all worldly

---

41. Itivuttaka, p. 29. (My translation)
Dvihi bhikkhave dhammehi samannāgato bhikkhu diṭṭhe va dhamme sukha somanassa bahulo viharati, yoniso āraddho hoti āsavānaṃ khayāya. Katame dvīhi ? Saṃvejanīyesu ṭhānesu saṃvejanena saṃvegassa ca yoniso padhānena.
42. Itivuttaka, p. 30. (My translation)
43. Vism., p. 135.
44. A.IV.118.
45. S.IV. 127. (My translation)

pleasures are dependently co-originated, they are in truth painful (*dukkhato*). But Buddhism would not have us merely attempt an escape from *dukkhato* for two reasons. First of all, any such attempted escape would be unsuccessful, as even the highest escape imaginable, that of birth among the *devā*, or of meditative bliss, are neither lasting nor ultimately satisfactory. This is not to say that the Buddha's attitude toward worldly pleasure was uncompromisingly negative. It was allowed for, in a limited sense, as the Buddha realized that, for the majority of people, it was the best that could be hoped for :[46] "Monks, the worldly person knows no other refuge from painful feeling than delight in sensuality." It seems that the bliss of the destruction of desire (*taṇhakkhayasukha*) was simply of a much greater magnitude than any conceivable worldly bliss, as we find stated in the *Udana* :[47] "That worldly happiness of sensuality, and that happiness of the *devā*, does not come to one-sixteenth part of the happiness of the destruction of desire." Following Buddhaghoṣa, then, we see that worldly pleasures of sensuality and of the *devā* may be seen as the closest approximation of spiritual accomplishment, but the purpose of the Buddha's doctrine was to see the superficiality of this type of pleasure. Religious emotion, according to Buddhaghoṣa, was the feeling of repugnance with all worldly pleasures. This disgust, repugnance and renunciative spirit was his use of the term '*saṃvega*.'

But it seems not to be the only one. We have seen that the Buddha taught that *saṃvega* could also mean a positive religious sentiment,[48] such as that arising from pilgrimage to the holy places. This trend seems to be more developed in the Singhalese commentaries. For example, the *Sāratthappakāsinī*[49] tells us that *saṃvega* arose in both monks and laypeople merely at the sight of the Mahācetiya at Anurādhapura. In the *Samanta-*

46. S.IV.208. (My translation)
na hi bhikkhave pajānāti assutavā puthajjano aññatra kāmasukhā dukkhāya vedanāya nissaraṇaṃ.

47. Udana, p. 11. (My translation)
yaṃ ca kāmasukhaṃ loke yaṃ c' idaṃ diviyaṃ sukhaṃ taṇhakkhaya-sukhassa te kalaṃ n' agghanti soḷasin ti.

48. A.IV.118.

49. *Sāratthappakāsinī*; cited in Adikaram, *EHBC*, p. 108.

pāsādikā[50] we learn of one monk named Phussadeva in whom arose the religious sentiment of *pīti* or joy while contemplating the Buddha (*buddhārammaṇapīti*). Māra, a personification of those forces which hinder one's spiritual growth, tried to combat this *Pīṭi*, but Phussadeva, in his stuggle with Māra to maintain that *pīti*, attains *arahattā* in such a situation. Govinda[51] makes the point that while sensuous desire (*kāmacchanda*), an emotion always rooted in egoism, is always seen as a prime enemy of spiritual growth, a desire for the Dhamma (*dhammacchanda*) is a positive emotion to be cultivated. Similarly, Johansson[52] makes a keen observation which could, however, be misleading. He says that"... by definition, *nibbāna* is... freedom from the emotions and desires by which egoism and attachment are created; all definitions are in complete agreement on this point." We would only wish to add, by way of caution and emphasis, that not all emotions, according to Buddhism, give rise to egoism (*asmimāna*) and attachment (*upādāna*).

Thus far we have limited ourselves to discussions of *taṇhā* and *chanda*, and of *saṃvega*. We have seen that while *taṇhā* is always something to be overcome; and also that although *taṇhā* is, in some contexts, identical to *chanda*, nevertheless, we have shown other uses of *chanda*, such as Govinda's *dhammacchanda*, which are clearly positive; and also the role of *chanda* in the cultivation of the *iddhipādā*, a way leading to *nibbāna*.

Saṃvega seems to be used to indicate two distinct types of religious emotion. The first one, following Buddhaghoṣa and some *Sutta Piṭaka* sources, is that feeling of repugnance and renunciation for the misery of the world. The second sense of *saṃvega*, about which the Buddha spoke and the commentaries elaborated, is a type of religious sentiment arising on pilgrimage or at a shrine, useful to both monks and the laity, which is something like joy (*pīti*).

We shall now consider a Buddhist use of the term '*mettā*,' which is love or lovingkindness or perhaps friendliness, an emotion upon which was based a very significant part of the *bodhisattvayāna* teachings under the term '*karuṇā*' or compassion. We shall then return to the issue of how emotions are to be

50. *Samantapāsādikā*; cited in Adikaram, *EHBC*, p. 68.
51. Govinda, *PAEBP*, p. 119.
52. Johansson, *PN*, p. 22.

viewed in a Buddhist context in general. We shall argue that the Buddha took a middle path in his approach toward the emotions : some are to be avoided, some cultivated, and all analyzed. This case is against many interpretations of Buddhism, Theravāda in particular, which hold that the Buddha was categorically opposed to all emotionality. This, we feel, is based on a misunderstanding of many factors, including a Buddhist understanding of the world, motivation and perfection.

We will readily grant that in the instances of those emotions which give rise to egoism and attachment, which is to say, those emotions which give rise to the world, the Buddha was uncompromising in saying that they must be overcome in order for there to be spiritual growth. A paradigm for this sort of negative emotion would be sensual desire (*kāmataṇhā* or *kāmacchanda*), or lust for sensuality (*kāmarāga*). This sort of emotional tone distorts and perverts our mind and therefore the world. The Buddha says :[53]

> Suppose, brahmin, a bowl of water were mixed with lac or turmeric or blue or yellow dye, and suppose a man with good sight should look closely therein for the reflection of his own face. He would not know or see it as it really is. Just so, brahmin, when one dwells with his heart possessed by sensual lust, overwhelmed by sensual lust, and knows not in very truth any refuge from sensual lust that has arisen,—at such time he neither knows nor sees in very truth his own profit.

There is no question that such emotions have no place in the religious life, according to the Buddha; yet, just that lust (*rāga*), if directed toward the Dhamma rather than sensuality, can conduce to *arahattā*. This is explicitly stated[54] : "... yet by his

---

53. A.V.121-122. (PTS translation)
Seyyathāpi brāhmaṇa udapatto saṃsaṭṭho lākhāya va haliddiyā vā niliyā vā mañjeṭṭhāyā vā, tattha cakkhunā puriso sakam mukkhanimittam paccavekkhamāno yathābhūtaṃ na jāneyya na passeyya, evam eva kho brāhmaṇa yasmiṃ samaye kāmarāgapariyuṭṭhitena cetassā viharati kāmarāgaparetena, uppannassa ca kāmarāgassa nissaraṇam yathābhūtaṃ nappajānati, attattham pi tasmiṃ samaye yathābhūtaṃ na jānāti na passati, parattham pi, ubhayattham pi tasmiṃ samaye yathābhūtaṃ na jānāti na passati, dīgharattam sajjhāyakatā pi mantā na paṭibhanti pageva asajjhāyakatā.

54. A.V. 346. (My translation)
ten'eva dhammarāgena tāya dhammanandiyā pañcannaṃ orambhāgiyānaṃ saṃyojanānaṃ parikkhayā.

lust [*rāga*] or passion for the Dhamma, by his bliss in the Dhamma, he utterly destroys the five lower fetters."

A narrow interpretation of the Buddha's teachings on the emotions, especially lust or passion (*rāga*), led some Buddhists to insupportable conclusions. In the *Kathāvatthu*[55] we learn of a group called the Uttarāpathaka sect, who so narrowly defined passion (*rāga*) as to hold that since the Buddha was not impassioned (*arāgya*), therefore he was incapable of emotions like friendliness (*mettā*) or compassion (*karuṇā*). The Theravāda controversialist makes two points against such a position. He first of all says that such a narrow view of being non-impassioned (*arāgya*) entails that the Buddha was ruthless, which no Buddhist would contend. He then appeals to the Uttarāpathaka not to get intoxicated with his logic, and to please see the simple fact that the Buddha did act compassionately, and that one should not hold theses which do violence to the simplest observations. The rejoinder is couched in language about the four divine abodes (*brahmavihārā*) of friendliness (*mettā*), empathy (*muditā*), compassion (*karuṇā*) and equanimity (*upekkha*), all of which were taught by the Buddha. To say that the Buddha did not act compassionately because he was free from passion is to deny the teaching of these four *brahmavihārā*, which are the elementary Buddhist meditational practices.

The *Sutta Piṭaka* is most eloquent in its praises of *mettā*. In the Mettā Sutta[56] we find the *gāthā* :

Just as with her own life
a mother shields from hurt
her own, her only child,—
let all-embracing thoughts
for all that lives be thine,
an all-embracing love
for all the universe,
in all its heights and depths

55. Kathāvatthu, pp. 561f.

56. Suttanipāta, p. 26. (PTS translation)
Mātā yathā niyaṃ puttaṃ, āyusā ekaputtam anurakkho, evam pi sabbabhūtesu, mānasam bhāvaye aparimāṇaṃ. Mettañ ca sabbalokasmiṃ, mānasam bhāvaye aparimāṇaṃ, uddhaṃ adho ca tiriyañ ca, asambādhaṃ averaṃ asapattaṃ.

and breadth, unstinted love,
unmarred by hate within,
not rousing enmity.

Moreover, the disciple who cultivates other aspects of the Dhamma but neglects *mettā*, opens himself to spiritual dangers. The Buddha says on this point :[57]

> Monks, just as any clan which is populated largely with women is susceptible to attacks from thieves and robbers, just so it is, monks, that any monk who does not cultivate the freedom of the heart/mind by means of *mettā*, he is susceptible to attack from non-human beings.

One possible interpretation of 'non-human beings' (*amanussehi*) could be those psychological functions which endanger spiritual growth, with Māra as the paradigm, or perhaps something like the *yakkhā*, demons which cause psychopathological problems. To say the least about this verse, the neglect of *mettā* in one's spiritual practices leads to a weakening of the results of those practices. To say the most, unless spiritual practices are infused with *mettā*, one runs a great psychological risk.

Having demonstrated that the emotions play a role in the spiritual life as understood by the Buddha, one might raise the question of how these emotions are to be viewed. The Buddha tells us[58] that the spiritual life must be preceded by a healthy view of the worldly life. One must understand what satisfaction is found in the emotions, and also that those which are related to self and sensuality are ultimately unsatisfactory :

> So long, brethren, as beings have not understood, as they really are, the satisfaction as such, the misery as such, the way of escape as such, in this sixfold personal sphere of sense,

---

57. S. II.264. (My translation)
Seyyathāpi bhikkhave yāni kānici kulāni bahutthikāni appapurisāni tāni suppadhaṃsiyāni honti corehi kumbhattenakehi. Evam eva kho bhikkhave yassa kassaci bhikkhuno mettā cetovimutti abhāvitā abahulikatā, so suppadhaṃsiyo hoti amanussehi.

58. Yava kivañca bhikkhave sattā imesaṃ channam ajjhattikānam āyatanānam assādato ādīnavañca ādīnavato nissaraṇañca nissaraṇato yathābhūtam nābbaññāsuṃ, neva tāva bhikkhave sattā sadevakā likā sabrahmakā sassamaṇabrāhmaṇiyā pajāya sadevamanussāya nissaṭā visaṃyuttā vippamuttā vimariyādakatena cetasā vihariṃsu.

so long, brethren, beings have not remained aloof, detached, separated, with the barriers to the mind done away with, nor have the world with its *devas*, its Māras, its Brahmās, nor the host of recluses and brahmins, of *devas* and mankind.

This is a very balanced view of ordinary human life which holds that the spiritual life must be preceded by a full understanding of the senses, which is not merely to say that they are to be avoided, but that they yield their satisfactions and their sufferings.

Similarly, a balanced view, or middle path, is taken regarding the self. The Buddha tells us[59] that there are three forms of pride (*māno*) : pride (*māno*); self-denigration (*omāno*); and excessive pride (*atimāno*). Belittling oneself, then, is as much a form of pride as self-aggrandizement, according to the Buddha, who herein displays an understanding of the psychological person, which corresponds to many developments within the western psychotherapeutic traditions.

The Buddha did not instruct his followers to suppress, ignore or view as pathological, the emotions as such. They are to be analyzed, or perhaps, in certain situations, to be used as a method of teaching. To this last point we find an example in the *Udana*.[60] One of the Buddha's disciples, Nanda, has become infatuated with a Sakyan girl and despairs of progressing in the spiritual life. The Buddha takes Nanda to one of the heavens, and shows him five hundred of the *kakuṭapādinī*, a type of goddess with bird-like feet. Nanda says that, when compared with these goddesses, his Sakyan girl friend looks like a deformed monkey. Thus his passion (*rāga*) is skilfully redirected by the Buddha, and Nanda eventually attains *arahattā*.

All emotions and feelings are, in Buddhism, a potential ground for spiritual growth; it merely becomes a question of our attitude towards these feelings and emotions. For example, the Buddha says :[61]

59. A.III.445.

60. Udana, pp. 21-24.

61. S.IV.207. (My translation)

Yatho kho bhikkhave bhikkhuno sukhā vedanā dukkhato diṭṭhā honti, dukkhā vedanā sallato diṭṭhā honti, adukkhamasukhā vedanā aniccato diṭṭhā honti. Ayaṃ viccati bhikkhave bhikkhu sammaddaso.

> Monks, by a monk happy feelings are seen as unsatisfactory; unhappy feelings are seen as a prod; and feelings which are neither happy nor unhappy are seen as impermanent. Monks, I call that monk one who sees rightly.

It is also important to note that this attitude towards emotions and feelings which the Buddha proscribes is not a mere neutrality. Neutrality or indifference is just another emotive tone, perhaps preferable to extreme agitation, elation or depression, but not ultimately satisfactory. He says :[62] "Monks, what is the nature of the faculty of neutrality or indifference ? [It is] that feeling of body or mind which is neither conscious nor unconscious." In our discussion of the *jhānā*, we have seen that that which is neither conscious nor unconscious is a product and therefore unsatisfactory, and we have also seen that *upekhindriyaṃ*, like the other *indriyāni—dukkha-*, *sukha-*, *domanassa-* and *somanassa-* — are to be treated in the same manner.

D. *Conclusions*

Rather than make categorical statements about the emotions, such as they should all be denied or sublimated or ignored, the Buddha is characteristically analytical. Those emotions which could be considered negative, such as grasping and worry (*upādāna* and *paritassanā*), are found to be negative to the extent that they are rooted in the self.[63] To say that something is rooted in the self, as we started this discussion on the psychology of the arahant, is to say that it is of the world (*loka*). Rather than saying, as some might,[64] that all emotions are worldly and therefore are to be left behind, we would prefer to employ the Buddha's more analytical and less categorical approach, and

---

62. S.V. 209. (My translation)

Katamañca bhikkhave upekhindriyaṃ ? Yaṃ kho bhikkhave kāyikaṃ vā cetasikaṃ vā neva sātaṃ nāsātaṃ vedatitaṃ.

63. S. III.18.

64. This seems to be the standard scholarly understanding of the arahant. See, for examples, Edward Conze, *BTI*; Surendranath DasGupta, *A History of Indian Philosophy*, vol. I; Har Dayal, *The Bodhisattva Doctrine in Buddhist Sanskrit Literature*; Nalinaksha Dutt, *Early Monastic Buddhism*; A.K. Warder, *Indian Buddhism*; Bhikshu Sangharakshita, *A Survey of Buddhism*; et cetera.

say something like : depending on the attitude one holds toward them, some emotions could be said to be worldly; and some, such as *mettā, saṃvega* and *karuṇā,* would be *nibbānic*, which is to say, those emotions appropriate to an arahant; and other emotions could be either worldly or *nibbānic,* depending upon their context and one's relation to them. This third category might include those emotions which are useful during one's period of spiritual growth, but which fall away in *arahattā.* One example of this sort has already been given by the Buddha, that of the desire to become an arahant, which falls away once the goal has been actualized. But certainly religious sentiment (*saṃvega*), and *mettā* and *karuṇā,* were held by the Theravāda and the Mahāyāna as emotions appropriate to an arahant, bodhisattva or Buddha, and therefore we would say that these could be called *nibbānic*, which is to say that they are not rooted in egoism (*asmimāna*), and therefore not connected with the world.

Chapter V

THE ARAHANT AND SOCIETY

A. *General*

Given that the mind of the arahant is not merely a psychological vacuum in which all emotion and motivation have been shrivelled by exacting meditation, we shall now consider the field in which this enlightened emotion and motivation expresses itself. It is this field of action which is meant by the interrelation of the arahant and society, as we contend that while in a very significant sense the arahant has left the world behind, he still does not abide in the mere hedonic tone of indifference (*upekhindriyaṃ*) but actively (*ātāpī*) engages in action that could be called social. Since the arahant is one who does not attach himself to any particular hedonic quality of experience, indifference included, therefore he is not beyond compassion for the sufferings of others, as the Theravāda debator in the *Kathāvatthu* argues. Since he is not merely indifferent about the plight of others, we propose to enquire into his interactions with those whom he has not quite left behind.

In order to pursue our enquiry, we shall view some of the practical injunctions of Buddhist monastic discipline (*vinaya*). We shall also investigate some claims in the *Sutta Piṭaka* as to what can and cannot be done by an arahant, which should serve to give a rough indication of the range of his activity.

As an immediate implication of what is said about an arahant in terms of his social interrelatedness, we shall consider the two key Buddhist ethical terms, *puñña* and *kusala*. While most scholars treat these terms as irreconcilable, the former governing the social organization of the laity and the latter that of the *saṅgha*, we find that if this distinction is over-emphasized, then one is left with a methodological bifurcation of the Buddhist world, one which unnecessarily bifurcates the lay and monastic systems. Experience in the field in Buddhist societies gives one the very strong impression that these two worlds, if they could be called as such, are interdependent and interacting. Rather than pursue a methodology which dictates conclusions, we propose to analyze what the early texts have to say about these two ethical terms. It is found that this analysis does not yield a bifurcation of Buddhism and Buddhist cultures; that *puññā* could better be seen as the habituating ground of *kusala*, just as we found that the highly structured practice of meditation is the habituating ground of utter spontaneity, so the practice of *puññā* and the practice of *kusala* are not separate and discrete, but continuous.

Given this theoretical basis of a reinterpretation of key Buddhist ethical terms, we shall then proceed to analyze the entire question of the arahant and the laity : his relation to it as exemplar and as active 'spiritual friend' (*kalyāṇamitta*). In this chapter, we shall also consider the crucial question of the relationship of the teaching by the arahant to the arahant's being an arahant. While we shall argue that it is not teaching *per se* which defines an arahant (or a Buddha) as such, we find that teaching is indeed intrinsic to the notion of an arahant, since the possibility of not teaching is considered by the Buddha to be an elementary form of pride which is overcome in the process of becoming an arahant. Therefore, an arahant who does not teach becomes a simple contradiction in terms : since the arahant has overcome pride (*asmimāna*), and since not teaching is a form of pride, then there cannot be an arahant who does notteach.

B. *What an Arahant Can and Cannot Do*

The *Pāṭimokkha* identifies itself as addressing two interrelated questions :[1] what are the characteristics of a lower course of moral practice (*heṭṭhimena pariyāyena sīlaṃ*); and of a higher course of moral practice (*uparimena pariyāyena sīlaṃ*). The former is defined as :[2]

> Here, a noble hearkener is restrained from destroying living creatures; is restrained from taking what is not given; is

1. *Pāṭimokkha,* ed. and tr. Ñāṇamoli Thera, *The Pātimokkha* : 227 *Fundamental Rules of a Bhikkhu*, intro. Phra Sāsana Sobhana, Bangkok : The Social Science Association Press of Thailand, 1966, Ovādapāṭimokkhādipāṭho, p. 21.

2. *Pāṭimokkha*, pp. 21-22. (Ñāṇamoli translation)

Idha ariyasāvako pāṇātipātā paṭivirato hoti, adinnādānā paṭivirato hoti, kāmesu micchācārā paṭivirato hoti, musāvādā paṭivirato hoti, surāmerayamajjappamādaṭṭhānā paṭivirato hoti 'ti. Evaṃ kho heṭṭhimena pariyāyena sīlaṃ sammadakkhātaṃ bhagavatā.

> restrained from wrong conduct in sexual relations; is restrained from false speech; is restrained from distilled and fermented intoxicants which are the occasion for carelessness. Thus it is that the lower course of moral conduct has been rightly expounded by the Lord.

The higher course is defined in this way :[3]

> Here, a bhikkhu is virtuous. He dwells restrained in accordance with the restraint of the *Pāṭimokkha*, perfect in conduct and resort, seeing danger in the slightest faults he trains himself by undertaking rightly the rules of training. Thus it is that the higher course of moral conduct has been rightly expounded by the Lord.

The way in which the problem is set up in the *Pāṭimokkha*, the essential character of monastic discipline is restraint. The *Abhidharmakośa-ṭīkā* gives this etymology for *prāṭimokṣa* :[4] "As it restrains [*sdom pa'i phyir*] body and speech [from misdeeds], thus it is called *prāṭimokṣa* [*so so thar pa*] restraints [or 'vows,' *sdom pa*]." As the term '*sdom pa*' in this passage may be translated either as 'vow' or 'restraint', we see the essential restraining character of the *Pāṭimokkha*, both from Theravāda and Mahāyāna sources. This would be especially true of the lower (*heṭṭhimena*) discipline. From the Pali source, it seems that the restraints implicit in the specific *pañcasīla* precepts mentioned have been internalized, and the bhikkhu may begin a more positive approach to action. It says that he is virtuous (*sīlavā*), the virtue perhaps entailing positive action. Kong sprul certainly takes this higher moral conduct to be something positive. He says :[5]

> According to the *śrāvakayāna*, the example [*mtshan gzhi*] of the *prāṭimokṣa* is : 'morality which is not merely aspiring for the refuge of protection from fear, and the wish for something good, but the thought of gaining peace for oneself

3. *Pāṭimokkha*, p. 23. (Ñāṇamoli translation)
Idha bhikkhu sīlavā hoti paṭimokkhasaṃvarasaṃvuto viharati ācāragocara sampanno aṇumattesu vajjesu bhayadassāvī samādāya sikkhati sikkhāpadesū 'ti. Evaṃ kho uparimena pariyāyena sīlaṃ sammadakkhātaṃ bhagavatā.

4. As cited by Kong sprul, *Shes bya kun khyab*, 'grel II.38. (My translation) lus ngag sdom pa'i phyir so so thar pa'i sdom pa zhes bya'o.

5. Kong sprul, *Shes bya kun khyab*, 'grel II.37. (My translation)

[*rang nyid zhi ba*] and developing a strong feeling of disgust [or 'renunciation,' *nges par 'byung pa*] for the whole cycle of *saṃsāra*.' Of course, Kong sprul the Mahāyānist follows his particular hermeneutical tradition of distinguishing the *śrāvakayāna* from the *bodhisattvayāna* in terms of motivation : 'peace for oneself' as opposed to 'the salvation of all sentient beings.' We shall explore this type of Buddhist hermeneutics in detail later. The point to note at this time is that, fundamentally, *Pāṭimokkha* is a system of restraints which leaves open the possibility of positive activity, although it never explicitly discusses such possibilities. For such a discussion, we must return to the *Sutta Piṭaka*. It should be noted that the lack of positive ethical statements in the *Pāṭimokkha*, unlike as in much of the *bodhisattvayāna* literature, should not lead one to the hasty conclusion that all that could be said about the arahant must be of a negative character in keeping with the tradition of vows and restraints in the *Pāṭimokkha*. For Kong sprul and some other Buddhists, the wish to escape from suffering entails the wish for positive good; for others it does not. But the convention of limiting the range of discussion in the *Pāṭimokkha* does not lead one to conclude that the arahant is inactive or that positive statements about him, about *nibbāna*, et cetera, could not be made. Rather, the *Pāṭimokkha* follows the tradition within Buddhism of saying the minimum about the solution itself and spending a great deal of time analyzing the problem and the means to its solution.

Following the *Pāṭimokkha's* methodology of beginning with restraints, we shall view some of the actions which the *Sutta Piṭaka* says the arahant is incapable of. Of these we find two lists, one with five members and one with nine.

The five things which an arahant cannot do are found in the Saṅgīti Suttanta[6] and repeated without significant alteration in the Sansaka Sutta :[7]

6. D.xxxiii. 2.1. x. (PTS translation)
Pañca abhabba-ṭṭhānāni. Abhabbo āvuso khīṇāsavo bhikkhu sañcicca pāṇaṃ jivitā voropetuṃ. Abhabbo khīṇāsavo bhikkhu adinnaṃ theyya—saṃkhātaṃ ādātuṃ. Abhabbo khīṇāsavo bhikkhu methunaṃ dhammaṃ paṭisevituṃ. Abhabbo khīṇāsavo bhikkhu sampajānamusā bhāsitum. Abhabbo khīṇāsavo bhikkhu sannidhi kārakaṃ kāme paribhuñjituṃ, seyyathā pi pubbe agāriyabhūto.

7. M.I.523.

> Five impossibilities, to wit, for an arahant intentionally to take life, or to take what is not given, so as to amount to theft, or to commit sexual offense, or to lie deliberately, or to spend stored-up treasures in worldly enjoyments, as in the days before he left the world.

These 'impossibilities' (*abhabba-ṭṭhānāni*) are identical to the *pañcasila* of the *Pāṭimokkha* save for its last member. Whereas in the *pañcasīla* the fifth member is refraining from intoxicants, in these *Sutta Piṭaka* verses it is the accumulation of wealth as a householder accumulates it. We shall return to this point in our discussion of the arahant and the *saṅgha*/ laity issue below; for the moment we only indicate these five actions which were considered as so inimical to the nature of the arahant as to be said to be impossibilities.

We find two listings of nine impossibilities for the arahant, and these two lists are identical. They are from the *Dīgha*[8] and the *Aṅguttara Nikāya* :[9]

> ...the arahant monk... cannot transgress nine standards : a monk, in whom the cankers [*āsavā*] are destroyed, cannot deliberately take the life of any living thing; cannot, with intention to steal, take what is not given; cannot engage in carnal intercourse; cannot intentionally tell a lie; cannot enjoy pleasures from savings, as of yore when a householder; a monk in whom the cankers have been destroyed, cannot go astray through desire; cannot go astray through hate; cannot go astray through delusion; cannot go astray through fear.

Nothing here alters the restraining character of Buddhist practice. We find the same five impossibilities as mentioned in the earlier citation, along with any action motivated by the three

8. D.xxix.26.

9. A.IV.370. (PTS translation)

yo so bhikkhu arahaṃ...abhabbo so nava ṭhānāni ajjhācarituṃ : abhabbo khīṇāsavo bhikkhu sanicca pāṇaṃ jīvitā voropetuṃ, abhabbo khīṇāsavo bhikkhu adinnaṃ theyyasaṃkhātuṃ ādātuṃ, abhabbo khīṇāsavo bhikkhu methunaṃ dhammaṃ paṭisevituṃ, abhabbo khīṇāsavo bhikkhu sampajānamusā bhāsituṃ, abhabbo khīṇāsavo bhikkhu sannidhikārake kāme paribhuñjituṃ seyyathā pi pubbe agāriyabhūto, abhabbo khīṇāsavo bhikkhu chandāgatiṃ gantuṃ, abhabbo khīṇāsavo bhikkhu dosāgatiṃ gantuṃ, abhabbo khīṇāsavo bhikkhu mohāgatuṃ, abhabbo khīṇāsavo bhikkhu bhayāgatiṃ gantuṃ.

mūlakilesā of ignorance, attraction or aversion, or by fear. This last factor, incidentally, has led to a variety of Singhalese commentatorial speculations, as mentioned earlier in this essay. However, that which is motivated by the three *mūlakilesā* could well include the notion of an arahant not teaching, which is said to be rooted in pride (*asmimāna*). This line of reasoning shall be continued below.

It is also said of an arahant that he is incapable of carelessness :[10] "Since they have practised so diligently, carelessness is an impossibility." However, to say that an arahant is incapable of carelessness is not to say that he need not be diligent. We find in another place :[11] "He constantly wards over all actions and intentions." To conjoin these two citations, the arahant, then, is incapable of any careless action because it is his nature to be vigilant. This, of course, was one of the most crucial issues considered at the Council of Pāṭalīputra, where Mahādeva said that an arahant was prone to some minor flaws. This position was held by the Mahāsaṅghikas and the later Mahāyāna; maintaining the integrity of the arahant concept was the position of the Sthaviravāda. We indicate these two citations to demonstrate the attitude found in the Pali canon, which clearly affirms the perfection of the arahant. Were one to read only the *Aṅguttara* verse, which in effect holds that the arahant must remain meticulous in action and intentionality, then perhaps one could find the roots of Mahādeva's position. Considering both verses together clearly indicates that this was contrary to the original textual position.

Except for the *iddhividhā*, the arahant was not capable of going against what we understand as the laws of nature. This point is made in the context of discussing indefinite extension of the arahant's life span. Here the Buddha says,[12] and I translate :

Mahārāja, there is no [life] other than life-and-death. ... Mahārāja, even those monks who are arahants, who have

---

10. S.IV.125. (My translation)
katam̩ tesam̩ appamādena, abhabbā te pamajjitum̩.

11. A.I.110. (My translation)
rakkhāvaraṇaguttim̩ sam̩vidahati kāyakammasmim̩.

12. S.I.71. (My translation)

> destroyed the *āsavā*, who have lived the life, accomplished what was to be accomplished, who have laid down their burden, who have won their goal, who have utterly destroyed the fetters which bind to existence, who by wisdom are completely freed, even for them this compounded body is such that it must decay and must be put aside.

The *Sutta Piṭaka* admits to some ambivalence on this point, however. In the Mahāparinibbāna Suttanta,[13] we recall that the Buddha rather blatently hinted to Ānanda that, if requested earnestly by his disciples, the Buddha could prolong his life span indefinitely. However, judging from other internal evidences, this section of the *suttanta* seems to be apocryphical. These other evidences indicate that the body of the Buddha was prone to old age, sickness and death. In the Jāra Sutta,[14] Ānanda notices that the Buddha's body had become wrinkled, and when questioned about it, the Buddha gives Ānanda a discourse on impermanence. In another place,[15] the Buddha is unable to continue a discourse due to back pains, and Ānanda finishes it for him. The commentaries on both these points explain away the Buddha's wrinkles and pains. The wrinkles, we are told, could be seen only by Ānanda as they were really very, very tiny; and his backache was very minor, but the Buddha wanted to give Ānanda the opportunity to discourse.[16] A reading of the primary sources gives the impression that the Buddha suffered these aches and ageing as we all do. The commentaries admit to miniscule aches and pains. Yet here we see a tendency to elevate the status of the Buddha, to supernaturalize him; a tendency which reached its culmination in the docetic view of the Buddha as found in the *Saddharmapuṇḍarīka Sūtra*, which tells us that the Buddha actually spent his time in rapture in some heaven, while some contrived body (*nirmāṇakāya*) gave

---

Natthi kho mahārāja aññatra jarāmaraṇā...Ye pi te mahārāja bhikkhū arahanto khīṇāsavā vusitavanto katakaraṇiyā ohitabhārā anuppattasadatthā parikkhīṇabhava-saṃyojanā sammadaññā vimuttā, Tesaṃ pāyaṃ kāyo bhedana-dhammo nikkhepana-dhammo ti.

13. D.xvi.3.3.
14. S.V. 216-217.
15. M.I. 354.
16. Adikaram, *EHBC*, pp. 96-97.

the appearance of teaching and aching in the world. At least this is the common scholarly interpretation of these sections of this major Mahāyāna text, an interpretation which need not be the only one, as it may well symbolically indicate the Buddha's meditative absorption despite his activity, which, we feel, became the paradigm for the bodhisattva's teaching method. At this point we merely wish to indicate that, despite commentatorial tendencies to deify the Buddha and his body, one impossibility for the arahant, and explicitly so, was the indefinite prolongation of his life span. Whether or not this was an impossibility for the Buddha as well was something of an open question in Buddhism, although our reading of the primary sources indicates that this was thought to be impossible, some sections from the Mahāparinibbāna Suttanta and some commentaries notwithstanding.

To summarize this discussion of what an arahant can and cannot do, we would offer the following observations :

1. The arahant could not go against any of the fundamental ethical injunctions of Buddhism, as expressed in the *pañcasīla;* nor was he capable of adequate greed to accumulate wealth;

2. The arahant could in no way be motivated by delusion, attraction or aversion, the three *mūlakilesā*, or by fear. While almost all ethical talk in early Buddhism is done in the context of restraints, this particular impossibility could serve to indicate a whole sphere of positive action for the arahant. For example, we have seen that the idea of not teaching is rooted in pride (*asmimāna*); so since the arahant is incapable of being motivated by the three *mūlakilesā*, we would argue that he is incapable of not teaching. This is to say that of which an arahant is incapable includes retreat from the sufferings of the world.

3. Despite repeated attempts at deification, and despite some canonical ambivalence on this point, the arahant and the Buddha possess a body which is subject to death and decay, which is to say that they are not beyond the physical laws as we understand them, although they are certainly beyond the world, in the Buddhist sense of the term.

4. The arahant is incapable of any carelessness because he is by nature mindful of his actions and intentions and is diligent about them.

C. *Puññā* and *Kusala*

The question to be investigated in this section is whether Melford Spiro's observation, immediately below, poses a substantial issue for Buddhists, or whether it is one rooted in his own methodological presuppositions. Having done some field work in Burma, Spiro wrote :[17]

> Since, in *nibbānic* Buddhism, the soteriological goal consists in the cessation of rebirth, and since *karma* is the cause of rebirth, the aim of soteriological action is the extinction of *karma*. With the shift in soteriological goal to the persistence and enhancement of rebirth rather than to its cessation, the aim of soteriological action is the improvement rather than the extinction of one's *karma*. Hence, in *nibbānic* Buddhism salvation is achieved, not by works (and certainly not by faith), but only by knowledge (*paññā*); and since meditation alone produces knowledge requisite for salvation, meditation is *the* soteriological act of *nibbānic* Buddhism. Any other kind of action, even moral action, is subversive to salvation, for morality produces *karma*, which in turn causes rebirth. Among contemporary Theravāda Buddhists, on the other hand, not knowledge but merit is the goal of religious action, for merit alone improves one's *karma*, and good *karma* is prerequisite for *their* soteriological aim, viz., a happy rebirth.

We intend to investigate this claim not by questioning Spiro's field data, although our experiences in Sri Lanka and elsewhere seem to indicate a greater doctrinal sophistication on the part of rural Buddhists than Spiro found, and it seems that Gombrich[18] got similar results as we did; we propose to analyze the same question in the Buddhist terms of *puññā* (analogous but not identical with Spiro's '*kammatic* Buddhism'), and *kusala* (analogous but again not identical with Spiro's '*nibbānic* Buddhism'). Our question is whether textual evidence could be found for such a radical distinction between *puññā* and *kusala* as Spiro finds between *kammatic* and *nibbānic* Buddhism.

---

17. Melford Spiro, *Buddhism and Society : A Great Tradition and its Burmese Vicissitudes*, New York : Harper & Row, 1970, pp. 92-93.

18. Richard F. Gombrich, *Precept and Practice : Traditional Buddhism in the Rural Highlands of Ceylon*, London : Oxford University Press, 1971, *passim.*

By *kammatic* Buddhism, Spiro means that ethical system which leads to rebirths understood as desirable. *Puññā* means those actions (*kamma*) which lead to pleasing (in some sense of the term, *sukha*) results (*kammaphala*). According to Spiro, *kammatic* Buddhism is that Buddhism upon which society, especially lay society, bases its ethical structures.

Nibbānic Buddhism, according to Spiro, is that Buddhism in pursuit of *nibbāna*, which is fundamentally (or, according to some traditions, exclusively) in the domain of the *saṅgha*. We find that the term *kusala*, which could be translated as 'good'[19] or perhaps as 'skill' or 'skilfulness,'[20] has a wide range of usages,[21] one of which would be used to discuss the activity of the Buddha or an arahant. It is found that the term '*kusala*' is particularly Buddhist, although some precedents could be found in the *Chāndogya Upaniṣad*.[22] The term is applicable to the Buddha and the arahant in the sense that actions thought to be *kusala* were those with no result of action (*kammaphala*).[23]

To rephrase Spiro's problem, we are asking whether or in what sense could action which has pleasing fruit be ethically or logically connected with that type of action which, by virtue of its being *kusala*, has no fruit. Spiro contends implicitly that this could not be.

Textual sources on this issue are ambivalent. In some places it seems that the Buddha would support Spiro. For example, in the Mahācattāri Sutta,[24] the Buddha distinguishes two types of 'right view' (*sammā-diṭṭhi*). One type of right view is said to be "with the *āsavā*, inclining towards *puññā* and culminating in clinging" : *sāsavā puññābhāgiyā upadhivepakkā*. The other

19. Rhys-Davids employs this term in translating D.I.26., in *Sacred Books of the Buddhists*, London : P.T.S., 1956, Vol. II, p. 37.

20. As Isaline B. Horner's translation of the *Majjhima*, *The Middle Length Sayings*, II, p. 89.

21. As discussed at length by P. D. Premasiri, "Interpretation of Two Principal Ethical Terms in Early Buddhism," *Sri Lanka Journal of the Humanities*, II, 1, June 1976, pp. 63-74.

22. *Chāndogya Upaniṣad*, I, 11, 1, in Sarvepalli Radhakrishnan, ed. and tr., *The Principal Upaniṣads*, London : George Allen & Unwin, 1969 (1953).

23. A.V. 2.

24. M.III.72.

type of right view is "without the *āsavā*, beyond the world and connected with the path" (*anāsavā lokuttarā maggaṅgā*). Of the first type of right view, the Buddha expands his comment to say :[25]

> And what, monks, is that right view which is with the *āsavā*, which inclines toward *puññā*, and which culminates in clinging ? There is gift, there is offering, there is sacrifice, there is the result of the fruition of actions performed well or wrongly, there is this world, there is another world, there is mother, there is father, there are beings which arise spontaneously, there are in the world disciples and brahmins who talk about this world, other world, actualized by *abhiññā*.

As for the second type of right view, the Buddha says :[26]

> And what, monks, is that noble right view which is without the *āsavā*, beyond the world, and connected with the path ? [It is] whatever is of a noble heart-mind [or thought], of a heart-mind without the *āsavā*, of a part of the noble path, that which develops the noble path, is wisdom, is the controlling faculty of wisdom; is the power of wisdom, is the faculty of investigating the Dhamma, that is the right view which is connected with the path.

From this lengthy discussion, we see that the Buddha's comments on the two types of right view might be seen as correlating with Spiro's categories of *kammatic* and *nibbānic* Buddhism. To some extent it does, but the point we wish to underscore is that the distinction between ordinary and noble right view is one of attitude. The ordinary right view clings to language as referrential, believing in worlds, parents, various beings and a naive understanding of the religious language of the *samaṇas* and

---

25. M.III.72. (My translation)
Katamā ca bhikkhave sammādiṭṭhi sāsavā punnābhāgiya upadhivepakkā ? Atthi dinnaṃ, atthi yiṭṭhaṃ, atthi hutaṃ, atthi sukaṭadukkaṭānaṃ kammānaṃ phalaṃ vipāko, atthi ayaṃ loko, atthi paro loko, atthi mātā, atthi pitā, atthi sattā opapātikā, atthi loke samaṇabrāhmaṇā sammaggatā sammāpaṭipannā, ye imañ ca lokaṃ parañ ca lokaṃ sayaṃ abhiññā sacchikatvā pavadentīti.

26. M.III.72. (My translation)
Katamā ca bhikkhave sammādiṭṭhi ariyā anāsavā lokuttarā maggaṅgā ? Ya kho bhikkhave ariyacittassa anāsavacittassa ariyamaggassa samaṅgino ariyamaggaṃ bhāvayato paññā paññindriyaṃ paññābalaṃ dhammavicayasambojjhaṅgo sammādiṭṭhi maggaṅgā.

brāhmaṇas. That type of right view which is noble is one rooted in a purified mind-heart, in wisdom, and in analytic thought. For the moment, nothing is said about actions *puññā* and *kusala per se.* Yet we already see that the Buddha's methodology in responding to questions of this sort is not to make categorical claims which would radically distinguish two types of thought ('right view') or action (*puññā* and *kusala*). It seems that he would rather analyze them in terms of one's attitude.

In an analysis of *kamma*, the Buddha says[27] that there are essentially three types of *kamma* : dark *kamma* which yields dark fruits (*kammaphala*); bright *kamma* which yields bright fruits; and *kamma* which is neither dark nor bright, which is neither dark nor bright in its fruition, but which leads to the destruction of all deeds. It is in this sense that the arahant is called 'beyond all good and evil action' : *puññāpāpaphīnassa.*[28] Were this all the Buddha had to say about the topic of *puññā*, then one might be more inclined to accept Spiro's analysis. However, the Buddha also admonished his disciples not to be afraid of puññā :[29] "Monks, do not fear *puññā.* Monks, it is a name for happiness. That which is *puññā* is pleasant, benevolent, beloved and delightful."

In another place,[30] the Buddha is even more explicit in saying that skilful morality can lead to the highest :

> So you see, Ānanda, good conduct [*kusalāni sīlāni*] has freedom from remorse as object and profit; freedom from remorse has joy; joy has rapture; rapture has calm; calm has happiness; happiness has concentration: concentration has seeing things

---

27. M.I.389.
28. Dhammapada.III.7.
29. Itivuttaka, pp. 14-15. (My translation)
Mā bhikkhave puññānaṃ bhāyittha sukkhass' etaṃ bhikkhave adhivacanaṃ, iṭṭhassa kantassa piyassa manāpassa, yad idaṃ puññāni.
30. A.V.2. (PTS translation)
Iti kho Ānanda kusalāni sīlāni avippaṭisāratthāni avippaṭisārānisaṃsani, avippaṭisāro pāmujjattho pāmujjānisaṃso, pāmujjaṃ pītatthaṃ pītānisaṃsaṃ, pīti pasaddhatthā passadhānisaṃsā, passaddhi sukhatthā sukhānsaṃsā, sukhaṃ samādhatthaṃ samādhānisaṃsaṃ, samādhi yathābhūtañāṇadassanattho yathābhūtañāṇadassanānisaṃso, yathābhūtañāṇadassanaṃ nibbidāvirāgatthaṃ nibbidāvirāgānisaṃsaṃ, nibbidāvirāgo vimuttiñāṇadassanattho vimuttiñāṇadassananānisaṃso. Iti kho Ānanda kusalāni sīlāni anupubbena aggāya parentī ti.

as they really are; seeing things as they really are has revulsion and fading of interest; revulsion and fading of interest have release by knowing and seeing as their object and profit.

Thus a skilful kind of morality is directly connected with the Buddha's notion of release, and a fear of *puññā* as binding to *saṃsāra* is found by him to be superficial because it is not the action itself but one's attitude of detachment towards that action that is primary in his notion of *kamma*. Since *puññā* is connected with the goal in some sense, we have to reject Spiro's radical distinction of *kammatic* and *nibbānic* types of Buddhism, as we are led to reject Lynn A. de Silva's observation that[31] "This development of the idea of a proximate goal of a happy rebirth and of the ultimate goal of final release—a double morality so to say—was of very great significance since it enabled laymen to find a place within the structure of Buddhism."

We shall discuss below the relation of the arahant to the *saṅgha*/ laity question, so we wish to hold de Silva's observation in mind as to the problem of the role of the laity within Buddhism. This was a cardinal concern of the early Mahāyā-nists, who did not find the earlier solutions to it satisfactory; but we do not support de Silva's contention that the laity and the *saṅgha* operate on different ethical bases, as we do not support Spiro's claim of binary patterns of social organization, lay and monastic. A Buddhist analysis of the role of the various ethical systems usually associated with the laity is presented by H. Saddhatissa in his *Buddhist Ethics* :[32]

> ...the Precepts [and, by implication, all such 'lay' ethical structures] were never ends in themselves, confined to the mundane life, but were the essential preliminaries, as also the permanent accompaniments, to the attaining to the Highest State.

Having rejected Spiro's and others' analyses, we shall proceed to develop our own. We wish to argue that morality (*puññā*, *sīla*, etc.) is connected with *nibbāna*, which is said to be beyond good and evil,[33] in a way similar to that between meditation and

31. Lynn A. de Silva, *Buddhism : Beliefs and Practices in Sri Lanka*, Wellawatte : L. A. de Silva, 1974, p. 94.

32. H. Saddhatissa, *Buddhist Ethics : Essence of Buddhism*, London : George Allen & Unwin, 1970, p. 113.

33. Dhammapada.III.7.

arahattā or *nibbāna*. Earlier we argued that meditation is the habituating ground for *nibbāna*, which is pure spontaneity. Similarly, ethics condition us for enlightened activity (*kusala*).

We get an indication of the relationship between '*puññā*-type' Buddhism and '*nibbāna*-type' Buddhism, to adapt Spiro's categories, in the Dhānañjali Sutta.[34] Here we find a discussion between Sāriputta and the brahmin Dhānañjali. The discussion is of the various types and realms of rebirth, and Dhānañjali is making a case that rebirth in Brahmaloka would be the highest rebirth possible. Sāriputta sees that the brahmin is indeed very devoted to and intent on this rebirth, so he teaches him the method for attaining such a rebirth, although he knows that no rebirth at all would be better than the best rebirth. At the end of this *sutta*, the Buddha confirms that Sāriputta has taught properly. Dhānañjali dies, and the Buddha clairvoyantly confirms that he was reborn in Brahmaloka. There are some other examples of this type of specialized and personalized teachings. It seems to indicate that the goal of a high rebirth and the cessation of rebirth are not necessarily contradictory, that the Buddha's notion of spiritual growth was a very gradual one, and that while any rebirth was certainly unsatisfactory in the ultimate sense, it could provide an impetus for full spiritual actualization, much as he made use of the divine realms in instructing Nanda.[35] Discussing a similar incident, however, Walpola Rahula comes to the conclusion that this served to indicate the utter incompatibility of *nibbāna* and the laity. Rahula writes :[36]

> ...in the Sīgala-sutta of the *Dīgha Nikāya*...the Buddha lays down that one of the six duties of a monk towards the laity is to show them 'the way to heaven' (*sagga*). It is of great significance that it is 'the way to heaven' (*saggassa maggaṃ*) and not 'the way to emancipation' (*mokkhassa maggaṃ*) that the monks are expected to show to the laity. Obviously, the way to *nibbāna* was too difficult for the general masses to traverse.

We do not find Rahula's conclusion quite so obvious. If spiritual progress in the highest sense is understood as habituated by more

34. M.II.184-197.
35. Udana, pp. 21-24.
36. Rahula, *HBC*, pp. 251-252.

modest practices, such as *puññā* or meditation, then we could interpret the Buddha's method of teaching heaven to the laity as not postulating a separate, or even proximate, goal as a concession to those of inferior capabilities or situations, but as a stage in a gradual progress towards *nibbāna* or *arahattā*. Certainly if one reads the primary texts on this issue, one learns of numerous lay arahants. The position of the *Sutta Piṭaka* on this issue is overwhelmingly that laymen and laywomen could attain *arahattā*, which was understood as having nothing to do with such mundane distinctions as *saṅgha* and laity. By the time of the *Milindapañha*, however, a growing conservatism among saṅghika commentators led to the belief that lay life and *arahattā* were incompatible. We shall investigate this controversy shortly; what we wish to offer at this time is that, following by analogy the premise that *asaṅkhārika-kusala-citta* is rooted in *sasaṅkhārika-kusala-citta*,[37] that a free and spontaneous heart-mind is rooted in a well-trained, disciplined heart-mind. Just as rigorous meditation inclines toward *arahattā*, so *puññā* (and other ethical categories) inclines one toward *arahattā*, the cessation of rebirth. Further, following the Buddha,[38] the distinction between those actions which lead to pleasant fruitions and those actions which are spontaneous and therefore have no fruition, lies in the mind, in one's intentionality and relationship toward that given action. The Buddha never categorically says that all actions as such lead to continued death and rebirth. Shunning such dogmatic categoricality, the Buddha rather investigates the mind which acts, and not the bare action itself. Therefore the difference between *puññā* and *kusala* is the concomitant mental *dhammā* which are the matrix of that action. By performing *puññā*, a Buddhist could, having habituated himself to a certain ethical modality, begin to develop his mind, regarding such activity in such a way that these same ethical actions no longer would lead to continued rebirth, but to the cessation of rebirth. It is not a question of mere typology of actions into *kammatic* and *nibbānic* modes; nor is it that, as Rahula[39] holds, "...the way to *nibbāna* was too difficult for the general masses to

---

37. See chapter II, section A, part 3.
38. A.V.2.
39. Rahula, *HBC*, p. 252.

traverse"; rather, we offer that *puññā* was a type of action which leads to pleasurable results of action and by which the laity or the *saṅghikas* could develop that attitude which, when habituated, leads to the type of activity which we characterize as free and spontaneous, and which was exemplified by the Buddha and his arahant disciples. Far from leading to merely another rebirth, then, *puññā* could be and was used as a way leading to *arahattā* :[40] "So you see, Ānanda, good conduct leads gradually up to the summit."

D. *The Arahant and the Saṅgha/ Laity*

1. *General*

In the introduction to her translation of the *Dīgha Nikāya*,[41] Mrs. Rhys-Davids observes : "Who, in the oldest period, could be an Arahant ? The answer is : Anyone—men or women, old or young, lay or religieux." As we shall evidence, this observation is undoubtedly accurate. The *Sutta Piṭaka* has numerous instances of the attaining of *arahattā* by all sorts of the Buddha's disciples. Yet, by the time of the writing of the *Milindapañha*, the idea was being advanced that *arahattā* was in the domain of the *saṅghikas* alone;[42] at least one controversial verse of the *Milindapañha* was interpreted in this way. We shall consider this text's position on this question in the light of some comments by the Buddha in the *Majjhima Nikāya*[43] to see whether the position has been fairly represented. Unquestionably, however, one of the dominant themes in the rise of Mahāyāna Buddhism was its disenchantment with the strong emphasis placed on the *saṅgha* by robed commentators on and interpreters of the Pali texts. The vitality of this question at the Council of Pāṭalīputra, the scene of the most significant Buddhist schism, is evidenced by the fact that those who broke away from the *saṅgha*-oriented Sthaviravāda named themselves the Mahāsaṅghika, or 'the larger *saṅgha*,' This could indicate one of two things : first, that they were the larger group numerically at the

40. A.V. 2. (PTS translation)
Iti pi kho Ānanda kusalāni sīlāni anupubbena aggāya parentīti.
41. Rhys-Davids, *Dialogues of the Buddha*, III, p. 5.
42. See *Milindapañha*, pp. 264-265.
43. M.I. 483.

Council; or, that their conception of '*saṅgha*' was more all-embracing so as to provide a more vital role for the laity. Quite possibly both considerations came into play in arriving at the name 'Mahāsaṅghika,' which serves to indicate the importance for Buddhist history of the first issue we shall be considering in this section, namely the arahant in relation to the *saṅgha* and to the laity. The arahants especially, but all *saṅghikas* in general, defined their relationship with the laity in three broad categories. They were 'fields of merit' (*puññākkheta*) for the laity in the sense that by serving them, honoring them, et cetera, the lay Buddhist accumulates *puññā*. Similarly, they were, in a sense, the manifestation of all social and aesthetic graces for Buddhist culture. Secondly, they were understood as exemplars of the ideal Buddhist life, to be emulated by all. Of exemplars, of course, the Buddha was the paradigm. While this train of thought is indeed found in the *Sutta Piṭaka*, we find that the notion of the arahant as *kalyāṇamitta*,, 'spiritual friend,' or *guru*, 'teacher,' is the much more dominant *leitmotif* of the arahant's relationship with the laity. We shall be considering, then, these three somewhat distinct but interrelated themes which depict the arahant's relationship with society : that of *puññākkheta*, that of exemplar, and that of the active spiritual friend (*kalyāṇamitta*).

2. *Lay and Saṅghika Arahants*

That the lay arahant was well-known in the *Sutta Piṭaka* is clearly evident. Rhys-Davids[44] cites the following instances of members of the laity attaining to *arahattā* : Vin.I.17; S.V.94; A.III.451; Kathāvatthu, p. 267; Dhp. Comy. I.308; Jāt.II.229; and Milinda.II.57, 96 and 245. While this is clear, we find such laymen as the son of Asibandhaka approaching the Buddha and asking :[45] "How is it that the Lord teaches Dhamma in full to some, but to others he does not teach it in full ?" It is significant and, we believe, only possible that this question could be posed by a layman (*gahapati*). The Buddha replies without regard to the *saṅgha*/ laity division. He says that one

44. Rhys-Davids, *Dialogues of the Buddha*, III, p. 5, fn 1.
45. S.IV.314. (PTS translation)
Atha kiñcarehi bhante Bhagavā ekaccānaṃ sakkaccaṃ dhammaṃ deseti, ekaccānaṃ no tathā sakkaccaṃ dhammaṃ sesetīti ?

applies one's greatest efforts in those areas where one has reason to expect the most result, just as a farmer first tends his best fields, and only then turns his attention to the poorer ones. From this instance, it seems that the householder felt somewhat slighted, and attributed it to his lack of *saṅghika* status. The Buddha's response, however, was simply in terms of the capabilities of his disciples, with no mention of such status.

We find a more forceful example of the same feeling of discontent among the laity in the Anāthapiṇḍikovāda Sutta.[46] Anāthapiṇḍika was, of course, one of the most devoted and influential of the Buddha's lay disciples. He was the Buddha's foremost patron. Many of the Buddha's dialogues were said to be held at a grove generously provided by Anāthapiṇḍika, and some historians have suggested that much of the rapid early success of the Buddha's *sāsana* could be attributed, in part at least, to Anāthapiṇḍika's patronage. All of this information is necessary to appreciate the poignancy of his position in his discussion with Ānanda and Sāriputta. In this *sutta*, Anāthapiṇḍika is dying, and these two disciples attend his deathbed. Sāriputta gives a discourse about the meditational techniques for detaching consciousness from objects of consciousness, which leads Anāthapiṇḍika to remark : "I, reverend Ānanda, am not holding on, I am sinking. Although the Teacher and monks who were developing their minds visited me for a long time, I have never yet heard reasoned talk such as this." This is a powerful statement by Anāthapiṇḍika. As he was one of the closest and foremost disciples of the Buddha, it seems somewhat bizarre that it was not until his deathbed that he received such fundamental meditational instructions.

Ānanda replies to Anāthapiṇḍika :[47] "Reasoned talk such as this, householder, does not really occur for householders clad in white. It is for those that have gone forth, that reasoned

46. M.III.261. (PTS translation)
Nāhaṃ bhante Ānanda olīyāmi na saṃsiddāmi. Api me dīgharattaṃ Satthā payirupāsito, manobhāvanīyo ca bhikkhū na ca me evarūpī dhammī kathā sutapubbā ti.

47. M.III.261. (PTS translation)
Na kho gahapati gihīnaṃ odātavasanānaṃ evarūpi dhammī kathā paṭibhāti. Pabbajitānaṃ kho gahapati evarūpī dhammī kathā paṭibhātīti.

talk such as this usually occurs." Thus Ānanda and, by implication, Sāriputta here are represented as affirming a dichotomization of Buddhists into *saṅghikas* and householders (*gahapati*). Yet Anāthapiṇḍika emerges from this *sutta* as the real teacher. His next statement is reminiscent of Brahmā's exhortation to the Buddha shortly after his *bodhi* :[48]

> Well then, reverend Sāriputta, let there occur such talk as this for householders clad in white. There are, reverend Sāriputta, young men of family with but little dust in their eyes who, not hearing Dhamma, are declining, but they could be learners of Dhamma.

One must bear in mind that the redactors of the *Sutta Piṭaka* were well aware of the power of an aptly applied symbol, and it was not accidental that this powerful speech of Anāthapiṇḍika was addressed to Sāriputta. One might recall that, after hearing Brahmā's admonition to teach, which was phrased nearly identically to Anāthapiṇḍika's, the Buddha clairvoyantly surveyed the worlds, and it was Sāriputta upon whom his attention was drawn.[49] For this statement to be addressed to this same Sāriputta is, in effect, to call the Buddha and Brahmā as its witness. This incident could well be taken as an example of a layman giving teachings to the foremost disciples of the Buddha, Ānanda and especially Sāriputta. The drama of the deathbed scene serves to underscore Anāthapiṇḍika's point that Sāriputta and Ānanda had too narrow a view of how the Dhamma should be taught; he emerges as the stronger character in this *sutta*. It also serves to indicate the strong ambivalence felt by such eminent disciples about the whole issue of whether the Dhamma could properly be taught to the laity.

We need not go into detailed lists of accounts of householders who became arahants. In one place[50] we find a list of twentyone

48. M.III.261. (PTS translation)

    Tena hi bhante Sāriputta gihīnaṃ odātavasanānaṃ evarūpī dhammī kathā paṭibhātu. Santi hi bhante Sāriputta kulaputtā apparajakkhajātikā assavanatā dhammassa parihāyanti bhavissanti dhammassa aññātāro ti.

49. M.I.330-331; and cf. S.I.136-138.

50. A.III.450-451.

Other scholars[51] have previously presented such lists and occasions. We find examples of householders doing everything that *saṅghikas* do, including attaining *arahattā*, preaching (as Anāthapiṇḍika),[52] expressing *aññā*[53], and so forth. However, we find in the *Milindapañha* :[54] "For whomever attains *arahattā*, there are two courses and no others : either immediate going forth [or entry into the *saṅgha*] or total extinction [*parinibbāyati*], because he cannot go on beyond that."[55]

Now, the Buddha was never one for rigid categories of spiritual growth, as in one place[56] he complains to Mahā-Kassapa that the reason why there were fewer arahants nowadays than there were before was the proliferation of monastic precepts (*sikkhāpadāni*). In fact, he expresses differently the sentiment found in the *Milindapañha*. He says[57] that there is no layman who, without putting away the bonds that bind laymen, obtains after death the end of ills. In this place he is referring to the fruit of the anāgāmī rather than that of the arahant, but the point is the same. Rather than talk about one's being a householder or a *saṅghika*, it would be better to examine those conditions given which one understands oneself as being a householder or a *saṅghika*. As Saddhatissa[58] comments on this *Milindapañha*, "It is obvious that a householder after becoming an arahant does not remain attached to his home or family," which is a far cry from saying that one cannot be a householder and an arahant at the same time. The *Milindapañha* claim becomes coherent if one takes a more internalized meaning for 'householder.' In this sense, the term 'householder' would be used in talk about

51. Such as : Rhys-Davids, *Dialogues of the Buddha*, III, p. 5; and Johansson, *PN*, pp. 117-118.

52. A.IV.185-192.

53. A.III.211.

54. *Milindapañha*, pp. 364-365. (My translation)
Yo gihī arahattaṃ patto dve v' assa gatiyo bhavanti anaññā : tasmiṃ yeva divase pabbajati vā parinibbāyati vā, na so divaso sakkā atikkametun ti.

55. This is discussed by Bimala Churn Law, "Nirvāṇa and Buddhist Laymen," *Annals of the Bhandarkar Oriental Research Institute*, 1933, Vol. 14, pp. 80-86, p. 84.

56. A.II.224.

57. M.I. 483.

58. Saddhatissa, *op. cit.*, p. 120.

one ensnared by the passions such that these passions express themselves in a wife, family, accumulation of wealth, et cetera. In our discussion of the five or nine 'impossibilities' for an arahant, the fifth member of the list was the impossibility of his enjoying accumulated wealth as does a householder. But the dichotomization, if any there be, is not between *arahattā* and a householder status. The tension here is between the *saṅgha* and the laity, and this was an historical tension.

Although this is not explicit in the *Sutta Piṭaka*, one could well make the case that one not only ceases to be a householder upon the attainment of *arahattā*, but one ceases to be human as well. Remembering the incident where the Buddha is asked what sort of being he is, whether human, divine or whatever, the Buddha replies that none of these categories apply to him, as he is the Buddha. Since, in an important sense, the world ceases for the arahant, so of course would one's position as 'householder.' But were this *Milindapañha* verse taken in too literal and rigid a sense, as there is some evidence that in certain cases it has been, the one ends up with a formalism and a condescending attitude towards the laity that was one of the contributing factors to the schism at Pāṭalīputra and the rise of the Mahāyāna, one of whose professed aims was a more vital spiritual position for the laity. Thus the *saṅgha*/ laity tension was an historical one, and not one stemming from the *Sutta Piṭaka* itself.

3. *The Arahant as Puññākkheta and Exemplar*

We can distinguish two modalities of the arahant's inter-relation with the laity : a passive modality, which would include his role as the field of merit (*puññākkheta*) for the laity, and his being an exemplar for the laity and non-arahant *saṅghikas*; and an active modality, that of a teacher (*guru*) or spiritual friend (*kalyāṇamitta*). We find the references to this active modality much more numerous and significant than those to the passive modalities.

A classic statement of his role as *puññākkheta* is found in the *Itivuttaka* of the *Khuddaka Nikāya* :[59]

---

59. Itivuttaka, pp. 111-112. (PTS translation)
Sāgārā anāgārā ca ubho aññoññanissitā /
ārādhayanti saddhammaṃ yogakkhemam anuttaraṃ //

> Home-dwellers and the homeless, both alike dependent on each other, come to win true Dhamma, utter safety from the yoke. From home-dwellers the homeless ones accept the robe, the means of life and bed and seat, dispelling hardships. But relying on him, the Wellfarer [Sugata], home-loving householders who trust the Ariyan wisdom of the worthy, musing, in this life Dhamma practicing, walking the Way that leads to a happy bourn, glad in the heaven world to win the bliss they seek.

According to this verse, the relationship of the arahant and the laity could be defined as one wherein the laity provides livelihood to the arahant. By so doing and by following his meditational instructions faithfully, the laity gains merit to facilitate their rebirth in some heavenly realm. This is a classical statement of the problem, and the type of statement from which Spiro most likely developed his distinction of *nibbānic* and *kammatic* Buddhism, which has been discussed above. However, the interdependence of *saṅgha* and laity of which the *Itivuttaka* speaks, when considered in the light of other canonical and commentatorial references is not quite so simple a matter as an exchange of livelihood for merit and some rudimentary meditational instructions. In the *Manorathapūraṇī*,[60] for example, we read of a layman named Dārubhaṇḍaka Mahātissa, a poor man of Mahāgāma, Lanka. Having saved all his earnings for six months of work in a sugar mill, he was able to present a generous gift to the *thera* of Ambariya Vihāra. Learning of how arduously Dārubhaṇḍaka had to work to enable him to present the gift, the *thera* became inspired and fortified his meditational efforts to the extent that he became an arahant, all so that this gift could have the most possible *puññā*. Thus the notion of an arahant's being a *puññākkheta* does not mean a passive accepting of gifts from the laity. The role of *puññākkheta* is such that it entails a very active receiving; it provides strong motivation for the

---

Sārāgesu ca cīvaraṃ paccayaṃ sayanāsanaṃ /
anāgārā paṭicchanti parissayavinodanaṃ //
Sugataṃ pana nissāya gahaṭṭhā gharam esino /
saddahāna arahataṃ ariyapaññāya jhāniyo //
Idha dhammaṃ caritvāna maggaṃ sugatimāminaṃ /
nandino devalokasmiṃ modanti kāmakāmino ti //

60. Cited in Adikaram, *EHBC*, p. 117.

monk to progress spiritually in order to fulfil the *puññākkheta* role.

Similar to the role of *Puññākkheta*, the arahant adds his own type of aesthetic to the world. As the Buddha says in *gāthā* :[61]

The varied beauties of the park, the grove,
Or lakes of lotuses and lovely line
For man's enjoyment are of little worth.
In village or the wild, in vale, or hill,
Where'ere the 'men of worth'—the Arahants—
Their dwelling make, that is the spot
By situation most enjoyable.

Again, this type of aesthetic enhancement indicates a passive interaction with those who are not arahants, which is very similar to the role of the arahant as exemplar : one who by living in a certain manner provides an example and inspiration for the rest of us, as is discussed at some length in the *Aṅguttara Nikāya.*[62]

However, the primary function of the arahant in his more or less passive interactions is that of the *puññākkheta.* However, we would add a caution here against taking the terminology of 'passive/active' too literally. These are meant only as modalities of interactions, and as we have seen with the *puññākkheta* modality, the arahant's passivity as *puññākkheta*, exemplar, or whatever, is not all that passive; he must maintain very strict standards to function adequately in these modalities. However, in the *Sutta Piṭaka*, most of the talk about the arahant as *puññākkheta* centers around the devotee and not around the arahant. As we read in the *Dhammapada* :[63]

He who reverences those worthy of reverence, whether Buddhas or their disciples; Those who have overcome the impediments

---

61. S.I.232-233. (PTS translation)
Ārācamcetyā venacetyā / pokkharaññā sunimmita /
ṃanussarāmaṇeyyassa / kalaṃ nāgghanti soḷasmiṃ //
Gāme vā yadivāraññe / ninne vā yadivā thale /
yattha arahanto viharanti / tam bhūmirāmaṇeyyakan 'ti //

62. A. IV.388-390.

63. Dhammapada.XIV.17-18. (Nārada translation)
Pūjārahe pūjayato—buddhe yadi vā sāvake
Papañcasammatikkante—tiṇṇasokapariddave.
Te tādise pūjayato—nibbute akutobhaye
Na sakkā puññaṃ saṅkhātuṃ—im' ettam' iti kena ci.

and have got rid of grief and lamentation—The merit of him who reverences such peaceful and fearless ones cannot be measured by anyone as such and such.

To summarize this passive modality of the arahant's interaction with the laity and non-arahant *saṅghikas*, we find that it is not necessarily so passive an interaction as might be thought; that to be an exemplar or a *puññākkheta* involves very rigorous standards, and that living up to these standards is as much an incentive for spiritual progress for the arahant as for the laity. However, much of *puññākkheta*-talk found in the *Sutta Piṭaka* revolves not around the arahant, but around the devotee of the arahant. So great was the merit resulting from these practices that it was said that one simple act of worship of the arahant was more meritorious than a century of tending sacrificial fires according to the Brahmanical traditions.[64] Of course, the roles of *puññākkheta* and exemplar are not necessarily totally distinguishable. Involved in worshipping an arahant, presumably, would be observing and emulating him. This would tend to follow our position that *puññā* and *kusala* are continuous and not discrete; and this, of course, leads us to a discussion of the arahant as teacher and spiritual friend, which we characterize as the active modalities of interrelation.

4. *The Arahant as Kalyāṇamitta*

The term '*kalyāṇamitta*' (Sanskrit : *kalyāṇamitra*; Tibetan : *dge shes*), which we have been translating as 'spiritual friend,' derives from the Vedic roots √*kan* or √*kā*, which is also the root of *kāma*, meaning 'to be pleased' or 'to enjoy';[65] and *mitra*, 'friend.' Thus the *kalyāṇamitta* is the friend who brings one into contact with that which is pleasing.

In the *Sutta Piṭaka*, the term '*kalyāṇa*' is used in many contexts, such as : (a) *kalyāṇapaṭipadā*,[66] the 'path leading to that which is pleasing,' a synonym for the noble eightfold path; (b) *kalyāṇaṃ karoti*,[67] to perform good deeds; (c) *kalyāṇakāma*,[68] with the sense

64. Dhammapada.VIII.8.
65. Whitney, p. 17.
66. J.III.342.
67. S.I.72.
68. S.I.227.

of religious sentiment which seeks that which is pleasing. In one place,[69] we are told that one who observes the moral precepts (*sīlapadaṃ*) could be said to be '*kalyāṇa*'; and in the *Dīghanikāya Aṭṭhakathā*[70] we find '*kalyāṇamitta*' and *seṭṭha* ('teacher') given as synonyms.

Edgerton[71] gives us : "good friend, regularly said to be one (not as a rule a Buddha) who helps in conversion or religious practice." The *P.T.S. Dictionary*[72] gives beautiful, charming, auspicious, helpful and morally good for '*kalyāṇa*'; and it offers two senses for *kalyāṇamitta* : "1. a good companion, a virtuous friend, an honest, pure friend...and 2. as a spiritual guide, a spiritual advisor. The Buddha is the spiritual friend par excellence, but any other Arahant can act as such..."

While the theme of the importance of the *kalyāṇamitta* for the spiritual growth of the disciple is found throughout the *Sutta Piṭaka*, the most direct and frequent reference is found in the *Khuddaka Nikāya*. We shall cite two examples of praise for the *kalyāṇamitta*. In the first, the arahant Kisāgotamī says :[73]

> Friendship with noble souls throughout the world
> The Sage hath praised. A fool, in sooth, grows wise
> If he but entertain a noble friend.
> Cleave to the men of worth ! In them who cleave
> Wisdom doth grow; and in the pious love
> From all your sorrows shall ye be released.

A similar sentiment is found in the *Itivuttaka* :[74]

> The monk who has a lovely friend, who pays
> Deference and reverence to him, who does
> What friends advise,—if mindful and composed,
> Such in due course shall win all fetters' end.

---

69. A.II.222.
70. DA.I.146.
71. Edgerton, *BHSD*, p. 174.
72. *P.T.S. Dictionary*, pp. 199-200.
73. Thig., verses 213-214. (PTS translation)
kalyāṇmittatā munimā lokaṃ ādissa vaṇṇitā /
Kalyāṇmitte bhajamāno api bālo paṇḍito assa //
bhajitabbā sappurisā paññā tatha pavaḍḍhati bhajantānaṃ /
bhajamāno sappurise sabbehi pi sukkhehi mucceyya //
74. Itivuttaka, p. 10. (PTS translation)
Kalyāṇamitto yo bhikkhu sappatisso sagāravo /
karaṃ mittānaṃ vacanaṃ sampajāno patissato /
pāpuṇe anupubbena sabbasaṃyojanakkhayan ti //

The *kalyāṇamitta*, then, is a person, usually an arahant and, following the paradigm of *kalyāṇamitta* in the life of the Buddha, who teaches disciples the Dhamma. One cannot judge from the Pali whether the term originally connoted one who is friendly with spirituality, or a friend who leads one spiritually; however, some intimacy is indicated by the use of the term 'friend' (*mitta*). According to the testimony of Kisāgotamī, the *kalyāṇamitta* can be of vital importance in the spiritual development of the disciple, and if we are to follow from the premise that the Buddha is the *kalyāṇamitta* par excellence, we might conclude that, except in the case of the Buddha, the *kalyāṇamitta* is indispensable in becoming an arahant. The *kalyāṇamitta* is the Buddhist *guru*, and all forms of Buddhism—Theravāda, Mahāyāna or Tantrayāna—are single in affirming his crucial position. To the largest extent, he fulfils his role by teaching, and we now propose to investigate three related questions in order to get a sense of what it might mean to be a *kalyāṇamitta*. The first issue is to show that the arahant does in fact teach. We find that much is said on this point, and we conclude from the sheer volume of canonical discussions on this point that it was a very important issue for Buddhists, and that they had a great deal at stake in affirming that the arahant does in fact teach.

To digress for a moment on this point : in our field work in countries with significant Buddhist and Hindu populations, i.e., Sri Lanka, one of the significant distinctions that rural, indigenous Buddhists made between their religion and Hinduism is as follows. Granted that both religions have a role for the gods (*devatā*), how does one distinguish the function of the gods in Hinduism and Buddhism ? Their answers usually ran along the lines that while the same gods were propitiated in both religions, the Hindus thought that the gods could in some sense aid the devotee's life in a spiritual sense. According to Buddhism, they told us, while the gods were indeed powerful in such realms as assuring the success of a venture or for the growth of crops, or for exorcism, cursing, et cetera, no Buddhist would ever say that the gods could be of any help spiritually. Spiritual growth, which is Dhamma, was totally in one's own hands, so to speak, and beyond the sphere of influence of any of the gods. For there to be spiritual progress, one had to pay close heed to the preaching (*bane*) of the bhikkhus, and practise *puññā* and some *bhāvanā*; for there to be material progress, the gods must be propitiated. These two 'religious' functions are perceived as radically discrete.

This bit of native Buddhist exegesis serves to underscore the importance of the role of the *kalyāṇamitta* in Buddhism. If spiritual progress could be accomplished by grace, by mystery, or by gods, as the Buddhists perceive the Hindus to believe, then the role of the human agent in spirituality would be diminished. However, if spiritual progress were entirely a matter of one's own efforts and the guidance of the *saṅgha*, then of course the *kalyāṇamitta* emerges as a highly significant and potent religious force. We have found this to be the case in several Buddhist countries : that while the gods were worshipped and propitiated, the *kalyāṇamitta* were revered and became the object of the most profound religious sentiments of that culture.

Returning to our immediate case, then, after demonstrating that the arahant does in fact teach, we shall enter into a discussion of how he does that, what teaching might mean in a Buddhist sense. We shall conclude our discussion with a consideration of whether this teaching is accidental or essential to the notion of the arahant.

That an arahant should teach is rooted in that a Buddha does teach. Therefore, we shall first consider the two major themes found in the *Sutta Piṭaka* by which is related the Buddha's famous confrontation with Māra shortly after his attainment of *bodhi* under the tree at Buddha Gayā. These two themes are the case in which the Buddha's defeat of Māra was mediated through Brahmā, and the case wherein he directly confronts Māra.

The first type is reported in the *Saṃyutta Nikāya*.[75] In this account, Māra puts the thought to the Buddha that he should not teach, and the Buddha reflects :[76]

This that through many toils I've won,
Enough ! Why should I make it known ?
By folk with lust and hate consumed

75. S.I.136-138.

76. S.I.136. (PTS translation)
Kicchena me adhigataṃ / halandāni pakāsituṃ /
rāgadosaparetehi / nāyaṃ dhammo susambuddho //
paṭisotagāmiṃ nipuṇaṃ / gambhīram duddasan aṇuṃ /
rāgarattā na dakkhinti / tamokkhandhena āvutā ti //

Not this a Norm [Dhamma] that can be grasped.
Against the stream (of common thought),
Deep, subtle, fine, and hard to see,
Unseen it will be by passion's slaves,
Cloaked in the murk (of ignorance).

The distinguishing feature of this rendition of the Buddha's confrontation with Mara is that in this one he wavers; he indicates some ambivalence on the part of Buddhism about whether teaching is essential to enlightenment. In this *sutta*, Brahmā-Sahampati argues with the Buddha;[77] he tells him that there are many who are not so caught up with hatred and with passion, who are near to supreme *bodhi* and need only some small indication from him in order to attain to *arahattā*. The Buddha then clairvoyantly surveys the worlds and focuses on the likes of Sāriputta, those who have little dust on their eyes, and resolves to turn the wheel of the Dhamma.

The unmediated account of this incident is found in the Brahmanimantaṇika Sutta of the Majjhima Nikāya.[78] In this account, Māra approaches the Buddha and tells him that it is useless to teach, that there had been many fully perfect Buddhas (*sammāsambuddhā*) before him, and that they never taught to any disciples, and that the Buddha should simply remain at ease and untroubled with the sufferings of others. The Buddha replies that he knows who Māra is, perhaps the personification of those psychological forces which run against spiritual growth. He says that while Māra is a very uncompassionate fellow, he is compassionate and that any before him who claimed to be a *sammāsambuddha* but did not teach were not in fact truly *sammāsambuddha*. The Buddha says that whether he is teaching or not, he is still untroubled by the world, and is still a Tathāgata; but he shall compassionately teach.

A short digression on these comments by the Buddha leads one to consider the origins of the *paccekabuddha* concept. The *paccekabuddha* (Sanskrit : *pratyekabuddha*; Tibetan : *rang sangs rgyas*) has attained to *bodhi*, but

> ...is not able to overcome the anxiety that the teaching will be too difficult to be made understood by others, is not capable of

77. S.I.136-138.
78. M.I.330-331.

> setting aside the disadvantage of having to find disciples and of having to incite them to go against the stream, and finds it difficult to be taken out of his concentration and to establish contacts with other people.[79]

Since it is understood in Buddhism that all *sammāsambuddhā* teach the same Dhamma, and since the Buddha here readily admits that there are some who had attained to *bodhi* and who did not teach the Dhamma, perhaps the *paccekabuddha* concept originally arose in order to accommodate within the Buddhist world-view, those saints who were not Buddhist (and, therefore, did not teach the same Dhamma as did the Buddha), but were nevertheless able to resolve their own multi-lemma of human existence, as did the Buddha. We are suggesting, albeit tentatively as further research on this point would be in order, that the *paccekabuddha* concept was originally the Buddha's way of dealing with 'other religions' within his system; it was his acknowledgement of the possibility of human perfectability outside of his formulation of the Dhamma. Of course, the *paccekabuddha* concept as it became known within the Buddhist commentatorial traditions is vastly different from this simpler and more primitive conception.

Returning to these two accounts of the Buddha's confrontation with Māra, we see that the canon redactors' attitude towards the question of the Buddha's response to Māra was ambivalent; or at least that the redactors of the different *nikāyas* had different views on the matter. In the *Saṃyutta* version, the Buddha is equivocal; he needs Brahmā's aid in order to inspire him to defeat Māra. This would indicate that the redactors' attitude towards the Buddha's teaching was ambivalent; that in this *sutta* it seems that not teaching appeared to the Buddha, even for a moment, as a live option. In the *Majjhima* we find the Buddha unequivocal. He replies to Māra's seductive offer immediately; he must and does teach because he is moved by compassion, although this teaching in no way effects his spiritual equilibrium. There is no one Buddhist canonical attitude, then, towards the Buddha and teaching, and this canonical ambivalence led to some hermeneutical difficulties for the Buddhist commentators, as we shall see. The point to note, however, is that the Buddha, whether spontaneously or through Brahmā's inspiration, must and does teach.

79. Kloppenborg, *op. cit.*, p. 77.

And the reason he teaches is because he is moved by compassion (*hitānu-kampī*). This is explicit in one place[80] where the Buddha says : "The fully enlightened one feels love and compassion while teaching others." This is more fully developed in another place.[81] While staying at Rājagaha, a *yakkha* named Sakka approaches him and says : "It is not proper that you, a *samaṇa* who has given up all bonds [*gantha*], should teach to others." The Buddha replies :[82]

> Sakka, for whatever reason men of caste congregate and live, [those reasons] do not apply to the arahant. Compassion motivates him. By trusting in mind, he teaches others, but is not thereby bound since he is with compassion and empathy [*sānukampā anuddayā*, an emphatic repetition].

We would now recall our point made about emotions and motivations in the arahant : that that type of motivation which is not rooted in the *kilesā* is not *kammatically* binding; therefore the Buddha's activity is not binding because it is motivated by or accompanied by compassion. The emphatic repetition of *sānukampā anuddayā* underscores the great significance of the idea that selfless motivation is radically different than the usual type of motivation of which modern psychologists speak.

The arahant teaches for the same reasons that the Buddha teaches. This is explicitly clear when he admonishes them :[83]

---

80. S.I.111. (My translation)
hitānukampīsambuddho yad aññam anusāsati.

81. S.I.206. (My translation)
Sabbaganthapahīnassa vippamuttassa te sato, samaṇassa na taṃ sādhu yad aññam anusāsatī ti.

82. S.I.206. (My translation)
Yena kenaci vaṇṇena saṃvāso Sakka jāyati, na tam arahati sappañño manasā anukampituṃ, manasā ce pasannena yad aññam anusāsati, na tena hoti saṃyutto sānokampā anuddayā ti.

83. S.I.131-132. (My translation)
Mutto 'ham bhikkhave sabbapāsehi ye dibbā ye ca mānusā. Tumhe pi bhikkhave muttā sabbapāsehi ye dibbā ye ca mānusā caratha bhikkhave cārikaṃ bahujana-hitāya bahujana-sukhāya lokānukampakāya atthāya hitāya sukhāya devamanussānaṃ. Mā ekena dve agamettha desetha bhikkhave dhammam ādikalyāṇaṃ majjhe kalyāṇaṃ pariyosāṇa kalyāṇaṃ sāttham savyajanaṃ kevalaparipuṇṇaṃ parisuddhaṃ brahmacariyaṃ pakāsetha. Santi sattā apparajakkha-jātikā assavanata

> Monks, I am freed from all entanglements, both divine and human. Monks, you are freed from all entanglements, both divine and human. Monks, carry out your work for the good of the masses, for the happiness of the masses, out of compassion for the world, for the aim, the good and the happiness of gods and humans. No two of you should go in the same way. Monks, teach the Dhamma which in the foundation, middle and end is for spiritual progress [*kalyāṇaṃ*], which is a fully meritorious and purified method for spiritual striving [*brahmacariyaṃ*]. There are beings for whom but a little dust clouds their vision; they die for a lack of the Dhamma, yet would become otherwise from the Dhamma. Monks, I, too, am going to preach the Dhamma at Uruvelā.

The Buddha is admonishing his disciples to teach for the same reasons and in the same way that he does : that they are both freed from all entanglements.

There is an appeal to self-evidence in Udāyin's response to a question posed by a brahmin lady of the Verahaccāni.[84] The lady is asking how it is that an arahant teaches :

> Prithee, reverend sir, because of the existence of what does an arahant make known happiness and suffering, and because of the absence of what does an arahant not make known happiness and suffering ?

Udāyin's response, while appealing to self-evidence, is nevertheless of wide implications :[85]

> Sister, because of the existence of eye, an arahant makes known happiness and suffering; because of the absence of eye, the arahant does not make known happiness and suffering; ...Tongue...Mind...et cetera.

---

dhammassa parihāyanti bhavissanti dhammassa aññātāro. Aham pi bhikkhave yena Uruvelā Senānigamo ten-upa-saṅkamissāmi dhamma desanāyā ti.

84. S.IV.123-124. (My translation)

Kisminnu kho bhante arahanto sukhadukkham paññāpenti kismim asati arahanto sukhadukkhaṃ na paññāpentīti ?

85. S.IV.123-124. (My translation)

Cakkhusmiṃ kho bhagini sati arahanto sukhadukkham paññāpenti. Cakkhusmim asati arahanto sukhadukkhaṃ na paññāpenti... la ... Jivhāya ... Menasmiṃ. ...

This is to say that, given sensory apparati, the suffering which follows from those apparati compels the arahant to teach; and that his role as teacher is coterminous with the suffering of the world, as he does not teach only when there is absence of sensory apparati. The sentiment herein expressed by Udāyin bears striking resemblance to the vows taken by a bodhisattva, and which is the fundamental generator of relative *bodhicitta* : that the bodhisattva will teach in the worlds so long as there are worlds in which he may teach. Udāyin says that so long as there is sensory apparati, which is to say so long as there is a world, the arahant teaches, and his task is completed only when there is absence of sensory apparati, which is to say when the world ceases.

The *Sutta Piṭaka* is firm in maintaining that it is natural for an arahant to teach. One *tirthika* named Lohicca[86] approached the Buddha with the idea that an arahant should not teach; that, in fact, for him to do so would be a form of lust (*rāga*), which is tantamount to holding the position represented in the *Kathāvatthu*[87] as belief in compassion as rooted in passion. The Buddha summarily dismisses Lohicca's position, and goes on to discuss the structures given which a teaching might be acceptable or one that should be rejected. His dismissal of Lohicca is so offhanded, so casual, that it gives the impression of his not even considering Lohicca's claim seriously at all.

We may recall our discussion of *satipaṭṭhāna* meditation, wherein we maintained[88] that meditation itself was a method for both warding oneself and warding others. So, apparently, was the way the Buddha considered teaching the Dhamma. The Buddha sees a direct connection between teaching and spiritual attainment,[89] that he considered teaching *per se* as part of the monk's religious practice :

---

86. D.xii.9ff.
87. Kathāvatthu, pp. 561ff.
88. A.V.168-169.
89. A.III.21. (My translation)
Idha bhikkhave bhikkhuno Satthā dhammaṃ deseti aññataro vā garuṭṭhāniyo sabrahmacārī. Yathā yathā bhikkhave assa bhikkhuno Satthā dhammaṃ deseti aññataro vā garuṭṭhāniyo sabrahmacārī, tathā tathā so tasmiṃ dhamme atthapaṭisaṃvedī ca hoti dhammapaṭisaṃvedī ca. Tassa atthapaṭisaṃvedino dhammapaṭisaṃvedino

> Monks, take the case when the Master, or some fellow in the spiritual life who acts as a teacher, instructs a monk in the Dhamma. While he teaches, that monk partakes of both the spirit and the letter of the Dhamma. From this experience, gladness [*pāmujja*] springs up; from that, zest [*pīti*]; in such a state his whole being calms down; when he is calm, ease is experienced; and for him who dwells at ease, the mind is composed. Monks, this is the first sphere of release....

Thus, according to the Buddha, teaching can be a spiritually opening process both for the teacher and the disciple, and when his disciples are admonished to go out and teach, one assumes, that was equally for their own benefit as for those whom they taught.

Having demonstrated that an arahant does in fact teach, and does so for the same reasons as does the Buddha, we may now address ourselves to a brief study of what characterizes his teaching methodology; or, given that he teaches, we shall now enquire into how he teaches. After this analysis we may address a fundamental question : is this teaching by the arahant essential or accidental to his nature *qua* arahant ?

The arahant teaches in the same way that the Buddha teaches, just as we have shown that he teaches for the same reasons.[90] As with the Buddha's teaching, faith or conviction (*saddhā*) is a prerequisite to exposition of the Dhamma :[91] "Insight is gained by trust that the Arahants hold saving doctrine; next, by diligent and close attention to their homilies." Like the Buddha, they teach with ease and effortlessly :[92]

---

pāmujjam jāyati, pamuditassa pīti jāyati, pītamanassa kāyo passambhati, passaddhakāyo sukhaṃ vedeti, sukhino cittaṃ samāshiyati : idaṃ bhikkhave paṭhamaṃ vimuttāyatanaṃ. ...

90. S.I.131-132.
91. Suttanipāta, p. 33. (HOS translation)
Saddhahāno arahatam dhammaṃ nibbānapattiyā sussūsā labhate paññaṃ appamatto vicakkhaṇo.
92. M.I.396. (My translation)
Evam eva kho rājakumāra ye te khattiyapaṇḍitā pi brāhmaṇapaṇḍitā pi gahapatipaṇḍitā pi samaṇapaṇḍitā pi pañhaṃ abhisaṅkharitvā Tathāgataṃ upasaṅkamitvā pucchanti, ṭhānaso v' etaṃ Tathāgataṃ paṭibhāti, taṃ kissa hetu : Sā hi rājakumāra Tathāgatassa dhammadhātu suppaṭividdhā yassā dhammadhātuyā suppaṭividdhattā ṭhānaso v' etaṃ Tathāgataṃ paṭibhātīti.

> So it is, Prince, that when a wise noble, wise brahmin, wise householder, or wise *samaṇa* who has framed a question comes to the Tathāgata and poses it, [the answer] comes to the Tathāgata at once. For what reason ? Prince, there is full comprehension of the realm of Dhamma by the Tathāgata, and because of this full comprehension of the realm of Dhamma, [the answer] comes to the Tathāgata at once.

However, when the arahant or the Buddha answers a question, or poses a formulation of the Dhamma, they do so in such a way that the answer or position has validity in the context of the situation in which it arises. Much has been said and written about the provisional, pedagogical structure of Buddhist religious language. This provisional nature is underscored in the Buddha's famous analogy of the raft. Since we have already discussed water and crossing-over symbolism in Buddhism, we need only mention the Buddha's famous analogy of the raft. Since we have already discussed water and crossing-over symbolism in Buddhism, we need only mention that the Buddha said[93] that the raft, symbol of crossing over, is not to be retained after the crossing (of the floods) has been accomplished and the other shore (*nibbāna*, in the language of this analogy) has been reached. The Buddha makes explicit the implications of this analogy :[94]

> Monks, so it is that the analogy of the raft is taught by me as Dhamma for crossing over [the floods] , not for keeping [once the crossing is accomplished]. Monks, by understanding the analogy of the raft, you should abandon Dhamma [teachings], all the more that which is not-Dhamma.

Remembering the centrality of this-shore/other-shore symbolism for the whole structure of the Buddha's teaching, as he employed this symbol set for talk about suffering and the cessation of suffering, which is the central theme of all of Buddhism, the wide implications of the *Dhammapada* verse might well be appreciated :[95]

---

93. M.I.134-135.

94. M.I.135. (My translation)
Evam eva kho bhikkhave kullūpamo mayā dhammo desito nittharaṇatthāya no gahaṇatthāya. Kullūpamaṃ vo bhikkhave ājānantehi dhammā pi vo pahātabbā, pag eva adhammā.

95. Dhammapada.XXVI. 3. (My translation)
Yassa pāraṃ apāraṃ vā pārāpāraṃ na vijjati.
Vītaddaraṃ visaṃyuttaṃ, tad ahaṃ brūmi brāhmaṇaṃ.

> For whom the terms 'this shore,' 'other shore,' 'both this shore and other shore,' do not apply; free from sorrow and detached, him I call a brahmin.

Here the Buddha is saying that he who understands his method of employing religious and symbolic language, he who understands the way in which the Buddha teaches, he is the one who could be called brahmin or arahant.

K. N. Jayatilleke[96] does an excellent job of demonstrating that the Buddha does not teach simply by means of an appeal to authority (*anussava*) or reasoning (*takka*), and it would be redundant to repeat his findings here. An analysis of what the Buddha does teach, which he himself undertakes,[97] shows that he teaches only what is (a) fact, (b) true, (c) connected with the goal, and (d) what may or may not be pleasing to others, but only given that the Tathāgata is expert at knowing the contexts and situations in which such teaching may be fruitful for his disciples.

We shall discuss some of the philosophic implications of these criteria of what should and should not be taught in the next chapter on the philosophy of the arahant, but it does not seem to follow, as Jayatilleke contends, that the Buddha was talking a kind of empiricism, since it is a tenet of empiricism that that which is meaningful is that which could be said to be fact and true without regard for any connection with any goal, and especially without regard for the personality of the observer, and this last factor, as this *sutta* says, seems to be the Buddha's most crucial criterion for what is to be taught. The Buddha concludes this discussion not with any talk about a correspondence theory of truth, or by postulating any principle of verifiability, as Jayatilleke might lead one to expect, but with a summary of the humanistic ground out of which he teaches. He concludes :[98] "And what is the reason [for this method of teaching] ? Prince, it is because the Tathāgata feels compassion for beings."

---

96. Jayatilleke, *op. cit.*, pp. 169-276.
97. M. I.395.
    Tathāgato vācaṃ jānāti bhūtaṃ tacchaṃ atthasaṃhitaṃ, sā ca paresaṃ appiyā amanāpā, tatra kālaññū Tathāgato hoti tassa vācāya veyyākaraṇāya.
98. M.I.395. (PTS translation)
    Taṃ kissa hetu ? Atthi rājakumāra Tathāgatassa sattesu anukampā ti.

This type of Buddhist compassion is one which feels for and understands the psychological matrix of a question, one which knows that a significant philosophico-religious question could not be answered apart from a full appreciation of the sufferings of the questioner which led him to raise an issue in the first place; compassion becomes the ultimate criterion for religious language and not, as Jayatilleke concludes, correspondence theories of truth or the notion of verifiability. Our reading of this passage leads us to conclude that the Buddha held to be the most important consideration in teaching not any empiricism, but the psycho-contextual history of the questioner : *tatra kālaññū Tathāgato hoti tassā veyyākaraṇiyā.*[99] This appreciation, which is what a Buddhist means by compassion, allows the Buddha to employ symbolically such religious talk as 'this shore' and 'other shore,' without becoming so fascinated with his language that the language and supposed principles of significant language (such as verifiability) that the language itself becomes religiously significant, losing the contextual, existential nature of the way a Buddha or an arahant teaches.

The arahant or the Buddha teaches primarily out of compassion;[100] he teaches in a way similar to that by which a kindly man might protect a flock of deer from danger.[101] He teaches some even the way to rebirth with Brahmā if that is suitable to the psychological context of the disciple.[102] He teaches by using his *iddhividhā.*[103] He becomes a linguist to teach all beings.[104] He does not, however, teach in a way that would threaten his own welfare,[105] although this caution would apply more to non-arahant bhikkhus than to arahants, since the arahant is incapable of carelessness.[106]

Given that an arahant teaches in all sorts of ways, and is very skilful at employing religious language in a specific Buddhist

99. M.I.395 : tatra kālaññū Tathāgato hoti tassa veyyākaraṇiyā.
100. S.IV.133.
101. M.I.117-118.
102. M.II.184-197.
103. S.V. 269-270; and cf. Vism. 392.
104. Vin.II.139; cf. Lamotte, *HBI*, pp. 610-614.
105. Dhammapada.XII.10.
106. S.IV.125

sense, all of this rooted in compassion, we are left with one remaining question as to whether or not teaching is essential or accidental to an arahant's being an arahant. Miss Horner[107] finds fault with some commentators who held that it was not essential. She says "... it is argued... by those wishing to condemn the arahant-concept, that if he did teach the laity this was not at all essential to his main business in life, which was to win his own perfection." We shall examine later on the Mahāyāna hermeneutical principle that the arahant or *śrāvaka* was concerned with pacification of only himself, while the bodhisattva, whom they raise as an alternate expression of the perfected human, was concerned with pacification for all sentient beings. Part of the problem seems to be with the way of interpreting the Buddha's comment made to Māra in the Brahmanimantaṇika Sutta :[108]

> For, Evil One, whether a Tathāgata is teaching Dhamma to disciples, he is such a one; whether, Evil One, a Tathāgata is not teaching Dhamma to disciples, he is such a one; whether, Evil One, a Tathāgata is communicating it to disciples, he is such a one; whether, Evil One, a Tathāgata is not communicating it to disciples, he is such a one. What is the reason for this ? Evil One, in a Tathāgata those cankers [*āsavā*] which are connected with the defilements [*kilesā*], with again-becoming, fearful, whose results are anguish, which make for birth, ageing and dying in the future, those are got rid of, cut off at the root, made like a palm-tree stump, so that they can come to no further existence in the future.

We extend the Buddha's comments to all arahants as well as himself. If one were to hold that the arahant was arahant because of his teaching others, then all sorts of conceptual problems would arise. Was he an arahant while he was sleeping,

---

107. Horner, *EBTMP*, p. 187.

108. M.I.331. (PTS translation)

Desento pi hi pāpima Tathāgato sāvakānaṃ dhammaṃ tādiso vā, adesento pi hi pāpima Tathāgato sāvakānaṃ dhammaṃ tādiso vā; upanento pi hi pāpima Tathāgato sāvake tādiso vā, anupanento pi hi pāpima Tathāgato sāvake tādiso vā; taṃ kissa hetu : Tathāgatassa pāpima ye āsavā saṅkilesikā ponobhavikā sadarā dukkhavipākā āyatiṃ jātijarāmaraṇiyā te pahīnā ucchinnamūlā tālāvatthukatā anabhāvakatā ayatiṃ anuppādadhammā.

or doing something other than teaching ? If one were arahant because of teaching others, then could the question not arise that teaching somehow was a cause of *arahattā*, which would be in contradiction to the fundamental notion that *arahattā* or *nibbāna* was unconditioned (*asaṅkhāta*), while all *dhammā* which are unsatisfactory are so because of their conditionality ? What the Buddha is saying is that the arahant's being arahant is not a result of teaching, and he is very diligent to affirm this point. This does not mean, as some Theravāda commentators and most Mahāyāna hermeneuticians hold, that an arahant does not or may not teach, or even that his fundamental interest is his own self-pacification. We have tried to show that an arahant does in fact teach. For him not to do so, according to the Buddha, would be a 'form of lust' (*rāga*),[109] and the arahant is one who by definition is free from all lust. Therefore, he must by nature teach, and he does so. But his being arahant is not in any sense dependent on his teaching, as the Buddha affirms that one is arahant whether teaching or not. We conclude, then, that while an arahant invariably teaches, he is not an arahant because he teaches, but because he is *khīṇāsavo*. However, being *khīṇāsavo* means being free from all lust, and if not teaching is a form of lust, as the Buddha says, the teaching does seem to be essential to the arahant notion as found in the *Sutta Piṭaka*.

---

109. D.xxi. 9ff.

CHAPTER VI

THE PHILOSOPHY OF THE ARAHANT

A. *General*

Any discussion of any philosophy of the arahant must be prefaced by the type of caution which the Buddha expressed as the parable of the blind men and the elephant.[1] In this well-known story, several blind men touch various parts of an elephant, and they are asked to report on what they have encountered. Some reply that they are touching a tree, others a rock, others a brush, and so on. So in any attempt at pointing to a philosophy of the arahant, or of the Buddha, one is in much the same position as the blind men; one cannot 'say it all' with regard to Buddhism, and it is this philosophically elusive (or, as some have said, non-entangling) character of Buddhist philosophy that has led many onto academic shoals in attempts to steer a middle course (*majjhima paṭipāda*) between various conceptualizations. Our reading of primary texts from several Buddhist traditions leads us to the conclusion that there is no one 'central philosophy' of Buddhism, and that precisely the dynamic of the history of Buddhist ideas has been repeated correctives against one-sided interpretations of the *sāsana* of the Buddha. As we shall demonstrate, one finds many conceptual gestalts, or constellations of notions, within the Pali canon. Various Buddhist systems, from the so-called 'eighteen schools' through late Mahāyāna developments, have taken some of these conceptual constellations and built them into systems. In the Pali canon, one finds a germinal theory of momentariness, one finds a sophisticated analysis of language, one finds the foundations for later metaphysical systems, and so forth. Our position is that all of the later Buddhist systems (*siddhānta*) can and do trace their philosophies to the Buddha of the Pali canon quite authenticly. For the scientific scholar of Buddhism, however, there can be no contentment with taking any one of these systems as the true or best interpretation of what the Buddha had to say; to do so would

1. Udana, pp. 66-69.

be to miss the fundamental dynamic of the Buddha's encounter with his disciples. The dynamic manner by which he taught is understood only by an appreciation of the contexts in which he spoke, by understanding that the Buddha dealt with questions on a spiritual and psychological, and not on a philosophic, level. It was never a question *per se* to which the Buddha responded; it was the spiritual-psychological matrix given which a question could be raised. Therefore, in a sense, the Buddha was philosophically unsystematic. But this was not a weakness on the part of the Buddha; rather, it was his greatest strength. As long as philosophical claiming is met solely on its own ground, one remains within the circularity of philosophy (*diṭṭhivāda*), a circularity from which the Buddha worked to emancipate us.

We are not here offering merely a psychological reduction of philosophy, although this would undoubtedly be one important aspect of the Buddha's teaching method. As the Buddha says,[2] some questions would require this psychological reduction by means of either a refusal to accept the question on its own terms, or by means of a Socratic process of counter-questioning. Other questions, he says, require a straightforward reply (*ekaṃsavyākaraṇīyo*), and others require further analysis (*vibhajjavyākàraṇīyo*). The point to note is that rather than simply offer a psychological reductionism as the method for responding to questions, the Buddha tells us that the type of answer to be given depends upon the matrix from which the question emerges, the spiritual and psychological condition of the questioner.

Rather than present any one conceptual constellation as *the* philosophy of the arahant, therefore, we shall content ourselves with indicating what we find to be the most significant and the dominant philosophic threads running through the Pali canon. We do not propose, by way of support, a statistical analysis of how often the Buddha responds in various modalities throughout our texts, although this could be a useful undertaking. What we do propose is to show four main themes : that of the arahant as one who invites us to 'come and see' (*ehipassako*) for ourselves, a theme which has been taken by some scholars to be a type of logical positivism; that of the arahant as critical philosopher,

2. A.II.46.

one who rejects all philosophic formulations (*diṭṭhi*); that of the arahant as language analyst, one who does not take language as referrential (*svabhavavāda*) and who is an expert at everyday, that is non-philosophic, language (*loke vohārā*); and, finally, the arahant as one about whom nothing could be claimed, one whose comings and goings cannot be known (*vattaṃ tesaṃ na 'tthi paññāpanāya*).

B. *Ehipassako*

While there is no final word on what type of philosophy the Buddha was presenting, he did give us some indications of the sort of teaching he was and was not giving. In the most general sense, he said that what he was teaching was not dogmatic but reasonable. He said in the Mahātaṇhāsaṅkhaya Sutta[3] that the Dhamma could be characterized in this way : "Monks, I say that the Dhamma is to be seen for onself, is timeless, is come-and-see (*ehipassako*), going further, to be actualized individually by the wise." In the well-known Kālāma Sutta of the *Mahāvagga* of the *Aṅguttara Nikāya*[4] the Buddha again calls the Dhamma '*ehipassako*.' In this *sutta*, the Kālāmas are confused by the proliferation of various teachings at the time of the Buddha, and they ask him quite bluntly which of these teachings are right and which are wrong. The Buddha tells them that their question is a wrong one; that they should not rely upon dogmatism, but should try some analysis (*vibbhaja*). He then proceeds to question them about ethical concerns, about the three *mūlakilesā* of attraction, aversion and ignorance, and about the absence of these *mūlakilesā*. He asks them to follow that which they can observe or infer to lead to the absence of these *kilesā*. Rather than giving categorical criteria for accepting or rejecting a given teaching, then, the Buddha asks his interlocutors to use their powers of reason and observation, and to please not bother him with questions that are not his own. Here the Buddha is following his dictum of not contending with others,[5] and is redirecting the

3. M.I.265. (My translation)
Sandiṭṭhiko ayaṃ bhikkhave dhammo akāliko ehipassako opanayiko paccattam veditabbo viññuhīti.

4. Soma Thera, ed. and tr., *Kālāma Sutta : The Buddha's Charter of Free Inquiry*, Kandy : Buddhist Publication Society, Wheel Series, No. 8, second impression, 1963.

5. S.III.138.

responsibility for the kālāmas' religious search back upon themselves. He has given them very basic guidelines for accepting or rejecting teachings, but without any of the elaboration which is found, for example, in the Brahmajāla Sutta,[6] where he himself analyzes various systems of teaching. This *sutta* then, which Soma Thera calls "the Buddha's charter of free inquiry,"[7] is given in a context which necessitates that the responsibility for judging teachings returns to the individual. As Soma Thera comments :[8]

> The reasonableness of the Dhamma, the Buddha's teaching, is chiefly evident in its welcoming careful examination at all stages of the path to enlightenment. Indeed the whole course of training for wisdom culminating in the purity of the consummate one (the arhat) is intimately bound up with examination and analysis of things internal.

Undoubtedly there is a strong emphasis on the individual's responsibility to analyze and, in some sense, to test out the Buddha's teachings. In one place,[9] the Buddha is discussing with Anuruddha the 'seven thoughts of a great man' (*satta mahāpurisa vittake*), which generally discuss his accomplishment at meditations and his ethical purity. The Buddha is pleased with Anuruddha's discussion, but cautions him not to forget an eighth member to the list of these thoughts, namely : "This Dhamma is for those who are without diffuseness (*papañca*), for those who enjoy non-diffuseness of thought; not for those who are diffuse in thought and enjoy diffuseness of thought."[10]

To say that one should approach the Dhamma in a *nippapañcārāmassāyaṃ* manner is to say that it should not be the object

---

Nāhaṃ bhikkhave lokena vividāmi loko ca mayā vividati.
Na bhikkhave dhammavādī kenaci lokasmiṃ vividati.

6. D. i.
7. Soma Thera, *op. cit.*
8. *Ibid.*, p. 1.
9. A.IV. 229. (My translation)
nippapañcārāmassāyaṃ dhammo nippapañcaratino, nāyaṃ dhammo papañcārāmassa papañcaratino ti.
10. We are aware of the unsatisfactoriness of the translation of the term '*papañca*' by 'diffuseness of thought,' although this translation does carry some of its literal as well as conceptual meaning. For an extended, excellent treatment of this key early Buddhist term, see Bhikkhu Ñāṇananda, *Concept and Reality in Early Buddhist Thought*, Kandy : Buddhist Publication Society, 2nd ed., 1976 (1971).

of our cognitive projections, that one should be clear-headed in considering it. A similar point is made when the Buddha announces five *dhammā* by which a monk can fully understand the unmovable (*akuppaṃ*), which the commentary equates with *arahattā*.[11] These five *dhammās* are : "He is a master of logical analysis; a master in analyzing causal relations; a master of grammatical analysis; a master in analyzing things knowable; and he reflects on the mind as freed (*ānāpānasati*)." Certain analytic faculties were considered by the Buddha to be of vital importance for spiritual progress. In another place,[12] the Buddha poses and then answers a question. He asks rhetorically : "Is there, brethren, any method, by following which a brother, apart from belief, apart from inclination, apart from hearsay, apart from argument as to method, apart from reflection on reasons, apart from delight in speculation, could affirm insight.... ?" Here the problem posed by the Buddha reflects his analysis of reason and authority as unsatisfactory grounds for spiritual knowledge.[13] Yet his answer gives us a meditational sort of analysis :[14]

> Herein, brethren, a brother, beholding an object with the eye, either recognizes within him the existence of lust, malice and illusion, thus : "I have lust, malice and illusion," or recognizes the non-existence within him, thus : "I have not lust,

---

11. A.III.119-120. (PTS translation)
Idha bhikkhave bhikkhu atthapaṭisambhidāpatto hoti, dhammapaṭisambhidāpattohoti, nirut.ipaṭisambhidāpatto hoti, paṭibhānapaṭisambhidāpatto hoti, yathāvimuttim cittaṃ paccavekkhati.
12. S.IV.138-139. (PTS translation)
Atthi nu kho bhikkhave pariyāyo yam pariyāyam āgamma bhikkhu annatreva saddhāya annatra ruciyā annatrānussavā annatrākāraparivittakā annatra diṭṭhinijjhānakhantiyā annam vyākareyya....
13. Jayatilleke, *op. cit.*, pp. 169-276.
14. S.'IV.138-139. (PTS translation)
Idha bhikkhave bhikkhu cakkhunā rūpaṃ disvā santam vā ajjhattaṃ rāgadosamohaṃ Atthi me ajjhattaṃ rāgadosamohoti pajānāti, asantam vā ajjhataṃ rāgadosamohaṃ Natthi me ajjhatam rāgadosamohoti pajānāti. Yantam bhikkhave bhikkhu cakkhunā rūpaṃ disvā santam vā ajjhataṃ rāgadosamohaṃ Atthi me ajjhataṃ rāgadosamohoti pajānāti, asantaṃ vā ajjhatam rāgadosamohaṃ Nattjo me ajjhataṃ rāgadosamohoti pajānāti, api nu me bhikkhave dhammā saddhāya vā veditabbā ruciyā vā veditabbā anussavena vā veditabbā ākāraparivitakkena vā veditabbā diṭṭhinijjhānakhantiyā vā veditabbā ti.

malice and illusion." Now as to that recognition of their existence or non-existence of these qualities within him, are these conditions, I ask, to be understood by belief, or inclination, or hearsay, or argument as to method or reflection on reasons, or delight in speculation ?

In this *sutta* we see that the Buddha is advocating an introspective type of analysis of motivation and psychodynamics which underlies the acceptance or rejection of any given statement of religio-philosophic import. So while the Buddha sets up the problem such that one expects to see him dispel any reliance on cognitive faculties for the understanding of the Dhamma, he returns us to another form of analysis : psychoanalysis rather than analysis of philosophy. One may infer from this *sutta* that that philosophy which is rooted in the *mūlakilesā* of lust, malice and delusion (*rāgadosamoha*), is found to be unsatisfactory, while that which is found in the absence of these *mūlakilesā* could be satisfactory. The point is that in this *sutta* the Buddha is affirming a meditational sort of analysis, and we continue to find that, indeed, analysis often is understood by the Buddha as being of vital importance.

Just as we saw earlier in our discussion of the arahant and meditation, the Buddha seemed to accept the standard Hindu meditational practices, such as the *jhānā,* but what he added was a significantly new analysis of these meditational or mystical experiences as ultimately unsatisfactory. There we argued that it was precisely this finding of meditational states as unsatisfactory that was the Buddha's vital contribution to meditation, and not especially the establishment of new meditational practices in themselves. In the Alagaddūpama Sutta[15] we find the same

15. M.I.133-134. (PTS translation)
Te taṃ dhammaṃ pariyāpuṇitvā tesaṃ dhammānaṃ paññāya atthaṃ na upaparikkhanti, tesaṃ te dhammā paññāya atthaṃ anupaparikkhataṃ na nijjhānaṃ khamanti, te upārambhānisaṃsā c' eva dhammaṃ pariyāpuṇanti itivādappamokkhānisaṃsā ca, yassa c' atthāya dhammaṃ pariyāpuṇanti tañ c' assa atthaṃ nānubhonti, tesaṃ te dhammā duggahitā dīgharattaṃ ahitāya dukkhāya saṃvattani, taṃ kissa hetu : duggahītattā bhikkhave dhammānaṃ. Seyyathā pi bhikkhave puriso alagaddatthiko alagaddagavesī alagaddapariyesanaṃ caramāno, so passeyya mahantaṃ alagaddaṃ, tam evaṃ bhoge vā naṇguṭṭhe vā gaṇheyya, tasso so alagaddo paṭiparivattitvā hatthe vā bāhāya vā aññatarasmiṃ vā aṅgapaccaṅge ḍaseyya, so tato nidānaṃ maraṇaṃ vā

point being made. The Buddha says that any mystical experience, in this case that of 'the mastery of the Dhamma' (*dhammaṃ pariyāpuṇanti*), becomes dangerous if not thoroughly and properly analyzed in Buddhist perspective. The text is significant enough in the context of our discussion of the role of analysis in Buddhism to merit citation at length :

> These, having mastered Dhamma, do not test the meaning of those things by intuitive wisdom; and these things whose meaning is untested by intuitive wisdom do not become clear; they master this Dhamma simply for the advantage of reproaching others and for the advantage of gossiping, and they do not arrive at that goal for the sake of which they mastered Dhamma. These things, badly grasped by them, conduce for a long time to their woe and sorrow. What is the reason for this ? Monks, it is because of a wrong grasp of things. Monks, it is like a man walking about aiming after a water-snake, looking about for a water-snake. He might see a large water-snake, and he might take hold of it by a coil or by its tail; the water-snake, having rounded on him, might bite him on his hand or arm or on another part of his body; from this cause he might come to dying or to pain like unto dying. What is the reason for this ? Monks, it is because of a wrong grasp of the water-snake. Even so, monks, do some foolish men here master Dhamma.... Monks, it is because of a wrong grasp of things.

Thus, a lack of analysis of the path itself, including those concepts and mystical experiences one is likely to encounter along the path, is as spiritually dangerous as a hastily-grabbed snake is physically dangerous. It was precisely with this same analogy that Nāgārjuna and Candrakīrti warned of the dangers of a badly-grasped Dhamma; but we would argue that, in their case, this poor grasp indicated a lack of specifically linguistic analysis.[16]

This 'come-and-see' (*ehipassako*) quality of the Buddha's teaching has at least one constellation of usages : that of anlysis,

---

nigaccheyya maraṇamattaṃ vā dukkhaṃ, taṃ kissa hetu : duggahītattā bhikkhave alagadassa ... evaṃ eva kho bhikkhave idh' ekacce moghapurisā dhammaṃ pariyāpuṇanti ... diggahītattā bhikkhave dhammānaṃ.

16. Candrakīrti, *dBu ma tshig gsal*, *op. cit.*, chapter 24, pp. 400-439.

both intellectually in the sense of the general reasonableness of the Dhamma; and also and perhaps more significantly, in the sense of meditational analysis of religious experiences, as well as the more commonly understood teaching of the Buddha of meditational analysis of ordinary experiences. We restate our earlier claim that *all* experience, according to the Buddha, be it 'ordinary' or 'mystical,' is to be understood as unsatisfactory, and that this understanding of it as unsatisfactory is to be achieved by a particular type of meditational analysis.

The Buddha also tells us some things that the Dhamma is not. One thing which the Buddha said it was not was that it was not an extreme. This claim certainly was not unusual for religious teachers of India, but it seems that what the Buddha meant by that which is not an extreme, or that which he calls 'the middle path' (*majjhima paṭipāda*), was of a different order.

One extreme into which the Buddha refused to fall was that of overly-severe ascetic practice. He says :[17] "Those recluses and brahmins who uphold self-mortification, who make self-mortification essential, who remain clinging to self-mortification,—they are incapable of crossing the flood." Of course, the Buddha was no antinomian : the sensual life was for him as unsatisfactory as an overly-severe religious life. So, one meaning of 'the middle path' is a religious commitment that falls somewhere between hedonism and an overly-rigorous asceticism.

But the principle of a 'middle path' was of equal significance conceptually as it was practically. A naive and prejudicial view of Buddhism has led some scholars to the type of position wherein it is believed that so-called early Buddhism taught a practical middle path, and that it was up to such great commentators as Nāgārjuna and his followers to show us the conceptual and psychological implications of this middle path. But the Buddha equally maintained both aspects : the middle path for him means discarding the raft of *sammādiṭṭhi* or 'right view', since holding them after having crossed over the floods would be an absurdity; the middle path also means, as the Brahmajāla Sutta tells us,[18] avoiding the extremes of eternalism and nihilism.

17. A.II.200. (PTS translation)
Ye te Sāḷha samaṇabrāhmaṇā tapojigucchāhetuvādā tapojigucchāsārā tapojigucchā-allīnā viharanti abhabbā te oghassa nittharaṇāya.

18. D.i.

This latter charge of nihilism was to plague almost all Buddhist authors, and the charge, we have found, is based on a naive, referrential notion of language : that a grammatical negation entails some sort of 'existential' negation and to say, for example, that things have no 'self-nature' is to negate a real. However, Nāgārjuna was not up against anything new. The Buddha himself reports similar pseudo-criticisms during his lifetime. In the Alagaddūpama Sutta[19] the Buddha considers the charge that he is a nihilist, and says that he is not negating an existent entity,[20] but that he is merely talking about suffering and the cessation of suffering.[21]

Another extreme which the Buddha avoided would be that which revolves around a western notion of 'faith.' In and of itself, *saddhā*, a notion analogous to but not identical with 'faith,' could not resolve our human multi-lemma. However, a faith based on careful observation and reflection can be of spiritual significance. In the Vīmaṃsaka Sutta,[22] a *sutta* which deals primarily with the role of cognitive analysis, the Buddha takes up the question of faith, and he says :

> Monks, in anyone in whom faith [*saddhā*] in the Teacher is established, supported by these methods, by these sentences, by these words, that faith is called reasoned, strong; it is indestructible by a recluse or a brahmin or *devā* or Māra or a Brahmā or by anyone in the world. Thus, monks, does there come to be a study of the Tathāgata's Dhamma, and thus does the Tathāgata come to be well studied in the proper manner.

This type of 'reasoned faith which is based on vision (*saddhā dassana-mūlikā daḷhā*) clearly could be opposed to a type of

19. M.I.140.
20. Venayiko samaṇo Gotamo sato satassa ucchedaṃ vināsaṃ vibhavaṃ paññāpetīti.
21. Pubbe cāhaṃ bhikkhave etarahi ca dukkhañ c' eva paññāpemi dukkhassa ca nirodhaṃ.
22. M.I.320. (PTS translation)
Yassa kassaci bhikkhave imehi ākārehi imehi padehi imehi byañjanehi Tathāgato saddhā niviṭṭhā hoti mūlajātā patiṭṭhitā, ayaṃ vuccati bhikkhave ākāravatī saddhā dassanamūlikā daḷhā, asaṃhāriyā samaṇena vā brāhmaṇena vā devena vā Mārena vā Brahmunā vā kenaci vā lokasmiṃ. Evaṃ kho bhikkhave Tathāgato dhammatā susamanniṭṭho hotīti.

faith which accepts reports, scriptures, and that which could not be experienced for oneself. Of course, this was one of the ways in which he criticized the Jaina's faith in the omniscience (*sabbaññā*) of their teacher; that one who was not himself omniscient could not have reason to claim another to be so. But the Buddha goes further in rejecting as incompetent for reasoned discussion (*akaccha*) those who accept, on the one hand, report, tradition or hearsay (*anussavena mā paramparāya mā itikirāya*); and also those who accept that which is based merely on logic, philosophic and personal tastes (*takkahetu mā nayahetu mā ākāraparivitakkena mā diṭṭhinijjhānakkhantiyā*).[23] Just as the type of faith in the Tathāgata of which the Buddha speaks should lead one to observe and consider the Tathāgata, to 'come-and-see' the Tathāgata as exemplar and *kalyāṇamitta* for oneself, so logic and tradition, in and of themselves, are as unlikely to lead to spiritual progress as is a blind faith. In the final analysis, the Buddha's teaching must be seen for oneself : *ehipassako*. The Buddha himself cannot be taken as the ultimate guarantor of his teaching, however much 'faith' one has in him, however revered he may be and however much our reverence for him is to our spiritual advantage. The ultimate guarantor of the correctness of the Dhamma is our experience of it, our analytical and meditative insights which culminate in *paññāvimutto*. This is a very human-rooted position, one in which the textual tradition is responsible to the individual, rather than posing the ultimate responsibility for the individual to submit himself to any textual tradition; the person is primary, even in regard to the Tathāgata. As the Buddha says :[24] "Monks, an inquiring monk, learning the range of another's mind, should make a study of the Tathāgata so as to distinguish whether he is a fully Self-awakened One or not."

For these reasons, we certainly affirm Jayatilleke's characterization of the way in which the Buddha taught as 'experientialism,'[25] but we would not hold with his conclusion that because the

23. A.II.191.
24. M.I.317. (PTS translation)
Vīmaṃsakena bhikkhave bhikkhunā parassa cetopariyāyaṃ ājānantena Tathāgato samannesanā kātabbā, sammāsambuddho vā no vā iti viññāṇāyāti.
25. Jayatilleke, *EBTK*, pp. 170-173.

Buddha referred all questions of the ultimate validity of his teaching back to the individual, that he was therefore any type of empiricist or logical positivist. There would be several reasons for our rejecting Jayatilleke's conclusion, including the self-imposed limitation of scope of the verification principle and scientific method in general, a limitation to clearly prsocribed issues; but it would not be to the point of this essay to engage in an extended dialogue with Jayatilleke on this entire issue. What is significant in this context is that while there is most certainly a verificationism in a very loose sense in the Buddha's teaching, namely his call to 'come-and-see,' and his ultimate referring of questions of ultimate validity of his Dhamma back to the individual and not to authority, logic, et cetera, it is also undeniable that it is the very heart of the scientific method and verificationism that the personhood of the enquirer not enter into the problem at hand. Cohen and Nagel[26] tell us precisely that it is this removal of the personhood of the enquirer that is the hall-mark of the scientific method and, we would add, of verificationism : "...its [the scientific method's] successful use depends upon seeking, in a deliberate manner, and *irrespective of what men's desires are*, to recognize, as well as to take advantage of, the structure which the flux possesses." Of course, for Buddhism these notions of the person and that which the person desires are not separable, and we might also make the type of case which claimed that any structure which the so-called 'flux' might possess could not be arrived at separately from our desire that there be structures to it. However, our point is more limited : that verificationism is rooted in the impersonality of the observer(s), and that this impersonality is thought to be guaranteed by bringing into the picture the bugaboo notion of 'consensus'; which is to say that while one individual observer, it could be held, could not rid himself of his personhood to the extent necessary for 'objective' observations, then certainly a large enough group should be able to observe without any considerations of personality. This seems patently absurd : that history has repeatedly shown us that even very large groups are

26. Cohen and Nagel, *An Introduction to Logic and Scientific Method*, Bombay : Allied Publishers, Indian reprint edition, 1976, p. 391. Emphasis added.

as prone to psychoses as is the individual, and there seems to be no reasonable grounds for assuming that simply because a large number of people, rather than an individual, hold something to be the case, that it follows then that this would be the case. The Buddha proceeded in just the opposite way from these verificationists and scientists. When an issue arose during discourses with his disciples, the Buddha taught contextually, in full regard of the person with whom he spoke. No claim of the Buddha's could be seen apart from the context of the spiritual growth of the person with whom he was engaged in discussion. While that individual might be asked to 'come-and-see,' it could not be held that the problem on the table could be solved by removing the personhood of the one who had that problem; the metaphysical belief in an objectively observable did not cloud the Buddha's pedagogical vision. The problems which he entertained were human problems, and their dis-solution was also fully human and not impersonal as is science and logical positivism. Those seeking to impose an impersonal consistency on the Buddha do him injustice that the blind man does to the elephant in calling him a tree. It is precisely this human-rootedness which the Buddha meant by 'middle path'; that positions and claims were secondary to the human situation, and that we do violence to the suffering person by treating him as secondary to our principles, be they metaphysical, logical, traditional or verificationist. Simply because the Buddha understood his system as reasonable does not entail that his system was derived through reason, and simply because the individual, in becoming an arahant, can discover for himself that the Buddha's teaching was in fact true, does not imply that impersonal criteria for truth and falsity need be brought into the picture to enable us to understand the way in which he taught.

C. *Diṭṭhi*

Nearly every book on Buddhist thought, be it introductory or technical, devotes a great part of its discussion to analyses of the Buddha's position vis-a-vis 'views' or *diṭṭhi* (Sanskrit : *dṛṣṭi*; Tibetan : *rtogs pa*). The *P.T.S. Dictionary*[27] lists the following usages for *diṭṭhi* : view, belief, dogma, theory, speculation, esp.

27. *P.T.S. Dictionary*, p. 321.

false theory, groundless or unfounded opinion. Edgerton[28] adds heresy, as indicated in the Saddharmapuṇḍarīka[29] where the Buddha says that he is one who can straighten out bent heretical views : *dṛṣṭiṃ kurvāmi ujjukām.* So important in the eyes of Buddhaghoṣa was the abandonment of *diṭṭhi* that in one place he says that *nibbāna* is escape from *diṭṭhi*, which we would here translate as 'opinionatedness' : *nissaraṇan ti diṭṭhinissaraṇaṃ nāma nibbānaṃ taṃ yathābhūtaṃ nappajānāti.*[30]

What we propose to explore in this section is what the Buddha had to say about *diṭṭhi*, and how that relates to the arahant as one who teaches or expresses *nibbāna* in a way that is not merely the formulation of simply another *diṭṭhi*. To understand how Buddhist teaching was not merely a case of new *diṭṭhi*, we must appreciate the Buddha's position as to what could be called correct view of *sammādiṭṭhi*, which is to say the leaving behind of all views and opinionatedness in such a way that the teaching of an arahant becomes a non-entangling expression of *nibbāna.* Structurally this is similar to the ancient Buddhist practice of *aññā vyākaroti*, or expression of *arahattā*, in the sense that that which was said in these situations was not merely another stage on the usual procedure of claiming and counter-claiming, but an open, spontaneous expression. To help us in our exploration of *diṭṭhi*, we shall consider, in the next section, the arahant as a sort of language analyst. One point on which the Buddha was never confused was about the way in which he employed language : heuristically, pedagogically, symbolically, expressively, but never in a technical philosophic sense of claiming x such that x negates y. In order to elucidate some of the Pali texts on this subject, we shall not hesitate to show the development of this linguistic criticism of Buddhism through some later Mahāyāna authors.

The Buddha, for very good reasons which shall be discussed in this section, devoted more of his teaching to an analysis of what conditions a wrong view (*pāpadiṭṭhi*) than to what could be said to be a correct view (*sammādiṭṭhi*). Therefore, we shall commence our discussion of views with an analysis of wrong views.

28. Edgerton, *BHSD*, p. 269.
29. *Saddharmapuṇḍarīka.* 125.14.
30. MA.II.144.

The principle by which the Buddha held some views to be wrong is simply those views which are rooted in self, which conduce to continued suffering rather than to the cessation of suffering. This point is made when Vaccha asks the Buddha[31] why it is that other religious teachers do not reach the same conclusions as the Buddha. He replies :

> The wanderers of other views, Vaccha, regard the eye thus : "This is mine. This am I. This is my self." They so regard the ear, nose, tongue, body and mind. That is why, Vaccha, the Arahant, who is a Fully Enlightened One, does not so regard the eye, ear, nose, tongue, body and mind. Therefore when questioned on these matters he does not reply that the world is eternal or not eternal, and so forth, or say whether or no the Tathāgata exists after death.

In another place,[32] the Buddha says that all grasping and worry (*upādā-paritassanā*) can be reduced to the view that identifies the body, or any of the five *kkhandā*, with a supposed self. He says :

> And how, brethren, is there grasping and worry ? Herein, brethren, the untaught many folk [*puthujjanā*] have this view : "This body is mine. I am this. This is my self." Of such a one the body alters and becomes otherwise. Owing to the altering and otherwiseness of body, sorrow and grief, woe, lamentation and despair arise in him.

So far we see, then, that according to the Buddha there was a close connection between wrong views, a false belief in self, and spiritual-psychological disease. Thus, views for the Buddha were more amenable to psychoanalysis than to philosophic

---

31. S.IV.394. (PTS translation)
Aññatitthiyā Vaccha paribbājakā cakkhuṃ Etam mama eso ham asmi eso me attā ti samanupassanti ... pe ... jivham Etam mama eso ham me attā ti samanupassanti ... pe ... manaṃ Etam mama eso ham asmi eso me attā ti samanupassanti. Tasmā aññatitthiyānam paribbājakānaṃ evam puṭṭhānam evam vyākaraṇaṃ hoti. Sassati loko ti vā ... pe ... Neva hoti na na hoti tathāgato param maraṇā ti vā.

32. S.III.18. (PTS translation)
Katham ca bhikkhave upādā-paritassanā hoti ? Idha bhihhave assutavā puthujjano Rūpam etam mama eso ham asmi eso me attāti samanupassati. Tassa taṃ rūpaṃ vipariṇamati aññathā hoti. Tassa rūpapariṇamaññathābhāva uppajjanti sokaparidevadukkhadomanas-supāyāsā.

analysis, and we find that this is his striking methodology in his most extensive treatment of heterodox views, the Brahmajāla Sutta,[33] in which, for example, views of the continuity of self, or of its eternality, are found to be rooted in a misinterpretation of the meditative experience of remembering past lives, and assuming therefrom that there is some self which is continuous through these lives;[34] or where the view which is called 'fortuitous origination,' a view which holds that the world is mere chance in a chaotic universe, the view that believes the world sprang up for no reason, is found[35] to be rooted again in a misinterpretation of past lives, wherein one ends a life as an unconscious being (*asaññā sattā*) and is reborn later consciously, and since he cannot recall what was before that conscious life, assumes wrongly that the world came into being at the same time as his conscious rebirth, that is, fortuitously (*adhicca samuppannikā*); or of those forerunners of the Buddha who refused to express any opinion on the eternality or finitude of the world, those whom the Buddha called 'eel wrigglers' (*amarā vikkhepaṃ*) because their metaphysical silence on such issues was found to be rooted in a psychological timidity, a fear of being found wrong, whereas his own setting aside of such metaphysical questions was not rooted in timidity but in an assuredness of the spiritual dysfunction of such views.[36] Such teachers, according to the Buddha, were resorting to mere sophistry and verbal jugglery; their opinions forced them to negate their opposition in such a way that entailed the maintaining of their position; put otherwise, the philosophic negations of other heterodox teachers were relative negations in the sense that the negation of x entailed some y; for the Buddha, negation became absolute in the sense that the negation of x did not entail any y. He makes this point in the famous verse from the *Saṃyutta Nikāya*:[37] "I quarrel not with the world, brethren. It is the world that quarrels with me. No preacher of the norm [*dhamma*], brethren, quarrels

33. D.i.
34. D.i.2.28-36.
35. D.i.2.30-34.
36. D.i.2.23-29.
37. S.III.138. (PTS translation)
Nāham bhikkhave lokena vivadāmi loko ca mayā vivadati.
Na bhikkhave dhammavādī kenaci lokasmiṃ vivadati.

with anyone in the world"; and again we find in the Dīghanakha Sutta of the *Majjhima Nikāya* :[38] "A monk whose mind is thus freed, Aggivessana, does not concur with anyone, he does not dispute with anyone. He makes use of the common phrases of the world without adhering to them." In this *Majjhima* verse, we find the same point being made in the more well-known *Saṃyutta* verse, but with one highly significant addition. Here the arahant, the one whose mind is freed, is said to have the ability to make use of common phrases (*loke vohārā*) without entanglements, either psychological or metaphysical. Shortly we shall be developing this very crucial notion of 'common phrases in use in the world,' or simply 'worldly speech,' as this not only provides us with a key interpretative principle for dealing with Buddhist texts, but also clearly is talking about something similar to what Ludwig Wittgenstein meant by 'everyday language,' which for him was not only a philosophic methodology, but a way of rescuing us from the savagery of philosophy.[39]

As for wrong views, then, we find that this notion in Buddhism is closely connected with suffering, and it is also connected with a false belief in self. This is explicit in the Aggi-Vacchagotta Sutta :[40]

---

38. M.I.500. (PTS translation)
Evaṃ vimuttacitto kho Aggivessana bhikkhu na kenaci saṃvadati na kenaci vivadati, yañ ca loke vuttaṃ tena voharati aparāmasan ti.

39. Ludwig Wittgenstein, *Philosophical Investigations*, tr. G. E. M. Anscombe, New York : Macmillan, 3rd edition, 1968 (1958), sect. 124. [hereinafter : *P.I.*].

40. M.I.485-486. (PTS translation)
Sassato loko ti kho Vaccha diṭṭhigatam—etaṃ diṭṭhigahanaṃ diṭṭhikantāraṃ diṭṭhivisūkaṃ diṭṭhivipphanditaṃ diṭṭsaṃyojanaṃ. sadukkhaṃ savighātaṃ saupāyāsaṃ sapariḷāhaṃ, na nibbidāya na virāgāya na nirodhāya na upasamāya na abhiññāya na sambodhāya na nibbānāya saṃvattati. Asassato loko ti kho Vaccha ... pe ... antavā loko ti kho Vaccha. —anantavā loko ti kho Vaccha—taṃ jīvaṃ taṃ sarīran ti kho Vaccha—aññaṃ jīvaṃ aññaṃ sarīran ti Vaccha—hoti tathāgato param maraṇā ti kho Vaccha—na hoti tathāgato param maraṇā ti kho Vaccha—hoti ca na hoti tathāgato paraṃ maraṇā ti kho Vaccha—n' eva hoti na na hoti tathāgato param maraṇā ti kho Vaccha—diṭṭhigataṃ etaṃ diṭṭhigahanaṃ diṭṭhikantāraṃ diṭṭhivisūkhaṃ diṭṭhivipphanditaṃ diṭṭhisaṃyojanaṃ sadukkhaṃ savighātaṃ saupāyāsaṃ sapariḷāhaṃ, na nibbidāya na virāgāya na nirodhāya na upasamāya na abhiññāya na sambodhāya na nibbānāya saṃvattati. Imaṃ kho ahaṃ Vaccha ādīnavaṃ sampassamāno evaṃ imāni sabbaso diṭṭhigatāni anupagato ti.

Vaccha, to think that 'the world is eternal'—this is going to a speculative view, holding a view, the wilds of views, the wriggling of views, the scuffling of views, the fetter of views; it is accompanied by anguish, distress, misery, fever; it does not conduce to turning away from, nor to dispassion, stopping, calming, super-knowledge awakening, nor to *nibbāna*. Vaccha, to think that 'the world is not eternal'...to think that 'the world is an ending thing'...to think that 'the life-principle and the body are the same'...to think that 'the life-principle is one thing, the body another'...to think that 'the Tathāgata is after dying'...to think that 'the Tathāgata is not after dying'...to think that 'the Tathāgata both is and is not after dying'...to think that 'the Tathāgata neither is nor is not after dying'—this, Vaccha, is going to a speculative view... etc.... I, Vaccha, beholding that this is a peril, thus do not approach any of these speculative views.

The Buddhist notion of wrong view is usually expressed in terms of the ten issues regarding the world, the *jīva* and the body, and the after-death status of the Tathāgata, as in the *sutta* cited above, and also as raised by one of the Buddha's foremost disciples, Māluṇkyaputta, in the Cūlamāluṇkya Sutta,[41] wherein he demands that the Buddha give him answers to these issues. Māluṇkyaputta's philosophic outburst is silenced by the Buddha, who tells him that his teaching the Dhamma does not presuppose that any answers to these issues would be formulated. The Buddha then preaches the parable of the arrow,[42] wherein the ludicrousness of the warrior's demanding to know the origin, wood-type, feather-type, et cetera, of an arrow by which he is impaled before he will allow for its surgical removal, is likened to Māluṇkyaputta's demand for answers to these pseudo-issues before he will consent to do some meditation. In another place,[43] the Buddha is asked why such questions as Māluṇkyaputta's are left unanswered, and he replies :

41. M.I.427-429.
42. M.I.429-430.
43. D.ix.28-30. (PTS translation)
Na h' etaṃ Poṭṭhapāda attha-saṃhitaṃ na dhammasaṃhitaṃ na ādibrahmacariyakaṃ, na nibbidāya na virāgāya na nirodhāya na upasamāya na abhiññāya na sambodhāya na nibbānāya saṃvattati. Tasmā taṃ mayā avyākatan ti.

> This question is not calculated to the profit, is not concerned with the Norm [*Dhamma*], it does not redound even to the elements of right conduct, nor to detachment, nor to purification from lusts, nor to quietude, nor to tranquillization of heart, nor to real knowledge, nor to the insight [of the higher stages of the Path], nor to Nirvāṇa. Therefore it is that I express no opinion on it.

The Buddha is then asked what it is that he does teach, and he replies[44] that he teaches about suffering, the patterning of suffering, the cessation of suffering, and the way going to that cessation of suffering; furthermore, this is taught for the reason that it does lead to detachment, quietude, et cetera.

Given that some things were considered to be wrong view, and that those things are connected with suffering and the belief in self, and are therefore more amenable to psychoanalysis than to philosophical analysis, we might now proceed to consider what might be the opposite of 'wrong view'; or, put differently, what was it that the Buddha taught as 'right view ?' We shall see that this is quite a tricky question, and one which played a major role in the differentiation of Buddhist schools.

That right view (*sammādiṭṭhi*) is not simply a matter of negating wrong view and consequently upholding a contrary right view, is expressed by the Buddha quite clearly. He is asked by Kaccāyana[45] to explain just what he means by right view, and the response is :

---

44. D.ix.28-30. (PTS translation)
Idam dukkhan ti Poṭṭhapāda mayā vyākataṃ. Ayam dukkhasamudayo ti kho Poṭṭhapāda mayā vyākataṃ. Ayam dukkhanirodho ti kho Poṭṭhapāda mayā vyākataṃ, Ayaṃ dukkhanirodha-gāminī patipadā ti kho Poṭṭha-pāda mayā vyākataṃ ti.

45. S.II.17. (PTS translation)
Dvayanissito khvāyaṃ Kaccāyana loko yebhuyyena atthitañ ceva natthitañ ca. Lokasamudayaṃ kho Kaccāyana yathābhūtaṃ sammappaññāya passato yā loke natthitā sā na hoti, lokanirodhaṃ kho Kaccāyana yathābhūtaṃ sammapaññāya passato yā loke atthitā sā na hoti. Upāyupādānabhinivesavinibandho khvāyaṃ Kaccāyana loko yabhuyyena, tañcāyaṃ upāyupādānam cetaso adhiṭṭhānam abhinivesānusayaṃ na upeti na upādiyati nādiṭṭhāti attā na me ti. Dukkham eva uppajjamānam uppajjati dukkhaṃ nirujjhamānaṃ nirujjhatīti na kaṇkhati na vicikicchati aparapaccayā ñāṇam evassa ettha hoti.

> The world, Kaccāyana, usually bases [its views] on two things : on existence and on non-existence. Now he, who with right insight sees the uprising of the world as it really is, does not hold with the non-existence of the world. But he, who with right insight sees the passing away of the world as it really is, does not hold with the existence of the world. Grasping after systems, imprisoned in dogmas is this world, Kaccāyana, for the most part. And the man who does not go after that system-grasping, that mental standpoint, that dogmatic bias, who does not grasp after it, does not take up his stand upon it, [does not think]—'It is my soul !'—who thinks :—'that which arises is just Ill, that which passes away is Ill'—that man is not in doubt, is not perplexed. Knowledge herein is his that is not merely another's. Thus far, Kaccāyana, he has right view.

Thus, right view in the Buddhist sense, is not merely holding to non-existence as opposed to the wrong view of existence, or vice-versa, but it is the middle path (*majjhima paṭipāda*) between both these extremes. Thus, it seems that speaking about wrong view is tantamount to speaking about extreme views.

In the Mahācattāri Sutta,[46] which we have already discussed at length, we learn of two types of *sammādiṭṭhi* : one that is *anāsava* and one which is *sāsava*, one with the *āsavā* and one without them. That right view which could be said to be with the *āsavā* is that type of view upon which ethics, morality and religion is based; namely, the belief in the efficacy of action (*kamma*), that of religious progress, that of 'this shore' and 'other shore' symbolism. That right view which is without the *āsavā* is simply called wisdom (*paññā*), and in another place we learn that this type of wisdom entails that no *dhamma* should be clung to (*dhammā nālaṃ abhinivesāya*).[47] To say that no *dhamma* should be clung to is to say, as we read in the *Dhammapada* :[48] "For whom there exists neither the hither nor the farther shore, nor both the hither and the farther shore, he who is undistressed

46. M.III.72.
47. S.IV. 50.
48. Dhammapada.XXVI.3. (Nārada translation)
Yassa pāraṃ apāraṃ vā, pārāpāraṃ na vijjati. Vītaddaraṁ visaṃyuttaṃ, tad ahaṃ brūmi brāhmaṇaṃ.

and unbound—him I call a brāhmaṇa." This is a very similar statement to the one which concludes the famous parable of the raft in the Alagaddūpama Sutta :[49]

> So it is, monks, that this teaching (*dhamma*) of the analogy of the raft is preached by me for crossing over, not for holding onto. You, monks, by understanding this analogy of the raft, should get rid of *dhammas*, all the moreso non-*dhammas*.

Of course, the parable of the raft tells that once one has crossed over the floods (*oghā*) of sensuality, hatred and views, then since one has already crossed over them, the raft by which one has made the crossing is not to be retained. Thus the raft, which, in the context of this discussion of right views, is in fact, Buddhism itself, could be said to be a right view only insofar as it is used in the context of the disciple's spiritual progress, and also in the sense that it is taught by the arahant. Beyond this situation of teaching and learning, however, it becomes a wrong view to the extent that it should be discarded and might not be discarded. Then, in addition to our earlier contention that a wrong view is that which is based on self and connected with suffering, such as eternalism, fortuitous origination, nihilism and eel-wriggling; we learn that even a right view becomes a wrong view when abstracted from the teaching context, which we would offer is its true linguistic home. As long as it is kept within its everyday language, in its *loka vohārā*, in its contextuality of teaching, the Buddha calls it *sammādiṭṭhi* or right view. When abstracted from this context, when something 'more' is made of it than its heuristic and pedagogical value, then it becomes wrong view, and is to be discarded, as we learn from the *Dhammapada* verse and from the parable of the raft. We shall see that this method could be applied to all Buddhist notions; all of them are contextual and heuristic, and that trouble arises if and when these teachings become abstracted from their contexts and are seen as a basis for philosophizing.

Taking a Buddhist notion as the basis for philosophizing is, according to the Buddha, speaking beyond which one has grounds

---

49. M.I.134-135. (My translation)
Evaṃ eva kho bhikkhave kullūpamo mayā dhammo desito nittharaṇatthāya no gahaṇatthāya. Kullūpamaṃ vo bhikkhave ājānantehi dhammā pi vo pahātabbā, pag eva adhammā.

for so speaking. There are many examples in the *Sutta Piṭaka* of the Buddha's rather strong criticisms for such self-assured speech, but we shall mention only three in this discussion. One very famous example, and one which has been discussed before in this essay, is found in the Mahāparinibbāna Suttanta,[50] where Sāriputta hails the Buddha as omniscient, and is rebuked by the Buddha for speaking beyond what he knows. The Buddha says there that Sāriputta's words are too grand and too bold, and that since he has not personally known all the Buddhas of the past, present and future, nor even the present Buddha entirely, then he does not know what he is saying; therefore, the Buddha requests him to kindly refrain from speaking, given that he does not know what he is speaking about.

Another example is found in the Poṭṭhapāda Sutta[51] where the Buddha criticizes those religious teachers who maintain that the soul is happy after death. The Buddha finds that these teachers do not even know happiness in this life, so how could they postulate such an unknown into the future ?

In the same *sutta*,[52] the Buddha scorns the man who loves the most beautiful woman in the world without ever having seen her. He should be psychoanalyzed : can he describe this beautiful woman ? does he know her caste, her family, or her village ? The Buddha is questioning the man's assumption that one can love, or speak about, that which he does not know, and in principle cannot know, and the Buddha finds his talk to be stupid (*bhāsitaṃ sampajjatīti*).

In these examples, we find the Buddha's interlocutors to be afflicted with a psychosis wherein one becomes so fascinated with one's linguistic conventions and designations that one builds all sorts of psycho-philosophical constructs upon these conventions. In one place,[53] the Buddha talks about a *rājah* who, upon first hearing the sound of a veena (an Indian stringed instrument) becomes so enamoured of the sound that he demands that it be brought to him. When his courtiers bring him a veena, he is disappointed as he had asked for the sound, and not this peculiar

50. D.xvi.1.16.
51. D.ix.38.
52. D.ix.35.
53. S.IV.197-198.

contraption. On being told that the sound emitted from the instrument, which itself is made up of so many parts, the *rājah* proceeds to demolish the poor veena in order to find its sound. The *rājah* is making a linguistic mistake; he naively believes that the terms 'sound' and 'veena' both refer to entities, and that just as one can grab hold of a veena, so he should be able to grab hold of a sound. The *rājah* concludes that people are led astray by this veena, because it is not its sound, which he found so enticing.

Such a naively-understood language can lead to all sorts of pseudo-questions which the Buddha set aside (*avyākarana*), such as : Who is it that craves ?[54]; Where do the four great elements (*mahābhūtā*) cease ?[55]; and What is the resort of *nibbāna* ?[56]. In all of these instances, the question goes beyond its mark, it is an uncritical question because it presupposes that words correspond to reality. Very similarly, Candrakīrti considered the questions of the Naiyāyika about *svabhāva* to have gone beyond their mark, because they, too, treat as established a term, in this case *svabhāva*, which has not been established. In negating the 'intrinsic nature' (*svabhāva*) of phenomena, the Naiyāyika would say that Nāgārjuna is nihilistic because he negates a real entity; however, as Candrakīrti points out,[57] the question itself is wrongly put because to say that Nāgārjuna has negated a real entity is to assume the establishment of the category of *svabhāva* in the first place, and that since it is precisely Nāgārjuna's point that *svabhāva* has no reality in the first place, then the question itself entails what is contrary to what Nāgārjuna is saying, and therefore that question, like the three cited above, is to be set aside.

All of these pseudo-issues, like the Naiyāyika's fear of the Mādhyamaka negation of his cherished *svabhāva*, like asking who it is that craves, and so on, are all questions that are to be set aside because they are questions that assume a certain view. If, when knowing an office to be empty, one were asked the identity of the person in the office, the category "person-in-the-

54. S.II.13-14.
55. D.XI.68-85.
56. S.V.218.
57. Candrakīrti, *dBu ma tshig gsal, op. cit.*, XVIII.8.

office" is not established. If the reply were "no one," the term "no one" does not become the name of an antity in the office, although this is precisely what the Naiyāyika would claim. It is not the same to say "No one is in the office" as to say "Frank is not in the office because Bill is there." The former would be the type of negation found in Buddhism; that the negation of x does not entail y. In the second case we find what Indian philosophy would call a relative negation, wherein the negation of x does entail y. In characterizing himself as 'contentionless,'[58] the Buddha is saying that his negations do not entail counter-positions that must be defended; similarly, Nāgārjuna is called 'positionless' (*vaitaṇḍika*). The type of *sammādiṭṭhi* of which Buddhism speaks, therefore, is not simply a matter of negating a false view (*pāpadiṭṭhi*) and substituting another correct view in its place. Rather, right view in a Buddhist sense is absolute in the sense that it is not merely another view, but the escape from all views, as Buddhaghoṣa tells us.[59]

The Buddha speaks metaphorically of both those addicted to views, and of those who are freed from them. Of the former, perhaps the most famous parable is that of the blind men and the elephant.[60] In this story, a king produces an elepahnt before several blind men, and they are each asked to touch it and report on what the object is. The one touching the tail says that it is a broom, the one touching the foot says it is a stone, the one touching the trunk says it is a tree, and so on. The blind men fall into violent arguments about the truth and falsity of their claiming, as those addicted to views quarrel over the validity of their views. The Buddha concludes the story :[61]

O how they cling and wrangle, some who claim
Of brahmin and recluse the honoured name !
For, quarrelling, each to his own view they cling.
Such folk see only one side of a thing.

On the other hand, one who does not cling to views is an

---

58. S.III.138.
59. MA.II.144.
60. Udana, pp. 66-69.
61. *Ibid.*, p. 69. (PTS translation)
imesu kira sajjanti eke samaṇabrāhmaṇā, viggahya naṃ vivadanti janā ekaṅgadassino 'ti.

arahant. In *gāthā*, the Buddha tells us :[62]

Man, 'ware alone of what is told by names,
Take up their stand on what is so expressed.
If this they have not rightly understood,
They go their ways under the yoke of death.
He who hath understood what is expressed
Concerning him-who-speaks no fancies builds;
For by his mind he hath attained release;
Won is the abode of peace incomparable.
He truly with this gift of knowing names
Is calm, and in the abode of calm delighting
With calm, deliberation lives the life,
Standing on *dhamma*; such as one goes not
By any name; perfect in lore is he.

It may seem something of an overstatement on the part of the Buddha to hold that freedom from *diṭṭhi* is freedom from suffering, and that addiction to view is suffering. If one so views the matter, then he would be requested to see that, according to Buddhism, it is not the world *per se* that is problematic for human life, but that the world as constucted by one's desires, beliefs, fears and opinions that is the problem—which, as we have shown, is the Buddhist sense of the term 'world' (*loka*). Belief in the world as eternal, et cetera, or our desire that there be a world, is the primary category; not in any *a priori* sense, but in the sense that one's willing that there be a world produces a world. Therefore the Buddha says :[63]

That which in the world is called 'being' or 'non-being,'
desire sufficiently gives rise to it.
Having seen the becoming and annihilation of form,
beings in the world make judgements.

---

62. Itivuttaka, pp. 53-54. Also found at S.I.11. (PTS translation)
Akkheyyasaññino sattā akkheyyasmiṃ patiṭṭhitā
akkheyyaṃ apariññāya yogam-āyanti maccuno.
Akkheyhañca pariññāya akkhātāraṃ na maññati
phuṭṭo vimokkho manasā santipadam anuttaraṃ.
Sa ve akkheyyasampanno santo santipade rato
saṇkhāya sevī dhamaṭṭho saṇkhaṃ nopeti vedagū 'ti.

63. Suttanipāta, p. 169. (My translation)
'Sātaṃ, asātan' ti yam āhu loke,
tam ūpanissāya pahoti chando,
rūpesu disvā vibhavaṃ bhavañ ca,
vinicchayaṃ kurute jantu loke.

In one place,[64] the Buddha discusses *diṭṭhi* in precisely the same language usually reserved for talk about *dukkha*, namely : views (*diṭṭhi*); the patterning of views (*diṭṭhisamudayaṃ*); the cessation of views (*diṭṭhinirodhaṃ*); and the way leading to the stopping of views (*diṭṭhinirodhagāminiṃ*). In this case at least, to the extent that the cardinal notion of dependent co-arising (*paṭicca samuppāda*) could be said to be referential, it refers not to events or entities 'out there,' but the way in which the 'out there' is psycho-existentially interpreted through the process of the formulation of *diṭṭhi*.

Of course, it is not so much any particular *diṭṭhi* as such that was the chief focus of the Buddha's criticisms, but the very possibility of formulating any *diṭṭhi* that was central. In his excellent book, *Concept and Reality in Early Buddhism*,[65] Bhikkhu Ñāṇanda discusses the key terms relating to the 'profuseness of views,' *papañca* and *papañcasaññāsaṇkhā* :

> . . . in the Pali canon we noted some basis for a distinction between *papañca* on the one hand and *papañcasaññāsaṇkhā* on the other. While *papañca* in a dynamic sense was used to denote the triple proliferating tendency of the mind, *papañcasaṇkhā* and *papañcasaññāsaṇkhā* signified the apparently static concepts tinged with or characterized by that particular tendency. As such, in a case of *papañca* the accent was more on the deep-seated psychological tendency centering on the ego notion, rather than on its external counterpart, the concept or linguistic convention. By eradicating *papañca* at its very source, the sage puts an end to *papañcasaṇkhā* or *papañcasaññāsaṇkhā*, but he is at liberty to use worldly concepts (*lokasamaññā, lokaniruttiyo, lokavohārā, lokapaññattiyo*) without any fear of being overwhelmed by them. Hence, the true struggle was fought within, rather than in debate.

We shall return to the arahant's skill in using common language without entanglement, as Ñāṇanda suggests, in the next section. The point to note is the very close connection in Buddhism between the tendency of the mind to formulate *diṭṭhi*, to contend and to make philosophies, and the whole wheel of human

64. A.IV.68.
65. Ñāṇanda, *op. cit., passim.*, especially pp. 126-127.

sufferings. Given this close connection, the Buddha's statement of the four noble truths in terms of *diṭṭhi* becomes more coherent, as does his famous expression that neither he nor any of his true disciples have any quarrels in the world.[66] Thus, the *Suttanipāta*[67] tells us that one who grasps any particular view of the world and the religious life merely begets suffering for himself.

In so many places in the *Sutta Piṭaka* the Buddha reiterates that it is not by the cultivation of views, especially wrong views, but even so-called right views, that one attains *arahattā*. Two general types of reasons are given for this : In the first place, we are very often told that views do not conduce toward *nibbāna*.[68] We are also shown a connection between views and suffering, as we have discussed immediately above. The right view, to the extent that there could be any right view in Buddhism, is seen precisely as the heuristic contextuality of whatever expressions and teachings that the Buddha happened to give; this point is also made repeatedly, but is most evident in such parables as the raft, the arrow, and the blind men and the elephant. Views are a psycho-spiritual problem for Buddhism, as is suffering. The Buddha at certain places seems to go so far as to equate views and the psychological matrix of views with suffering itself, and, as Buddhaghoṣa and so many other commentators tell us, ***nibbāna*** is none other than escape from views.

D. *Language Analysis*

Given that it is a crucial step on the Buddhist path that one overcome *diṭṭhi*, we are left to consider one method for so doing, and that is the method of language analysis.. We do not mean to imply that language analysis is the only method for overcoming *diṭṭhi*, as the successful attainment of the *jhānā*, as we have seen, leads to the same freedom from conceptualization. However, we would offer that language analysis is both the most philosophically interesting method, and it is also the most predominant in terms of textual references in the *Sutta Piṭaka*. This train of thought was the mainstay of Nāgārjuna

66. S.III.138 and M.I.500.
67. Suttanipāta, p. 156.
paraman 'ti diṭṭhīsu paribbasāno yad uttariṃkurute jantu loke, 'hina' ti aññe tato sabba-m-āha, tasmā vivādāni avitivatto.
68. S.V.448, and D.xxix.31.

and his Mādhyamaka followers, so it seems appropriate that our discussion of language analysis not restrict itself to sources from the Pali *Sutta Piṭaka*, but also consider some Mādhyamaka writings.

Since by language analysis most of us think immediately of the philosophy of Ludwig Wittgenstein, we shall not refrain from comparative discussions in this section. We find that, despite significant divergences in presuppositions—especially in regard to our everyday cognizing of the world, and the range of application of this language analysis—Wittgenstein's philosophical method bears strong resemblances to that found in Buddhism. We feel this particular comparison to be a useful tool in understanding Buddhism.

Wittgenstein, in that oft-quoted passage from the *Tractatus*, tells us that, at a point, the philosopher must revert to silence.[69] For Buddhism, this silence is not the mere absence of verbiage, but a way of liberating language from its metaphysical uses to heuristic, pedagogical ones. It may strike one as enigmatic that the Buddha says that because he has understood silence, then he may use pedagogical language in a variety of ways. He tells Ānanda :[70]

> If, Ānanda, when asked by the Wanderer : "Is there a self ?" I had replied to him : "There is a self," then, Ānanda, that would be siding with the recluses and brahmins who are eternalists. But if, Ānanda, when asked : "Is there a self ?" I had replied that it does not exist, that, Ānanda, would be

69. Ludwig Wittgenstein, *Tractatus Logico-Philosophicus*, tr. C. K. Ogden and F. P. Ramsey, London : Routledge & Kegan Paul, 1922, 7.

70. S.IV.400-401. (PTS translation)
Ahañ c' Ānanda Vacchagottassa paribbājakassa Atthattā ti puṭṭho samāno Atthattā ti vyākareyyaṃ, ye te Ānanda samanabrāhmaṇā sassatavādā tesaṃ etaṃ saddhim abhavissa. Ahañ c' Ānanda Vacchagottassa paribbājakassa Natthattāti puṭṭo samāno Natthattāti vyākareyyaṃ, ye te Ānanda samaṇabrāhmaṇā ucchedavādā tesaṃ etam saddhim abhavissa. Ahañ c' Ānanda Vacchagottassa paribbājakassa Atthattā ti puṭṭho samāno Atthattā ti vyākareyyaṃ, api nu me taṃ anulomam abhavissa ñāṇassa upādāya Sabbe dhammā anattāti. No hetam bhante. Ahañ c' Ānanda Vacchagottassa paribbājakassa Natthattāti puṭṭho samāno Natthattāti vyākareyyaṃ, sammuḷhassa Ānanda Vacchagottassa bhīyyo sammohāya abhavissa Ahu vā ma nūna pubbe attā, so etarahi natthīti .

> siding with those recluses and brahmins who are annihilationists. Again, Ānanda, when asked by the Wanderer : "Is there a self ?" had I replied that there is, would my reply be in accordance with the knowledge that all things are impermanent ? —Surely not, Lord. —Again, Ānanda, when asked by Vacchagotta the Wanderer : "Is there not a self ?" had I replied that there is not, it would have been more bewilderment for the bewildered Vacchagotta, for he would have said : "Formerly indeed I had a self, but now I have not one any more."

Certainly Vacchagotta finds himself in a linguistic dilemma, one which involves a naively understood notion of negation which somehow affirms the negated. We shall see that this sort of philosophizing is relentlessly under attack by the Buddha and his followers, and the attack is mounted against language naively understood as referential.

To pose the initial analyses of Wittgenstein and the Buddha, we might say that one of the most important points Wittgenstein is making repeatedly and throughout his *Philosophical Investigations* is that a word is not necessarily the name of a thing, and that philosophic problems arise when one abstracts a word from its context—that is, from the everyday workings of language—and tries to understand that word apart from its functional matrix. Buddhism, especially in its more dialectical writings and encounters with heterodox systems, seems to be telling us that our words and concepts neither adequately explain nor describe reality. There are similarities and differences in just these two statements. Both would imply that the proper business of philosophy would be a criticism of language, which is what in fact both do. But Wittgenstein maintains that language describes reality just fine—it *works* in our business of conducting life. We get into difficulties only when we abstract words from this working language and try to do philosophy. It is not so much that words are *inadequate* ; rather, philosophers tend to make nonsense out of perfectly good words. Buddhism would agree with this much at least : that philosophers do indeed make nonsense.

In a very important sense, neither the Buddha (nor his followers) nor Wittgenstein could be considered 'philosophers' at all—if we take 'philosopher' to mean one who goes about developing philosophic systems. Rather, both are critics of philosophy; both would want to render philosophy, in the sense just indicated, an impossibility. As critics, neither are cocerned with maintaining consistent positions, as the Buddha says in the *Saṃyutta* verse just cited—unless one would want to call the very methodology of criticism a 'position'. Wittgenstein writes :[71] "My aim is : to teach you to pass from a piece of disguised nonsense to something that is patent nonsense," a statement which would serve as a very fine characterization of Nāgārjuna's *prasaṅga* methodology of refutation as well.

While an extended discussion of Wittgenstein's philosophy would not directly pertain to this study, nevertheless it will be necessary to outline some of his major points in order to get a clearer view of the Buddhist idea of language analysis. What we wish to entertain is Wittgenstein's keen observation that words do not refer, that they do not have a 'meaning' or 'stand for' things. This is precisely the point made by some later Buddhists, especially Candrakīrti, in their encounters with Nyāya realism (*bāhyārthavāda*), which we find to be an analogue to what Strawson[72] calls 'logical atomism.' Perhaps the fundamental misconception about the way our language works considered at length in his *Philosophical Investigations*, from the first to the 137th sections more or less, is the belief that a word has a 'meaning,' a reference, that words 'stand for' things.

One of the ways by which he analyzes how language *works* is by imagining a very simple language indeed : that of a builder and his assistant who get along very well by pointing and saying "Slab," "Pillar" and "Block" and specifying numbers.[73] This system of language, or 'language game,' is offered as an alternative to our more common belief that we learn the word "Slab" by *ostensive definition*, by pointing to the 'meaning' of the word. What Wittgenstein is telling us is that when the builder says "Slab," he is not conveying information or 'communicating' with his assistant; rather, he wants him to bring the slab ! The

71. *P.I.*, section 464.

72. P. F. Strawson, "Critical Notice of Wittgenstein's *Philosophical Investigations*," reprinted in Harold Morick, ed., *Wittgenstein and the Problem of Other Minds*, New York : McGraw Hill, 1967, pp. 3-42.

73. *P.I.*, sections 6-10.

idea that words have meanings and that language is the communication of these meanings is shown to be absurd. If we see what Wittgenstein is trying to show us—that belief in meanings of words, and language as communication, is not a useful model—then we would come to realize that the builder's "Slab" was not aimed at communicating anything at all. Rather, words are used to tell us to do something. Thus Wittgenstein's rule :[74] "For a *large* class of cases—though not for all—in which we employ the word 'meaning' it can be defined thus : the meaning of a word is its use in the language."

Quite similarly, we find the Buddhist use of the burning house image, one which also makes a statement about the way our language works. In this famous analogy from the *Saddharmapuṇḍarīka*,[75] the kindly father finds his children in the upper storey of a burning building. He calls to them to warn them of their danger, but they do not heed until he promises them all sorts of toys and goodies were they to vacate the building. Upon hearing such promises, the children exit the house to safety. Now if one were to follow a referential model of language, one might conclude that what the Buddha is teaching is a pedagogically useful lie. In a sense this is true, but the Buddha is making an even stronger statement about the nature of our language. What he is saying is that language is an imperative, not a proposition, and that religious language is an invitation, not a turth claim. Therefore, he can skilfully employ language (*upāya kauśalya*) in a way that is unencumbered from any referential models of language, such that the truth or falsity of any given religious statement is not to be determined by any external criteria of truth and falsity, such as a principle of verification, but by an existential analysis of the context or situation in which that language is expressed. Thus, the *Saddharmapuṇḍarīka,* a crucial early Mahāyāna text which many see as polemical vis-a-vis that type of Buddhism as found in the Pali canon, is not saying that the early Buddhist texts are lying; rather, it is telling us that we have no external criteria for adjudicating truth and falsity beyond the contextuality of a statement. Since the purpose of language is to get us to do something, and therefore the purpose

74. *P.I.*, section 43.
75. *Saddharmapuṇḍarīka*, chapter II.

of religious language is to get us to do something important, then getting the children out of the burning house is the only criteria by which the Buddha's expressions could be evaluated. Since it did so, the teaching is appropriate and 'true' insofar as it is not removed from that context and made into philosophizing.

Belief in some external, that is non-contextual, criteria for evaluating language, such as a correspondence theory of truth which would entail a referential model of language, is just the mistaken type of assumption that leads us into philosophical dilemmas. Wittgenstein, following St. Augustine's lead, considers the word 'time,' a word we all know and use more or less successfully when we ask each other the time, when we're on time for a seminar, when we time our three-minute eggs, and when we keep time to the music by tapping our feet. Wittgenstein observes, following Augustine's lead in the *Confessions* :[75a] "*Quid est ergo tempus ? Si nemo me quaerat, scio; si quarenti explicare velim, nescio.*" ["What, then, is time ? If no one asks me, I know; but if someone asks me to explain, I don't know."] The question—"what is time ?"—has led philosophers in Europe and India to some of the most remarkable conclusions. For Zeno it is unreal. For some Kālacakra-tāntrikas it seems like an absolute. Yet we have no reason to doubt, just as Hume could play billiards after 'disproving' causality, that both Zeno and the Tāntrika could answer the question, "What time is it ?", or, if trained musically, "What is the time signature of this piece ?" with no difficulty. The word 'time' is a technique we learn for quite a variety of purposes : so as not to be late for dinner, so as to keep rhythm with our fellow musicians, and so our eggs won't be too runny. But it is the assumption of a referential model of language, the dogma that a word has a meaning, which leads us astray. Some of us have gotten into similar difficulties with words like 'knowledge,' 'being,' 'object,' 'I,' 'proposition' and 'name'—to follow Wittgenstein's examples.[76] He cautions us that when we try to deal with such words :[77] "One must always ask oneself : is the word ever actually used in this way in the language-game which is its original home ?

75a. *P.I.* section 89.
76. *P.I.*, section 116.
77. *Idem.*

What *we* do is to bring words back from their metaphysical to their everyday use."

Buddhism is also highly critical of the assumption that all words have meanings and refer to things. Of course, given the central position of Buddhism as *anātmavāda*, this becomes manifestly clear in discussions of the word 'I' (*ahaṅkāra*), as we find in the *Sutta Piṭaka.* It was also a chief concern of later Sanskrit and Tibetan writers, especially Diṅnāga's Sautrāntika school and Nāgārjuna's Mādhyamaka school, in their encounters with the Nyāya realists (*bāhyārthavāda*). We shall look at some of the arguments given at different stages in the history of Buddhist thought in this section, and we shall be commenting upon some similarities and divergences from Wittgenstein's position.

In the *Sutta Piṭaka* we find the Buddha arguing against a naively-understood language. In the Poṭṭhapāda Sutta[78] we find him saying :

> Just so, Citta, when any of the three modes of personality [*i.e.*, past, present or future] is going on, it is not called by the name of the other. For these, Citta, are merely names, expressions, turns of speech, designations in the common use of the world. And of these a Tathāgata makes use indeed, but is not led astray by them.

The question of personal identity was a crucial one at the time of the Buddha, and different systems of thought had covered it from every possible angle. Here the Buddha is telling his interlocator that terms thought to be referring to a self are merely turns of speech, useful in the business of everyday life, but not referring to an entity, not mysteriously carrying a 'meaning' beyond these everyday usages. The wisdom of a Tathāgata consists, in part, in that he doesn't make the type of grammatical mistake that the *ātmavāda* philosophers make. In an

78. D.ix.53. (PTS translation)
Evam eva kho Citta yasmiṃ oḷāriko atta-paṭilābho hoti ... pe ... Tasmiṃ Citta samaye manomayo attapaṭilābho hoti ... pe ... Yasmiṃ Citta samaye arūpo atta-paṭilābho, n' eva tasmiṃ samaye olāriko atta-paṭilābho te saṇkham gacchati, na manomayo atta-paṭilābho ti saṇkham gacchati, arūpo attapaṭilābho tveva tasmiṃ samaye saṇkham gacchati. Itimā kho Citta loka samaññā ḷoka-niruttiyo, loka vohārā loka paññattiyo yāhi Tathāgato voharati aparāmasan.

insightful commentary to the Mahātaṇhāsaṇkhaya Sutta,[79] Buddhaghoṣa[80] observes that Sāti, a bhikkhu, is confused about personal identity because he has abstracted a continuing self from *jātaka*-talk, and he is instructed in seeing that these types of discourses must be kept separately; that the homiletic value of a *jātaka* tradition should not be confused with claiming a continuing personal identity.

The Buddha's position here must be clearly distinguished from that of other heterodox teachers of his day. He does not, as the Cārvāka, merely negate the view of the *ātmavādin* and claim that the self is identical with the body and does not exist beyond the body after death. He also does not, as Sañjāya, opt for a sceptical position, which merely refuses to affirm or deny any thesis about the self. The Buddha rather skilfully examines the language of talking about the self and finds that the mistake is grammatical : that learning to use the word 'I' does not entail an entity corresponding to it. Of course, the Buddha goes on to psychoanalyze the conditions given which one claims there to be an 'I' in terms of *paṭicca samuppāda,* and goes on to teach a therapy (*magga*) for quieting these psychoses—which is far more than Wittgenstein would care to attempt. The point to note, however, is the nature of the Buddha's analysis of the language of talking about 'I,' and its similarity to Wittgenstein's.[81]

A bit later in the history of Pali literature, in the *Milindapañha,* we find perhaps the most famous example of the Buddhist critique of 'I'-language.[82] King Milinda is discussing with the monk, Nāgasena, the Buddha's teaching of no-self (*anattā*). He is confused, as many of us are, by the apparent contradiction based on a naive understanding of the workings of language : if there is no self, to what does the term 'Nāgasena' refer ? Nāgasena answers in two ways, by grammatical and analogical methods. He first replies :[83]

---

79. M.I.259.

80. MA.II.305.

81. One possible Wittgensteinian critique of the notion of 'I' has been worked out by Peter Geach in "The Fallacy of 'Cogito Ergo Sum,' " in H. Morick, ed., *op. cit.*, pp. 211-214.

82. Milindapañha. II.1.1.

83. *Idem.* (PTS translation)

> I am known as Nāgasena, O king, and it is by that name that my brethren in the faith address me. But although parents, O king, give such names as Nāgasena, or Sūrasena, or Vīrasena, or Sīhasena, yet this, Sire—Nāgasena and so on—is only a generally understood term, a designation in the common use. For there is no permanent individuality involved in the matter (*na puggalo upalabbhati*).

Then Nāgasena offers the famous analogy of the chariot[84] wherein the term 'chariot' is found to be a convention for speaking about the functioning of certain parts, but not the name of an entity (essence). As Wittgenstein has shown us with the example of the sword Excalibur,[85] language is not necessarily referential, but it is useful. Milinda thanks Nāgasena and goes on his way, muttering to himself.[86]

The parallel between the Buddhist notion of a 'convenient designation' and Wittgenstein's 'everyday language' is clear. Both are saying that because a word may be *used*, we should not get carried away with philosophies about essences and the like. The method of the Buddha and that of Wittgenstein is also similar : Wittgenstein wants to return a word from its metaphysical to its everyday use. In the instance just cited, Nāgasena de-metaphysicalizes the terms 'chariot' and 'Nāgasena' and shows us that a convenient designation (*loke vohārā*) does not imply a metaphysical entity. One of the powers (*balāni*) of an arahant is his grammatical skilfulness (*loke samaññaṃ kusalo*). He is praised for this ability :[87]

> He among the monks who is an arahant, slayer of the *āsavā*, doer of what was to be done, can say 'I say' or 'It is mine,' skilfully employing worldly, natural language, and aware of its value; yet he speaks only in conformity with these usages.

So important was this point that the Buddha himself declared that all grief, woe, lamentation and despair could be traced to a naively-understood grammar of 'I.'[88]

---

84. Milindapañha. II.I.1.
85. *P.I.*, section 39.
86. Milindapañha.II.1.3.
87. S.I.14-15. (My translation)
Yo hoti bhikkhu arahaṃ katāvī, khīṇāsavo antimadehadhārī, ahaṃ vadāmīti pi so vadeyya, vohāraṃattena so vohareyyāti.
88. S.III.18 : ... tassa rūpapariṇāmaññathābhāva uppajjanti lokaparidevadukkhasomanassasupāyāsā.

The type of position which Wittgenstein has been criticizing has been called 'logical atomism' by Strawson,[89] and has as its counterpart in India the Nyāya school. Fundamentally the Nyāya holds that that which could be meaningfully asserted in terms of 'is' and 'is not' (*asti* and *nāsti*) alone is real; that which could not be so asserted is nonsense.[90] Religiously this could be expressed as : the sickness of life (*duḥkha*) is due to a sick understanding of life, and this sickness could be remedied by appropriate, healthy, referential language. It is precisely against this school that later Buddhists, most notably Nāgārjuna and Diṅnāga, launch their most telling arguments. Nāgārjuna's *Vigrahavyāvartanī*[91] devotes its first twenty verses to a restatement of the Nyāya notion of *svabhāva*, a difficult concept used to denote the reality, literally 'self-existence,' of an object. The remaining fifty verses comprise Nāgārjuna's attack on this notion. In verses 52 to 55, Nāgārjuna makes a temporal case similar to Wittgenstein's Excalibur[92] when he argues that the notion of *svabhāva* is incompatible with temporality. He is objecting to the ontologization of the verb 'to be' (*bhava*). A similar argument is found in his most famous work, the *Mūlamadhyamaka-kārikā*,[93] in Chapter V which deals with the notion of an element (*dhātu*). The *dhātu* are earth, water, fire, wind, space and consciousness, and in this argument he takes space (*ākāśa*) as a paradigm. He argues that space cannot be separated from the characteristic of space (*ākāśalakṣaṇa*). He then employs a temporal argument : if space is said to precede its characteristic, then we would be left with a characteristicless element—an impossibility according to Nyāya epistemology; also, if the characteristic precedes the element, then there would be no

89. Strawson, *op. cit.*

90. A masterful discussion of these and other tenets of the Nyāya system is found in Dharmendra Nath Shastri, *A Critique of Indian Realism*, Agra : Agra University Press, 1964.

91. Tibetan text and English translation in Giuseppe Tucci, ed. and tr. *Pre-Diṅnāga Buddhist Texts on Logic from Chinese Sources*, Gaekwad's Oriental Series, XLIX, Baroda : 1929.

92. *P.I.*, section 43.

93. Sanskrit text and English translation in Kenneth K. Inada, ed. and tr., *Nāgārjuna : A Translation of his Mūlamadhyamakakārikā with an Introductory Essay*, Tokyo : Hokuseido, 1970. In this discussion we shall be concentrating on Chapter V, verses 1-4. [Hereinafter : *MMK*].

place for the characteristic to reside—this point also contradicts the Nyāya tenet that "So long as the properties exist, they can only exist as residing in their substance":[94] and if the element and its characteristic are said to be simultaneous, then we are at a loss to explain from where the characteristic has come. What is behind this argument is the invitation for the Naiyāyika to see that simply because one may *speak* about elements and characteristics does not give one the right to speak about them *metaphysically*. While the surface grammar of 'element' and 'characteristic' may look as if they were two separate reals, which is what Nyāya doggedly affirms, a closer analysis of our language will reveal that these two are dependently co-originated, that is, these concepts take on meaning only when used in counterposition to each other. The error of Nyāya is to attribute to each *svabhāva*—here the antithesis of 'dependently co-originated' and which we would translate here as 'linguistic referability'—and to speak of them abstractly as reals.

Two other arguments of Nāgārjuna are worthy of our attention in this context of our discussion of Wittgenstein's comments about time. In one,[95] we are reminded that speech about time independent of a particular thing in time is incoherent. From this point, Nāgārjuna goes on to attack the notion of a 'thing,'[96] but the point of interest to us is Nāgārjuna's refusal to allow his opponent to speak of time in the abstract, that is, in metaphysical rather than everyday language. A similar argument is found in Nāgārjuna's examination of the cardinal Buddhist notions of 'birth' and 'old age/death.'[97] To those who would speak about birth and old age/death apart from *somebody's* being born, ageing and dying, Nāgārjuna launches another temporal argument, similar to the one regarding 'element' and 'characteristic' : if birth is prior to, implying separate from, old age/death, then we are left with a deathless being, a contradiction in Buddhist terms. If death is prior to birth, again implying separation, then we are left with something dying which is unborn; and if they are

94. D. N. Shastri, *op. cit.*, p. 139
95. *MMK*.19.6.
96. For a Wittgensteinian criticism of the notion of a 'fact,' analogous to the Nyāya concept of a 'thing', see Paul M. van Buren, *The Edges of Language*, New York : Macmillan, 1972, pp. 58-59.
97. *MMK*.11.1-7.

simultaneous, this would be tantamount to saying that they are uncaused, that is, having no antecedent condition. Unlike the person who loves humanity in general but is repelled by real people, the Buddha's horror at the chain of suffering, as expressed by birth and old age/death, was not an abstract horror. It was lived, not theoretical, suffering that is Buddhism's point, and to theorize about these vital matters is to kill them. For those who do theorize, Nāgārjuna and the Buddha are willing to use their own presuppositions to demonstrate the incoherence of their claims.

Wittgenstein writes :[98] "The philosopher's treatment of a question is like the treatment of an illness." This would also hold for Nāgārjuna, but he would be a homeopathic physician : the principle of like healing like is shown in his use of logic to cure us of our metaphysical insistence that the world conform to our logic. Nāgārjuna wants to show us that the world is indeed older than our logic, that our logic is a malignancy rooted in our being so fascinated with language that our conventions become convictions. He wishes, along with Wittgenstein, that language could be returned to its everyday, conventional home; but, as we shall see below, it may be that Nāgārjuna finds that home far removed from us indeed.

Wittgenstein contends that :[99] "Philosophical problems arise when language goes on holiday," and it is this view that comes through in his treatment of words like 'to know,' 'to understand,' 'to intend,' et cetera—words which have caused great philosophic confusions. Such words give the appearance of something mysterious, something beyond the investigator's empirical ken.[100] Both Wittgenstein and the Mādhyamaka find these problems, like all metaphysical issues, to evolve out of sloppy grammar. One modern example of otherwise intelligent people getting themselves carried away by such metaphysics, which the Buddhists characterize as a 'dispositional disease,' is found in scholarship on the term '*prajñā*' and has led many to the conclusion that Nāgārjuna is some sort of absolutist. We shall examine the grammar of such claims.

98. *P.I.*, section 225.

99. *Ibid.*, section 38.

100. For a discussion of the grammar of these terms, see Paul M. van Buren, *op. cit.*, pp. 55-56.

The grammar of '*prajñā*' is closely connected with terms like '*yathābhūtadarśana*' and '*dharma-cakṣus*'—Wittgenstein would call them grammatical cousins. We are not concerned here with its etymology or translation: we shall accept Murti's 'intuition.' But because '*prajñā*' looks like, in terms of surface grammar, words like '*jñāna*,' '*vijñāna*,' et cetera, scholars like Murti,[101] Stcherbatsky[102] and Shayer[103] have thought it to work in the same way. Since *jñāna* cannot be thought of without *jñāpti*, since the *abhidharma* always speaks about the object-of-vision co-arising with the consciousness-of-object-of-vision, then one might be misled into thinking that there could be no intuition apart from 'intuition-into-something'—in this case, an absolute. *Prajñā* no more implies an absolute than 'to understand' implies a 'mental event'; yet it is precisely this type of reasoning, based on superficial grammatical considerations, that had led to Nāgārjuna's being thought of as an absolutist. However, were one to consider the deeper grammar of '*prajñā*,' then the case for Nāgārjuna as absolutist would collapse. There are strong family resemblances between '*prajñā*,' '*yathābhūtadarśana*,' and '*dharma-cakṣus*,' as we have already indicated. Yet no one would think that the 'eye of *dharma*' sees objectively in the same way as the 'eye of flesh.' Why, then, need *prajñā* be directed toward any object, absolute or otherwise ?

According to Nāgārjuna, the Buddha is a being free from metaphysics. In the *dPe med par bstod ba*[104] he writes :

---

101. T. R. V. Murti, *The Central Philosophy of Buddhism : A Study of the Mādhyamika System*, London : George Allen & Unwin, 1974 (1955). Cf. Jacques May's review, "Kant et le Mādhyamaka : a propos d'une livre récent," *Indo-Iranian Journal*, III, 2, 1959, pp. 102-111. For a restatement of his position by new arguments, see his "*Samvṛti* and *Paramārtha* in Buddhism and Vedānta," in Mervyn Sprung, ed., *The Problem of the Two Truths in Buddhism and Vedānta*, Dordrecht : D. Reidel, 1973, pp. 9-26.

102. Th. Stcherbatsky, *The Conception of the Buddhist Nirvana*, Leningrad : Academy of the U.S.S.R., 1927, *passim.*, and a whole series of articles which formed an exciting debate between himself and Louis de la Vallée Poussin.

103. Stanislav Schayer holds Nāgārjuna to be an absolutist in two articles : "Notes and Queries on Buddhism," *Rocznik Orjentalistyczny*, XI, 1935, pp. 206-213; and "Das Mahāyānistische Absolutum nach der Lehre der Mādhyamikas," *Orientalistische Literaturesitung*, XXXVIII, 1935, pp. 401-415.

104. Tibetan and Sanskrit texts with English translation in Guiseppe Tucci, "Two Hymns of the *Catuḥ-stava* of Nāgārjuna," *Journal of the Royal Asiatic Society*, 1932, pp. 309-325, p. 317.

10. Thy mind, O Lord, is not attached to the multifarious opinions as regards pleasure and pain, existence of an ego, non-existence of an ego, affirmation of some eternal being, negation of some eternal being.
11. Thy belief is that things do not go [changing into some other condition], nor do they come [into existence by agency of some force]; nor dost Thou admit that there is a whole as the conglomeration of many parts. Therefore Thou knowest absolute truth....
12. Thou, the Irreproachable One, didst understand that this world is neither unity nor multiplicity; it is like an echo, it is neigher subject to changing [into other forms] nor to destruction.
13. Thou, my Lord, didst know that the cycle of existence is neither eternal nor impermanent, that in it there ss no predicable nor predicate, [since it is] similar to a dream or to a magic play.

An analysis of these devotional verses will yield an insight into Nāgārjuna's position regarding the arising of metaphysical opinions (*dṛṣṭi, prapañca*), and will show how an absolutist reading of his works is an instance of sloppy grammar.

Verse 10 is rather straightforward; we have already discussed Chapter XI of the *Mūlamadhyamakakārikā*—and a similar point is made in Chapter XII—wherein talk about birth and death apart from somebody's being born and dying is incoherent. *Duḥkha* is not a proposition; it is an invitation to see clearly our human condition. To treat *duḥkha* as propositional is to engage in worthless disputation, as the Buddha taught in the parable of arrow.[105] When the Buddha's invitational language about *duḥkha* is taken as propositional, philosophic problems arise—problems which Nāgārjuna is trying to dissolve by returning birth/old age/ death talk to its original language-game. The Buddha is : (1) a being free from suffering; and (2) a being free from metaphysics. These two statements are intimately bound up.

In the *Ātma-parīkṣā* (Chapter XVIII), Nāgārjuna tells us that the teaching of *anātman* is not a metaphysical position in contradistinction to the *ātmavāda*. He writes :[106]

105. Cūḷa-māluṇkya Sutta, M, *sutta* 63.
106. *MMK*.18.6. (Inada translation)
ātmetyapi prajñāpitamanātmetyapi deśitam buddhanairātmā na sānātmā kascidityapi deśitaṃ.

> The Buddhas have provisionally employed the term *ātman* and instructed on the true idea of *anātman*. They have also taught that any [abstract] entity as *ātman* or *anātman* does not exist.

Thus Nāgārjuna's understanding of the Buddha's teaching of *anātman* is structurally similar to his own teaching of *śūnyatā*. Both *anātman* and *śūnyatā* are correctives and neither can be understood apart from this corrective language-game. Seeing either term as other than dependently co-originated, that is, other than as having 'meaning' only in relation to the view (*dṛṣṭi*) for which they were offered as correctives—in these cases, the views of *ātmavāda* and *bāhyārthavāda* ('substantialism' and 'realism')—is to treat them away from their original homes. Neither *anātman* nor *śūnyatā* are the bases for any metaphysics. It is not for nothing that Nāgārjuna's school is called the '*mādhyamaka*' ('middle position'), as it steers a middle course between all extremes, and any metaphysical position whatsoever is considered an extremity. Candrakīrti[107] compares *śūnyatā* with a snake; if wrongly grasped, the snake can be extremely dangerous, just as a metaphysically-understood *śūnyatā* is dangerous. He writes :[108]

> It is true that a useful thing when wrongly seized does not give service, but how could it be injurious ? The seed, sown in contempt of nature, does not destroy the sower. Thus the Master gives an example to clarify this regard : '[It is] just like a serpent clumsily grasped, like the magical sciences wrongly applied.'

Thus *śūnyatā* has as its use (read : 'meaning') the negation without counter-position of extreme (read : 'metaphysical') views. Other interpretations of *śūnyatā* as absolutism, according to Candrakīrti, are instances of faulty grammar.[109]

---

107. Candrakīrti, *Prasannapadā-Mādhyamakavṛtti*, XXIV.11. Tibetan text and French translation in Jacques May, *Candrakīrti, Prasannapadā Mādhyamakavṛtti : Douze chapitres, traduits du sanscrit et du tibétain en français, et accompagnés d'une introduction, du notes et d'une édition critique de la versionne tibétaine*, Paris : Libraire d'Amérique et d'Orient, 1959.

108. *Ibid.*, p. 232.

109. Louis de la Vallée Poussin supports the same conclusion by a different method. See his "Réflexions sur le Mādhyamaka," *Mélanges chinois et bouddhiques*, II, 1933, pp. 4-59, especially pp. 38-47.

As both Nāgārjuna and Wittgenstein are critics of language (Nāgārjuna has been called one without any position, a *vaitaṇḍika*),[110] one might expect them to have some interesting thoughts on negation, since it would be the business of a critic to negate what he considers to be errors. And here we find strong parallels. All sorts of questions, such as the status of the negated, which was a key issue in the Nyāya-Sautrāntika debates,[111] and the absolute or relative quality of the negation itself, which was a focus of the Prasaṅgika-Svātantrika debates,[112] have been raised.

Wittgenstein notices that there is something curious about the grammar of negation. He writes :[113] "The feeling is as if the negation of a proposition had to make it true in a certain sense, in order to negate it," which is precisely the point Nyāya was making in their encounters with the Sautrāntikas. A meaningful negation, according to Nyāya, is possible only if the opposite of the negated, which they called *pratiyogin* or counter-positive, is a real. Remember that it is a basic tenet of Nyāya that anything which could be meaningfully asserted is real, and it will not be difficult to see their consistency in insisting that in the case of 'the pot is not on the ground,' the 'absence of pot' is said to be a real, albeit a negative real (*abhāva*) . For both the Buddhists and Wittgenstein, this position is absurd. Speaking for Buddhism, a Sautrāntika would say that the perception 'the pot is not on the ground' is not a true perception at all, but a 'determinate perception' (*savikalpa*), which is a mental and not a sensory object (*vikalpa*). What is being cognized, he would argue, is the 'empty ground' (*kaivalya*) in the context of one's expecting

---

110. Just as Nāgārjuna is 'positionless,' so the Buddha characterizes himself as 'contentionless.' See S.III. 138 : Nāham bhikkhave lokena vivadāmi loko ca mayā vivadati. Na bhikkhave dhammavādī kenaci lokasmiṃ vivadati.

111. D. N. Shastri gives a very lucid, blow-by-blow account of the issues raised in the course of these debates. See *op. cit.*, pp. 395-487.

112. For a thorough treatment of these issues, see Nathan Katz, "An Appraisal of the Svātantrika-Prasaṅgika Debates," *Philosophy East and West*, 26, 3, July 1976, pp. 253-267.

113. *P.I.*, section 447.

pot to be there. Again, the Buddhist is asking the Naiyāyika to see that the speaking of *x* does not entail the being of *x*.[114]

Wittgenstein gives a similar analysis, but along explicitly linguistic lines. He writes :[115]

> It would be odd to say : 'A process looks different when it happens from when it doesn't happen.' Or 'A red patch looks different when it is there from when it isn't there'—but language abstracts from this difference, for it speaks of a red patch whether it is there or not.

It is a pecularity of our language, and not of reality as Nyāya would have us believe, that "The assertion of a negative proposition contains the proposition which is negated, but not the assertion of it.'"[116] To take our mode of speaking for what is given is one of the fundamental types of error for both Nāgārjuna and Wittgenstein. In this instance, taking our language of negation and abstracting it into untenable theses such as the existence of absence (*abhāvaḥ vastu*) is a fine example of such philosophic nonsense for which Buddhism and Wittgenstein are offering remedies.

Both Wittgenstein and Nāgārjuna are explicit in stating that in their negations, they are not negating anything real—which is consistent with our characterization of them as both being positionless. Wittgenstein says :[117] "What we are destroying is nothing but houses of cards and we are clearing up the ground of language on which they stand." When we say 'there is no red patch,' it is only by convention that we may say 'red patch' when it is not there. When such language critics refute metaphysical talk about 'Being,' they are doing just that—refuting *talk about* 'Being.' Since name does not imply thing, as we have discussed, then the negation involved is grammatical and not ontological. And 'grammar' is certainly not a 'thing.'

Nāgārjuna recapitulates the Nyāya position in his *Vigrahavyāvartanī*.[118] He says :

---

114. A masterful discussion of these issues is found in Bibhuti S. Yadav, "Negation, Nirvāṇa and Nonsense," *Journal of the American Academy of Religion*, XLV, 4, 1977, pp. 451-471.

115. *P.I.*, section 446.

116. *P.I.*, section 447.

117. *P.I.*, section 118.

118. Nāgārjuna, *Vigrahavyāvartanī*, XI. This time we are following the

> Negation is seen to be only of an existent (*sata eva pratiṣedho... dṛṣṭaḥ*), as in the following : 'There is no pot in the house' (*nāsti ghaṭo geha ity ayam*). Consequently, this negation is that of an existent intrinsic nature (*pratiṣedho' yaṃ sataḥ svabhāvasya te tasmāt*).
>
> It is only an existent object that is negated, not a non-existent one. For instance, when it is said : 'There is no pot in the house,' it is an existent pot that is negated, not a non-existent one (*sato ghaṭasya pratiṣedhaḥ kriyate nāsataḥ*).
>
> In like manner it follows that the negation 'The things have no intrinsic nature' (*nāsti svabhāvo dharmāṇāṃ*) is a negation of an existent intrinsic nature, not of a non-existent one. In these circumstances, the statement that all things are devoid of an intrinsic nature is not valid. By the very fact that a negation is possible, the intrinsic nature of all things is non-negated.

As we have seen, the claim of Nāgārjuna that things have no 'intrinsic nature' (*svabhāva*) is a grammatical rather than an ontological statement. To say that things have *svabhāva* is to say that one can coherently speak of them apart from their everyday language, that a word has a referent, which is to say that a word is more than a convenient designtion. It is precisely this naive conception of language that Nāgārjuna is negating when he says that things have no *svabhāva*. Candrakīrti[119] says that the objection of the Naiyāyika is meaningless, that it amounts to saying as little as 'the son of a barren woman is handsome,' since it wants to treat as established an unestablished term, *svabhāva*. Their argument is not well founded because it wants to admit, by virtue of its negation, the existence of *svabhāva*, when the Mādhyamika does not accept it due to grammatical considerations.

---

translation by Kamaleswar Bhattacharyya in "The Dialectical Method of Nāgārjuna : Translation of the 'Vigrahavyāvartanī' from the Original Sanskrit with Introduction and Notes," *Journal of Indian Philosophy*, I, 1, 1971, pp. 217-261. Compare Giuseppe Tucci, ed. and tr., *Pre-Diṅnāga Buddhist Texts on Logic*, pp. 18-19.

119. Candrakīrti, *Prasannapadā-Mādhyamakavṛtti*, XVIII.8. Tibetan text and French translation in Jan Willem de Jong, *Cinq chapitres de la Prasannapadā*, Leiden : E. J. Brill, 1949, pp. 11-12.

It has not been unusual for Buddhism in general, and the Mādhyamika in particular, to be misunderstood as nihilism.[120] This misunderstanding is precisely because their negations are taken as ontological rather than grammatical, leading to the false idea that Nāgārjuna negates reals. One argument against this view given by Candrakīrti[121] is analogical : Imagine that a theft has been committed. One man, who has not witnessed the theft, but out of malice for the accused, testifies against him. Another man, having seen the accused commit the crime, also testifies against him. While both are making the same claim —that the accused did commit the crime—in one case we have an untruth and in the other, truth. The nihilist who negates is like the first witness; Nāgārjuna is like the second. There are two reasons for this : (1) Nāgārjuna's negation is a corrective, an enquiry into the grammar of talking about the world, while the nihilist's negation is, according to the Mādhyamaka, just another view; and (2) Nāgārjuna's negation is absolute in the sense that it offers no countr-thesis, not even a negative counter-thesis, whereas the nihilist's negation is relative to a particular view which is being negated, which is tantamount to saying that he is indulging in mere play of concepts (*prapañca*). Comparing Candrakīrti's analogy with the method employed by the Buddha to examine claims about the self, as discussed above, and we see that the Buddha does not negate self, as the Cārvāka, nor does he assume a sceptical stance, as Sañjāya. Rather, the Buddha analyzes our talking about the self and makes some grammatical observations. Of course, for Buddhism grammar is rooted in psychology, not ontology, which is to say that grammatical confusions involved in talk about the self require a psychotherapy rather than mere philosophizing.

Due to the grammatical nature of the negations employed in Buddhism and by Wittgenstein, both eschew easy definitions of what might be meant by the negated, or what is meant by an error, a philosophic mistake. Rather than offer such definitions, we have attempted to show how they work. In considering such mistakes, Wittgenstein comments :[122] "A main cause of philos-

120. See, for example, Harsh Narain, "Śūnyavāda : A Reinterpretation," *Philosophy East and West*, 13, 4, January 1964, pp. 311-318.

121. Candrakīrti, *Prasannapadā*, XVIII.13, in de Jong, *op. cit.*, p. 26.

122. *P.I.*, section 593.

ophic disease—a one-sided diet : one nourishes one's thinking with only one kind of example." And he cautions :[123] "Say what you chose, so long as it does not prevent you from seeing the facts. And when you see them, there is a good deal that you will not say." We tend to look at only one type of usage of a word, and to hypothesize a meaning from this diet of one-sided examples.

Wittgenstein's philosophy neither negates anything real nor proposes to modify our everyday language :[124] "Philosophy may in no way interfere with the actual use of language; it can in the end only describe it. For it cannot give any foundation either. It leaves everything as it is." And as for those who would do philosophy in a metaphysical sense ? :[125] "When we do philosophy we are like savages, primitive people, who hear the expressions of civilized men, put a false interpretation on them, and draw the queerest conclusions from it."

The question of Wittgenstein's diet becomes, in Buddhist parlance, the well known question of the relationship of the two truths : *paramārtha-satya and saṃvṛti-satya.* Nāgārjuna's famous verse on this subject is :[126]

> Those who do not know the distinction between the two truths cannot understand the profound nature of the Buddha's teaching.

Many scholars, both western and Buddhist, have been confused by statements like that one and :[127]

> No *dharma* relating to any person or place has ever been taught by the Buddha.

It does seem unusual to claim that the Buddha, whose teachings have been compiled into five full *nikāyas*, never taught anything. What is involved with this statement is an invitation to see that when the Buddha does teach, he does so in a very different way from our mundane methods. Much has been said about how

---

123. *P.I.*, section 79.
124. *P.I.*, section 124.
125. *P.I.*, section 194.
126. *MMK*.24.9. (Inada translation)
ye 'nayorna vijānanti vibhāgaṃ satyayordvayoḥ
te tattvaṃ na vijānanti gambhīraṃ buddhaśāsane.
127. *MMK*.25.24. (My translation)
na kva citkasya citkaściddharmo buddhena deśitaḥ.

the Buddha's teaching is really silence, et cetera; the point to consider in this context is that the Buddha never confused the relative discourse (*saṃvṛti-satya*) with the ultimate (*paramārtha-satya*), which is beyond any specifications whatsoever (*āparyāya*). To take the *words* of the Buddha as ultimate, as did the Lokattaravādins and, to a lesser extent, as do the Theravādins,[127a] is to involve oneself in a one-sided diet—from the Mādhyamaka standpoint. Their distinction (*vibhāṣa*) of *saṃvṛti* and *paramārtha* is a caution to us to see *any* statement (including the Buddha's) as a convenient designation, as an exercise in skilful means (*upāya kauśalya*), as heuristic and pedagogical, as everyday language—but never as referring or absolute. Thus, to take the four noble truths, much less any other statement, as ultimate, to treat them as propositional, is to refuse to see that when the Buddha preached, he preached contextually.[128] This is not to deny the *value* of the Buddha's teaching; it is to remove it from the realm of metaphysical discoursing.[129]

If for Wittgenstein the philosopher is a savage, for the Buddha he is a very sick man. His problem, like that of the metaphysician who would predicate the Tathāgata in terms of fourfold logical alternatives (*catuṣkoṭi*),[130] is the desire to make cognitive claims where the grounds for such claims is lacking. He is like the man who loves 'the most beautiful woman in the world,' without even knowing who she is.[131] His one-sided diet is likened by the Buddha to the case of the six blind men and the elephant.[132] It has been said that Nāgārjuna wrote his *Mūlamadhyamakakārikā* as a commentary on the Buddha's silence when asked about the predication of the Tathāgata by the members of the *catuṣkoti*,[133] and that he is showing how all philosophic

127a. André Bareau, *Les sectes bouddhiques du petit véhicule*, Paris; École française d'Extrême Orient, 1955, p. 70. The Lokattaravāda holds that *all* words of the Buddha are ultimately true. The Theravāda holds that *some* words of the Buddha are ultimately true.

128. *MMK*.24, *passim*.

129. It seems that Bhāvaviveka and his Svātantrikas better understood this point than did Buddhapālita and the Prasaṅgikas. See Nathan Katz, "An Appraisal ...," *op. cit*.

130. See *MMK*.22.

131. D.ix.36-37.

132. Udana, VI.4.

133. D.xxix. 31.

claiming follows the same model wherein one claims despite lack of grounds to do so. As discussed earlier, the Buddha even rebuked his beloved disciple, Sāriputta, for hailing the Buddha as omniscient, since Sāriputta was speaking beyond what he could know.[134] Speaking despite a lack of grounds for so speaking, which is found to be at the very basis of Nāgārjuna's examination of errors—as is the one-sided diet at the basis of Wittgenstein's analysis—is found to be rooted in psychology.

The Indian paradigm for our dis-ease in the world is that of the rope and the snake.[135] The rope/snake metaphor goes like this : A person at twilight sees a coiled rope near a tree, but he sees the rope as a snake and responds in terms of snake. Later, when the light is clearer, he sees that the supposed snake is a rope. In Vedāntic parlance, the snake is no longer superimposed on the rope when the rope sublates the experience of snake. Our life, so the analogy goes, in terms of self and other is a case of seeing snake, with all the fear responses appropriate for that situation, instead of a rope. By intuition (*prajñā*) we come to know that what we'd thought was a snake was a rope all along. So it goes with *saṃsāra* and *nirvāṇa*, both interpretative experiences of the given. There are other similar paradigms : the case of a man with jaundiced eyes seeing the world as yellow, et cetera. The point to note is that, in the Indian *Weltanschauung*, our daily cognizing of the world is faulty.

Wittgenstein considers unusual perceptual instances, such as Jastrow's duck/rabbit,[136] which is a figure that can be seen as either a duck or a rabbit. Wittgenstein comments :[137] " 'Seeing as...' is not a part of perception. And for this reason it is like seeing and again not like." The Buddhist, following his paradigm, would offer that, in the world of self and other (*saṃsāra*), there is no 'seeing' apart from 'seeing as.' Wittgenstein might reply that the Buddhist is unhealthy because of a one-sided diet : he is

134. D.xxviii. 31; and D.xvi.1.16.

135. For a commentatorial discussion of 'illusion' (*mig yor*) in Buddhism, see kLong chen rab 'byams pa, *Ngal gso skor gsum*, part III : *sGuy ma ngal so*, tr. by Herbert V. Guenther as *Kindly Bent to Ease Us*, part III : *Wonderment*, Emeryville : Dharma Publishing, 1976, pp. 63-69, and p. 128, fn. 1.

136. *P.I.*, page 194e.

137. *P.I.*, page 197e.

taking as a paradigm an unusual case, and then forcing our experience to conform to this unjustified paradigm. Wittgenstein has a lot at stake on this point, because if the Buddhist can convince him that our everyday perceptions are defective, then his crucial stance about everyday language might be in jeopardy.

The Buddhist might then ask Wittgenstein not to miss the context of his paradigm. The philosophical, for Buddhism, is rooted in the psychological. The belief in self, which Buddhism also holds to be a grammatical mistake, is deeply rooted in our desire that there be a self (*diṭṭhitaṇhā* is rooted in *bhava-taṇhā*).[138] Philosophic problems are a disease to be cured because life is a disease to be cured. If philosophers are savages, it is due to the savagery of our being born to be re-born. Having done this linguistic therapy, the Buddha would then invite us to do some psychotherapy. Nāgārjuna writes *Ratnāvalī* after completing *Mūlamadhyamakakārikā*; the Buddha, after having quieted Māluṇkyaputta's philosophic outburst, invites him to do some quiet meditation.[139] Philosophic problems do indeed arise when language goes on holiday, but this holiday is not only a problem for the philosopher. It is a disease with which we are all afflicted.

We are not concluding this section by saying that Nāgārjuna and Wittgenstein, had they met, would have ended up at these loggerheads. What we are saying is that their philosophic methodologies, as well as many of the points they make, are at times strikingly similar; however, Buddhism's concern is not primarily philosophic but religious. Therefore, for the Buddha, analytic philosophy is analogous to sweeping the floor before one sits on it to meditate. The cognitive defilements (*jñeyāvaraṇa*) are resolved in Buddhism only as a preliminary to the quieting of the emotive defilements (*kleśāvaraṇa*). In fact, the two cannot he separated.

E. *The Arahant as Ineffable*

Perhaps the most accurate thing that could be said about an arahant is stated by the Buddha in the Alaggadūpama Sutta :[140]

138. Padmasiri de Silva makes this type of case convincingly in *Buddhist and Freudian Psychology*, Colombo : Lake House, 1973.

139. M. *sutta* 63.

140. M.I.141. (PTS translation)
Ye tebhikkhū arahanto khīṇāsavā vusitavanto katakaraṇīyā ohitabhārā anuppattasadatthā parikkhīṇabhavasaṃyojanā sammadaññā vimuttā, vaṭṭaṃ tesaṃ na 'tthi paññāpanāya.

> Those monks who are perfected ones [*arahanto*], the cankers [*āsavā*] destroyed, who have lived the life, done what was to be done, laid down the burden, attained their own goal, the fetter of becoming utterly destroyed, and who are freed by perfect, profound knowledge—the track of these cannot be discerned.

As we shall see, this ineffability of the arahant is applicable both after death, a position which has been closely examined by Nāgārjuna,[141] but also during this life. We propose to adduce reasons for this statement in this section. First, we shall find that one who is preoccupied with the world, and therefore full of conflicting views, cannot actualize clarity of vision such that he could know about arahants. Secondly, following our earlier analysis of the philosophy of the arahant in terms of *ehipassaka*, we find that one lacks the cognitive, empirical grounds for predicating anything about the arahant. Thirdly, we shall see that according to the Buddha, any claim about an arahant is mere conceptual play (*papañca*), and is merely the formulation of yet another *diṭṭhi*. Fourthly, Buddhism would ask us to recognize that our referential notion of language must, at a point, collapse over the edges of language. Our analysis of the ineffability of the arahant, therefore, will follow our analysis of the philosophy of the arahant.

Any student of Buddhism is familiar with the Buddha's refusal to predicate the after-death status of the Tathāgata in terms of the *catuṣkoti*; given the amount of attention paid to this issue, one need not consider it at any length here. The Buddha also tells us that the same unpredicatability of after-death status applies to the arahant as well as to the Tathāgata :[142]

> A brother who is ardent, self-possessed, and from the substratae free, well understands in his awareness feelings of all kinds. He, understanding feelings, in this life is drug-immune [*anāsavo*] and, when the body dies, a saint, lore-perfect, past our reckoning.

141. *MMK*.XVIII.8.

142. S.IV.218. (PTS translation)
Yato ca bhikkhu ātāpī, sampajaño nirūpadhi, tato so vedanā sabbā parijānāti paṇḍito. Se vedanā pariññāya diṭṭhe dhamme anāsavo, kāyassa bhedā dhammaṭṭho, saṇkhyaṃ nopeti vedagūti.

But it is not simply a matter of unpredicatable after-death status; Sāriputta argues that just as the arahant cannot be known after death, so also he cannot be known in this life :[143]

> Then, friend Yamaka, since in this very life a Tathāgata is not to be regarded as existing in truth, in reality, is it proper for you to assert : 'As I understand the doctrine taught by the Exalted One, in so far as a brother who has destroyed the *āsavā*, he is broken up and perished when the body is broken up, he becomes not after death ?

Of course, Sāriputta is leading Yamaka to see that the same conditions hold for the arahant or the Tathāgata both before and after death, that he cannot be said to be this or that.

Perhaps the simplest reason for this unpredicatability of the arahant either during or after his life is that one who is immersed in this world is too intoxicated by its pains and pleasures to have clarity of vision. The Buddha says :[144]

> But surely, householder, it's a hard thing for you—a layman, engrossed in pleasures, encumbered with children, odorous with Kasi's sandalwood, decked with flowers and scented oils, merry with silver and gold—to tell which are arahants and which have won the arahant's way.

The Buddha makes the same observations to the king of Kosala, Pasenadi,[145] and in another place[146] he makes this observation into an imperative when he tells Ānanda :

> Wherefore, Ānanda, be ye not measurers of persons, take not the measure of persons. One is ruined, Ānanda, by taking

---

143. S.III.112. (PTS translation)
Ettha ca te āvuso Tamaka diṭṭheva dhamme saccato thetata tathāgato anupalabbhiyamāno, kallaṃ nu te taṃ veyyākaraṇam Tathāhaṃ Bhagavatā dhammaṃ desitam ājānāmi, yāthā khīṇāsavo bhikkhu kāyassa bhedā ucchijjati vinassati na hoti param maraṇā ti.

144. A.III.391. (PTS translation)
Dujjānaṃ kho etaṃ gahapati tayā gihinā kāmabhoginā puttasambādhasayanaṃ ajjhāvasantena Kāsikacandanaṃ paccanubhontena mālāgandhavilepanaṃ dhārayantena jātarūparajataṃ sādiyantena 'ime vā arahanto ime vā arahattamaggaṃ samāpannā ti.

145. S.I.77-79.

146. A.V.143. (PTS translation)
Tasmā ti h' Ānanda mā puggaleso pamāṇikā ahuvattha mā puggalesu pamāṇaṃ gaṇhitta. Khaññati h' Ānanda puggalo puggalesu pamāṇaṃ gaṇhato, ahañ c' Ānanda puggalesu pamāṇaṃ gaṇheyyaṃ, yo vā pan' assa mādiso.

> the measure of persons. But I myself, Ānanda, and whose is like unto me, could take the measure of persons.

One such as that is Mahā-Moggallāna, of whom it is said :[147] "The venerable Mahā-Moggallāna saw with his mind that their mind was freed without basis." So it is not that an arahant cannot in principle be known to be an arahant, but that only another arahant has sufficient clarity of mind to know this. As for his predicatability, either during or after this life, there is no evidence that this is possible. The simplest reason for this, as we have indicated, is that one involved with the world is in no position to do so, just as the Dhamma is inaccessible to one holding contrary views : *dudiṭṭhī na dukkhā pamuccare 'ti.*[148]

The second reason for the ineffability of the arahant is more significant. Remembering our discussion of the quasi-empirical trends in the *Sutta Piṭaka*, we find here that the cognitive grounds for making claims about an arahant are lacking. One basis of this lack of cognitive grounds is expressed in the *Suttanipāta*,[149] where the Buddha says that a person is defined by his psychological predelictions and latent *kammatic* tendencies, and that since these are utterly absent in the perfected person, as a definitional matter of what the notion of perfection entails in Buddhism, therefore there could be no grounds for claiming anything at all about the arahant. The arahant Kaccāna tells us that there are no grounds for claiming anything about the form of consciousness of the arahant :[150]

> Now as to the reason, the grounds, for describing him as embodied or disembodied, as conscious or unconscious, as neither conscious nor unconscious,—if such reason, such grounds, should cease in every way, entirely, wholly, utterly, and without remainder, by what definition could one describe him as embodied or disembodied, as conscious or unconscious, as neither conscious nor unconscious.

147. A.V.164 : cetasā ceto paricca.
148. Udana, p. 73.
149. Suttanipāta, p. 154.
150. S.IV.402. (PTS translation)
Yo ca Vaccha hetu yo ca paccayo paññāpanāya Rūpīti vā Arūpīti vā Saññīti vā Asaññīti vā Neva saññī nāsaññīti vā, so ca hetu so ca paccayo sabbena sabbaṃ sabbathā sabbam aparisesaṃ nirujjheyya, kena naṃ paññāpayamāno paññāpeyya Rūpīti vā Arūpīti vū Saññī vā Asaññīti vā Neva saññī nāsaññīti vāti.

Similarly, as one might expect, the arahant himself does not compare himself with anyone :[151] *Na samesu na omesu na ussesu vadate muni*, because any such claiming, given grounds or lack of grounds for claiming, is rooted in a psychological disorder, according to Buddhism, and as we have discussed, is especially emphasized in some of the writings of Nāgārjuna.

This discussion of the last of logical or empirical grounds for making claims about the arahant leads us to the fourth basis for the ineffability of the arahant : that any statement about the arahant is merely a *diṭṭhi*, something which must be overcome. Miss Horner[152] expressed some dismay at the Buddha's refusal to allow us to formulate any opinion about the arahant :

> In the *Majjhima* . . . it is said (M.I.141) 'there is no discovering the course (*vaṭṭa*) of arahans,' and nowhere in Pali literature is this elucidated; we are left in ignorance as to the ultimate destiny of arahans. They are no longer liable to be reborn, for by them death and birth have been overpassed. The silence shrouding this question is attributable to two causes : arahanship was regarded as its own reward, the goal itself; and speculative questions were not welcomed by Gotama.

We must take exception to Miss Horner's observations here. In the first place, we would argue that there is no single point more fully explained in Pali literature than why an arahant cannot be predicated. It is not as if, as Miss Horner suggests, that the Buddha had set the question aside and said no more about it, leaving us in ignorance. Rather, he very skilfully analyzes the reasons why this question is set aside, reasons which we have been examining in this section. It is also not so much the case that we are left in ignorance about the ultimate destiny of the arahant; rather, we are requested to see that our insistence that this 'ultimate destiny' be predicated is precisely our ignorance. There seems to be a rather naive understanding of what a Buddhist might mean by ignorance in the first place. In Buddhism and all of India, ignorance is not so much the absence of particular information, but ignorance means something like an overabundance of speculative and irrelevant (in terms of the dis-solution of the multi-lemma of *saṃsāra*) theorizing. A

151. Suttanipāta, p. 185.
152. Horner, *EBTMP*, p. 137.

careful reading of these texts will show that the Buddha does not leave us in ignorance about the arahant; he has demonstrated to us that our normal method of claiming and counterclaiming is itself ignorance, and that one does not simply overcome ignorance (lack of predication) by more ignorance (superfluity of information).

Statements about an arahant, or a Buddha, tend to be mere *diṭṭhivāda*. We have referred several times to the claim of Sāriputta that the Buddha was omniscient. Omniscience, at least for one who is not himself omniscient, is merely an opinion.[153] In one place the Buddha lists four 'unthinkables' (*acinteyyāni*),[154] the first of which is the range of a Buddha (or an arahant) : *buddhānaṃ bhikkhave buddhavisayo acinteyyo*. Also held to be unthinkable, because any predication thereof would be indulgence in *diṭṭhi*, are : meditation (*jhāyissa bhikkhave jhānavisayo*); the result of action or intentionality (*kamma vipāko bhikkhave acinteyyo*); and the world (*lokacintā bhikkhave acinteyyā na cintetabbā*). This is to say that any statement about a Buddha or an arahant, about meditation, about *kamma* and its fruit, or about the world, is mere *diṭṭhi*. In the commentatorial literature,[155] it is said that such *diṭṭhivāda* is so dangerous that poor Buddhism was forced to develop a system of *abhidhamma* in order to keep the mind of the bhikkhu from wandering to all sorts of metaphysical excesses : *abhidhamme duppaṭipanno dhammacittam atidhāvanto acinteyyāni pi cinteti, tato cittavikkhepaṃ pāpuṇāti*.

And finally, one reason why the arahant cannot be predicated is that the study of Buddhism leads one to a study of language. The Buddhist negation of *svabhāva* is the negation of referrential language. We find this theme expressed in a dialogue between the Buddha and Upasīva :[156]

153. S.V.160.

154. A.II.80.

155. Asl., p. 24 : abhidhamme duppaṭipanno dhammacittam atidhāvanto acinteyyāni pi cinteti, tato cittavikkhepaṃ pāpuṇāti.

156. Suttanipāta, p. 207. (HOS translation)
Atthaṇ gato so uda vā so n' atthi udāhu ve sassatiyā arogo, tam me munī sādhu viyākarohi, tathā hi te vidito esa dhammo. Atthaṇ gatassa na pamaṇam atthi, Upasīvā ti Bhagavā, yena naṃ vajju, taṃ

> Does he who 'disappears' quite cease to be ? or last forever hale and strong ? Explain this, sage; for, clear to thee this outlook shows. Whoso thus 'disappears' is measureless; he keeps nothing that can be named. When attributes have gone, denoting terms go too.

This is to say that the arahant knows that language is not referential, and therefore knows that 'nothing can be named'; therefore, all 'denoting terms go,' which is to say that referrential models of language are found to be dysfunctional in terms of one's spiritual development.

Thus the Buddha says of himself that a Tathāgata is untraceable,[157] just as he says of the arahants that their course cannot be known (*vaṭṭaṃ tesaṃ na 'tthi pannāpanāya*).[158] One who has destroyed the *āsavā* is called 'immeasurable' (*appameyyo*).[159] And it is also said that an arahant is one who is unknown by all the world, including by the *devā* of the divine worlds.[160]

The same point is also made by two metaphors, one which likens the arahant to fire, and one which likens the course of the arahant to the course of birds in the sky. The first of these metaphors is :[161]

> Just as the bourn of a blazing spark of fire struck from the anvil, gradually fading, cannot be known,—so in the case of those who've rightly won release and crossed the flood of lusts that bind, and reached the bliss unshaken, the bourn they've won cannot be pointed to.

---

tassa n' atthi, sabbesu dhammesu samūhatesu samūhatā vādapatha pi sabbe ti.

157. M.I.140.

158. M.I.141.

159. A.I.266 : Katama ca bhikkhave puggalo appameyyo? Idha bhikkhave bhikkhu arahaṃ hoti khīṇāsavo. Ayaṃ vuccati bhikkhave puggalo appameyyo.

160. Udana, p. 77 : yassa papañcā ṭhiti ca n' atthi, sandhānaṃ palighañ ca vītivatto, na taṃ nittaṇhaṃ muniṃ carantaṃ n' āvajānāti sadevako pi loko.

161. Udana, p. 93. **(PTS translation)**
ayoghanahatass' eva jalato jātavedasso, anupubbūpasantassa yathā na ñāyate gati, evaṃ sammāvimuttānaṃ kāmabandhoghatārinaṃ, paññāpetuṃ gati n' atthi pattānaṃ acalaṃ sukhan ti.

We find two very similar verses which liken the arahant to the bird of the sky. The first is from the *Dhammapada* :[162]

> They for whom there is no accumulation, who reflect well over their food, who have deliverance which is void and signless as their object—their course is like that of birds in the air which cannot be traced.

Similarly, the Therāgāthā[163] reports the arahant Vijayo as saying :

> In whom the intoxicants [*āsavā*] are dried up; whose happiness dependeth not on food; whose range is in the Void and the Unmarked, and Liberty;—as flight of birds in air, so hard it is to track the trail of him.

The arahant, then, is sort of a test case; in understanding how and why he is beyond our speaking and referring, in understanding how and why he cannot be predicated, and in understanding how and why he comes to be free of such opinions, the follower of the Buddhist path comes to learn that the arahant is free from all psychological, verbal and philosophic constraints; so as the world ceases for the arahant, it comes to cease for those who pay heed to him.

---

162. Dhammapada.VII.3. (Nārada translation)
yesaṃ sannicayo natthi, ye pariññātabhojanā, suññato animitto ca, vimokkho yassa gocaro, ākāse 'va sakuntānaṃ, gati tesaṃ durannayā.

163. Thag., verse 92 (PTS translation).
Yassāsavā parikkhīṇā āhāre ca anissito, suññato animitto ca vimokkho yassa gocaro, ākāse va sakuntānaṃ padan tassa durannayan ti.

CONCLUSIONS

A. *Genera*

We run across very tricky exegetical and hermeneutical problems when confronted with some of the claims made about the arahant in later Buddhist Sanskrit and Tibetan literatures. We find statements about the arahant that are at times conflicting, we find a complex grammar of terms such as 'arhat'/'bodhisattva,' as *śrāvaka* and arhat; as the *triyāna* and *ekayāna* teachings; and so forth. As a way of concluding this study of the arahant, then, our procedure will be to survey some of these Mahāyāna and Tantric claims, and then to attempt to sort out their grammar. We shall then view these claims in the light of what we have seen of the arahant from our Pali sources.

Most fundamentally, there are two general types of statements made about the arhat and the bodhisattva in Mahāyāna literature. The first claims that the arhat is inferior to the bodhisattva; the second says that they cannot be distinguished, that they are equals. Since our method is that we should view the context in which such statements regarding these controversial matters are being made, it will be necessary to enter upon a somewhat extended discussion of these competing claims. We shall then consider whether or not these claims are in fact competing, or if they can be exegetically reconciled.

B. *The Arhat as Inferior to the Bodhisattva*

In the *prajñāpāramitā* literature, we find the theme repeated that the realization attained by the arhat is quite different from that attained by the bodhisattva. In the *Aṣṭasāhasrikā*,[1] we find Subhuti saying : "The concentrated insight of a Bodhisattva is called 'the non-apprehension of all *dharmas*.' It is vast, noble,

---

1. *Aṣṭasāhasrikā-Prajñāpāramitā*, ed. P. L. Vaidya, Buddhist Sanskrit texts, No. 4, Darbhanga : Mithila Institute, 1960; tr. Edward Conze, *The Perfection of Wisdom in Eight Thousand Lines and Its Verse Summary*, Bolinas : Four Seasons Foundation, 1973, ed. p. 5; tr. p. 85. [Hereinafter : *Aṣṭa*]

unlimited and steady, not shared by any of the Disciples or Pratyekabuddhas." Here the bodhisattva is differentiated from the arhat by the insight known as 'the non-apprehension of all *dharmas*,' a specific topic to be considered below. However, it should be pointed out here that the term 'disciple' (*śrāvaka*) is employed, rather than the term 'arhat.' In some cases, these two terms are interchangeable, as we shall see. However, there are certain senses in which the terms '*śrāvaka*' and 'arhat' are distinct in their Mahāyāna contexts. We merely wish to raise the issue at this point of the terminology of '*śrāvaka*' and 'arhat,' an issue to which we shall return.

In the *Ratnaguṇasañcayagāthā*, another *prajñāpāramitā* text, we find the Buddha saying that the teachings particular to the *bodhisattvayāna* are much more highly valued than those of the *śrāvakayāna* :[2]

> If someone would discipline in Arhatship as many beings as there are in fields equal to the sands of the river Ganges; and if someone else, having copied this perfection of wisdom, would give this book to another being,—his would be the more distinguished merit.

Once again, a significant issue is raised. While it cannot be denied that, historically, the teachings which were known as the *prajñāpāramitā* were closely associated with the rise of the bodhisattva ideal, we offer that, in its Mahāyāna context, the term '*prajñāpāramitā*' refers to the highest wisdom in all of Buddhism, be it that type of Buddhism specific to the *bodhisattvayāna,* or that type of Buddhism found in the Pali canon.[3] One must not confuse such terminology in terms of its 'outer horizon,' which is to say its historical matrix, and its 'inner horizon,' which is to say the text's own conceptual systematizations. This seems to be a possible ground for confusion

---

2. *Ratnaguṇasañcayagāthā*, ed. E. Obermiller, St. Petersburg : Bibliotheca Buddhica, XXIX, 1937; tr. Edward Conze, "Verses on the Accumulation of Precious Qualities," *Indo-Asian Studies*, Pt. I, ed. R. Vira, Śata-Piṭaka Series, Vol. 31, New Delhi : 1963, pp. 126-178; p. 135. [Hereinafter : *Ratna*]

3. *Pañcaviṃśatisāhasrikā-Prajñāpāramitā*, tr. Edward Conze, *The Large Sūtra on the Perfection of Wisdom*, Berkeley : University of California Press, 1975; p. 237. [Hereinafter : *Pañca*].

regarding the arhat and the bodhisattva : the identification of the historical use of the term '*prajñāpāramitā*' with its contextual use. To repeat our position, the contextual use of the term '*prajñāpāramitā*' is such that it refers to that insight by which the person becomes perfected, regardless of whether this perfection is understood in terms of the symbols of the arahant, the bodhisattva or the mahāsiddha. Historically, the term refers to a body of literature which identifies itself with the Mahāyāna and which was fundamental in the rise of the bodhisattva ideal. We also offer that it is precisely this confusion of the historical 'outer horizon' with the contextual 'inner horizon' that has led both western and traditional scholars into vast confusions regarding the arhat/bodhisattva issues. Our text is telling us that the promulgation of the *prajñāpāramitā* is far more meritorious than the training of the arhat; we offer that the term is employed in its contextual, 'inner horizon' sense.

The Tibetan writer, sGam po pa, psychoanalyzes the arhat, to whom he refers by the term '*śrāvaka*.' He says :[4]

> The '*Śrāvaka* family' are those who are afraid of *Saṃsāra*, yearn for *Nirvāṇa* and have little compassion. As has been said about them : 'Having seen the misery of *Saṃsāra*, they become afraid and yearn for *Nirvāṇa*; they do not delight in working for the benefit of sentient beings;—endowed with these three characteristics is the *Śrāvaka* family.

And he continues :[5] "...the *Nirvāṇa* which they claim is not the real one," and he cites the *Saddharmapuṇḍarīka*[6] as authority.

This certainly raises several crucial issues in this controversy; in fact, it crystallizes the problem. sGam po pa has more or less given us a definition of what he takes to be the *śrāvaka*, a definition which contains four key elements : (a) a renunciation of *saṃsāra*; (b) a desire for *nirvāṇa*; (c) a lack of compassion; and (d) that their *nirvāṇa* is not the true *nirvāṇa*. Certainly

---

4. sGam po pa, *The Jewel Ornament of Liberation*, tr. Herbert V. Guenther, Berkeley : Shambhala, 1971; p. 4. [Hereinafter : *Jewel*].

5. *Jewel*, p. 5.

6. *Saddharmapuṇḍarīka Sūtra*, ed. P. L. Vaidya, Buddhist Sanskrit Texts, No. 6, Darbhanga : Mithila Institute, 1960; tr. H. Kern, *Saddharma-Puṇḍarīka, or The Lotus of the True Law*, Sacred Books of the East, ed. F. Max-Müller, Vol. XXI, repr. New York : Dover, 1963 (oxford : Clarendon Press, 1884); V.74. [Hereinafter : *Saddharma*].

these conclusions are utterly incompatible with the Pali materials we have considered; yet, we must point to the use of the term '*śrāvaka*' rather than 'arhat.' Here we wish to make a clear distinction, and since sGam po pa refers us to the *Saddharmapuṇḍarīka* by way of support for his contention, we shall look there for guidance in this matter.

The *Saddharmapuṇḍarīka* is one of the most influential early Mahāyāna texts. It introduces us to such important Mahāyāna notions as '*upāya kauśalya*,' a notion to which the entire second chapter is devoted, and which holds that the Buddha's early teachings were like so many toys offered to rather dull-witted children. This is a major Mahāyāna hermeneutical tool, one by which disparities between the new Mahāyāna teachings and the older 'Hīnayāna' teachings were explained, and it introduces the notion that the entire career of the Buddha as reported in the Pali canon was simply a display for the dull disciples. To return to our immediate problem, we wish to indicate two important points made in the text.

We are told[7] that the Buddha was about to preach to the effect that he knows more than he had taught to his disciples by his skilful means. At that point, some five thousand monks, nuns, laymen and laywomen get up and walk out of the lecture hall. The Buddha says that those who had left were those who "...imagined having attained what they had not." He then turns to Śāriputra and tells him that the chaff had been winnowed from his audience, and he proceeds to teach. The crucial point to note is that nowhere in this incident does the Buddha refer to those who had left the lecture hall as 'arhats,' but merely by the term '*śrāvaka*.'

That these terms 'arhat' and '*śrāvaka*' were clearly distinct in this text is made explicit when Śāriputra, after hearing the Buddha's discourse, proclaims :[8]

> ...today, O Lord, I have reached complete extinction; today, O Lord, I have become calm; today, O Lord, I am wholly come to rest; today, O Lord, I have reached Arhatship; today, O Lord, I am the Lord's eldest son, born from his law....

7. *Saddharma*, p. 23; tr. pp. 38-39.
8. *Saddharma*, p. 44; tr. p. 61.

While this incident in the *Saddharmapuṇḍarīka* is thought by many to affirm a distinct and lower status of the arhat *vis-à-vis* the bodhisattva, we find that a contextual reading shows that arhatship is truly attained by Śāriputra while listening to these teachings, and that by '*śrāvaka*' the text means 'one who thinks he has attained arhatship but had not truly done so.' It is this use of the term '*śrāvaka*' that is employed to refer to those who walked out of the lecture hall; those who stayed, like Śāriputra, are said to rightfully be arhats.

We find a similar point made in the *Ratnaguṇasañcayagāthā*,[9] where the Buddha is discussing the profundity of the *prajñāpāramitā* teachings. He says :

> Four kinds of persons are not alarmed by this teaching : Sons of the Jīna skilled in the truths; saints unable to turn back [a level of the *bodhisattvayāna*]; Arhats free from defilements and taints, and rid of doubts; those whom good teachers mature are reckoned the fourth kind.

This verse tells us that one who is truly an arhat has no difficulty with these new teachings, that he understands them without difficulty. Clearly, this use of the term 'arhat' is strikingly dissimilar to the *Saddharmapuṇḍarīka's* use of the term '*śrāvaka*,' who is so threatened by the Mahāyāna teachings that he must leave the presence of the Buddha himself, rather than hear what he has to say. Therefore, sGam po pa's characterization of the '*śrāvaka* family' should not be understood as referring to the arahant, but to a certain psychological type of person (hence the use of the term 'family,' *rigs*) who is so arrogant as to think he has attained what he has not attained, who is fearful of *saṃsāra* and seeks *nirvāṇa*, the object of his desire, as a kind of escape from that which he fears, who lacks compassion and because of all this, has not truly attained *nirvāṇa*. Thus, the *Prajñāpāramitā Sūtra of* 700 *Lines*[9a] says that "...the greatly conceited Disciples should wake up to what is really true."

Śāntideva, in his *Śikṣā Samuccaya*, is adamant that the follower of the *bodhisattvayāna* understand that the way he is practising is not the way of the *śrāvakayāna*. He cites Mañjuśrī in the

9. *Ratna*, pp. 131-132.

9a. Edward Conze (tr.), *The Short Prajñāpāramitā Texts*, London : Luzac & Co., 1973, p. 84. [Hereinafter : *Short P.*].

Bodhisattva-Prāṭimokṣa-Sūtra :[10] "...a Bodhisattva devotes himself to the highest enlightenment and has given his mind to it, and does not intermediately give his mind to the spiritual stage of the mere Disciple or Pratyeka-Buddha." Here we find the notion of an intermediate stage of spiritual achievement which is attained by the *śrāvakas*, an idea which was first introduced in the *Saddharmapuṇḍarika*, where we find it claimed :[11]

> ...the Tathāgata...to give a repose to the creatures, very skilfully teaches and proclaims two stages of *Nirvāṇa*, viz., the stage of the disciples and that of the Pratyeka-buddhas and, monks, when the creatures are there halting, the Tathāgata... himself pronounces these words : 'You have not finished what you had to do. But behold, monks, the Buddha-knowledge is near; behold and be convinced [*vyavakārayadhvam*]. What to you seems *Nirvāṇa*, that is not *Nirvāṇa*. Nay, monks, it is an able device of the Tathāgatas...that they expound three vehicles.

We shall consider what is meant by 'vehicle' or 'career' (*yāna*) below; the notion here cogent to our discussion is the idea that there is some sort of intermediate resting-place, which is identified with what the *śrāvakas* call '*nirvāṇa*,' but which is not the '*nirvāṇa*' which the text preaches as superior. In the *Laṅkāvatāra Sūtra*[12] this 'resting-place which the *śrāvakas* call *nirvāṇa*' seems to be identified with the *dhyānā* (Pali *jhānā*). We read : "...by disciplining thyself well in *samādhi* and *samāpatti*, follow not the state realized by the *śrāvakas*, pratyeka-buddhas and philosophers, which rises from thę imagination of those who discipline themselves according to the practice of the puerile philosophers." It would be well to recall our earlierd iscussion of the arahant and meditation. There we demonstrated that it was not so much the case that the Buddha taught new medita-

---

10. Śāntideva (Zhi ba lha), *Śikṣā-samuccaya*, ed. Cecil Bendall, St. Petersbourg : Bibliotheca Buddhica, 1897; tr. Cecil Bendall and W. .H. D. Rouse, *Śikṣa-samuccaya : A Compendium of Buddhist Doctrine*, Delhi : Motilal Banarsidass, 1971; p. 17; tr. p. 19. [Hereinafter : *Ś-S*].

11. *Saddharma*, p. 121; tr. pp. 182-183.

12. *Laṅkāvatāra Sūtra*, ed. Bubyu Nanjo, Kyoto : Otani University Press, 1923; tr. Daisetz T. Suzuki, *The Laṅkāvatāra Sūtra : A Mahāyāna Text*, London : Routledge & Kegan Paul, 1968 (1932), p. 11; tr. pp. 10-11. [Hereinafter : *Laṅka*].

tional systems, but that he analyzed traditional Indian meditational systems in a new way. This new way of analyzing the meditations was to see their ultimate unsatisfactoriness. This identification of the intermediate stage of the *śrāvakas* wih the *dhyānā* is also found in the *Aṣṭasāhasrikā*[13] when the Buddha says:

> The decision to win seclusion, to win the fruits of the holy life, from the fruit of a Streamwinner to Pratyekabuddhahood, to enter *Parinirvāṇa* after one has, in this very life, freed thought, without further clinging, free from the outflows [*āśravā*; *āsavā*],—that means to be 'associated with the level of a Disciple or a Pratyekabuddha.'

Thus the *śrāvaka*, in the Mahāyāna sense of the term, is one who 'gets stuck' in the *dhyānā*, and we have seen that the Buddha cautions his disciples in the Pali canon to avoid just this difficulty.

Because of these considerations, Kong sprul[14] tells us that in order to generate *bodhicitta*, which is the basis of all *bodhisattvayāna* practices, one needs both a feeling of disgust with *saṃsāra* (*'khor bar skye pa*) as well as not clinging to *nirvāṇa* (*myang 'das la mi zhen pa*). This is to say, as the Buddha says in the Pali canon, that one must not confuse the means with the end, and that proficiency at the *jhānā* is not *arahattā*, which involves an understanding of the *jhānā* as unsatisfactory, and which proceeds from insight (*paññā*; *prajñā*; *shes rab*).

Another Mahāyāna hermeneutical device for distinguishing the *śrāvaka* from the bodhisattva is to claim, as does Kong sprul,[15] that the *śrāvaka* is interested only in 'self-pacification' (*rang zhi*). The *Aṣṭasāhasrikā*[16] makes a similar point:

> ...a Bodhisattva should not train in the same way in which persons belonging to the vehicle of the Disciples of Pratyekabuddhas are trained. How then are Disciples and Pratyekabuddhas trained? They make up their minds that 'one single self we shall tame, one single self shall we lead to *Nirvāṇa*.' Thus they undertake exercises which are intended to bring about wholesome roots for the sake of taming themselves, pacifying themselves, leading themselves to *Nirvāṇa*.

---

13. *Aṣṭa*, p. 116, tr. p. 164.
14. Kong sprul, *Shes bya kun khyab*, 'grel, II, p. 114.
15. *Ibid.*, rTsa, p. 42.
16. *Aṣṭa*, p. 116; tr. p. 164.

> A Bodhisattva should certainly not in such a way train himself. On the contrary, he should train himself thus : 'My own self I will place in Suchness, and, so that all the world might be helped, I will place all beings into Suchness, and I will lead to *Nirvāṇa*, the whole immeasurable world of beings !'

In our chapter on the arahant and society, we made the case that the arahant is one who is intrinsically and not accidentally a teacher; that this 'pacification of self' of which Kong sprul speaks is the overcoming of all egoism and its roots, such that one then actualizes a new modality of being in the world, a modality which entails that the arahant is an exemplar, a *puññākkheta*, a *guru*, and a *kalyāṇamitta*. Having practised the four divine abodes of friendliness (*mettā*), empathy (*muditā*), compassion (*karuṇā*) and equanimity (*upekkhā*), he is actively (*ātāpī*) engaged in helping others as the natural expression of his having attained to *arahattā*.

Asaṅga, in his *Bodhisattvabhūmi*, asks himself which powers of the Buddhas and bodhisattvas are held in common with the *śrāvakas* and which are not held in common.[17] He finds that there are only three which are not held in common, and these are : (a) 'subtle' power (*cha phra ba*), which means that 'Buddhas and bodhisattvas have inconceivable, innumerable means of power; thus he has the means for benefitting inconceivable, innumerable sentient beings'; (b) 'aspect' power (*rnam pa*), which means that the 'Buddhas and bodhisattvas possess all aspects of power of *abhijñā*, Dharma, and spontaneous powers'; and (c) 'aptitude' or 'realms' power [*khams*], of which he says that "all the realms [*khams*] of the world and the aptitudes [*khams*] of all sentient beings are objects of his power; the object of the *abhijñā* of the *śrāvakas* is up to the realm of the sentient beings of two thousand universes; the object for the pratyekabuddhas is up to three thousand universes; and these limitations are due to their original motivation for entry into training—to train self and not others." Asaṅga[18] concludes that "other than these three points, all powers of Buddhas, pratyekabuddhas

---

17. Asaṅga, *rNal 'byor spyod pa'i sa las byang chub sems dpa'sa, bsTan 'gyur*, Peking ed., Sems tsam, Vol. Zhi, fascs. 49b-50a. [Hereinafter : *Bo. Bhū.*].

18. *Bo. Bhū.*, fasc. 50a.

and *śrāvakas* are the same." Asaṅga seems to have nothing especially new to say, except that whatever powers the *śrāvakas* have, the bodhisattvas have them to a greater degree. He attributes this difference in degree of powers to a different motivation : that the *śrāvaka* is motivated by the quest for self-pacification, whereas the bodhisattva is motivated by a desire to save all sentient beings.

Now, one way in which Mahāyānists talk about the motivation of a bodhisattva is in terms of *bodhicitta*. However, Kong sprul finds that the question of the motivation of a bodhisattva as compared with that of a *śrāvaka* is one of degree, and not one of kind. He tells us[19] that *bodhicitta* is rooted in *maitrī* (Pali : *mettā*; Tibetan : *'byams pa*), through the intermediary of *karuṇā* (Tibetan : *snyin rje*) :

> *Maitrī* is the attitude of wishing prosperity and happiness for others. Its practice gradually generates *karuṇā*, which is the attitude of wishing the total detachment or separation of the sufferings of sentient beings, along with the causes of those sufferings. Its cultivation leads to *bodhicitta*, which is the aspiration for Buddhahood.

In this sense, *maitrī* is different in degree but not in kind from the motivation of a bodhisattva, expressed as *bodhicitta*. However, since Kong sprul's definition of *maitrī* is much more modest than what we have seen said of *mettā* in the Pali canon, where it is said to be felt for all beings as a mother feels for her only son.[20] Since Kong sprul holds that *bodhicitta* proceeds from the cultivation of *maitrī*, and since his claims about *maitrī* are so modest, then one could be led to conclude that *bodhicitta* in the Mahāyāna sense, and *mettā* as found in the Pali texts, are not so fundamentally different. In fact, insofar as there could be said to be any difference at all, it is merely one of degree, and that would be even less of a degree than Kong sprul allows.

Returning to Asaṅga's postulation of some special powers that are attributable to a bodhisattva and which could not be said of an arhat, we find a similar analysis in the *Pañcaviṃśatisāhasrikā*,[21] where eighteen special *dharmas* of a Buddha are

19. Kong sprul, *Shes bya kun khyab*, 'grel, II, p. 101. (My translation)
20. *Suttanipāta*, p. 26.
21. *Pañca*, pp. 159-160.

enumerated.[22] We need not go into the specifics of these *buddhadharmas*, but they were used to indicate some special abilities and characteristics of those who follow the *buddhayāna* as opposed to those who follow the *śrāvakayāna*. However, in the same text[23] we find it said in a discussion of the twenty-four varieties of bodhisattvas, that these eighteen *buddhadharmas* are attained by an *anāgāmī*. In this discussion, the arhat, who is one of these varieties of bodhisattvas according to our text, has attained these eighteen *buddhadharmas* as well as the six perfections (*pāramitā*), which are characteristic of the *bodhisattvayāna*; that he has the power to illuminate others without obstruction, a point which we considered at length based on Pali sources in our discussion of the Buddha and the arahant; and "do not lack the splendor of Buddhahood even before they attain it." Talk about special characteristics or abilities of the bodhisattva do not differ significantly from those characteristics and abilities of the arhat, either from Pali or Sanskrit sources.

From time to time, our Sanskrit and Tibetan texts speak about the *śrāvakayāna* as a spiritual danger to the bodhisattvas; that the bodhisattva might 'fall' into the *śrāvakayāna* if he does not carry out his religious practices effectively. Śāntideva[24] cites the *Upāyakauśalya Sūtra* by way of a warning to the bodhisattva: "...if he have not ... renounced those thoughts of Disciples and Pratyekabuddhas, [he] is incapable of final release at the stage of a Buddha." This warning is emphasized in the same text[25] when he cites the *Ākāśagarbha Sūtra*:

> Again, fair sir, the inceptor Bodhisattva may speak thus to certain hearers [*śrāvaka*] : 'Avoid, young sirs, the preaching of the Disciples' Way; hear it not, study it not, teach it not to others; ... no great fruit will you get from it, nor will you be able to make an end to sin as a result of it.'

Similarly, in the *Aṣṭasāhasrikā*, we find a discussion of detachment which is expressed in terms of detachment from the *śrāvakayāna*.[26] This text tells us that whereas many think of

22. See Chapter III, fn. 129.
23. *Pañca*, pp. 159-160.
24. *Ś-S*, p. 66; tr. p. 70.
25. *Ś-S*, p. 61; tr. p. 64.
26. *Aṣṭa*, pp. 194-196; tr. pp. 233-234.

detachment in terms of living in forests, real detachment means being uncontaminated by the thoughts associated with the *śrāvakayāna.* It concludes by claiming that detachment is fully a question of the mind, and not one of externals.

That the Mahāyāna understanding of the *śrāvakayāna* presented a threat to those practising the *bodhisattvayāna* is explicit in the *Pañcaviṃśatisāhasrikā*,[27] in a discussion of how it comes to be that a bodhisattva falls into the *śrāvakayāna* :

> Not taking hold of the perfection of giving [and the other perfections], meaning practising with a mind that has fallen into I-making and mine-making [*ahaṅkāra*],... he falls on the level of a Disciple ... and does not go forth to the knowledge of all modes.

This citation raises two issues. The first is whether or not, or in what sense, the *śrāvakayāna* could be equated with the *bodhisattvayāna* when practised in an egoistic modality. While it is perfectly clear that this was not the sort of religious practice which the Buddha of the Pali canon had in mind, as he was adamant about maintaining that the practice of his methods entailed a negation of egoism, and therefore that this admonition of the *Pañcaviṃśatisāhasrikā* could not be understood as referring to the arahant of the Pali literature; we do find that this Mahāyāna understanding of the *śrāvaka* is consistently repeated here. What we are suggesting is that the *śrāvaka* is defined in Mahāyāna literature as one who thinks he has attained more than he actually has, and that this mentality would certainly be disastrous to any Buddhist path, Mahāyāna or otherwise. The Mahāyāna notion of the *śrāvaka* is one who is arrogant and conceited; therefore, this *sūtra* merely requests us to avoid such arrogance and conceit. As we find Śāntideva cited in the *Lam rim man ngag* :[28] "Whatever suffering there is in the world is all due to the selfish wish for one's own happiness alone," do such a seeking after one's own happiness alone must be discarded in all the teachings of Buddhism.

Thus far we have merely given an indication of the types of claims found in various Mahāyāna *sūtras* and commentaries

27. *Pañca*, p. 365.

28. dGe shes Ngag dbang dar rgyas, *Lam rim man ngag*, Berzin tr., pp. 469-470 : 'jig rten sdug bsngal ji snyid pa de kun bdag bde 'dod las byung.

which tell us that the arhat, or the *śrāvaka*, is inferior to the bodhisattva. To make a typology out of these sources, we find the following grounds for these claims of the inferiority of the *śrāvaka* :

1. That the *śrāvaka* does not understand the 'non-apprehension of all *dharmas*,' a topic to which we shall return below.

2. That the teachings of the *bodhisattvayāna* are more valuable than those of the *śrāvakayāna*, a claim which we have found necessitates a clear distinction of the historical and the contextual usages of the term '*prajñāpāramitā*,' another topic which shall be held for further considerations.

3. The type of claim made by sGam po pa and others to the effect that the *śrāvaka* family is an inferior psychological type, one characterized by a fear of *saṃsāra*, a desire for *nirvāṇa*, a lack of compassion, and the tendency to claim *nirvaṇa* when it has not in fact been actualized. We offer that sGam po pa is talking about a psychological type called the '*śrāvaka*' in Mahāyāna literature. An analysis of his claims about the *śrāvaka* has found that they do not apply to the arahant of the Pali canon. We have followed sGam po pa's reference to the *Saddharmapuṇḍarīka*, and found that while the *śrāvakas* walk out on the Buddha, those who remain in the audience are said to attain arahattā, indicating the clear distinction between what the Mahāyāna understands by the terms '*śrāvaka*' and 'arhat.'

4. The claim that the *nirvāṇa* actualized by the *śrāvaka* is not the *nirvāṇa* attained by the bodhisattva, but some sort of intermediate resting-place. In analyzing the contexts in which some statements arise, we have found that they are invariably couched in meditational language. Thus, another characteristic of the Mahāyāna usage of the term '*śrāvaka*' is one who 'gets stuck' in the *dhyānā* (*jhānā*); remembering our discussions of the arahant and meditation, we find that the Buddha of the Pali canon equally cautioned his disciples there about not confusing these *jhānic* states with *arahattā* itself. Therefore, we conclude that the Mahāyāna is simply restating what the Buddha said in the Pali texts, and that this intermediate resting-place is merely the *jhānā*/*dhyānā* themselves. Once again, we find that our methodology which entails close contextual reading of these materials leads us to a separation of the Mahāyāna notion of the *śrāvaka* from the Pali notion of the arahant.

5. The claim that the arhat is interested only in self-pacification while the bodhisattva is interested in the welfare of all sentient beings, is likewise found to refer to the Mahāyāna notion of the *śrāvaka* and not to the Pali concept of the arahant. Earlier in this essay,[29] we went to pains to demonstrate at length that the arahant is one who is intrinsically involved with the active teaching of others; thus this criticism can be levelled against what the Mahāyāna understands as the *śrāvaka*, but not against the arahant itself.

6. There is also the Mahāyāna claim that the bodhisattvas and the Buddhas have some special characteristics or abilities which the arhats don't have. However, we found that even Asaṅga in his monumental work on the bodhisattva path, the *Bodhisattvabhūmi*, concluded that what the bodhisattvas have by way of powers and characteristics differ from those of the arhat merely in degree, but not in kind.

7. Finally, we have found the position that the motivation of the arhat differs from that of the bodhisattva. However, from Mahāyāna commentatorial texts, we found that the motivation of the bodhisattva, which is expressed throughout the Mahāyāna as *bodhicitta*, is itself rooted in *maitrī* (*mettā*); so once again the difference, if there could be said to be one, is only in degree, not in kind. As Kong sprul says :[30] "*Maitrī* is the root of all virtues," and we have seen that this *maitrī* is practised by the arahants extensively, and that it plays a key role in the *Sutta Piṭaka*.

Now that we have briefly surveyed and considered some Mahāyāna claims as to the distinction between the arhat or *śrāvaka* and the bodhisattva, we may consider other Mahāyāna claims that the arhat and the bodhisattva cannot be distinguished.

C. *The Arhat and the Bodhisattva as Equals*

One would misrepresent the attitude of early Mahāyāna texts about the arhat were one to consider only those sections which claim some sort of distinction between the arhat or *śrāvaka* and the bodhisattva. There are approximately an equal number of

---

29. See chapter V on the arahant and society.

30. Kong sprul, *Shes bya kun khyab*, 'grel, II, p. 101. (My translation) byams pa ni chos dkar thams cad kyi rgyu yin pa.

references which uphold the equality or identity of the arhat and the bodhisattva, and they do so in various ways.

For example, the *Aṣṭasāhasrikā*[31] tells us that the teachings of the *prajñāpāramitā* are equally understood by the arhat and the irreversible bodhisattva : "Bodhisattvas who cannot fall back will grasp it [the perfection of wisdom], or persons who have reached sound views, or Arhats in whom the outflows have dried up," which is a theme we find often repeated throughout the *prajñāpāramitā* literature. One may surmise that if the arhats readily understand this *prajñāpāramitā* teaching, then it is not alien to their attainments.

The *Saddharmapuṇḍarīka* makes exactly the opposite point :[32] that these new teachings which the Buddha is giving are equally difficult for all Buddhists to understand, be they *śrāvakas*, pratyekabuddhas, bodhisattvas or even irreversible bodhisattvas. In another place in the same text,[33] it is said that the ignorant cannot understand these new teachings (*sahanti bālā na im' indriṣāni*). One might assume that by the ignorant is meant those *śrāvakas* who walked out on the Buddha. But apparently it is not intended to refer to the arhats like Subhut, Śāriputra, Mahā-Katyāyana, Mahā-Kāśyapa and Mahā-Maudgalyāyana, all of whom declare, upon hearing the teachings :[34]

> Now, O Lord, we are disciples, and we shall proclaim supreme enlightenment everywhere, reveal the word of enlightenment, by which we are formidable disciples (*śrāvaka bhīṣmakalpa*). Now we have become Arhats, O Lord; and deserving of the worship of the world, including the gods, Māras and Brahmās, in short, of all beings.

We find precisely the same point in the *Aṣṭasāhasrikā*[35] where we are told that, upon hearing the promulgation of the *prajñāpāramitā* by the Buddha, some five hundred monks, two hundred nuns, and six thousand of the laity, attained"...the pure, dispassionate, unstained eye of Dharma."

In many places in the *prajñāpāramitā* literature, these teachings are recommended to all Buddhists, whether they are following

31. *Aṣṭa*, p. 21; tr. p. 99.
32. *Saddharma*, pp. 22-23; tr. pp. 32-34.
33. *Saddharma*, p. 83; tr. p. 116.
34. *Saddharma*, p. 82; tr. p. 115.
35. *Aṣṭa*, p. 137; tr. p. 181.

the career of the *śrāvaka*, that of the pratyekabuddha, or on the *bodhisattvayāna*. For example, in the *Fifty Lines Prajñāpāramitā*[36] we read : "If someone wants to train in Discipleship or Pratyekabuddhahood, they should hear this Perfection of wisdom, should take it up, bear it in mind, recite and master it." Śāriputra says precisely the same thing in the *Aṣṭasāhasrikā*,[37] but adds that they should" . . . spread it among others, and in this very perfection of wisdom should one be trained and exert one-self."

While it is one thing to say that the *śrāvakas should* study the *prajñāpāramitā*, it is quite another thing to say that the *śrāvakayāna already* has this wisdom. But this is precisely what is said in many *prajñāpāramitā*[38] texts, including the *Pañcaviṃśatisāhasrikā*, the *Aṣṭasāhasrikā*, and the *Fifty Lines Prajñāpāramitā.* In the *Pañcaviṃśatisāhasrikā* we find it said that"...in the perfection of wisdom are contained all the *dharmas* which act as wings of enlightenment, be they Disciple-*dharmas*, Pratyekabuddha-*dharmas*, Bodhisattva-*dharmas* or Buddha-*dharmas*." In the *Aṣṭasāhasrikā*[39] we find : "...just so, whatever *dharmas* of Buddhas, Pratyekabuddhas or Disciples there may be, they are all entrusted to the perfection of wisdom." And in the *Fifty Lines Prajñāpāramitā* :[40]

> Subhuti, whatever wholesome *dharmas* there are, as *dharmas* leading to enlightenment, be they Disciple-*dharmas*, or Pratyekabuddha-*dharmas*, or Bodhisattva-*dharmas*, or Buddha-*dharmas,* since they are all included in the perfection of wisdom, contained and embodied in it, one should apply oneself diligently to it.[41]

Thus we find that the *prajñāpāramitā* teachings, which are said to be the quintessential Mahāyāna teachings, are said in their own literatures to be equally contained in the *śrāvakayāna*, which is to say that they are equally actualized by the arhat.

One might think that the reason for such claims is that, in one sense, the *prajñāpāramitā* contains all, and by virtue of its

36. *Short P.*, p. 154.
37. *Aṣṭa*, p. 3; tr. p. 84.
38. *Pañca*, p. 237.
39. *Aṣṭa*, p. 140; tr. p. 181.
40. *Short P.*, p. 154.
41. See also *Pañca*, p. 98 and p. 58.

containing all it could be stated that it equally contains the *śrāvakayāna*. But this statement would only be operative from the level of highest truth (*paramārtha-satya*), but certainly there should remain some valid distinction between the arhat and the bodhisattva at the relative level of truth (*saṃvṛti-satya*). Indeed, this whole point is made in the *Pañcaviṃśatisāhasrikā*[42] when it is said that not only the bodhisattvas and *śrāvakas*, but even the common people (*pṛthagjana*) equally abide in the *prajñāpāramitā*. But this would not be the complete story. In the *Aṣṭasāhasrikā*,[43] Subhuti tells us that "the perfection of wisdom...is also the perfection which [allows them not to] lean on any *dharma*, because [it shows that] all *dharmas* have no support ..." But this point is made most forcibly by Nāgārjuna in his *Rin po che'i phreng pa* :[44] "The teaching of the Mahāyāna of non-production and of extinction in the Hīnayāna are the same emptiness [since they show that inherent existence] is extinguished, and that nothing [inherently existent] is produced." What the *Aṣṭasāhasrikā* and Nāgārjuna are telling us is that the *śrāvakayāna* and the *bodhisattvayāna* cannot be distinguished in terms of wisdom; that extinction (*nirodha*) and non-production (*akaraṇiyā*) are just the same *śūnyatā*; in effect, this is to say that the arhat and the bodhisattva are identical.

This is not a simple point to comprehend. Indeed, Kong sprul[45] tells us that only a bodhisattva of the seventh *bhūmi*, a highly advanced spiritual level, can see that the goal (*artha*, *don*) of all the Buddha's teachings is identical : *bdun par mdo la sogs ba'i chos kyi mtshan ma tha dad pa med pa'i don dang*. This is difficult to understand because it involves an understanding of *dharmas*, as the *Suvikrāntavikrāmiparipṛcchā Sūtra*[46] tells us that the meaning of '*prajñāpāramitā*' is "the actual transcendental understanding of all *dharmas* that cannot be expounded" : *gang chos thams cad kyi tshu rol rtogs pa ste*. It is precisely this 'transcendental' understanding of all *dharmas*, which is to say,

42. *Pañca*, p. 388.
43. *Aṣṭa*, p. 15; tr. p. 94.
44. Nāgārjuna (kLu sgrub), *Rin po che'i phreng pa*, tr Jeffrey Hopkins, *et al.*, *The Precious Garland*, London : George Allen & Unwin, Wisdom of Tibet Series, No. 2, 1975, verse 386, p. 75. [Hereinafter : *Phreng pa*]
45. Kong sprul, *Shes bya kun khyab*, 'grel, III, p. 534.
46. *Short P.*, pp. 23-24.

the leaving behind of all *dharmas* once the 'other shore' has been attained, that is herein meant by '*prajñāpāramitā*.' As the *Vajracchedaka*[47] says : "Those who know the discourse on *dharma* as like unto a raft should foresake *dharma*, still more so no-*dharmas*," which is precisely the same thing the Buddha says after preaching the analogy of the raft in the *Majjhima Nikāya*.[48]

It is for this reason that the arhat of the *Vajracchedaka*[49] speaks about his attainment of *arahattā* in precisely the same way as the bodhisattva expressed his attainment. There we find the Buddha in conversation with Subhuti, and he asks :

> "What do you think, Subhuti, does it occur to the Arhat, 'By me has Arhatship been attained ?' " Subhuti replied : "No indeed, O Lord. And why ? Because no *dharma* is called 'Arhat.' That is why he is called an Arhat. If, O Lord, it would occur to an Arhat, 'by me has Arhatship been attained,' then that would be in him a seizing on a self, seizing on a being, seizing on a soul, seizing on a person."

This is to say that the arhat (*dgra bcom pa*) attains *arahattā* (*dgra bcom pa nyid*) in the same way as the bodhisattva reaches his attainments.[50]

---

47. *Vajracchedaka-Prajñāpāramitā*, Tibetan poṭi text, '*Phagaspa shes rab kyi pha rol tu phyam pa rdo rje gcod pa zhes bya ba theg pa chen po'i mdo bzhugs so*, Dharmsala : Tibetan Press, n.d.; tr. Edward Conze, *Buddhist Wisdom Books*, New York : Harper Torchbooks, 1972 (1958), fasc. 8a; tr. 124. [Hereinafter : *Vajra*] chos kyi rnam grangs 'di gzings lta bur shes pa rnams kyis chos rnams kyang spang bar bya na/ chos pa yin pa rnams lta ci smos.

48. M.I.135.

49. *Vajra*, fasc. 11b; tr. p. 121.

bcom ldan 'das dka' tsal pa/ rab 'byor' di ji snyam du sems/dgra bcom 'di snyam du bdag gis dgra bcom pa nyid thob po snyam du sems snyam mam rab 'byor gyis gsol pa/ bcom ldan 'das de ni ma lags so/de ci'i slad du nye na' gang dang dgra bcom pa zhes bgyi ba'i chos de gang yang ma mchis pa'i slad du'o/bcom ldan 'das gal te dgra bcom pa 'di snyam du bdag gis dgra bcom pa nyid thob bo snyam du sems par gyur na/de nyid de'i bdag du 'dzin par' gyur lags so//sems can du 'dzin pa dang/srog tu' dzin pa dang' gang zag tu 'dzin par' gyur lags so//

50. Śāriputra and the Buddha have a very similar discussion in the *Aṣṭa*, p. 178; tr. p. 217.

In the *Fifty Lines Prajñāpāramitā*,[51] the Buddha says that all three—the *śrāvaka*, the bodhisattva and the pratyekabuddha—equally practise and actualize the following *dharmas* : (1) the six *pāramitā*; (2) the eighteen emptinesses; (3) the four applications of mindfulness; (4) the four right efforts; (5) the four *ṛddhipādā*; (6) the five *indriya*; (7) the seven *bojjhaṅgā*; (8) the eightfold path; (9) the four noble truths; (10) the four *jhānā*; (11) the eight *vimokkhā*; (12) the four *sampatti*; (13) the nine stations; (14) emptiness, signlessness and wishlessness; (15) the *abhijñā*; (16) the concentrations; (17) the *dharani*; (18) the ten *Tathāgatabalāni*; (19) the four grounds of self-confidence; (20) *maitrī*; (21) *karuṇā*; (22) the eighteen *buddhadharmas*; (23) the four *maggā* and the four *phalāni*; and (24) *sarvajñā* : in short, all significant doctrinal formulae of all forms of Buddhism are practised by accomplished Buddhists of all *yānas*, be they *śrāvakayāna, pratyekabuddhayāna, bodhisattvayāna, buddhayāna*, or whatever-*yāna*. The *Pañcaviṃśatisāhasrikā*[52] goes so far as to say, in its discussion of the five paths (a highly technical way of speaking about the Buddhist path in general), that at the final stage of the path, the fruition of the arhat is identical to the tenth *bhūmi* of the bodhisattva, which is complete buddhahood.

To review what we have offered so far by way of conclusions, we have demonstrated that the Mahāyāna texts speak in two distinct ways about the arhat. The first way of speaking is to show that the arhat is spiritually inferior to the bodhisattva; however, we have demonstrated that there is a conceptual distinction between the *śrāvaka* as one who thinks he has attained more than he actually has, and the true arhat. When speaking about the *śrāvaka* pejoratively, the standard contest is in talk about meditation, and the *śrāvaka* is one who has mistakenly identified proficiency at meditation with *arahattā* itself, a danger about which the Buddha of the Pali canon warned repeatedly, as we have seen much earlier in this essay.[53]

The second way of speaking about the arhat in these early Mahāyāna texts is to identify the arhat with the bodhisattva.

51. *Short P.*, p. 155.

52. *Pañca*, p. 668.

53. On the identification of the perjorative usage of the term '*śrāvaka*' with the *dhyānā*, see also : *Ratna*, p. 165 and p. 167; *Aṣṭa*, p. 58, tr. p. 127; and *Laṅkā*, p. 212, tr. p. 183; and p. 51, tr. p. 46.

This is done in terms of *prajñāpāramitā*, which means that the arhat as well as the bodhisattva go beyond all *dharmas* once the 'other shore' is attained. We find this to be especially cogent to our earlier discussions of both the symbolism and the philosophy of the arahant from Pali sources, and is the strongest basis for claiming their identity, which we do.

D. *The Meaning of the Term 'Yāna'*

Let us now pose a new but related problem. We have demonstrated the spiritual equality of the arhat and the bodhisattva. Given that they are equal, how does it remain coherent for Buddhists to speak about different *yānas* ? This issue has been one with which Buddhist hermeneuticians have been grappling for centuries, and it is not resolved by positing differences between arhats and bodhisattvas, as many scholars have done. The issue is a complex one, and while we only wish to indicate the general structure of some resolutions which Buddhist texts offer, the issue itself does entail a total reevaluation of the very tidy 'Hīnayāna'/Mahāyāna dichotomization of which scholars speak. Tsong kha pa[54] poses the issue very succinctly : "There is no contradiction in the fact that for a Mahāyānist, Hīnayāna is an obstacle to full enlightenment, but for one in the Hīnayāna lineage, it is a method for full enlightenment." What Tsong kha pa wants to do, and we would like to present a similar case, is to affirm both (a) the identity of the arhat and the bodhisattva, and (b) a real distinction between what is termed as 'Hīnayāna' and 'Mahāyāna.' To do so, we shall have to remain very close to the contextual homes of our sources.

As a brief preliminary, we must consider what is meant by the term '*yāna*' in the first place. The term derives from the Sanskrit root √yā, 'to go,' and[55] gives the sense of going or proceeding, as well as the means of carriage or vehicle,[56] and is very close in some connotations to '*magga*' or '*mārga*.'[57] Its usage in pre-Buddhistic literature, according to Dayal,[58] gives the

54. Tsong kha pa, *sNgags rim chen mo* (Hopkins translation), p. 103.
55. Whitney, p. 131.
56. *P.T.S. Dictionary*, p. 553.
57. Edgerton, *BHSD*, p. 446.
58. Har Dayal, *The Bodhisattva Doctrine in Buddhist Sanskrit Literature*, Delhi : Motilal Banarsidass, 1970 (1932), p. 321, fn. 22.

sense of a way or path, as in the *Chāndogya Upaniṣad* :[59] *pathor-devayānasya pitṛyānasya ca vyāvartanā.* Sukumar Dutt[60] distinguishes its usage in the *sūtras* as 'way' or 'career' from that found in the later *śāstras* as 'vehicle.' This is certainly the sense we find offered by Kong sprul in his definition of '*yāna*' (Tibetan : *theg pa*) :[61] "Like a vehicle or conveyance by riding on which one goes beyond suffering, so it is known as '*yāna*.'" Thus the term '*yāna*,' deriving from 'to go,' carried the range of meanings from a path or way to a conveyance or vehicle, the latter connotation deriving in later Mahāyāna literatures.

Many Mahāyāna texts assert the identity of these *yānas*. The *Saddharmapuṇḍarīka,* which popularized the whole of *yāna*-language, also tells us that there is only one *yāna*. As the Buddha says there :[62] "By means of one sole vehicle [*yāna*], to wit, the Buddha-vehicle, Śāriputra, do I teach creatures the law; there is no second vehicle, nor a third." That there were no two vehicles entails that there could be no two *nirvāṇas*, which the Buddha also affirms in the same text :[63] "*Nirvāṇa,* Kaśyapa, is a consequence of understanding that all [*dharma*] are equal. Hence there is but one *Nirvāṇa*, not two, not three." Śāntideva, quoting from the *Sarvadharmavaipulyasaṅgraha Sūtra*, cites the Buddha in discussion with Mañjuśrī on the same point :[64]

> I have never preached the Law [Dharma] in separate portions, one for the Disciples' Way, one for the PratyekaBuddhas' Way, one for the Great Way [Mahāyāna]. Therefore are they children of confusion who make divisions in this my Law, saying, 'This belongs to the Disciples, that to the Pratyekas, and that to the Bodhisattvas.' He who says this rejects the Good Law by describing it as being divided.

Nāgārjuna, in his *Rin po che'i phreng pa*,[65] makes the same point : "If emptiness and the great nature of a Buddha are

---

59. *Chāndogya Upaniṣad*, v.3.2.

60. Sukumar Dutt, *Buddhist Monks and Monasteries in India*, London : George Allen & Unwin, 1962, pp. 274-275.

61. Kong sprul, *Shes bya kun khyab*, 'grel, II, p. 495. (My translation) gang la nyon pa ste de la brten nas mya ngan las 'das par' gro bas theg pa' am bnyon pa dang 'dra ba'i cha nas theg pa zhes khyang bya'o.

62. *Saddharma*, p. 27; tr. p. 40.

63. *Saddharma*, p. 91; tr. p. 129.

64. *Ś-S*, p. 95; tr. pp. 96-97.

65. *Phreng pa*, verse 387, p. 75. (Hopkins translation)

viewed thus with reason, how cou!d what is taught in the two vehicles be of unequal value for the wise ?" Thus, on the one hand, we have a canonical denial that there was ever more than one vehicle in the first place.

On the other hand, we find the type of position which says that while the wisdom involved in each of the vehicles is identical, and while the goal (*artha*; *don*) of each is the same complete enlightenment, yet the Buddha taught in differing methods of different people as an example of his methodological skilfulness. Atīśa, in the auto-commentary to his *Bodhipathapradīpa*,[66] says : "The Blessed One has preached the individual paths of the vehicles because He knows the capability of persons, and their states and dispositions." Here we find the notion that, due to different faculties of his disciples, the Buddha taught different methods. But these different methods have precisely the same goal : namely, mental training, as the Seventh Dalai Lama writes :[67] "All the extensive teachings spoken by the Jīna—for example, the three *yānas*, the four classes of tantras, and so forth—in short, all the *sūtras* and tantras, are spoken only as a means solely for training our mental-continuums [*santāna*; Tibetan : *sems rgyud*]."

Let us make a provisional distinction of components of the Buddhist way : that of wisdom, that of ultimate goal, and that of method. We have seen that it is repeatedly claimed that, in terms of wisdom, all of these *yānas* are equally expressions of *prajñāpāramitā*. In terms of ultimate goal, which is the enligh-

---

66. Atíśa, *Byang chub lam gyi sgron ma, bsTan 'gyur*, Peking ed., Vol. Khi, fasc. 33b. (Sherburne translation)

theg pa dag ni rnam par thar pa bsre bar mi bya ba yin te/bcom ldan 'das kyis gang zag gi dband po khams dang bag la nyal mkhyen pas theg pa'i lam so sor gsungs pa yin no//

67. dGe slong blo bzang bskal bzang rgya mtsho (the Seventh Dalai Lama), *gSang chen rdo rje theg pa'i smin byed kyi dbang rjes gnang sogs kyi sngon 'gro'i chos kyi gtam du bya ba gzhan phan ra ster bzhugs*, Tibetan woodblock manuscript, L.T.W.A. accession no. 1081, fascs. 8a-8b. [Hereinafter : *gSang chen*] (My translation)

rgyal bas theg pa gsum dang/rgyud sde bzhi la sogs pa mdo sngags kyi chos tshul mtha' yas pa gsungs pa de dag thams cad rang re'i sems rgyud 'di khon ' dul ba lam sbyong ba'i thams su gsungs pa sha stag yin bas//

tenment of all beings, they are also the same, as Nāgārjuna writes :[68] "The aims of benefitting oneself and others and the meaning of liberation taught (in the Hīnayāna) by the Buddha are contained in the six perfections."

As for the method for attaining such wisdom and for actualizing such a goal, we find that Tsong kha pa allows that there is a difference. He writes :[69]

> Hīnayāna and Mahāyāna are not differentiated through their view (of emptiness); the Superior Nāgārjuna and his sons assert that the two vehicles are discriminated by way of the acts of skilful method. For instance, a mother is the common cause of her children, but the fathers are the cause of discriminating their children's lineage (Tibetan, Mongolian, Indian and so forth). In the same way, the mother—the perfection of wisdom—is the common cause of all four sons [Hearer, Solitary Realizer, Bodhisattva and Buddha Superior], but the cause of their being divided into the individual lineages of Mahāyāna and Hīnayāna are methods, such as the generation of an aspiration to highest enlightenment for the sake of all sentient beings.

Very similarly, the *Laṅkāvatāra Sūtra*[70] makes a distinction between the 'realization itself' and the teaching about it, the former remaining constant through the *yānas* and the latter being a methodological distinction. However, taking this pedagogical distinction as something real, according to the *Saddharmapuṇḍarīka*,[71] is simply *prapañca* and nothing real.

E. *The Vajrayāna and the Mahāsiddha*

If it is true, as Dayal says,[72] that "the bodhisattva ideal was taught in order to counteract this tendency to a cloistered, placid, inert monastic life," then we might look for similar circumstances in which a new ideal, that of the mahāsiddha, arose. And we do find that the reasons were very similar.

One finds, in studying the history of the Theravāda, a tendency toward self-limitation in terms of *saṅgha*/laity issues, as we have

---

68. *Phreng pa*, verse 382, p. 74. (Hopkins translation)
69. Tsong kha pa, *sNgags rim chen mo*, p. 99. (Hopkins translation)
70. *Laṅkā*, p. 149; tr. p. 128.
71. *Saddharma*, p. 65; tr. p. 68.
72. Dayal, *op. cit.*, p. 3.

discussed above. While in the *Sutta Piṭaka*, *arahattā* was open to all, both in principle and in fact, there was a growing tendency among later Theravāda *saṅghikas* to restrict *arahattā* to those wearing the robe Earlier, we indicated a *Milindapañha* verse[73] which held that while *arahattā* might be attainable by a layperson, within one day of its attainment he would have to either enter the *saṅgha* or die. Of course, this verse could be explicated by saying that it was not the lay status itself that was a deterrent to *arahattā*, but the conditions given which one pursued the lay life that were obstacles : namely, lust, greed, and so forth. Nevertheless, there was such a trend in the Theravāda to exclude the laity, to some extent at least, from the very heart of the religious life, and we found that this tendency was quite contrary to what the Buddha himself taught in the *Sutta Piṭaka*.

Similarly, with the rise of the great monastic universities in northern India, we find that bodhisattva practices, which had been introduced, in part, as a way of including the laity within the central religious life of Buddhism, themselves began to fall more and more within the domain of the *saṅghikas*. One of the reasons for the rise of this new ideal person, the tantric master known as the mahāsiddha (*grub chen thob pa* or *grub thob* or *grub chen*), was the calling of Buddhism out of a monastic seclusion, a modality of lay religious expression. The mahāsiddhas themselves were invariably laypeople. Their rejection of *saṅghika* exclusivity is emphasized repeatedly in their hagiographies (*rnam thar*) wherein many of them, as a preliminary to pursuing this tantric method of training, were required to relinquish their monastic status. The most well known story to illustrate this point is found in the hagiography of Nāropa. Having the high post of western gate-keeper at Nālanda, Nāropa is approached by a woman with all thirty-seven marks of ugliness.[74] She asks him what he is looking at, and he replies that while looking at her, he is seeing Dharma. She asks him whether he understands this by words or by meaning, and he

73. *Milindapañha*, pp. 264-265.

74. Tsong kha pa, *gSang yig*, Vol. 2, Na, 5; cited by Khetsun Sangpo, *rGya gar paṇ chen rnams kyi rnam thar ngo mt[illegible]har padmo'i 'dzum zhal gsar pa*, Dharamsala : Library of Tibetan Works and Archives, 1973, pp. 827-835, esp. pp. 829-830.

replies that he knows it by its meaning, at which she begins to laugh hysterically. Nāropa asks the ugly woman why she is laughing, and she replies that he is lying to her; that, as a *paṇḍita*, a scholar, he couldn't possibly understand this by its meaning. The woman then tells him to give up his academic post and his monk's status, and to go and study with her brother, the tantrika Telopa.

This disenchantment with monastic exclusivity became symbolically expressed by the taking of a consort (*rig ma*), itself a symbol for wisdom (*rig*; *jñāna*). rDo rje gdan pa, in a poetic text of praises and entreaties to these mahāsiddhas, the *Grub thob brgyad bcu rtsa bzhi'i gsol 'debs*,[75] praises many of these saints for taking a consort. For example, Padmakāra is praised for having cultivated his consort while still a *bhikṣu*,[76] and such claims are standard aspects of the lives of these tantric saints.[77]

The taking of a consort is not the only symbolic expression of the Tantrayāna's weariness with monastic formalism. These saints repudiate all aspects of the monastic life : rDo rje dril bu pa[78] worships female pig farmers; Lohipa[79] chides some *paṇḍitas*, singing "Brahmin ministers give precedence to purity and caste, whereas I, who am a yogin, who eats meat and drinks chang [beer], do not care for these matters"; Kukuripa[80] falls in love with a dog; and all of these antinomian trends are cogently expressed in a *gīti* (*glu*; tantric song) by Saraha :[81]

Oh, I am a brahmin.
Together with a magician girl I enjoy myself.

---

75. rDo rje gdan pa (Vajrāsanaguru), *Grub thob brgyad cu rtsa bzhi'i gsol 'debs*, *bsTan 'gyur*, Peking ed., rgyud' grel, Vol. Nu, fascs. 326a-330a. [Hereinafter : *gSol debs*]

76. *gSol 'debs*, fasc. 327b.

77. We have investigated this theme in our essay, "Anima and mKha' 'gro ma : A Critical Comparative Study of Jung and Tibetan Buddhism," *op. cit*.

78. Bu ston, *Chos 'byung*, Vol. Cho., 40, 4;; cited by Sangpo, *op. cit*., p. 384.

79. Bu ston, *Chos 'byung*, Vol. cha, 37, 4; cited by Sangpo, *op. cit*., p. 406.

80. bLa ma chen po Mi 'jigs pa sbyin pa dpal, *'Phags yul grub chen brgyad cu rtsa bzhi'i byin rlabs skor lus/lo rgyus rnam par thar pa rnams bzhugs so*, Varanasi : E. Kalsang, 1972, pp. 154-155.

81. Tāranātha, *bKa' bab bdun ldan gyi brgyud pa'i rnam thar*, Vol. 2, Na, 3; cited by Sangpo, *op. cit*., pp. 161-162. (My translation)

I don't see caste or no-caste.
One who is abiding as a *bhikṣu* with shaved head,
I wander together with a mistress.
There is no division between attachment and non-attachment;
Impurity is merely a mental construct (*vikalpa*),
And this is not known by others.

And Indrabhūti[82] puts the matter succinctly. He says : "I request a method to achieve enlightenment while I enjoy the huge group of women, along with the five objects (of *kāmadhātu*)," and then he chides those who adhere to a more traditional understanding of the Buddha's teachings :

In the magnificent garden of Dzambu
I become like a fox.
"Liberation by abandonment of sensual objects."
I don't ever want Gotama.

Thus the Vajrayāna was a rebellion against monastic regulations and scholasticism; the five traditional subjects taught at Nālanda were to be repudiated after having been mastered; the texts they wrote were much more poetic, expressive and symbolic than they were academic.

For these reasons, the *Guhyasamājatantra*[83] tells us that the bodhisattvas fell into comas upon hearing the preaching of the tantras, just as many of the *srāvakas* of the *Saddharmapuṇḍarīka*[84] had heart attacks upon hearing the *prajñāpāramitā* teachings. Once again, those bodhisattvas who fell into comas, like those *śrāvakas* who walked out on the Buddha, were those who were not true bodhisattvas, but ones who were puffed-up with pseudo-learning. The mahāsiddha is not antithetical to the bodhisattva, just as the bodhisattva is not antithetical to the arahant; in fact, the mahāsiddha is understood, within the tantric tradition, as a special case of bodhisattvas who are distinguishable by method alone.

As the bodhisattva ideal developed, especially as expressed in such texts as the *Bodhisattvabhūmi,* his ultimate goal became more and more remote; that to attain the Buddha-body at the eleventh or tenth *bhūmi*, one had to exert oneself for countless

82. *Ibid.*, 16, Na, 1; cited by Sangop, *op. cit.*, p. 118. (My translation)

83. Quoted by Lal Mani Joshi *Studies in the Buddhistic Culture of India*, Delhi : Motilal Banarsidass, 2nd rev. ed., 1977 (1967), p. 264.

84. *Saddharma.*

koṭis of aeons. Certainly, this is a far cry from the arahant concept in the *Sutta Piṭaka*, who could attain *arahattā*, which we have equated with Buddhahood, in this very life (*diṭṭhe va dhamme*). So the Tantrayāna also taught a way to complete *nirvāṇa* in this very life; it perceived itself as a better method for actualizing the same goal. The Seventh Dalai Lama[85] discusses the slowness of the Pāramitāyāna (another name for the Mahāyāna or Bodhisattvayāna) and the relative speed of the Vajrayāna, which he calls "a quick way" (*myur lam*).

Tsong kha pa, who was a very keen Buddhist hermeneutician, closely analyzes the use of the term '*yāna*' in this context. He writes :[86]

> Individual vehicles are posited (1) if there is a great difference of superiority or inferiority between them in the sense that a vehicle is a fruit or goal toward which one is progressing; and (2) if there are different stages or paths that give a different body to a vehicle in the sense that a vehicle is a course by which one progresses. However, if the bodies of the paths have no great difference in type, then a series of vehicles cannot be assigned merely because the paths have many internal divisions or the persons who progress along them differ in superiority or inferiority.

Just as the so-called 'Hīnayāna' and the Mahāyāna cannot be distinguished in terms of wisdom, nor in terms of their goal, they do present different methods for actualizing this wisdom and this goal; so the same structure holds for the division of the Mahāyāna into the Pāramitāyāna or the *bodhisattvayāna* and the Vajrayāna or Tantrayāna. Tsong kha pa says :[87] "...the Mahāyāna cannot be divided into two vehicles from the viewpoint of the enlightenment sought"; however :[88] "...the division of the Mahāyāna into two is not made on account of the wisdom cognizing the profound emptiness, but on account of method."

Now we may consider very briefly just what this methodological difference between the path of the bodhisattva and the tantric path is. Tsong kha pa[89] cites Jñānapāda (Ye shes zhabs) from

85. *gSang chen*, fascs. 8b-9a.
86. Tsong kha pa, *sNgags rim chen mo*, p. 142. (Hopkins translation)
87. *Ibid.*, p. 110.
88. *Ibid.*, p. 115.
89. *Ibid.*, p. 132.

his bDag sgrib pa la 'jug pa, a tantra of the highest Anuttarayoga class : "...the vast deity yoga (*yi dam gyi rnal 'byor*) constitutes the difference in method between the Perfection and Mantra vehicles."

The bodhisattva teachings are an adaptation from the Pali tales of the previous lives and births of the Buddha. Essentially it holds that all Buddhists should emulate the Buddha's career (*yāna*) through numerous life-spans in order to attain finally a full Buddha-body, replete with all the marks of the *mahāpurisa*, in order to best teach Dharma to others. An extended discussion of the manner in which the bodhisattva assumes a Buddha-body at the tenth and eleventh *bhūmis* is narrated by Kong sprul.[90] While we shall not go into the details of this process, it fundamentally involves the attaining of the various powers (*dbang po*) which enable one to teach unobstructedly and perfectly.

Tantrayāna takes this talk about assuming a Buddha-body, and converts it into meditational practices which are known as 'deity-yoga' (*yi dam gyi rnal 'byor*), a practice which involves the visualization of a personal aspect of Buddhahood, and ultimate identification of the meditator with the visualized object, which is the tantric expression of the *bodhisattvayāna* notion of attaining a Buddha-body. The *yi dam* is the Buddha, and this type of body (or intentionality to teach perfectly) is attained meditatively in this life, rather than after aeons of progression through *bhūmis*. As Tsong kha pa says :[91] "...on the former [*bodhisattvayāna*] one cannot, and on the latter [*mantrayāna*] one can become fully enlightened without relying on countless aeons."

The *yi dam* is understood as the convergence of the ultimate (*paramārtha*) and the relative (*saṃvṛti*). It is relative in the sense that its particular form is consequent upon the particular abilities (*dbang*), thoughts (*bsam*) and sensitivities (*khams*) of the practitioner, according to the Seventh Dalai Lama.[92] Thus, this and all tantric practices utilize the particularity of the practitioner, a particularity which is identified with individuality and which is the generator of *saṃsāra*, as a basis for spiritual practice. For this reason, the *Hevajratantra*[93] says :

---

90. Kong sprul, *Shes bya kun khyab*, 'grel, II, pp. 536-538.
91. Tsong kha pa, *sNgags rim chen mo*, p. 142.
92. *gSang chen*, fasc. 8b.
93. *Hevajra Tantra*, ed. & tr., David L. Snellgrove, *The Hevajra Tantra : A*

> That by which the world is bound, by that same its bonds are released, but the world is deluded and knows not this truth, and he who is deprived of this truth will not gain perfection.

By 'that by which the world is bound' is meant the passions, the *skandhas*, and so forth; and it is the hallmark of the Tantrayāna that it employs just these passions and *skandhas* (which become identified with the five Buddha-families)[94] which enable the tantrika to attain his goal. Thus the *yi dam* is ultimate (*paramārtha*) because it is Buddhahood; but this is not to deny that it is also relative (*saṃvṛti*) as it is also an expression of the meditator's personality. Thus, the Tantrayāna methodologically transmutes the relative into the ultimate; put differently, Milarepa[95] says that any thought of ultimate and relative are merely interpretative experience of the given; that they are *savikalpa.* He offers a new term, *mahāmūdra* (*phyags rgya chen po*) as a linguistic device for talking about the existentially given which is apart from and beyond all interpretative experiences, including *saṃsāra* and *nirvāṇa.*

Thus, any distinction of *yānas*, which is to say, any distinction of the arhat, bodhisattva and mahāsiddha, is merely a provisional and pedagogical distinction. *Yānas*, according to Tsong kha pa, are distinguished only in terms of method employed, and never in terms of either wisdom or goal. Thus, the continuity of the images of the perfected person in Buddhism is the continuity of their wisdom and their goal; all distinctions are merely questions of method.

F. *Final Conclusions*

The continuity of Buddhism is the continuity of the teaching of enlightenment, the resolution of the multi-lemma of *saṃsāra.* The divergences are methodological : that, due to differing

---

Critical Study, 2 vols., London : Oxford University Press, London : Oriental Series, Vol. 6, 1959, p. 35, tr. p. 80.

gang dang gis 'jig rten 'ching' gyur ba/de dang des ni 'ching ba las grol te/de nyid mi shes 'jig rten mi grol nyin/ de nyid rnam apangs dngos grub rnyed my 'gyur//

94. Indrabhūti, *rDo rje theg pa'i rtsa ba dang yan lag gi ltung ba'i bshags pa, bsTan 'gyur*, sNar thang ed., Vol. Phu, rgyud 'grel, verse 8.

95. Mi la ras pa, *sKu gsum ngo spyod*, rapid handcopy of text and translation by Herbert V. Guenther.

psychological natures of individuals, there are different practices that can be followed. This is the conclusion we have reached by way of a very close, contextual study of the arahant concept in the *Sutta Piṭaka*, and a view of the bodhisattva and mahāsiddha ideals from Sanskrit and Tibetan texts. What we have done, in addition to a close and detailed study of the arahant ideal, is to provide a basis for future researches into both the dynamic structure of the history of Buddhist thought, as expressed in these ideals, and into what it means, in a Buddhist sense, to be a perfected human.

Our method has been contextual and textual because of the nature of the Buddhist understanding of language as something useful, pedagogical, heuristic; but never something referential or formally philosophic. This contextual study began with an overview of the expressions, occasions and symbols of the arahant. This was so that one could gain a picture, rather than a restrictive definition, of what an arahant is in its original contexts. Then we analyzed the arahant by several methods. First we analyzed him in the context of meditation, maintaining that meditation itself could never be confused with *arahattā*; on this point the Buddha was adamant. However, many of the meditational attainments of the arahant, such as his powers, were essential to his equation with the Buddha, or at least the equation of one type of arahant with the Buddha, who is one who is able to discover the Dhamma and teach it unobstructedly.

We then analyzed his psychology : his relation to the world as his experience of the world, and his relation to his emotions. We found, contrary to many other such investigations, that the arahant is not without emotions, and that the Buddha was characteristically analytical about these emotions. He did not reject them out of hand, but found some to be spiritually dysfunctional, and others were found to be useful. In terms of his relationship with others, we found the arahant image to be a very active one, one which is involved in helping and teaching others, all natural expressions of his attainment of *arahattā*. Finally, the arahant has four philosophic dimensions : one which is pseudo-empirical, one which goes beyond all views, one which analyzes language, and one which is ineffable.

We then briefly analyzed Mahāyāna claims about the arhat *vis-à-vis* the bodhisattva, the new ideal person which the

Mahāyāna propounded. We found that a clear distinction between the *śrāvaka* as one who thinks he has attained more than he has, a very conceited fellow who is the rightful object of these Mahāyāna criticisms, and the true arhat, of whom Haribhadra[96] claims a greatness surpassing even that of the irreversible bodhisattva, and who is said to be identical with the Buddha. We then returned to the notion of a *yāna*, and followed Tsong kha pa's position that a *yāna* is a way of speaking about methodical, pedagogical distinctions, but never implies a difference about either wisdom or goals. And we also found that the difference in method between the arahant and the bodhisattva is the explicit dedication to the welfare of all beings; and that the methodical distinction between the bodhisattva and the mahāsiddha is one which centers around yogic practices involving the *yi dam*, an expression and symbolization of one's human potentiality.

Our analyses of these issues has entailed a new understanding of Buddhist religious language, and it involves an appreciation of the diversity of human psychological tendencies and expressions. It does not involve such notions as different *nirvāṇas* for *śrāvakas* and bodhisattvas; it does not involve treating the Tantrayāna as a degeneration from something perceived as a 'pure' Buddhism; it does not involve any sort of meta-language. Rather, our analyses insist upon a respect for the contexts in which claims are made; it reflects a dedication, we hope, to a serious discussion of Buddhism on its own terms, without imposing on Buddhism alien issues or alien methodological presuppositions. We have also not opted for the easy way of 'letting the texts speak for themselves.' We are convinced that the academic study of religion entails analyses, and our analyses have attempted to show rather than to define, which we feel follows the example of the Buddha : analyzing *nirvāṇa* is a disease, but showing *nirvāṇa* is health.

96. See *Pañca*, p. 66, fn. 22.

BIBLIOGRAPHY

PRIMARY TEXTS : SŪTRA-TYPE LITERATURE

Aṅguttara Nikāya — Vols. I and II, ed. Richard Morris, London : Pali Text Society, 1885 and 1888.
Vols. III, IV and V, ed. E. Hardy, London : Pali Text Society, 1897, 1899 and 1900.
tr. *The Book of Gradual Sayings*, Vols. I and II by F. L. Woodward, London : Pali Text Society, 1951 (1932) and 1952 (1933).
Vols. III and IV by E. M. Hare, London : Pali Text Society, 1952 (1934) and 1955 (1935).
Vol. V by F. L. Woodward, London : Pali Text Society, 1955 (1936).

Aṣṭasāhasrikā-Prajñāpāramitā — ed. P. L. Vaidya. Buddhist Sanskrit Texts, No. 4, Darbhanga : Mithila, 1960.
tr., *The Perfection of Wisdom in Eight Thousand Lines and Its Verse Summary*, by Edward Conze, Bolinas : Four Seasons Foundation, 1973.

Abhidhammattha-Saṅgaha — tr. *Compendium of Philosophy*, by Shwe Zan Aung and C. A. F. Rhys-Davids, London : Pali Text Society, 1972 (1910).

Bhikkhupāṭimokkhaṃ — tr. & ed., *The Pāṭimokkha : 227 Fundamental Rules of a Bhikkhu*, by Ven. Ñāṇamoli Thera, Bangkok : The Social Science Association of Thailand, 1966.

Dhammapada — ed. & tr., *Dhammapada : Pali Text and Translation*, by Nārada Thera, Delhi : Sagar, 1972.

Dīgha Nikāya — ed. T. W. Rhys-Davids & J. Estlin Carpenter, 3 vols., London : Pali Text Society, 1949, 1938 and 1911.

tr., *Dialogues of the Buddha*, by T. W. Rhys-Davids, 3 vols., London : Pali Text Society, 1899, 1910 and 1921.

Hevajratantra — ed. & tr., *The Hevajra Tantra : A Critical Study*, by David L. Snellgrove, 2 vols., London : Oxford University Press, London Oriental Series, Vol. 6, 1959.

Itivuttaka — ed. Ernest Windisch, London : Pali Text Society, 1889.

tr., *The Minor Anthologies of the Pali Canon*, by F. L. Woodward, London : Pali Text Society, 1948 (1935).

Kathāvatthu — ed. Arnold C. Taylor, London : Pali Text Society, 1894.

tr., *Points of Controversy*, by Shwe Zan Aung and C. A. F. Rhys-Davids, London : Pali Text Society, 1960 (1915).

Laṅkāvatārasūtra — ed. Bunyu Nanjo, Kyoto : Otani University Press, 1923.

tr., *The Laṅkāvatāra Sūtra : A Mahāyāna Text*, by Daisetz Teitaro Suzuki, London : Routledge & Kegan Paul, 1968 (1932).

Majjhima Nikāya — Vol. I, ed. V. Trenckner, London : P.T.S., 1888. Vols. II and III, ed. Lord Chalmers, London : P.T.S., 1898 and 1899.

tr., *The Middle Length Sayings*, by Isaline B. Horner, London : P.T.S., 1954, 1957 and 1959.

Pañcaviṃśatisāhasrikā-Prajñāpāramitā — tr., *The Large Sūtra on the Perfection of Wisdom*, by Edward Conze, Berkeley : University of California Press, 1975.

Ratnaguṇasañcayagāthā — ed. E. Obermiller, Bibliotheca Buddhica, XXIX, 1937. Corrected by Edward Conze, *Indo-Iranian Reprints* (*V*, 1960), and *Indo-Iranian Journal*, IV, 1960, pp. 37-58; also by F. Edgerton, *Indo-Iranian Journal*, V, 1961, pp. 1-18.

tr. "Verses on the Accumulation of

Precious Qualities," by Edward Conze, *Indo-Asian Studies*, Pt. I, ed. Raghu Vira, Śata-Piṭaka Series, Vol. 31, New Delhi, 1963, pp. 126-178.

Saddharmapuṇḍarīkasūtra — ed. P. L. Vaidya, Buddhist Sanskrit Texts, No. 6, Darbhanga : Mithila, 1960.

tr. *Saddharma-Puṇḍarīka, or The Lotus of the True Law*, by H. Kern, Sacred Books of the East, ed. F. Max-Müller, Vol. XXI, repr. New York : Dover, 1963. [Oxford : Clarendon Press, 1884.]

Saṃyutta Nikāya — ed. M. Léon Freer, 5 vols., London : P.T.S., 1960 (1884-1898).

Vols. I and II tr. by C. A. F. Rhys-Davids, *The Book of Kindred Sayings*, London : P.T.S., 1950 (1917), 1952 (1922).

Vols. III, IV and V tr. by F. L. Woodward, London : P.T.S., 1954 (1925), 1956 (1927) and 1956 (1930).

Sutta Nipāta — ed. Dines Andersen and Helmer Smith, London : P.T.S., 1948 (1913).

ed. and tr. *Buddha's Teachings*, by Lord Chalmers, Cambridge : Harvard University Press, Harvard Oriental Series, ed. C. R. Lanman, Vol. 37, 1932.

Thera and *Therīgāthā* — ed. Hermann Oldenberg and Richard Pischel, London : P.T.S., 1883.

tr. *Psalms of the Early Buddhists*, 2 vols., by C. A. F. Rhys-Davids, London : P.T.S., 1964 (1909) and 1964 (1913).

Udana — ed. Paul Steinthal, London : P.T.S., 1948 (1885).

tr. *The Minor Anthologies of the Pali Canon*, by F. L. Woodward, London : P. T. S., 1948 (1935).

Vinaya Piṭaka — ed. Hermann Oldenberg, 5 vols., London : P.T.S., 1964 (1879, 1880, 1881, 1882 and 1883).

tr. *The Book of Discipline*, by I.B. Horner, 6 vols. 1949,1957,1957,1951, 1952 and1966.

Vajracchedaka-prajñāpāramitā-sūtra	Tibetan poṭi text, *'Phags pa shes rab kyi pha rol tu phyam pa rdo rje gcod pa zhes bya ba theg pa chen po'i mdo bzhugs so*, Dharamsala : Tibetan Press, n.d. tr. *Buddhist Wisdom Books*, by Edward Conze, New York : Harper Torchbooks, 1972 (1958).

PRIMARY TEXTS : ŚĀSTRA-TYPE LITERATURE

Āryadeva ('Phags pa lha)	*bsTan bcos bzhi brgya pa shes bya ba* (*bZhi brgya pa*), pp. 87-161 in *rTsa ba shes rab/ bzhi brgya pa/ sum cu pa/ nyi shu pa/ bcas bzhugs so//*, Sarnath : The Pleasure of Elegant Sayings Printing Press, The Tibetan Monastery, 1974.
Asaṅga (Thogs med)	*rnal 'byor spyod pa'i sa las byang chub sems dpa' sa* (Yoga-caryā-bhūmau bodhisattva-bhūmi), Tibetan trans. Prajñāvarman (Ye shes sde), *bsTan 'gyur*, Peking ed., mDo *'grel*, *sems tsam*, Vol. Zhi, fascs. 1-245a, Otani no. 5538.
Atīśa (Jo bo rje)	*Byang chub lam gyi sgron ma* and *Byang chub lam gyi sgron ma dka' 'grel* (*Bodhi-patha-pradīpa* with auto-commentary), *bsTan 'gyur*, Peking ed., *dBu ma*, Vol. Khi, fascs. 274b-277b and 277b-339b, Otani nos. 5344 and 5345. tr. "A Study of Atīśa's *Commentary* on His *Lamp of the Enlightened Path*," by Richard Faust Sherburne, Ph.D. thesis, University of Washington, 1976.
Bhāvaviveka (Legs ldan 'byed pa)	*sDe pa tha dad par 'byed pa dang rnam par bshad pa* (*Nikāyabhedavibhaṅgavyākhyānc*), *bsTan 'gyur*, Peking edition, *mDo 'grel*, Vol. U, fascs. 177a-187b, Otani no. 5640.
Buddhaghosācariya	*Papañcasūdanī Majjhimanikāya-Aṭṭhakathā* 5 vols., Vols. I and II ed. J. H. Woods, and D. Kosambi; Vols. III, IV and V

ed. I. B. Horner, London : P.T.S., 1922, 1928, 1933, 1937, 1938.

Visuddhimagga, ed. Henry Clarke Warren, rev. Dharmananda Kosambi,Cambridge : Harvard University Press, Harvard Oriental Series, Vol. 41, 1950.

tr. *The Path of Purification : Visuddhi Magga by Bhadantācariya Buddhaghosa*, by Bhikkhu Ñāṇamoli, Kandy : Buddhist Publication Society, 3rd ed. 1975.

Bu-ston — *Chos 'byung*, tr. *History of Buddhism by Bu-ston*, by E. Obermiller, Heidelberg : Materialien zur Kunde des Buddhismus, 1932.

Candrakīrti (Zla ba sgrags pa) — *dBu ma tshig gsal* (*Mūlamadhyamakavṛttiprasannapadānāma*), Dharamsala : Council of Cultural and Religious Affairs of His Holiness the Dalai Lama, 1968.

ed. and tr. *Candrakīrti, Prasannapadā-Madhyamakavṛtti : Douze chapitres, traduit du sanscrit et du tibétain en français et accompagnés d'une introduction, du notes et d'une édition critique de la versionne tibetaine*, by Jacques May, Paris : Libraire d'Amérique et d'Orient, 1959.

ed. and *tr. Cinq chapitres de la Prasannapadā*, by Jan Willem de Jong, Leiden : E. J. Brill, 1949.

Cūlavaṃsa — tr. *Cūlavaṃsa : Being the More Recent Part of the Mahāvaṃsa,* by Wilhelm Geiger, 2 vols., tr. from the German by Mrs. C. Mabel Rickmers, Colombo : The Ceylon Government Information Department, 1953.

dGe shes Ngag dbang dar rgyas — *Lam rim man ngag*, tr., *A Standard Intermediate Level Textbook of the Graded Course to Enlightenment*, by Alexander Berzin, xeroxed unpublished edition, Dharamsala : Library of Tibetan Works and Archives, n.d.

Do-drup chen Rinpoche III — *O rgyan yul tr gyi nub byang mtshams,* Tibetan mss. in the author's collections.

Dudjom Rinpoche — *Bod snga rabs pa gsang chen rnying ma'i chos 'byung legs bshad gsar ba'i dga' ston gyi dbu 'drin gzhung don le'u'i ngos 'jin bzhugs,* Kalimpong : Madhav Nikunj, 1967.

N. Dutt (ed. & tr.) — *Bodhisattva Prāṭimokṣa Sūtra, Indian Historical Quarterly,* VII, 1931, pp. 259-286.

rGogs tshang ras pa sna tshogs rang grol — *gTsang smyon he ru ka phyogs thams cad las rnam par rgyal ba'i rnam thar rdo rje thes pa'i gsal byed nyi ma'i snying po bzhugs so,* ed. Likesh Chandra, intro. Ellis Gene Smith, *The Life of the Saint of Gtsang,* New Delhi : International Academy of Indian Culture, Śata-Piṭaka Series, Vol. 79, 1969.

Gos lo tsa ba gzhon nu dpal — *Bod kyi yul du chos dang chos smra ba ji ltar byung ba'i ram pa deb ther sngon po,* tr. *The Blue Annals,* by George N. Roerich, Delhi : Motilal Banarsidass, 1976 (1949).

dGe slong blo bzang bskal bzang grya mtsho (The Dalai Lama VII) — *gSang chen rdo rje theg pa'i smin byed kyi dbang rjes gnang sogs kyi sngoh 'gro'i chos kyi gtam du bya ba gzhan phan ra ster bzhugs, Tibetan wood-block mss.,* L.T.W.A. accession no. 1081.

Indrabhūti — *rDo rje theg pa'i rtsa ba dang yan lag gi ltu ba'i bshags pa* (*Vajrayāna-mūlāṅgā-patti-deśanā*), *bsTan 'gyur,* sNar thang edition, *rgyud 'grel,* Vol. Phu, fascs. 116a-118a, Otani no. 4626.

Kathāvatthuppa-karaṇa-Aṭṭhakathā — tr. *The Debates Commentary,* by Bimala Churn Law, London : P.T.S., 1969 (1940).

Kong sprul — *Theg pa'i sgo kun las btus pa gsung rab rin po che'i mdzod bslab pa gsum .legs par ston pa'i bstan bcos shes by a kun khyab* (*shesby a kun khyab*), ed. Lokesh Chandra and intro. Ellis Gene Smith, *Kongtrul's*

Encyclopaedia of Indo-Tibetan Culture, Parts I-III, New Delhi : International Academy of Indian Culture, Śata-Piṭaka Series, Vol. 80, 1970.

rNal 'byor dbang phyug Kun dga' legs — *rNal 'byor pa'i mid can kun dga' legs pa'i rnam thar byang tshul lhug par smras 'ba zhib mo'i rtsing mo ha le ho le sne zin nas bkod pa ces bya ba bzhugs so*, Tibetan handwritten mss., L.T.W.A., n.d.

Mahāvaṃsa — ed. Wilhelm Geiger, London : P.T.S., 1958 (1908).

tr. *The Mahāvaṃsa : or The Great Chronicle of Ceylon*, by Wilhelm Geiger, Colombo : The Ceylon Government Information Department, 1950.

Milindapañha — ed. V. Trenckner, London : Pali Text Society, 1962 (1880).

tr. *The Questions of King Milinda*, by T. W. Rhys-Davids, Delhi : Motilal Banarsidass, 2 vols., 1975 (London : 1890).

bLa ma chen po Mi 'jigs pa sbyin pa dpal — *'Phags yul grub chen brgyad cu rtsa bzhi'i byin rlabs skor lus/lo rgyus rnam par thar pa rnams bzhugs so*, Varanasi : E. Kalsang, 1972.

Nāgārjuna (kLu sgrub) — *rTsa ba shes rab*, pp. 1ff. in *rTsa ba shes rab/ bzhi brgya pa/ sum cu pa/ nyi shu pa/ bcas bzhugs so//*, Sarnath : The Pleasure of Elegant Sayings Printing Press, The Tibetan Monastery, 1974.

tr. *Nāgārjuna : A translation of his Mūlamadhyamakakārikā with an Introductory Essay*, by Kenneth K. Inada, Tokyo : Hokuseido, 1970.

Mahāprajñāpāramitāśāstra, tr. *Le Traité de la Grande Vertu de Sagessa*, by Étienne Lamotte, Louvain : Publications Universitaires, Bibliothèque du Muséon, Vol. 18, 1966 (1949).

and Sakya Pandita, *Elegant Sayings*,

Emeryville : Dharma Publishing, 1977.

and the Seventh Dalai Lama, *The Precious Garland and the Song of the Four Mindfulnesses,* tr. and ed., Jeffrey Hopkins, Lati Rinpoche and Anne Klein, London : George Allen & Unwin, Wisdom of Tibet Series, No. 2, 1975.

and Lama Mipham, *Golden Zephyr : Instructions from a Spiritual Friend,* tr. Leslie Kawamura, Emeryville : Dharma Publishing, 1975.

Khetsun Sangpo — *rGya gar paṇ chen rnams kyi rnam thar ngo mtshar padmo'i 'dzum zhal gsar pa* (*Biographical Dictionary of Tibet and Tibetan Buddhism. Vol. I : The Arhats, Siddhas and Panditas of India*), Dharamsala : Library of Tibetan Works and Archives, 1973.

Śāntideva (Zhi ba lha) — *Byang chub sems dpa' spyod pa la 'jug pa zhes bya ba bzhugs so* (*Bodhicaryāvatāra*), Dharamsala : Tibetan Press, n.d.

ed. P. L. Vaidya, Buddhist Sanskrit Texts, No. 12, Darbhanga : Mithila, 1960.

tr. *Entering the Path of Enlightenment : The Bodhicaryāvatāra of the Buddhist Poet Śāntideva,* by Marion L. Matics, New York : Macmillan, 1970.

Śikṣā-samuccaya, ed. Cecil Bendall, St. Petersbourg : Bibliotheca Buddhica, 1897.

tr. *Śikṣā-samuccaya : A Compendium of Buddhist Doctrine,* by Cecil Bendall and W.H.D. Rouse, Delhi : Motilal Banarsidass 1971.

Tārānātha — tr. *Mystic Tales of Lama Tārānātha,* by Bhupendra Nath Datta, Calcutta : Rama Krishna Vedanta Math, 1957 (1944).

Tsong kha pa — *rGyal ba khyab bdag rdo rje 'chad chen po'i lam gyi rim pa gsang ba kun gyi gnad rnam par phye ba,* Peking edition, Otani no. 6210.

tr. *Tantra in Tibet : The Great Exposition of Secret Mantra*, by Jeffrey Hopkins, London : George Allen & Unwin, Wisdom of Tibet Series, No. 3, 1977.

Vajrāsanaguru (rDo rje gdan pa) — *Grub thob brgyad cu rtsa bzhi'i gsol 'debs* (*Caturaśītisiddhābhyarthanā*), *bsTan 'gyur*, Peking ed., *rgyud 'grel*, Vol. Nu, fascs. 326a-330a, Otani no. 4578.

Vasubandhu (dByig gnyen) — *Chos mngon pa mdzod kyi bshad pa* (*Abhidharmakośa*), 2 vols., Dharamsala : Council of Cultural and Religious Affairs of His Holiness the Dalai Lama, n.d.

SECONDARY SOURCES : BOOKS

Adikaram, E. W., *Early History of Buddhism in Ceylon, Or State of Buddhism in Ceylon as Revealed by the Pali Commentaries of the 5th Century A.D.*, Colombo : M. D. Gunasena, 1953 (1946).

Aung, Shwe Zan, and C. A. F. Rhys-Davids (trs.), *Compendium of Philosophy : Being a Translation Now Made for the First Time from the Original Pali of the Abhidhammatha-Sangaha with Introductory Essay and Notes*, London : Pali Text Society, 1972 (1910).

Aung, Shwe Zan, and C. A. F. Rhys-Davids (trs.), *Points of Controversy, or, Subjects of Discourse, Being a Translation of the Kathā-Vatthu from the Abhidhamma Piṭaka*, London : Pali Text Society, 1960 (1915).

Bareau, André, *Les premiers conciles bouddhiques, Paris :* Presses universitaires de France, Annals du musée Guimat, Tome LX, 1955.

Bareau, André, *Les sectes bouddhiques du petit véhicule*, Paris : Ecole française d'Extrême Orient, 1955.

Barua, Benimadhab, *A History of Pre-Buddhistic Indian Philosophy*, Delhi : Motilal Banarsidass, 1970 (1921).

Barua, Benimadhab, *Prolegomena to a History of Buddhist Philosophy*, New Delhi : Munshriram Manoharlal, 1974 (1918).

Bendall, Cencil and W. H. D. Rouse (trs.), *Śikṣā-Samuccaya : A Compendium of Buddhist Doctrine*, Delhi : Motilal Banarsidass, 1971 (?).

Berzin, Alexander (tr.), *Lam rim man ngag : A Standard Intermediate Level Textbook of the Graded Course to Enlightenment*, by dGe shes Ngag dbang dar rgyas, xeroxed unpublished edition, Library of Tibetan Works and Archives, n.d.

Bharati, Agehananda, *The Tantric Tradition*, Garden City : Doubleday, 1970 (1965).

Bose, P. H. A. Nindranath, *Indian Teachers of Buddhist Universities*, Adyar, Madras : Theosophical Publishing House, 1923.

Burns, Douglas M., *Language, Thought and Logical Paradox*, Bangkok : World Fellowship of Buddhists, W.F.B. Book Series, No. 50, 1974.

Chalmers, Lord (ed. & tr.), *Buddha's Teachings, Being the Sutta-Nipāta or Discourse-Collection, edited in the Original Pali Text with an English Version Facing It,* Cambridge : Harvard University Press, Harvard Oriental Series, Vol. 37, ed. C. R. Lanman, 1932.

Chattopadhyaya, Alaka, and Lama Chimpa, *Atīśa and Tibet : Life and Works of Dipaṅkara Śrījñāna in relation to the History and Religion of Tibet with Tibetan Sources,* Calcutta : Indian Studies Past and Present, 1967.

Chaudhuri, Sukmao, *Analytic Study of the Abhidharmakośa,* Calcutta : Sanskrit College, Research Series, No. CXIV, 1976.

Cohen, Morris R., and Ernest Nagel, *An Introduction to Logic and Scientific Method,* Bombay : Allied Publishers, 3rd Indian reprint, 1976 (1968).

Conze, Edward, *Buddhist Thought in India,* Ann Arbor : University of Michigan Press, 1967 (1962).

Conze, Edward (ed. & tr.), *Buddhist Wisdom Books*, New York : Harper Torchbooks, 1972 (1958).

Conze, Edward (tr.), *The Large Sūtra on the Perfection of Wisdom,* Berkeley : University of California Press, 1975.

Conze, Edward (tr.), *The Perfection of Wisdom in Eight Thousand Lines and Its Verse Summary,* Bolinas : Four Seasons Foundation, 1973.

Conze, Edward (tr.), *The Short Prajñāpāramitā Texts,* London : Luzac & Co., 1973.

Dasgupta, Surendranath, *A History of Indian Philosophy*, 5 vols., Delhi : Motilal Banarsidass, 1975 (1922).

Datta, Bhupendra Nath (tr.), *Mystic Tales of Lama Taranatha,* Calcutta : Ramakrishna Vedanta Math, 1957 (1944).

Dayal, Har, *The Bodhisattva Doctrine in Buddhist Sanskrit Literature*, Delhi : Motilal Banarsidass, 1970 (1932).

Dhammaratana, U, *Guide through Visuddhimagga,* Sarnath : Maha Bodhi Society, 1964.

Dharmasiri, Gunapala, *A Buddhist Critique of the Christian Concept of God*, Colombo : Lake House, 1974.

Dutt, Nalinaksha, *Early Monastic Buddhism*, Calcutta : Firma K. L. Mukhopadhyay, 2nd ed., 1971 (1960).

Dutt, Nalinaksha, *Buddhist Sects in India,* Calcutta : Firma K. L. Mukhopadhyay, 1970.

Dutt, Sukumar, *Buddhist Monks and Monasteries in India : Their History and their Contribution to Indian Culture*, London : George Allen & Unwin, 1962.

Ergardt, Jan T., *Faith and Knowledge in Early Buddhism : An Analysis of the Contextual Structures of an Arahant Formula in the Majjhima Nikāya,* Leiden : E. J. Brill, Supplements to *Numen*, XXXVII, 1977...

Fromm, Eric, D. T. Suzuki, and Richard J. DeMartino, *Zen Buddhism and Psychoanalysis,* New York : Grove Press, 1960.

Gard, Richard A. (ed.), *Buddhism*, London : Prentice-Hall International, 1961.

Geiger, Wilhelm (tr.), *The Mahāvaṃsa : or The Great Chronicle of Ceylon,* Colombo : Ceylon Government Information Department, 1950.

Geiger, Wilhelm (tr.), *Cūlavaṃsa : Being the More Recent Part of the Mahāvaṃsa,* 2 vols., Colombo : Ceylon Government Information Department, 1953.

de Glasenapp, H., *Mystères bouddhistes : Doctrines et rites secrets du 'véhicule de diamant,'* French tr. Jacques Marty, Paris : Payot, 1944.

Govinda, Lama Anagarika, *The Psychological Attitude of Early Buddhist Philosophy, and Its Systematic Representation according to the Abhidhamma Tradition,* New York : Samuel Weiser, 1961.

Grünwedel, Albert (tr.), *Die Geschichten der Vierundachtzig Zauberer (Mahāsiddhas) : aus dem Tibetischen Ubersetz,* Leipzig und Berlin : Druck und Verkag von B. G. Teubner, *Baessler-Archiv, Band V,* 1916.

Guenther, Herbert V. (tr.), *The Life and Teaching of Nāropa : Translated from the Original Tibetan with a Philosophical Commentary based on the Oral Transmission,* London : Oxford University Press, 1963.

Guenther, Herbert V., *Philosophy and Psychology in the Abhidharma,* Berkeley : Shambhala, 1974.

Guenther, Herbert V. (tr.), *The Jewel Ornament of Liberation by Sgam. po. pa.,* Berkeley : Shambhala, 1971.

Guenther, Herbert V. (tr. & ann.), *The Royal Song of Saraha : A Study in the History of Buddhist Thought,* Berkeley : Shambhala, 1973 (1968).

Guenther, Herbert V., *Yuganaddha : The Tantric View of Life,* Varanasi : Chowkhamba, Chowkhamba Sanskrit Series, Vol. III, 2nd rev. ed. 1969 (1952).

Guenther, Herbert V. (tr.), *Kindly Bent to Ease Us,* by kLong chen rab 'byams pa, 3 vols., Emeryville : Dharma Publishing, 1975-1976.

Hare, E. M. (tr.), *The Book of Gradual Sayings* (*Aṅguttara Nikāya*), Vols. III and IV, London : Pali Text Society, 1952 (1934) and 1955 (1935).

Herold, A. Ferdinand (tr.), *The Life of the Buddha,* tr. Paul C. Blum, Tokyo : Charles E. Tuttle, 1954.

Hopkins, Jeffrey (ed. & tr.), *Tantra in Tibet : The Great Exposition of the Secret Mantra,* London : George Allen & Unwin, Wisdom of Tibet Series, No. 3, 1977.

Hopkins, Jeffrey, Lati Rinpoche and Anne Klein (trs. & eds.), *The Precious Garland and the Song of the Four Mindfulnesses,* by Nāgārjuna and the Seventh Dalai Lama, London : George Allen & Unwin, Wisdom of Tibet Series, No. 2, 1975.

Horner, Isaline B., *The Early Buddhist Theory of Man Perfected : A Study of the Arahan,* London : Williams & Northgate, 1936.

Horner, Isaline B. (tr.), *The Book of Discipline* (*Vinaya-Piṭaka*), 6 vols., London : Pali Text Society, 1949, 1957, 1957, 1951, 1952 and 1966.

Horner, Isaline B. (tr.), *The Middle Length Sayings* (*Majjhima Nikāya*), 3 vols., London : Pali Text Society, 1954, 1957 and 1959.

Inada, Kenneth K. (tr.), *Nāgārjuna : A Translation of his*

Mūlamadhyamakakārikā with an Introductory Essay, Tokyo : Hokuseido, 1970.

I-Tsing, *A Record of the Buddhist Religion as Practised in India and the Malay Archipelago* (*A.D.* 671-695), tr. Junjiro Takakushu, Delhi : Motilal Banarsidass, 1966 (1896).

Jacobson, Nolan Pliny, *Buddhism : The Religion of Analysis*, Carbondale : Southern Illinois University Press, 1970 (1966).

Jayasuriya, W. F., *The Psychology and Philosophy of Buddhism*, Kuala Lumpur : Buddhist Missionary Society, 1963.

Jayatilleke, K. N., *Early Buddhist Theory of Knowledge*, London : George Allen & Unwin, 1963.

Johansson, Rune E. A., *The Psychology of Nirvana : A Comparative Study of the Natural Goal of Buddhism and the Aims of Modern Western Psychology*, Garden City : Doubleday, 1970 (1969).

de Jong, Jan Willem (ed. & tr.), *Cinq chapitres de la Prasannapadā*, Leiden : E. J. Brill, 1949.

Joshi, Lal Mani, *Studies in the Buddhistic Culture of India* (*During the 7th and 8th Centuries A.D.*), Delhi : Motilal Banarsidass, 2nd rev. ed., 1977 (1967).

Kalupahanna, David J., *Buddhist Philosophy : A Historical Analysis*, Honolulu : University Press of Hawaii, East-West Center Book, 1976.

Karundasa, Y., *Buddhist Analysis of Matter*, Colombo : Department of Cultural Affairs, 1967.

Katz, Nathan (ed.), *Buddhist and Western Philosophy : A Critical Comparative Study*, New Delhi : Sterling Publishers, 1978.

Kawamura, Leslie (tr.), *Golden Zephyr : Instructions from a Spiritual Friend*, by Nāgārjuna and Lama Mipham, Emeryville : Dharma Publishing, 1975.

Keith, A. Berridale, *Buddhist Philosophy in India and Ceylon*, Varanasi : Chowkhamba, Chowkhamba Sanskrit Series, Vol. XXVI, 1963 (1923).

Kern, H. (tr.), *Saddharma-Puṇḍarīka, or The Lotus of the True Law*, New York : Dover, Sacred Books of the East Series, Vol. XXI, F. Max-Müller, ed., 1963 (1884).

Kimura, R., *A Historical Study of the Terms Mahāyāna and Hīnayāna and the Origin of the Mahāyāna Buddhism*, Calcutta : University of Calcutta Press, 1927.

King, Winston, *In the Hope of Nibbāna,* La Salle : Open Court, 1964.

Kloppenborg, Maria Anna Gertruida Theresia, *The Paccekabuddha : A Study of the Paccekabuddha in Pali Canonical and Commentatorial Literature,* Leiden : E. J. Brill, 1974.

Lamotte, Étienne, *Histoire du bouddhisme indienne : des origines à l'ère Saka,* Louvain : Publications Universitaires, Bibliothèque du Muséon, Vol. 43, 1958.

Lamotte, Étienne (tr.), *Le Traité de la Grande Vertu de le Sagesse* (*Mahāprajñāpāramitāśāstra*), by Nāgārjuna, Louvain : Publications Universitaires, Bibliothèque du Muséon, Vol. 18, 1966 (1949).

Law, Bimala Churn, *The Life and Work of Buddhaghosa,* Delhi : Nag Publishers, repr. 1976 (1923).

Law, Bimala Churn (tr.), *The Debates Commentary* (*Kathāvatthuppakaraṇa Aṭṭhakathā*), London : Pali Text Society, 1969 (1940).

Lhalungpa, Lobsang P. (tr.), *The Life of Milarepa,* by gTsang smyon he ru ka, New York : E. P. Dutton, 1977.

Maisonneuve, Adrien, (ed.), *Études tibétaines déidées à la mémoire de Marcelle Lalou,* Paris : Libraire d'Amérique et d'Orient, 1971.

Malalasekera, G. P., *The Pali Literature of Ceylon,* Colombo : M. D. Gunasena, 1958 (1928).

Marasinghe, M. M. J., *Gods in Early Buddhism : A Study in the Social and Mythological Melieu as Depicted in the Nikāyas of the Pali Canon,* Kelaniya : Vidyalankara Campus Publications Board, 1974.

Matics, Marion L. (tr.), *Entering the Path of Enlightenment : The Bodhicaryāvatāra of the Buddhist Poet Śāntideva,* New York : Macmillan, 1970.

May, Jacques (ed. & tr.), *Candrakīrti, Prasannapadā-Madhyamakavṛtti : Douze chapitres, traduit du sanscrit et du tibétain en français et accompagnés d'une introduction, du notes et d'une édition critique de la versionne tibétaine,* Paris : Libraire d'Amérique et d'Orient, 1959.

Mojumder, Atindra, *The Caryāpadas,* Calcutta : Naya Prokash, 1973 (1967).

Morick, Harold (ed.), *Wittgenstein and the Problem of Other Minds,* New York : McGraw-Hill, 1967.

Murti, G. Srinivasa and A. H. Krishna Aiyanger (trs.), *Edicts of Aśoka (Priyadarśin)*, Madras : The Adyar Library, 2nd ed. 1951 (1950).

Murti, T. R. V., *The Central Philosophy of Buddhism : A Study of the Mādhyamika System,* London : George Allen & Unwin, 1974 (1955).

Ñāṇamoli, Bhikkhu (tr.), *The path of Purification : Visuddhi Magga by Bhadantācariya Buddhaghosa,* Kandy : Buddhist Publication Society, 3rd ed. 1975.

Ñāṇamoli Thera (ed. & tr.), *The Pāṭimokkha : 227 Fundamental Rules of a Bhikkhu,* intro. Phra Sāsana Sobhana, Bangkok : The Social Science Association Press of Thailand, 1966.

Ñāṇanda, Bhikkhu, *Concept and Reality in Early Buddhist Thought: An Essay on 'Papañca' and 'Papañca-Saññā-Saṅkhā,'* Kandy : Buddhist Publication Society, 2nd ed., 1976 (1971).

Nārada Mahāthera, *The Buddha and His Teachings,* Colombo : Vajirārāma, 2nd ed., 1973 (1964).

Nārada Mahāthera (ed. & tr.), *A Manual of Abhidhamma : Being Abhidhammattha Sangaha of Bhadanta Anuruddhācariya, Edited in the Original Pali Text with English Translation and Explanatory Notes,* Kandy : Buddhist Publication Society, 3rd ed., 1975 (1956).

Nārada Thera (ed. & tr.), *Dhammapada : Pāli Test and Translation with Stories in Brief and Notes,* New Delhi : Sagar Publications, 1972.

Nyāṇaponika Thera, *The Heart of Buddhist Meditation,* New York : Samuel Weiser, 1965 (1962).

Nyāṇaponika Thera, *Abhidhamma Studies : Researches in Buddhist Psychology,* Kandy : Buddhist Publication Society, 2nd ed., 1965 (1949).

Nyāṇatiloka Mahāthera, *Fundamentals of Buddhism,* Colombo : Bauddha Sāhitya Sabhā, 3rd ed., 1968 (1949).

Nyāṇatiloka Mahāthera, *Guide through the Abhidhamma Piṭaka,* Kandy : Buddhist Publication Society, 1971.

Obermiller, E. (tr.), *History of Buddhism by Bu Ston,* Heidelberg : Materialien zur Kunde des Buddhismus, 1932.

Obeyesekere, Gananath, Frank Reynolds and Bardwell L. Smith, *The Two Wheels of Dhamma : Essays on the Theravāda Tradition in India and Ceylon,* Chambersburg :

American Academy of Religion, A.A.R. Studies in Religion, No. 3, 1972.

Pandeya, Ram Chandra (ed.), *Buddhist Studies in India,* Delhi : Motilal Banarsidass, 1975.

Prebish, Charles S., *Buddhist Monastic Discipline : The Sanskrit Prāṭimokṣa Sūtras of the Mahāsāṅghikas and Mūlasarvāstivādins,* University Park : Pennsylvania State University Press, 1975.

Radhakrishnan, Sarvepalli (ed. & tr.), *The Principal Upaniṣads,* London : George Allen & Unwin, 1969 (1953).

Rahula, Walpola, *History of Buddhism in Ceylon: The Anurādhapura Period,* Colombo : M. D. Gunasena, 2nd ed., 1966 (1956).

Rahula, Walpola, *What the Buddha Taught,* New York, : Grove Press, 2nd ed., 1974 (1959).

Rhys-Davids, C.A.F., *Buddhist Psychological Ethics,* London : Royal Asiatic Society, 2nd ed., 1923.

Rhys-Davids, C.A.F. (tr.), *The Book of Kindred Sayings* (*Saṃyutta Nikāya*), Vols. I and II, London : Pali Text Society, 1950 (1917) and 1952 (1922).

Rhys-Davids, C.A.F. (tr.), *Psalms of the Early Buddhists* (*Thera-Therigāthā*), London : Pali Text Society, 1964 (1909 and 1913).

Rhys-Davids, C. A. F. and Shwe Zan Aung (trs.), *Points of Controversy, or Subjects of Discourse, Being a Translation of the Kathā-Vatthu from the Abhidhamma Piṭaka,* London : Pali Text Society, 1960 (1915).

Rhys-Davids, C. A. F. and Shwe Zan Aung (trs.), *Compendium of Philosophy : Being a Translation Now Made for the First Time from the Original Pali of the Abhidhammattha-Sangaha with Introductory Essay and Notes,* London : Pali Text Society, 1972 (1910).

Rhys-Davids, C. A. F. and T. W. Rhys-Davids (trs.), *Dialogues of the Buddha* (*Dīgha Nikāya*), Vol. III, London : Pali Text Society, 1921.

Rhys-Davids, T. W. (tr.), *Dialogues of the Buddha* (*Dīgha Nikāya*), Vols. I and II (Vol. III with C. A. F. Rhys-Davids), London : Pali Text Society, 1899 and 1910.

Rhys-Davids, T. W. (tr.), *The Questions of King Milinda* (*Milindapañha*), Delhi : Motilal Banarsidass, 2 vols., 1975 (London : 1890).

Robinson, James Burnell (tr.), *The Eighty-Four Siddhas (Caturaśīti-siddha-pravṛtti)*, unpublished Ph.D. dissertation, Madison : University of Wisconsin, 1975.

Roerich, George N., *Izbrannye Trudy*, Moscow : 1967.

Roerich, George N. (ed. & tr.), *The Blue Annals*, Delhi : Motilal Banarsidass, 1976 (1949).

Saddhatissa, H., *Buddhist Ethics : Essence of Buddhism*, London : George Allen & Unwin, 1970.

Sangharakshita, Bhikshu, *A Survey of Buddhism*, Bangalore : Indian Institute of World Culture, 3rd ed. 1966 (1957).

de Saram, C., *The Pen Portraits of Ninety Three Eminent Disciples of the Buddha* (based on *Sravaka Sravika Carita* by Ven. Kirielle Gnanavimala, and the *Saddharma Sangaraya* by Ambalangoda Dhamma Kusala Mahathera, both in Singhalese), Colombo : Ceylon Readers' Bookshop, 1971.

Sarathchandra, E. R., *Buddhist Psychology of Perception*, Colombo : Ceylon University Press, 1958.

Sayadaw, Mahāthera Ledi, *The Manuals of Buddhism : The Expositions of the Buddha-Dhamma*, Rangoon : Union Buddha Sāsana Council, 1969.

Shastri, Dharmendra Nath, *A Critique of Indian Realism : A Study of the Conflict Between Nyāya-Vaiśeṣika and Buddhist Dignāga School*, Agra : Agra University Press, 1964.

Sherburne, Richard Faust (tr.), *A Study of Atīśa's Commentary on His Lamp of the Enlightenment Path*, unpublished Ph.D. dissertation, Seattle : University of Washington, 1976.

de Silva, Lynn A., *Buddhism : Beliefs and Practices in Sri Lanka*, Wellawatte : L. A. de Silva, 1974.

de Silva, M. W. Padmasiri, *Buddhist and Freudian Psychology*, Colombo : Lake House, 1973.

de Silva, M. W. Padmasiri, *Tangles and Webs : Comparative Studies in Existentialism, Psychoanalysis and Buddhism*, Colombo : Lake House, 2nd ed., 1976 (1973).

Singh, Jaideva, *An Introduction to Mādhyamaka Philosophy*, Delhi : Motilal Banarsidass, 1976 (1968).

Soma Thera (tr.), *The Way of Mindfulness : Being a Translation of the Satipaṭṭhāna Sutta of the Majjhima Nikāya; its Commentary, the Satipaṭṭhāna Sutta Vaṇṇanā of the*

Prapañcasūdanī of Buddhaghosa Thera; and Excerpts from the Linatthappakāsanī Tikā, Marginal Notes of Dhammapāla Thera on the Commentary, Kandy : Buddhist Publication Society, 4th ed., 1975 (1941).

Spiro, Melford E., *Buddhism and Society : A Great Tradition and Its Burmese Vicissitudes*, New York : Harper & Row, 1970.

Sprung, Mervyn (ed.), *The Problem of the Two Truths in Buddhism and Vedānta*, Dordrecht : D. Reidel, 1973.

Stcherbatsky, Th., *The Concept of the Buddhist Nirvana*, Leningrad : Academy of the U.S.S.R., 1927.

Stcherbatsky, Th., *The Central Conception of Buddhism and the Meaning of the Word 'Dharma,'* repr. Delhi : Motilal Banarsidass, 1974 (1923).

Suzuki, Daisetz Teitaro (tr.), *The Laṅkāvatāra Sūtra : A Mahāyāna Text*, London : Routledge & Kegan Paul, 1968 (1932).

Swearer, Donald K., *Secrets of the Lotus*, New York : Macmillan, 1971.

Thomas, Edward J., *The History of Buddhist Thought*, London : Routledge & Kegan Paul, 2nd ed., 1951 (1933).

Tilakasiri, J. (ed.), *Añjali : Papers on Indology and Buddhism : A Felicitation Volume Presented to Oliver Hector de Alwis Wijesekera on his Sixtieth Birthday*, Peradeniya : University of Ceylon, 1970.

Tucci, Giuseppe (ed. & tr.), *Minor Buddhist Texts*, Part I, Roma : Instituto italiano per il medio ed estreme oriente, Serie Orientale Roma, IX, 1956.

Tucci, Giuseppe (ed. & tr.), *Pre-Diṅnāga Buddhist Texts on Logic from Chinese Sources*, Baroda : Gaekwad's Oriental Series, XLIX, 1929.

Van Buren, Paul M., *The Edges of Language : An Essay in the Logic of a Religion*, New York : Macmillan, 1972.

Warder, A. K., *Indian Buddhism*, Delhi : Motilal Banarsidass, 1970.

Wayman, Alex, *The Buddhist Tantras : Light on Indo-Tibetan Esotericism*, New York : Samuel Wiser, 1973.

Wayman, Alex (ed. & tr.), *Yoga of the Guhyasamājatantra : The Arcane Lore of Forty Verses*, Delhi : Motilal Banarsidass, 1977.

Wijesekera, O. H. de A. (ed.), *Malalasekera Commemoration* Volume, Colombo : 1976.

Wittgenstein, Ludwig, *Philosophical Investigations,* tr. G. E. M. Anscombe, 3rd ed., New York : Macmillan, 1968 (1958).

Wittgenstein, Ludwig, *Tractatus Logico-Philosophicus*, tr. C. K. Ogden and F. P. Ramsey, intro. Bertrand Russell, London : Routledge & Kegan Paul, 1922.

Woodward, F. L. (tr.), *The Book of Gradual Sayings* (*Aṅguttara Nikāya*), Vols. 1, II and V, London : Pali Text Society, 1951 (1932), 1952 (1933) and 1955 (1936).

Woodward, F. L. (tr.), *The Book of Kindred Sayings* (*Saṃyutta Nikāya*), Vols. III, IV and V, London : Pali Text Society, 1954 (1925), 1956 (1927) and 1956 (1930).

Woodward, F. L. (tr,), *The Minor Anthologies of the Pali Canon* (*Udana* and *Itivuttaka*), London : Pali Text Society, 1948 (1935).

SECONDARY SOURCES : MONOGRAPHS

Buddhadasa Bhikkhu, *Extinction without Remainder,* Kandy : Buddhist Publication Society, Bodhi leaves series no. B33, 1967.

Dhargyey, Geshe Ngawang, *et al.* (trs.), *The Bodhicitta Vows and Lam Rim Puja*, Dharamsala : Library of Tibetan Works and Archives, 1974.

Dunnington, Jacqueline Miller, *Arahantship*, Kandy : Buddhist Publication Society, Bodhi leaves series no. B64, 1974.

Goonesekere, L. R., *Buddhist Commentatorial Literature*, Kandy : Buddhist Publication Society, Wheel series nos. 113/114, 1967.

Gorkom, Nina Van, *Perfections of Buddhahood,* Kandy : Buddhist Publication Society, Bodhi leaves series no. 75, n.d.

Gunaratne, V. F., *The Message of the Saints : Thera-Theri-Gāthā*, Kandy : Buddhist Publication Society, Wheel series no. 135, 1969.

Gyatsho, Tendzin (Dalai Lama XIV), *Key to Madhyamika*, Dharamsala : Library of Tibetan Works and Archives, 1976.

Hecker, Hellmuth, *Lives of the Disciples*, Kandy : Buddhist Publication Society, Wheel series no. 115, 1967.

Katz, Nathan, *Meanderings of the Wheel of Dhamma : A Comparative Study of Some Buddhist Missions*, Kandy : Buddhist Publication Society, Wheel series no. 257, 1978.

Khantipalo, Bhikkhu (tr.), *Forest Meditations : The Verses of the Arahant Talapuṭa,* Kandy : Buddhist Publication Society, Wheel series nos. 243/244, 1977.

Ñāṇamoli Thera (tr.), *The Greater Discourse on Voidness : Mahā-Suññatā Sutta and Commentary from the Papañcasūdanī,* Kandy : Buddhist Publication Society, Wheel series no. 87, 1965.

Nyāṇaponika Mahāthera, *The Power of Mindfulness,* Kandy : Buddhist Publication Society, Wheel series nos. 121/122, 1976 (1968).

Nyāṇaponika Mahāthera, *The Worn-Out Skin,* Kandy : Buddhist Publication Society, Wheel series nos. 241/242. 1977.

Nyāṇaponika Mahāthera, *The Life of Sāriputta*, Kandy : Buddhist Publication Society, Wheel series nos. 90/91/92, 1966.

Nyāṇaponika Mahāthera (tr.), *The Discourse on the Snake Simile : Alagaddūpama Sutta,* Kandy : Buddhist Publication Society, Wheel series nos. 48/49, 1974.

Perera, T. H., *The Four Cankers* (*Āsavas*), Kandy : Buddhist Publication Society, Bodhi leaves series no. B35, 1967.

Piyadassi Thera, *The Seven Factors of Enlightenment : Sattā Bojjhaṅgā,* Kandy : Buddhist Publication Society, Wheel series no. 1, 2nd imp., 1960 (?).

Piyadassi Thera, *The Psychological Aspect of Buddhism,* Kandy : Buddhist Publication Society, Wheel series no. 179, 1972.

Premasiri, P. D., *The Philosophy of Aṭṭhakavagga,* Kandy : Buddhist Publication Society, Wheel series no. 182, 1972.

Shan Shin Buddhist Institute, *The Sixteen Arhats and the Eighteen Arhats*, tr. Li Yung-hsi, Peking : The Buddhist Association of China, 1961.

de Silva, M. W. Padmasiri, *The Psychology of Emotions in Buddhist Perspective*, Kandy : Buddhist Publication Society, Wheel series no. 237, 1976.

de Silva, M. W. Padmasiri, *Persons and Phantoms*, Professor Gunapala Malalasekera Memorial Lecture, April 23, 1976, Kandy : T. B. S. Godamunne & Sons, 1976.

Soma Thera (tr.), *Kālāma Sutta : The Buddha's Charter of Free*

Inquiry, Kandy : Buddhist Publication Society, Wheel series no. 8, 1963.

Soma Thera and Piyadassi Thera, *The Lamp of the Law : Being Selected Excerpts from Gurulugomi's Dharmapradīpikā*, Kandy : Buddhist Publication Society, Wheel series no. 38, 1961.

SECONDARY SOURCES : ARTICLES

Aaronson, Harvey B., "Measureless States : The Relationship of the Karmic to the Nirvanic," A paper read at the first annual meeting of the International Association for Buddhist Studies, New York, 1978.

Bhattacharyya, Benoytosh, "Glimpses of Vajrayāna," *Proceedings and Transactions of the Third Oriental Conference*, Madras : Law Printing House, 1925, pp. 129-141.

An-Che, Li, "The Sakya Sect of Lamaism," Chengtu : *West China Border Research Society Journal*, XVI, Series A, 1945, pp. 72-86.

An-Che, Li, "Rñiṅma : The Early Form of Lamaism," *Journal of the Royal Asiatic Society*, 1949, pp. 142-163.

An-Che, Li, "The Bkah-Brgyud Sect of Lamaism," *Journal of the American Oriental Society*, 69, 2, 1949, pp. 51-59.

Ch'en, Kenneth K. S., "The Tibetan Tripitaka," Cambridge : *Harvard Journal of Asiatic Studies*, 9, 1945-47, pp. 53-62.

Barlingay, S. S., "Buddhism and Change," in Ram Chandra Pandeya (ed.), *Buddhist Studies in India*, Delhi : Motilal Banarsidass, 1975, pp. 71-81.

Bhattacharyya, Kamaleswar (ed. & tr.), "The Dialectical Method of Nāgārjuna : Translation of the 'Vigrahavyāvartanī' from the Original Sanskrit with Introduction and Notes," *Journal of Indian Philosophy*, I, 1, 1971, pp. 217-261.

Carter, John Ross, "Dhamma as a Religious Concept : A Brief Investigation of Its History in the Western Academic Tradition and Its Centrality within the Singhalese Theravāda Tradition," *Journal of the American Academy of Religion*, XLIV, 4, pp. 661-674.

Carter, John Ross, "Traditional Definitions of the Term *Dhamma*," *Philosophy East and West*, 26, 3, July 1976, pp. 329-337.

Chandra, Lokesh (ed. & tr.), "The Biography of Mitra-Yogin,"

Indo-Asian Studies, Part 2, Prof. Raghu Vira Memorial Volume, Śata-Piṭaka Series, Vol. 37, New Delhi : International Academy of Indian Culture, 1965, pp. 161ff.

Conze, Edward (tr.), "Verses on the Accumulation of Precious Qualities," (*Ratnaguṇasañcayagāthā*), *Indo-Asian Studies*, Part I, Śata-Piṭaka Series, Vol. 31, New Delhi : International Academy of Indian Culture, 1963, pp. 126-178.

Devaraja, N. K., "What is Living and What is Dead in Traditional Indian Philosophy," *Philosophy East and West*, 26, 4, October 1976, pp. 427-442.

Dutt, Nalinaksha (tr.), "Bodhisattva Prāṭimokṣa Sūtra," *Indian Historical Quarterly*, VII, 1931, pp. 259-286.

Guenther, Herbert V., "The Philosophical Background of Buddhist Tantraism," Hong Kong : *Journal of Oriental Studies*, 5, 1 & 2, 1959 and 1960, pp. 45-64.

Hisamatsu, Shin'ichi, "The Characteristics of Oriental Nothingness," *Philosophical Studies of Japan*, II, 1960, pp. 65-97.

Horner, Isaline B., "The Four Ways and the Four Fruits in Pāli Buddhism," *Indian Historical Quarterly*, December 1934, pp. 785-796.

Kalansuriya, A. D. P., "Wittgenstein, Meaning Model and Buddhism," *Indian Philosophical Quarterly*, VI, 3, April 1977, pp. 381-391.

Kalupahanna, David J., "Aññā," s.v. *Encyclopaedia of Buddhism*, I, fasc. 4, Colombo : Government of Ceylon, 1965.

Katz, Nathan, "An Appraisal of the Svātantrika-Prasaṅgika Debates," *Philosophy East and West*, 26, 3, July 1976, pp. 253-267.

Katz, Nathan, "Nāgārjuna and Wittgenstein on Error," in N. Katz (ed.), *Buddhist and Western Philosophy : A Critical Comparative Study*, New Delhi : Sterling Publishers, forthcoming.

Katz, Nathan, "Anima and mKha' 'gro ma : A Critical Comparative Study of Jung and Tibetan Buddhism," *The Tibet Journal*, II, 3, 1977, pp. 13-43.

Katz, Nathan (tr.), "A Translation of the Biography of the Mahāsiddha Indrabhūti with Notes," *Bulletin of Tibetology*, XII, 1, Februray 1975, pp. 25-29.

Katz, Nathan, and Kalsang Yeshi (trs.), "The Hagiography of Nāgārjuna," Kathmandu : *Kailash—A Journal of Himalayan Studies*, V, 4, 1977, pp. 269-276.

Lancaster, Lewis R., "Samādhi Names in Buddhist Texts," in Wijesekera (ed.), *Malalasekera Commemoration Volume*, pp. 196-202.

Law, Bimala Churn, "Nirvāṇa and Buddhist Laymen," *Annals of the Bhandarkar Oriental Research Institute*, 14, 1933, pp. 80-86.

Marasinghe, M. M. J., " 'Functional' Buddhism of Sri Lanka : A Mahindian Adaptation from Original Buddhism," Colombo : *The Buddhist*, XLVIII, 1, May 1977, pp. 9-11.

May, Jacques, "Kant et le Mādhyamaka : à propos d'une livre récent," *Indo-Iranian Journal*, III, 2, 1959, pp. 102-111.

Mookerjee, S., "The Omniscient as the Founder of a Religion," *The Nava-Nālandā-Mahāvihāra Research Publication*, I, Patna : Nava Nālandā Mahāvihāra, n.d. (ca. 1960), pp. 1-44.

Narain, Harsh, "Śūnyavāda : A Reinterpretation," *Philosophy East and West*, 13, 4, January 1964, pp. 311-318.

Poussin, Louis de la Vallée, "Studies in Buddhist Dogma : The Three Bodies of a Buddha," *Journal of the Royal Asiatic Society*, 1906, pp. 943-977.

Poussin, Louis de la Vallée, "The 'Five Points' of Mahādeva and the Kathāvatthu," *Journal of the Royal Asiatic Society*, 1910, pp. 413-423.

Poussin, Louis de la Vallée, "Réflexions sur le mādhyamaka," *Mélanges chinois et bouddhiques*, II, 1933, pp. 4-59.

Poussin, Louis de la Vallée, "Le Bouddha et les Abhijñās," *Le Muséon*, 1931, pp. 335-342.

Poussin, Louis de la Vallée, "Une dernière note sur le nirvāṇa," *Études d'Orientalisme publiées par Le Musée Guimet à la mémoire de Raymonde Linossier*, Tome II, Paris : Libraire Ernest Laroux, 1932.

Poussin, Louis de la Vallée, "The Mādhyamikas and the Tathatā," *Indian Historical Quarterly*, 1933, pp. 30-31.

Prebish, Charles S., "A Review of Scholarship on the Buddhist Councils," *Journal of Asian Studies*, XXXIII, February 1974, pp. 239-254.

Premasiri, P. D., "Interpretation of Two Principal Ethical Terms in Early Buddhism," *Sri Lanka Journal of the Humanities*, 2, 1, June 1976, pp. 63-74.

Rahula, T., "The Buddhist Arahant : Is His Attainment of Nirvāṇa as Perfect as the Buddha's Enlightenment ?" *Religious Traditions*, I, 1, April 1978, pp. 33-42.

Rahula, Walpola, "L'idéal du bodhisattva dans le therevāda et le mahāyāna," *Journal Asiatique*, 259, 1971, pp. 63-70.

Ray, Reginald, "Understanding Tantric Buddhism : Some Questions on Method," *Journal of Asiatic Studies*, XXXIV, 1, November 1974, pp. 169-175.

Ray, Reginald (tr.), "Laksminkari : A Woman Siddha," *Loka II*, Garden City : Doubleday, 1976, pp. 36-42.

Ray, Reginald, "The Vajrayāna Mahāsiddhas : Some Principles of Interpretation," A paper presented to the annual meeting of the American Academy of Religion, San Francisco, 1977.

Samtani, N. H., "The Conception of Ideal Man in Pali Canon," in R. C. Pandeya (ed.), *Buddhist Studies in India*. Delhi : Motilal Banarsidass, 1975, pp. 61-70.

Schayer, Stanislav, "Das Mahāyānistische Abosolutum nach der Lehre der Mādhyamikas," *Orientalistische Literaturseitung*, XVIII, 1935, pp. 401-415.

Schayer, Stanislav, "Notes and Queries on Buddhism," *Rocznik Orjentalistyczny*, XI, 1935, pp. 206-213.

Schleberger, Ecard, "Bodhisattva Iconography in Sri Lanka," *World Buddhism*, XXV, 9, April 1977, pp. 241-243, and XXV, 10, May 1977, pp. 272-273.

Sharma, Arvind, "A Note on the Use of the Word Hīnayāna in the Teaching of Buddhism," *The Eastern Buddhist*, IX, 2, October 1976, pp. 129-133.

Shendge, Malatij (ed. & tr.), "Śrīsahajasiddhi," *Indo-Iranian Journal*, X, 2/3, 1967, pp. 126-149.

Thurman, Robert A. F., "Buddhist Hermeneutics," *Journal of the American Academy of Religion*, XLVI, 1, March 1978, pp. 19-40.

Tucci, Giuseppe (ed. & tr.), "Two Hymns of the *Catuḥ-stava* of Nāgārjuna," *Journal of the Royal Asiatic Society*, 1932, pp. 309-325.

Tucci, Giuseppe, "Animadversiones Indicae," *Journal of the Royal Asiatic Society of Bengal*, 26, 1, 1930, pp. 125-160.

Wayman, Alex, "The Significance of Mantras, from the Veda down to Buddhist Tantric Practice," *Brahmavidya : The Adyar Library Bulletin*, XXXIX, 1975, pp. 65-89.

Wayman, Alex, "Observations on Translation from the Classical Tibetan Language into European Languages," *Indo-Iranian Journal*, 14, 3/4, 1972, pp. 161-192.

Wayman, Alex, "Regarding the Translation of Buddhist Terms *saññā/saṃjñā, viññāṇa/vijñāna,*" in Wijesekera (ed.), *Malalasekera Commemoration Volume*, pp. 325-335.

Wylie, Turrell, "A Standard System of Tibetan Transcription," *Harvard Journal of Asiatic Studies*, 22, 1959, pp. 261-267.

Yadav, Bibhuti S., "Negation, Nirvāṇa and Nonsense," *Journal of the American Academy of Religion,* XLV, 4, 1977, pp. 451-471.

REFERENCE AND LEXICAL MATERIALS

Angdu, Sonam (ed.), *Tibeto-Sanskrit Lexicographical Materials,* the *sGra rbyor bam po gnyis,* the *Dag yig za ma tog*, and the *Dag yig li shi'i gur khang,* Leh : Basgo Thongspon Publication, 1973.

Buddhadatta, A. P. Mahātjera, *Concise Pāli-English Dictionary*, Colombo : Colombo Apothecaries' Co,. 1968.

Chandra, Lokesh, *Tibetan-Sanskrit Dictionary*, 2 vols., Kyoto : Rinsen Book Company, 1976 (1959).

Chattopadhyaya, Alaka, *Catalogue of Indian (Buddhist) Texts in Tibetan Translation : Kanjur and Tanjur,* Clacutta : Indo-Tibetan Studies, 1972.

Dass, Sarat Chandra, *A Tibetan-English Dictionary*, repr. Delhi : Motilal Banarsidass, 1970 (Calcutta : Baptist Mission Press, 1902).

Edgerton, Franklin, *Buddhist Hybrid Sanskrit Dictionary*, Delhi : Motilal Banarsidass, 1970 (New Haven : Yale University Press, 1953).

Jäschke, H. A., *Tibetan-English Dictionary*, London : Routledge & Kegan Paul, 1968 (1881).

Mahāvyutpatti, ed. & tr. Alexander Csoma de Körös, *Sanskrit-Tibetan-English Vocabulary, Being an Edition and Translation of the Mahāvyutpatti,* Memoirs of the Royal Asiatic Society of Bengal, Vol. IV, No. 3, Calcutta : 1944.

Malalasekera, G. P. (ed.), *Encyclopaedia of Buddhism,* Colombo : Government of Ceylon Press, 1961 on.

Nyāṇatiloka Mahāthera, *Buddhist Dictionary : Manual of Buddhist Terms and Doctrines*, Colombo : Frewin & Co., 3rd ed., 1972 (1952)).

Rhys-Davids, T. W., and William Stede, *Pali-English Dictionary,* repr. New Delhi : Oriental Books Reprint Corp., 1976 (London : Pali Text Society, 1921-1925).

Suzuki, Daisetz T. (ed.), *Catalogue and Index to the Tibetan Tripitaka, Peking Edition*, Tokyo : Suzuki Research Foundation, 1962.

Webb, Russell, *An Analysis of the Pali Canon*, Kandy : Buddhist Publication Society, Wheel series nos. 217/218/219/220, 1975.

Whitney, William Dwight, *The Roots, Verb-Forms and Primary Derivatives of the Sanskrit Language*, repr. New Haven : American Oriental Society, American Oriental Series, Vol. 30, 1945 (Leipzig : Breitkopf und Härtel, Bibliothek Indogermanischer Grammatiken, Band II, Anhang II, 1885).

INDEX